FROM REEL TO DEAL

WARNING!

**After reading this book,
there are no excuses!**

For everything, *yes everything,*
**needed to succeed as an
independent filmmaker
is in these pages.**

FROM REEL TO DEAL

EVERYTHING YOU NEED
TO CREATE A SUCCESSFUL
INDEPENDENT FILM

Dov S-S Simens

WARNER BOOKS

NEW YORK   BOSTON

PUBLISHER'S NOTE: This publication is designed to provide competent and reliable information regarding the subject matter covered. However, it is sold with the understanding that the author and publisher are not engaged in rendering legal, financial, accounting, or other professional advice. Laws and practices often vary from state to state and if legal, financial, or other expert assistance is required, the services of a professional should be sought. The author and publisher specifically disclaim any liability that is incurred from the use or application of the contents of this book.

Copyright © 2003 by Dov S-S Simens
All rights reserved.

Warner Books

Time Warner Book Group
1271 Avenue of the Americas, New York, NY 10020
Visit our Web site at www.twbookmark.com.

Printed in the United States of America

First Printing: July 2003
10   9   8   7   6   5   4

Library of Congress Cataloging-in-Publication Data
Simens, Dov S-S
 From reel to deal : everything you need to create a successful independent film / Dov S-S Simens.
  p. cm.
 Includes index.
 ISBN 0-446-67462-1
 1. Motion pictures—Production and direction. 2. Motion picture authorship. 3. Motion pictures—Marketing. 4. Independent filmmakers.
I. Title.

PN1995.9.P7 S555 2003
791.43'023—dc21   2002038043

Book design and text composition by Stanley S. Drate / Folio Graphics Co. Inc.
Cover design by Tony Greco

Teiko Yamada is the one person to whom this book is dedicated. Why? The answer is simple. She is the driving force. She is the inspiration. She is the knowledge. She is the goddess of dreams. She is why creativity exists . . . and because of her this book exists.

Acknowledgments

After Teiko Yamada my sincerest thanks go to several groups that supported, worked, and nurtured this book into form. They are the staffs of my three film education ventures, The Hollywood Film Institute, www.WebFilmSchool.com, and THE BIZ; then the agent who made the dream attainable and the editor who made the dream tangible.

My senior staff members are Angela Taylor, Melissa Puch de Fripp, Luis Quijada, Michael Perlin, and Oscar Simens, who gave me daily support at work. The agent, whose understanding and business acumen started the journey, is Michael Hamilburg, along with his associate Joanie Kern. Finally, the editor, who grasped the book's importance and worked and worked and worked to mold it into its final stage, is John Aherne, with his colleagues Mari Okuda and Megan Rickman.

To everyone, my heart feels and mind says, "Thank you and God bless."

Contents

MEET YOUR TEACHER

To a first-timer, Hollywood is confusing. It's a glamorous puzzle filled with vagaries. It's a web that entraps wannabes armed with hopes of fame and fortune but no knowledge of the rules. Anyone wanting to be a player, a mover and shaker, in Hollywood needs a mentor, a guide. Someone to take your hand and lead you through the maze called Tinseltown. In the film industry, I'm that person. I have the information you've been looking for—with an ability to explain it, in a way that you can understand. I'm your mentor and this book is your road map.

The Spielbergs, Lucases, Coppolas, and Tarantinos might be great filmmakers, but they are rotten teachers. On the other hand, I am not a great filmmaker, but I am a great teacher—and that is what you want. I've made films. I've produced. I've directed. I've written checks. I've made mistakes. I did not succeed initially in Hollywood. Then out of necessity I stumbled into teaching. I became a film instructor with facts from my own experiences, learned to communicate them, and became known as "Hollywood's Greatest Independent Film Instructor."

By 1980 I had a degree in economics, had spent four years in the army (first lieutenant, Green Berets, Vietnam, 1968–69), had backpacked through Europe, retired to quaint Carmel, California, where I owned a successful bookstore for 10 years. My life was full. Then the big four-zero hit: 40!—I sold my store, sold my house, packed my bags, took my cash, and went to Hollywood in quest of fame and fortune.

The first project I created was a TV series called *Auto Test Point,* a 30-minute newsmagazine show featuring half a dozen segments with in-studio host wraparounds, focusing solely on the automobile. I tried to option the rights to *Car & Driver* or *Road & Track* magazines, but they wanted too much money.

Undaunted, I shot a pilot (with my own money—stupid me) and wrote 13 episodes, assuming it would air on weekend mornings instead of those boring hunting, fishing, and gardening shows. I also assumed hundreds of auto industry advertisers would want in on the show. I took the pilot to syndicators (TV salesmen), and although they said it had excellent production values (a "kiss of death" line), they passed. My show, they said—since it would air on weekend mornings—would barely get a 1.0 rating and have no rerun life.

I came away with one piece of practical information that lands in your lap only after you've failed. The advice was to produce a "strip show," a program that airs Monday through Friday between 3:00 and 5:00 P.M., or after the A.M. or P.M. news. This show would get a 3.0 to 6.0 rating five times per week, totaling 15–30 weekly rating points, with revenues 2,000 percent greater than my *Auto Test Point* show.

Undaunted, I put my thinking cap on and came up with *Soap Opera Update*, a 30-minute newsmag series about the daily soaps. It was to be presented as a news show in which the anchors report, with two-minute clips, treated as hard news, what dramatically occurred that day on each soap.

This time I didn't produce a pilot (I was now almost broke) but merely wrote an episode, outlined 13 additional shows, and went back to the syndicators. They all thanked me and passed on the idea. Three months later, at the NATPE (National Association of Television Program Executives) convention, where TV shows are sold to individual stations, I saw three of the syndicators that I had pitched *Soap Opera Update* to, who had passed, pitching their own versions! Another hard lesson from the school of hard knocks.

Back to the drawing board. I created *A Woman's POV*, another 30-minute newsmag show, this time for cable, with segments about sex, sensuality, and eroticism from the female perspective, featuring voluptuous women in bikinis and negligees. This program would easily attract male viewers. But I needed to secure the 25- to 40-year-old female viewer that advertisers love. I brainstormed and came up with the "hook"—everyone connected with the program, in front of the camera and behind it (executives, talent, crew, etc.), would all be women. Not a single male would come near the show. Voilà! Women on women.

I wrote, registered, and copyrighted the show, then partnered with someone in the inner circles of the cable industry, who pitched it. After rejections at HBO, Showtime, SelecTV, and Playboy we gave up. Three years later I received a late-night phone call from a hostile woman shouting, "You son of a bitch! You scum-sucking pig!" Turns out she was the woman I was going to use as the production manager for *A Woman's POV,* claiming she'd just seen the show on cable (with a slightly changed title) and demanding to know why I hadn't used her.

I quickly got a tape of the show. I wanted to cry. It was mine! Of course, I sued, spent eight years in the courts, collected a small check, and wasted a lot of energy. During the litigation, I entered AA (as of this writing I have 22 years clean and sober) and took night courses at UCLA Extension and the AFI (American Film Institute) with titles like "Financing and Distributing Independent Features," "Creative Means to Financing Films," "Writing Commercial Scripts," "International Co-productions and Hollywood," "Securing High Quality with Low Budgets," etc. I learned some buzzwords and transferred my attention from the small screen to the large one.

I called studio heads and development executives. I pitched remakes of English novels, bloodcurdling horror stories, unique fish-out-of-water plots, modernized Shakespearean plays, vampire tales with a twist, updated 3-D stories, etc. I pitched and pitched and pitched. Everyone said they'd get back to me (another kiss-of-death line), but no one ever did. Then I sank to pitching projects to the low-budget distributors who sell schlock to non–English speaking nations (they don't want great stories). I came up with projects with words like "Blood," "Zombie," "Nightmare," "Slime," "Massacre," or "Fatal" in the titles and budgets that were always "under $1 million."

Still nothing happened! No one would give me development money! Then, almost broke, I had a moment of clarity. Instead of hiring a writer, I'd write it myself. After a few screenwriting classes with the "structure gurus" (Syd Field, Bob McKee, Michael Hauge, David Freeman, Linda Seger, John Truby, Jeff Kichen), I wrote three scripts. Naturally, I thought they were *great.* In reality, they were only good, and sadly, good is not good enough for first-timers in Hollywood.

Then I got hit with a bolt of lightning—"Hey, kid, keep it simple"—from a low-budget executive who was 17 years my junior, and calling me "kid." What he meant was, when producing your first low-budget film, write a script with very few locations. I quickly penned two scripts: *Boobs,* the story of five teens in search of the Perfect American Bosom (five boys, one beach blanket; they never got off the blanket as 65 38DDDs saunter by) and *9 Lives of Rufus Johnson,* the story of a house and a cat (a kitten lives in a suburban house, and over 10 years as house buys and sells four times and four families come and go). It is shot from the satirical cat's POV (point of view) of American society. Each script could be shot in one location in one week. The scripts were imaginative, cheap to make, and still no one would fund me to make them.

Three years in Hollywood and I ran out of money. Luckily, one of my roommates, a cinematographer, had a job shooting a feature film for a soap actor who wanted to pull a *Rocky* (Stallone) or a *Sling Blade* (Billy Bob). He wrote, produced, directed, and starred in it. His script was horrible, but he had $30,000! He hired my roomie, who hired me (two weeks at $200 a week) to be the production manager. Nice, but I didn't really know how to make a film. Suddenly, I had to get a crew, buy film stock, find a film lab, rent cameras, create a shooting schedule, etc. God was on my side, and the film got made.

In the film industry, just like any other, one job done well leads to another. In the next two years, I worked as a production manager and line producer on seven low-budget features. As the line producer, I was in charge of the checkbook. By writing the checks, I learned not what those expensive theory-laden film schools say things cost but what they really cost. I should know—I wrote the checks.

Simultaneously, I supplemented my line-producing income (not enough to pay rent) by working as a reader for small film companies. For $25 to $35 each, I read more than 800 scripts and did "coverage" (two-page script book reports) during those two years. It was during this period that I got a call from a work associate who landed a great-paying line-producing gig and had to find a replacement for himself as a panelist at a UCLA seminar on "High Quality with Low Budgets," the same class I'd taken as a student four years earlier. I accepted the honor—lecture at UCLA!

Standing in front of 150 attendees for 30 minutes, I was extremely nervous, I talked super fast, petrified that someone might find out I was a phony. However, people approached me after the seminar and thanked me! So did the dean of UCLA's School of Theater, Film and Television, who invited me to give a class at UCLA. I jumped at the opportunity and gave a one-day seminar.

The seminar, "Producing Ultra-Low-Budget Features," drew over 200 enrollees at $125 each. It grossed $25,000 (I was paid $250) and was a success. I presented it several more times at UCLA. Then USC, a competing university, paid me $2,000 to teach it, and the following year I presented it several times at NYU, another competing university, for $5,000, along with flight, hotel, and per diem. I had stumbled into a career.

It was now 1989 and I took my act on the road. I said good-bye to UCLA, USC, and NYU and founded HFI, the Hollywood Film Institute (in Santa Monica, California), with an intensive crash course (one weekend) that became the 2-Day Film School™. I partnered with film societies, film commissions, and film festivals in smaller cities (Cincinnati, Seattle, Denver, Dallas, Minneapolis) and brought Hollywood know-how to middle America.

The numbers show the course's success: 3 percent of 2-Day Film School™ graduates either produce, write, or direct a feature film within six months. Three percent might sound low, but considering that not a single graduate of all the two- to four-year film schools in America makes a feature film for at least five years after graduating, if ever, 3 percent is extremely high. Alumni of the 2-Day Film School™ include Quentin Tarantino (*Reservoir Dogs, Pulp Fiction*), Matthew Vaughn (*Lock, Stock and Two Smoking Barrels*), Kirk Jones (*Waking Ned Devine*), Mark Archer (*In the Company of Men*), Philippa Braithwaite (*Sliding Doors*), Guy Ritchie (*Snatch*), Chris Nolan (*Memento*); numerous Sundance, Cannes, and Toronto festival winners' writers; and cinematographers of films like *Blade, Mortal Kombat,* and *X-Men.* Other alumni include musicians like Michael Jackson, Queen Latifah, and Roland Best who wanted to cross over into film, and actors like Sinbad, Valerie Bertinelli, Malcolm-Jamal Warner, and Will Smith who wanted to take control of their careers.

Orson Welles once said, "Everything you need to know about filmmaking can be learned in two to three days." I believe that Mr. Welles was correct, and I developed a way to teach "everything you need to know" by giving birth to the 2-Day Film School™ upon which this book is based.

This book is geared to any adult who wants to produce, write, or direct a feature film but doesn't want to waste four years and $70,000–$100,000 at film school (UCLA, USC, NYU, etc.) that preach and coddle. This book, like my weekend class, can't teach talent. No one can and no book can. Either you have it or you don't. But, if you have talent and a great idea, and want to launch a career in the film industry, this book will give you absolutely all the information you need.

Before proceeding you must understand that this book is based on the fact that 🕴️ *filmmaking is a business. It is not an art form.* In Hollywood, as in any industry, everything costs something. You write checks. And when making a feature film you negotiate and write approximately 38 bank checks. I present these 38 bank checks (chapters 17–41) as "the 38 Steps of Filmmaking™."

Contrary to what I just wrote, yes, I do agree that filmmaking is an art form. But I cannot teach art. I cannot teach talent. It can't be taught. You either have it or you don't. What I can teach is the business of making the art (how to write those 38 bank checks cheaply) and then the business of selling the art.

Another concept to understand is that 🧳 *Hollywood is not a film-making industry—it is a film-marketing industry.* Studios are corporations that must make profits. They do this by creating values, i.e., when a film is in theaters, there are newspaper ads, and when you, the consumer, see the ads you believe the film has a $10 (theater ticket price) value. Nineteen out of twenty consumers don't see the film in a theater. However, 17 of the 19 who don't go to the cinema think, "I'll rent it." Renting isn't free! Blockbuster, Hollywood Video, or any video store charges $3–$4, so, in essence, the $10 film was put on sale at a 60 to 70 percent discount—now the consumer pays to see it. No ads, no video store rentals. It's that simple.

Hollywood is a marketing industry. Distributors would love to split $10 with theater owners—they try every time for a "box office" winner—but if they don't get it, they'll gladly split $3–$4 with video store owners and add to the profits with lucrative pay-cable and broadcast sales. And this is only North America.

Don't get me wrong. It's not that Hollywood has no desire to make excellent films. It tries to make the best film possible every time. But four out of five films the studios make are poor to mediocre. Do they quit? No, they market the duds. They place ads, create a value, cash in, and make profits even with mediocre-to-rotten films because Hollywood is a business. It is a marketing machine.

Once again, I acknowledge that filmmaking is art and art takes talent. But talent can't be taught. You either have it or you don't. What can be taught is the nuts and bolts, which, once learned, frees up your talent to be utilized in the best way possible. *From Reel to Deal* does not teach art. However, it does teach the mechanics of making the art and the business of selling that art.

From Reel to Deal is written with 51 easy-to-follow chapters mirroring the actual stages of filmmaking (pre-production, production, post-production, and marketing) as you produce, write, direct, and distribute your first feature film—literally a producing-by-the-numbers.

> **IMPORTANT POINT** Don't skip around. I beg you. Please read the chapters in the order presented. Don't check out the more exotic chapters (financing, directing, dealmaking, negotiating, etc.) first, for this will only give you a snippet of information out of context. Filmmaking, like life, is one chapter at a time.

Chapters 1–16 involve the basics: getting an idea, obtaining the script, securing the financing, and readying for production. These chapters read a little slow but they're imperative for they give you a solid foundation. Chapters 17–41 will then fly by as you discover step-by-step (bank check by bank check) how to physically make a feature film. Finally, chapters 42–51 will take you through the glamorous process of marketing, selling, and distributing. They will also fly by, for who doesn't like reading about how to get rich and famous?

Further, each chapter is enhanced with a homework assignment and two indispensable lists. The first displays the specialized books and software available for in-depth information pertinent to that chapter's subject, with an order form at the book's end. And, second, each chapter contains a meticulously selected list of contacts (studio heads, A-list talent, foreign buyers, power agents, film financiers, etc.) relevant to that chapter, who you can instantly phone or e-mail. In essence this book is literally three books in one—a how-to, a resource manual, and a directory—all geared to help you launch your career.

 BOOKS

My First Movie
S. Lowenstein, 458 pp., $27.50
Twenty famous filmmakers detail their first feature film triumphs.

The First Time I Got Paid for It
P. Lefcourt, 254 pp., $15.00
Amazing first-time war stories from 60 writers, producers, and directors.

Breaking In: How 20 Directors Got Their Start
N. Jarecki, 316 pp., $14.00
The naked truth from successful directors on how they launched their careers.

Wannabe
E. Weinberger, 226 pp., $12.95
Scathing and hilarious book that describes the misadventures of this first-timer in Hollywood.

Surviving Hollywood
J. Rannow, 224 pp., $16.95
Features wise counsel for living in
Hollywood and pursuing a showbiz
career with a healthy mind.

Creative Careers in Hollywood
L. Scheer, 240 pp., $19.95
Perfect for career seekers looking for
the unusual, yet profitable, jobs that
are part of the film industry.

Filmmaker's Dictionary
R. Singleton, 358 pp., $22.95
Over 5,000 filmmaking terms from
technical to slang explained.

The Complete Film Dictionary
I. Konigsberg, 468 pp., $19.95
Know the talk—4,000 entries with line
drawings and photos.

*Technical Film and TV for
    Nontechnical People*
D. Campbell, 256 pp., $19.95
A guide that makes the technical
mumbo-jumbo of film and TV making easy to understand.

*The Complete Idiot's Guide to
    Filmmaking*
J. Parrent, 334 pp., $18.95
Don't let the title fool you. An
excellent primer on the craft and business of filmmaking.

 VIDEOS/DVDS

Video School
Six 30-minute VHS instructional
videos, $134.95
   1. *Basic Shooting*, $22.95
        The very basics for production.
   2. *Advanced Shooting*, $22.95
        The A–Z of camera moves to
        composition.
   3. *Light It Right*, $22.95
        An essential guide to lighting
        techniques.
   4. *Sound Success*, $22.95
        The audio basics from miking to
        post-production.
   5. *Video Editing*, $22.95
        Basic editing techniques and
        more.
   6. *Computer Video*, $22.95
        Computer video tips and
        techniques.

Videomaker/DVD
DVD/DVD-ROM, three instructionals,
$99.00
Learn on your computer with three
filmmaking how-tos on "Basic
Shooting," "Lighting," and "Sound
Techniques."

First Works, Volume 1
VHS, 122 minutes, $34.95
Compare yourself to the first films of
Roger Corman, Spike Lee, Oliver
Stone, Bob Zemeckis, and more.

First Works, Volume 2
VHS, 120 minutes, $34.95
More first films from Martin Scorsese,
Ron Howard, John Milius, John
Carpenter, and others.

 **MENTOR
PROGRAMS**

Program: AFTRA Mentoring Program
Contact: American Federation of Television & Radio Artists

5757 Wilshire Blvd, 9th Floor
Los Angeles, CA 90036
Attn: Jean Frost
Ph: 323-634-8181

Program: Project Involve
Contact: Independent Feature Project
   (West or East)
104 W 29th St, 12th Floor
New York, NY 10001
Attn: Katla Smith (IFP/East)
Ph: 212-465-8200
8750 Wilshire Blvd, 2nd Floor
Beverly Hills, CA 90211
Attn: Pamela Tom (IFP/West)
Ph: 310-432-1280

Program: Mentorship Program
Contact: Women In Film
8857 W Olympic Blvd, Suite 201
Beverly Hills, CA 90211
Attn: Diane Sherer
Ph: 310-657-5144

Program: Producer's Mentoring
   Program
Contact: Producers Guild of America
8530 Wilshire Blvd, Suite 450
Beverly Hills, CA 90211
Attn: Sabrina Wind
Ph: 310-358-9020

Program: Mentoring Program
Contact: Step Up Women's Network
8424-A Santa Monica Blvd, Suite 857
West Hollywood, CA 90069
Attn: J. J. Klein
Ph: 323-653-5588
Web: www.stepupwomensnetwork.org

Program: Talent Development
   Programs
Contact: ABC Entertainment Talent
   Development

500 S Buena Vista St
Burbank, CA 91521
Attn: Carmen Smith
Ph: 818-560-4000
Web: www.abcnewtalent.com

Program: Internship Program
Contact: American Cinema Editors
100 Universal City Plz, Bldg 2352B,
   Room 204
Universal City, CA 91608
Attn: Internship Committee
Ph: 818-777-2900
Fax: 818-733-5023
Web: www.americancinema
   editors.com

Program: Film Editor Training
   Program
Contact: American Cinema Editors
100 Universal City Plz, Bldg 2282,
   Room 234
Universal City, CA 91608
Ph: 818-777-2900
Fax: 818-733-5023

Program: Assistant Directors Training
   Program
Contact: Directors Guild of
   America/West
7920 Sunset Blvd
Los Angeles, CA 90046
Attn: Training Committee
Ph: 310-289-2000
Fax: 310-289-2029
Web: www.dgptp.org or www.dga.org

Program: New York Assistant
   Directors Training Program
Contact: Directors Guild of
   America/East
110 W 57th St
New York, NY 10019

Attn: Training Committee
Ph: 212-397-0930
Fax: 212-664-1626

Program: Production Assistant
   Program
Contact: Streetlights
650 N Bronson Ave, Suite B108
Hollywood, CA 90004
Attn: Minority Training Committee
Ph: 323-960-4540
Fax: 323-960-4546
Web: www.streetlights.org

Program: Warner Bros. Global Trainee
   Program
Contact: Warner Bros.
4000 Warner Blvd
Burbank, CA 91522
Attn: Global Trainee Committee
Ph: 818-954-5400
Web: www.wbjobs.com

Program: Documentary Filmmaking
Contact: International Documentary
   Association
1201 W 5th St, Suite M320
Los Angeles, CA 90017
Attn: Education Committee
Ph: 213-534-3600

Program: Intern Program
Contact: Black Entertainment
   Television
1235 W St, NE
Washington, DC 20018
Attn: Intern Committee
Ph: 202-608-2020

 JOB HOTLINES

BayTV (San Francisco)
Ph: 415-561-8662

Black Entertainment Television (BET)
Ph: 202-608-2800 ext. 2

C-SPAN
Ph: 202-626-7983

Cable News Network (CNN)
Ph: 404-827-5144
Web: www.turnerjobs.com

Cartoon Network
Ph: 404-885-2263 ext. 8

Children's Television
Ph: 212-875-6804

Corporation for Public Broadcasting
   (CPB)
Ph: 202-879-9600

Country Music Television
Ph: 615-335-3350

Discovery Channel
Ph: 301-986-0444 ext. 3

E! Entertainment Television
Ph: 323-954-2710

ESPN
Ph: 860-766-2000

Fox Networks
Ph: 310-444-8290

MSNBC
Ph: 201-583-5819

MTV Latino
Ph: 305-604-5388

MTV Network
Ph: 212-846-2500

NBC News
Ph: 212-664-4444

Public Broadcasting Services (PBS)
Ph: 703-739-5000

The Learning Channel
Ph: 301-986-0444 ext. 3

Time Life Video & Television
Ph: 703-838-7000

Turner Broadcasting System (TBS)
Ph: 404-827-5144
Web: www.turnerjobs.com

VH1
Ph: 310-752-8008
Web: www.MTVCareers.com

 JOB PLACEMENT SITES

Abacus Staffing
www.abacusstaffing.com

Apple One
www.appleone.com

Blaine and Associates
www.blaineandassociates.com

Career Quest
www.careerquest.com

Corestaff Services
www.corestaffservices.com

Employ Now
www.employnow.com

Eventure
www.getyourfirstjob.com

Headhunter.Net
www.headhunter.net

Hot Jobs
www.HotJobs.com

Journalism Jobs
www.jounalismjobs.com

Media Bistro
www.mediabistro.com

Reel Dirt
www.reeldirt.com

ShowBiz Data
www.Showbizdata.com

Showbiz Jobs
www.ShowbizJobs.com

TV and Radio Jobs
www.tvandradiojobs.com

TV Jobs
www.tvjobs.com

Ultimate TV
www.ultimatetv.com

RESOURCES AND TOOLS

"Your Homework"

Six months costing $2,000 to $3,000 is all that's needed to become a professional. Why spend $70,000–$100,000 at a four-year film school when, at a fraction of the cost, you can get more practical know-how by creating your own hands-on film school.

To accomplish this, acquire some books and software at $200–$500, then secure some filmmaking basics with a workshop or two at $300–$1,000, next spend $2,000 shooting a weekend short, and with the $67,500–$96,500 and three and a half years saved (by not attending a how-to-make-the-perfect-feature-film-when-everything-in-the-universe-is-available-to-you-whenever-you-want-it film school) you can make your first feature film like *Clerks; Easy Rider; sex, lies and videotape; The Blair Witch Project;* or *Barbershop.*

The following 12 sources will give you all the information needed to launch your career:

1. Production directories
2. Film commissioners
3. Film books
4. Film co-ops and programs
5. Production vendors
6. Film magazines and trades
7. Software programs
8. Paperwork and forms
9. Industry organizations

10. Screenplays
11. Entertainment contracts
12. Guilds and unions

1. PRODUCTION DIRECTORIES

These books are your regional filmmaking Yellow Pages. Every city and state has one that's filled with names and phone numbers. Need to hire a camera operator? Turn to this book. Need to buy film stock? Turn to the section that lists raw stock suppliers. Need camera equipment? Props? Production insurance? Qualified crew? Film processing? Once you know where you plan to shoot, the first phone call you'll make is to that area's respective film commissioner (Association of Film Commissioners, 406-495-8040) to procure your local production directory.

2. FILM COMMISSIONERS

Film commissioners are government bureaucrats who work for cities or states. They will help with location scouting and getting film permits. They act as your liaison with their respective police and fire departments, and they can also help refer cast and crew. However, don't expect much more help, for most of their time and money is spent hustling studios (Hollywood), networks (New York), and advertising producers (Madison Avenue) to bring productions to their city or state, to enhance the local economy.

3. FILM BOOKS

All film books have merit. My recommendations, by subject, for a basic filmmaker's library are:

1. Screenwriting
   The Complete Guide to Standard Script Formats (Cole)
   Adventures in the Screen Trade (Goldman)
   The Screenwriter's Bible (Trottier)
   Screenplay (Field)
   Story (McKee)
   Secrets of Screenplay Structure (Cowgill)
   The Writer's Journey (Vogler)

Writing the Character-Centered Screenplay (Horton)
Plots Unlimited (Sawyer)
Making a Good Script Great (Seger)
Writing Treatments That Sell (Atchitey)
The Complete Book of Scriptwriting (Straczynski)
The Script Is Finished, Now What Do I Do? (Callan)
Getting Your Script Through the Hollywood Maze (Stuart)

2. Filmmaking, Production, and Cinematography
   The Filmmaker's Handbook (Ascher & Pincus)
   Independent Feature Film Production (Goodell)
   Feature Filmmaking at Used-Car Prices (Schmidt)
   Persistence of Vision (Gaspard & Newton)
   The Grip Book (Uva)
   The Five C's of Cinematography (Mascelli)
   Cinematography (Malkiewicz)
   Painting with Light (Alton)
   Film Lighting (Malkiewicz)

3. Budgeting, Scheduling, and Paperwork
   Film Scheduling (Singleton)
   Film Budgeting (Singleton)
   Film and Video Budgets (Simon)
   Production Budget Book (Koster)
   The Complete Film Production Handbook (Honthaner)

4. Directing
   Film Directing Shot by Shot (Katz)
   The Film Director (Bare)
   On Directing (Clurman)
   Directing Actors (Weston)
   A Sense of Direction (Ball)
   Grammar of the Film Language (Arijon)
   The Film Director's Team (Silver and Ward)
   Art of Storyboarding (Hart)
   Directing Your Directing Career (Callan)
   From Word to Image (Begleiter)
   Directing and Producing for Television (Cury)
   The Director's Journey (Travis)

5. Financing and Dealmaking
   Contracts for the Film and Television Industry (Litwak)
   Dealmaking in the Film and Television Industry (Litwak)
   The Movie Business Book (Squire)
   Film and Video Financing (Wiese)
   Filmmakers and Financing (Levison)
   This Business of Television (Blumenthal)
   The Biz (Moore)
   Movie Money (Daniels, Leedy & Sills)
   The Independent Film Producer's Survival Guide (Erickson, Tulchin, and Halloran)

6. Digital Filmmaking
   The Filmmaker's Handbook (Ascher)
   The Digital Producer, with CD (Poole and Feldman)
   Easy Digital Video, with CD (Slaughter)
   Digital Video for Desktop, with CD (Pender)
   Digital Filmmaking (Ohanian & Philips)
   The Avid Digital Editing Room Handbook (Solomons)
   The Web Cam Book (Parker)
   Digital Moviemaking (Billups)
   Digital Video Handbook (Collier)
   Building a Home Movie Studio and Getting Your Films Online (Lancaster & Conti)

4. FILM CO-OPS AND PROGRAMS

Every city, from Seattle (911 Media Arts), to San Francisco (Film Arts Foundation), to Los Angeles (Independent Feature Project, aka IFP), to Atlanta (Image Film Video), to Chicago (Chicago Filmmakers), to Pittsburgh (Pittsburgh Filmmakers), to New York (Film Video Arts), has a film co-op that is a member of the National Association of Media Arts Center. These co-ops provide access to equipment, offer networking opportunities, sponsor festivals, host screenings, and give workshops. Every film co-op has a bulletin board, which is a great place to find out who has a camera, a script, a digital workstation, and, most importantly, money.

There are also 15 alternative independent film curricula programs that compete with the traditional four-year undergraduate film schools. The programs vary in length (two days to three years) and cost ($299 to $28,000).

Sundance Filmmakers Lab (801-328-3456, 3 weeks, N/A)
Hollywood Film Institute (800-366-3456, 2 days, $349)
American Film Institute (323-856-7690, 2 years, $28,000+)
London Film School (44-207-836-9642, 2 years, $30,000+)
NYU Intensive Program (212-998-7140, 2 months, $5,000+)
USC Summer Production Workshop (213-740-2235, 10 weeks, $5,500+)
New York Film Academy (212-674-4300, 4–8 weeks, $6,000+)
International Film and TV School (207-236-8581, 4 weeks, $2,700+)
Columbia College (818-345-8414, 3 years, $27,000+)
Vancouver Film School (800-661-4101, 1 year, $15,000+)
Los Angeles Film School (323-860-0789, 10 months, $28,000+)
IndieU (877-463-4375, weekends, $349+)
UCLA Extension Certificate Program (310-825-9971, 6–8 courses, $3,000+)
Filmmaker's Central (323-467-6580, 3–4 courses, $2,000+)
Raindance Lab (44-207-287-3833, 4–5 courses, $2,500+)

5. PRODUCTION VENDORS

There are vendors, in your region, who supply filmmakers with equipment and services. These suppliers know everyone and have a vested interest in getting your project going—they make money when you shoot. The vendors (see local production directory) to call are:

A. Film labs: They develop your film. If you shoot a 35mm feature, the lab gets a minimum of $25,000 from you. The lab salesmen will help you find an excellent camera crew, etc.

B. Camera rental houses: They rent you a 35mm camera to shoot a feature film for a minimum of $10,000. They'll also help you find crew, film stock, and equipment.

C. Insurance vendors: They issue completion bonds and production coverage and help you with dos and don'ts of contracts and releases.

D. Light/grip facilities: Need a gaffer? Need a key grip? They help get your crew together and minimize the equipment you'll need for your shoot.

E. Editing facilities: They assist in finding post-production personnel. They also know local directors.

F. Post-sound houses: They help you find a film editor, sound editor, and music composers.

6. FILM MAGAZINES AND TRADES

Magazines are a wonderful source of information, and they are topical. Some helpful publications are:

1. Screenwriting
   Creative Screenwriting (monthly, 323-957-1405)
   Written By (monthly, 323-782-4522)
   Script (monthly, 410-592-3466)
   Hollywood Scriptwriter (monthly, 818-845-5525)
   Scenario (quarterly, 800-222-2654)
   Fade In (monthly, 800-646-3896)
   Screentalk (bimonthly, 011-45-7670-1020)

2. Filmmaking
   Filmmaker (quarterly, 212-983-3150)
   MovieMaker (quarterly, 310-234-9234)
   Film & Video (monthly, 323-653-8053)
   Millimeter (monthly, 212-462-3580)

3. Cinematography
   American Cinematographer (monthly, 323-969-4333)
   International Photographer (monthly, 323-876-0160)

4. Hollywood gossip
   Premiere (monthly, 212-767-5400)
   Movieline (monthly, 760-745-2809)

5. Low-budget and digital filmmaking
   Independent Film & Video (monthly, 212-807-1400)
   Fade In (monthly, 800-646-3896)
   Indie Slate (bimonthly, 832-593-0405)
   Release Print (monthly, 415-552-8760)
   Digital Video (monthly, 888-776-7002)
   Res (quarterly, 212-320-3750)
   Computer Videomaker (monthly, 530-891-8410)
   Camcorder & Computer Video (monthly, 800-784-5709)

6. Directing
   DGA Magazine (monthly, 310-289-5333)

7. Acting
   Back Stage (weekly, 800-745-8922)

8. Business
   Variety (weekly, 800-323-4345)
   Hollywood Reporter (daily, 866-525-2150)
   Daily Variety (daily, 323-857-6600)

7. SOFTWARE PROGRAMS

Computer programs for screenwriting, budgeting, scheduling, storyboarding, and editing make things easier. The best place to purchase these programs is either at the Writer's Store in Westwood, California, or on the Web. The programs are:

1. Screenplay formatting
   Final Draft (Windows or Mac)
   ScriptThing (Windows or Mac)
   Scriptware (PC or Mac)
   Movie Magic Screenwriter 2000 (PC or Mac)

2. Screenplay storytelling
   Blockbuster (Windows or Mac)
   Collaborator III (Mac)
   Plots Unlimited (DOS or Mac)
   Dramatica Pro (Windows or Mac)

3. Budgeting and scheduling
   Turbo Budget (Windows or Mac)
   Movie Magic Budgeting (Windows or Mac)
   Easy Budget (DOS or Windows)
   Movie Magic Scheduling (Windows or Mac)
   MacToolkit Budgeting (Mac)
   MacToolkit Scheduling (Mac)

4. Storyboarding
   Storyboard Artist (Windows or Mac)
   Storyboard Quick (Windows or Mac)
   Boardmaster (Windows or Mac)

5. Business and contracts
   Industry Labor Guide (Windows or Mac)
   Automated Contracts for the Film and Television Industry (Windows or Mac)
   Film Profit (PC or Mac)

6. Desktop editing
   Avid Cinema (PC or Mac)
   Final Cut Pro 3.5 (Mac)
   VideoStudio (PC)
   Adobe Premiere 6.2 (PC or Mac)
   MediaStudio Pro (PC)

8. PAPERWORK AND FORMS

When producing, you need to fill out a lot of paperwork, and there is only one store, Enterprise Stationers, that sells blank budgets, forms contracts, checklists, agreements, and release forms for independent filmmakers. There also are two books that provide a majority of blank forms, checklists, etc. that you need. They are:

1. *The Complete Film Production Handbook* (Honthaner, $54.95). Includes instructions on the forms and a CD-ROM, so you can alter the forms and print them out.
2. *Movie Production and Budget Forms—Instantly* (Singleton, $19.95). A book of filmmaking forms you can pull out and photocopy.

9. INDUSTRY ORGANIZATIONS

Like any industry, the motion picture world has its organizations and associations. Most have prerequisites for membership, but at the very least, they publish membership directories that are great contact resources.

1. Guilds and unions
   Writers Guild of America (WGA, *writers*, 323-951-4000/LA, 212-767-7800/NY)
   Directors Guild of America (DGA, *directors*, 310-289-2000/LA, 212-581-0370/NY)
   Screen Actors Guild (SAG, *actors*, 323-954-1600/LA, 212-944-1030/NY)

American Guild of Variety Artists (AGVA, *singers/comics*, 818-508-9984/LA, 212-675-1003/NY)

American Federation of Television & Radio Artists (AFTRA, *TV and radio performers*, 323-634-8100)

International Alliance of Theatrical and Stage Employees (IATSE, *film crew*, Canada: 604-664-8910; LA: 818-980-3499; NY: 212-730-1770)

National Association of Broadcast Engineers and Technicians (NABET, *TV crew*, 323-851-5515)

2. Organizations

American Film Marketing Association (AFMA, *foreign sales agents*, 310-446-1000)

National Association of Television and Program Executives (NATPE, *TV sales agents*, 310-453-4440)

Academy of Motion Picture Arts and Sciences (AMPAS, *Oscar voters*, 310-247-3000)

National Association of Theatre Owners (NATO, *movie exhibitors*, 818-506-1778)

Video Software Dealers Association (VSDA, *video distributors*, 416-642-1565)

National Cable Television Association (NCTA, *cable networks*, 202-775-3669)

International Documentary Association (IDA, *documentary film-makers*, 213-534-3600)

Association of Film Commissioners (AFC, *film commissioners*, 406-495-8040)

3. Associations

American Society of Cinematographers (ASC, *cinematographers*, 323-969-4333)

Casting Society of America (CSA, *casting directors*, 323-463-1925/LA, 212-868-1260/NY)

Association of Independent Commercial Producers (AICP, *commercial production companies*, 323-960-4763/LA, 212-929-3000/NY)

10. SCREENPLAYS

If you want to succeed, you must read. You can purchase scripts from mail-order retailers, but you should go to a library where you can read several in a day and learn a genre. Other than your local university, the best script libraries are:

Academy Library (Beverly Hills, CA)
UCLA Theater Arts Library (Westwood, CA)
USC Cinema Library (Los Angeles, CA)
American Film Institute Library (Hollywood, CA)
THE BIZ Library (Santa Monica, CA)
NYU Cinema Library (New York, NY)

11. ENTERTAINMENT CONTRACTS

You need an entertainment attorney to handle contracts and negotiations. To save money, the books that have most of the contracts, which you can adapt for your own needs, are:

Contracts for the Film and Television Industry (Litwak, $35)
Dealmaking in the Film and Television Industry (Litwak, $29.95)
43 Ways to Finance Your Feature Film (Cones, $17.95)
Independent Producer's Guide to Film and TV Contracts (Alberstadt, $49.95)
The Producer's Business Handbook (Lee, $39.95)
The Biz (James, $26.95)
Automated Contracts for the Film and Television Industry (software, $199.95)
Independent Film Producer's Survival Guide (Erickson, Tulchin, and Halloran, $34.95)

12. GUILDS AND UNIONS

There are three guilds and one union that represent writers (Writers Guild of America), directors (Directors Guild of America), actors (Screen Actors Guild), and crew/technicians (International Alliance of Theatrical Stage Employees), which you'll either work with or without once you know your budget.

Each guild or union has a contract, a rule and rate book, and a low-budget agreement that you must get. But be sure not to sign (you're a "signator") any contract until you have consulted with your entertainment attorney and made sure that you've read all the rules and understand them.

The individual low-budget agreements include the Writers Guild

(WGA), with one low-budget agreement (budgets under $2.5 million); the Directors Guild (DGA), with one (budgets under $1.2 million); the Screen Actors Guild (SAG), with five agreements (experimental agreement, under $75,000; limited exhibition agreement, under $200,000; modified low budget, $80,000–$500,000; low budget, under $2 million; and affirmative action low budget, under $2.75 million), each with different rules and rates; and the International Alliance of Theatrical Stage Employees (IATSE), with one low-budget agreement that has three rate tiers ($1–$3 million, $3–$5 million, and $5–$7 million).

Don't Be Fooled

Just because they're called low-budget agreements doesn't mean, however, you can afford it. For instance, the Writers Guild calls anything under $2.5 million low-budget and, upon signing, you contractually agree to hire a writer for a treatment and two drafts. Sounds simple. Now let's look at the numbers. You've just agreed to pay the writer $23,540 for a treatment, $20,460 for a first draft, and $17,047 for a rewrite, which adds up to $61,047. Now add 12 percent–17 percent pension, health, and welfare dues, a 10 percent agent fee, and your total is more than $70,000. This is not low-budget!

The Directors Guild calls anything under $1.2 million low-budget. The DGA requires that you pay a director no less than $7,874 per week for a minimum of eight weeks. If your film is only a three-week shoot, you still must pay for eight weeks. Plus, you must hire the first assistant director ($3,400/week) and the unit production manager ($3,578/week) for the eight-week minimum. These three employees, with pension, health, welfare, and a 10 percent agent's commission, add up to $120,000–$150,000. This is not low-budget!

IATSE has three separate low-budget rates, for $1–$3 million, $3–$5 million, and $5–$7 million budgets. But each agreement only lowers hourly wages by 3–5 percent. And there is no provision if your budget is under $1 million.

The Screen Actors Guild is by far the most accommodating guild for independent filmmakers with its five low-budget agreements. Two of them, the experimental and the limited exhibition, are affordable. But when you sign them, you give actors power; keep in mind that you can hire SAG actors anyway, even if you haven't signed with the guild. The

Blair Witch producers probably didn't sign with SAG but used SAG actors! Ed Burns, a SAG member, probably didn't sign with SAG when he produced *The Brothers McMullen*—nor did Robert Rodriguez when he shot *El Mariachi*. They got away with it. How did this happen? What are the misconceptions surrounding the Hollywood guilds?

Misconceptions

#1. Can't hire: To hire anyone (actors, writers, directors, crew) who is in a guild or union, you must sign with that guild or union. This is incorrect. This is America. You can hire whoever you want, whenever you want, as long as you adhere to the laws pertaining to minimum wage and workers' compensation. If the person you desire to hire is in a guild or union, but you don't want to sign with that guild or union, you can do so. It is your potential employee's concern but it is not your problem.

#2. Can't sell it: If you hire an actor who's a member of SAG and you haven't signed with SAG, the guild will stop you from selling your film. This is not true. Distributors, networks, and buyers don't give a damn. They buy anything as long as they think it will make a profit. *El Mariachi,* a $7,500 feature, was picked up for distribution by Columbia Pictures. Do you think Robert Rodriguez (producer-director) signed with any guild or union to make his movie? Spike Lee's *She's Gotta Have It,* Kevin Smith's *Clerks,* Neil LaBute's *In the Company of Men,* and Darren Aronofsky's *pi* probably weren't guild or union either, but they got sold. How about *The Blair Witch Project*? Do you think it was guild or union? It got sold. Matter of fact, it grossed $150 million. 🔒 ***Studios don't care if your production is union or non-union. They only care if it'll make money.***

#3. Get in trouble: If you make a non-union film you'll be "blackballed from the industry." What a crock! Roger Corman (the "King of Bs"), who has produced and distributed over 500 feature films, has rarely signed with all the guilds and union and hasn't gotten into any trouble. In fact, he's heralded as a celebrity who is credited with launching Ron Howard, John Sayles, and Francis Coppola's careers, and they haven't gotten in trouble either. So stop worrying.

#4. Sign for life: Once you sign with a guild or union you've signed for life. This is true. However, everyone gets around this by signing not as a person but as a production company. And for every project they form a new production company.

#5. Mix and match: If you sign with one guild you are forced to sign with the other guilds. Not so. You can sign with the WGA, but not with SAG, DGA, and IATSE. Or you can sign with SAG and IATSE, adhere to their rates and rules, but not sign with the WGA and DGA. Each guild or union is a separate entity that operates independently from the others.

#6. At least SAG: I want professional actors, therefore I should sign with SAG. 🏷 ***You don't have to sign with SAG to hire an actor who is a member of SAG.*** You can hire whomever you want to hire. Once again, this is America! If a SAG member wants to work for you, but your company is not a signator of SAG, the actor still can work for you. It is his/her decision. It is his/her problem, not yours!

There are approximately 98,000 actors in SAG looking for starring roles. How many stars can you name? Fifty? Maybe a hundred? The rest barely make a living by selling shoes, driving limos, or waiting tables. Give your great script to 20 SAG actors, who discover that the part you're casting has them in 75 out of 90 pages. It's a leading part with an opening title credit, and up until now they've only had "number" parts—Cop #4, Hooker #4, Thug #5—in a rear title crawl. They'll take the part in a split second, whether it's a SAG shoot or not. Willis did it. Stallone did it. Schwarzenegger did it. Costner did it. They all did it when starting their careers, and they're not in trouble.

Then Why Sign?

You may be wondering why anyone signs with a guild or union. The answer is simple. Money! 🏷 ***The financing source for the project will dictate whether it is a guild or union shoot.***

If you get funding from a studio, network, or production company that is a signator with the guilds and union, then your project must also be a signator. For, since a signator company is funding it, it is actually their project, which you are contracted to make.

Next, if you're financing by pre-selling at film markets (chapter 45), you don't initially get money from those territories you pre-sell to. What you'll get are contracts, instead of cash, from foreign buyers confirming that when you deliver the final product, they will pay X number of dollars. Suppose you return from a film market with 10–35 contracts from foreign buyers to purchase your movie—when it is done. Then you must find a bank to loan you money, utilizing those pre-sale contracts as collateral.

The bank, however, only loans money if you get a completion bond, and the bonding company will demand that your film be a guild and union shoot. In that case, you'll sign with the guilds and union in a New York minute because you have to get the bond, to get the loan, to get the financing.

Let's go down to the lowest level. Assume your uncle Joe is one of the wealthiest people in North America. He has a $3 billion net worth. His interest (5 percent tax free) is more than $3 million per week and he will give you $500,000 (that's a day's interest) to make a feature, but he stipulates that you must have a good writer. Who are you going to bring, as the alleged good writer, to Uncle Joe? What I would do is to first ask him what TV shows he likes. Maybe he likes *Law & Order* or *ER* or *Friends*.

These shows are massively successful and have each had 30–50 writers. The writers, although talented, are mostly unknowns. Can you name a *Law & Order* writer? Hire one of them. An episodic TV writer receives $25,000–$75,000 per episode. However, if they write just one successful feature film script, they start receiving $250,000–$1 million per script. You, with your feature film project, are providing TV writers the opportunity to leap into the amazingly lucrative movie industry.

The problem is, this writer who is not struggling is probably a WGA member and has enough power to dictate terms. He will tell you he'll gladly write the script for you, but at WGA minimum, which is still a healthy $60,000. Therefore, knowing that if this writer commits, Uncle Joe will give you $500,000, I bet you sign with the Writers Guild—to get the writer, to get Uncle Joe's money.

If, however, you are self-financed, meaning it's your own money, you already have it! Then it is the stupidest thing in the world to sign with any guild or union. You can still hire people (actors in SAG, directors in the DGA, writers in the WGA, or crew in IATSE, etc.) that are in the guilds or union.

However, if your own money isn't funding the film, then probably the amount of money you are about to obtain will determine which guilds or union you can afford. For instance:

1. A $1,000–$50,000 budget is non-union with SAG on an experimental filmmaker's agreement.
2. A $50,000–$300,000 budget can be only SAG on a limited exhibition or experimental agreement.

3. A $300,000–$500,000 budget is usually SAG and sometimes WGA also.
4. A $500,000–$700,000 budget is normally SAG and WGA, but no "names," or just SAG with a small name or two.
5. A $700,000–$1 million budget is commonly SAG, WGA, and DGA with a completion bond.
6. $1–$1.5 million budget is usually SAG, WGA, and DGA, with a completion bond but shot in Canada.
7. $1.5–$2.5 million budget is SAG, WGA, and DGA, with a completion bond, and shot in the USA.
8. $2,500,000-plus budget is SAG, DGA, WGA, and IATSE, with a completion bond, and shot in the USA.

With the above twelve categories you have the resources, contacts, and educational tools needed at one-tenth to one-hundredth the cost of attending UCLA, USC, or NYU, save almost $70,000 to $100,000, and you'll still be able to launch your career within the year with your own feature.

TO DO:

1. Call your film commissioner and get the local film directory.
2. Read books on filmmaking.
3. Take one production and two screenwriting workshops.
4. Get the guild and union low-budget agreements.

 BOOKS

LA 411
Variety staff, 946 pp., $79.00
Shooting in Hollywood/Southern California? The directory for all vendors, suppliers, and crew you'll need.

NY 411
Variety staff, 837 pp., $49.00
Shooting in New York/Tri-State area?

This is the directory you'll use for crew, vendors, and suppliers.

Reel Directory
632 pp., $35.00
Shooting in San Francisco/Northern California? This is the directory you'll use to procure equipment and crew.

Knowledge
972 pp., $110.00
Shooting in London/England? Replete with 4,000 companies,

names, and addresses, this is the directory you'll use.

The Blu-Book
Hollywood Reporter staff, 636 pp., $74.95
The best directory: lists all the dealmakers, studios, networks, and production companies needed to finance and sell your film.

Distributors
HCD staff, 224 pp., $59.95
Lists 800 companies that distribute film and video to the theatrical, TV, and cable buyers.

Producers
HCD staff, 399 pp., $59.95
Lists 1,750 companies with film financing contracts and development deals.

Agents & Managers
HCD staff, 304 pp., $59.95
Lists over 5,000 talent agents, personal managers, and casting directors.

 FILM BOOKSTORES

Samuel French Bookstore (Books)
7623 Sunset Blvd
Los Angeles, CA 90046
Ph: 323-876-0570

The BIZ (Books, software, and scripts)
1223 Olympic Blvd
Santa Monica, CA 90404
Ph: 310-399-6699
    800-366-3456
Web: www.webfilmschool.com

Applause Bookshop (Books)
211 W 71st St

New York, NY 10023
Ph: 212-496-7511

Drama Book Shop (Books)
250 W 40th St
New York, NY 10019
Ph: 212-944-0595

Cinema Bookshop (Books)
13-14 Great Russell St
London WC1B 3NH England
Ph: 44-207-637-0706

Theatre Books (Books)
11 St Thomas St
Toronto, ONT M5S 2B7 Canada
Ph: 416-922-7175

Performing Arts Bookshop (Books and scripts)
302/262 Pitt St
Sydney, NSW 2000 Australia
Ph: 61-2-9267-2257

Enterprise Printers (Forms, paperwork, and books)
7401 Sunset Blvd
Los Angeles, CA 90046
Ph: 323-876-3530

Studio Depot (Expendables and books)
900 N La Brea Ave
Hollywood, CA 90038
Ph: 323-851-0111

Writers Store (Software and books)
2040 Westwood Blvd
Los Angeles, CA 90025
Ph: 310-441-5151
Web: www.Writerstore.com

Screenwriters Store (Software and books)
10-11 Moor St
London W1V 5LJ England
Ph: 44-207-7287-9009

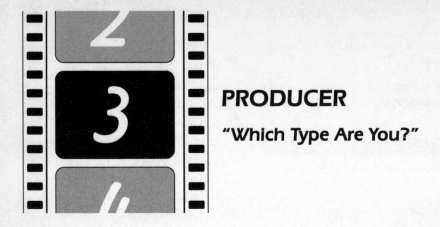

PRODUCER

"Which Type Are You?"

Everyone's a producer and the proliferation of "producer" credits has become the beast of the day. Opening title credits are still popping up during the climax to act III, but do you know the difference between a producer, an associate producer, and an executive producer? Here are the seven producer titles that appear at the front (opening title credits) and end (rear title crawl) of a movie, and an explanation of what these people actually do:

1. Producer
2. Executive producer
3. Co-producer
4. Associate producer
5. Line producer
6. Production manager
7. Executive in charge of production

PRODUCER: *"I'll get the film made."*

A film producer is a jack-of-all-trades: a dreamer (he/she has an idea, a vision, and nurtures it into reality); a salesman (he/she obtains the money and talent to manufacture the dream); an artist (he/she transfers the dream to paper and celluloid in an innovative manner); a mechanic (he/she understands the physical craft of making film); a manager (he/she directs the individual personalities of the crew toward a single goal); and a businessperson (he/she keeps a bottom-line point of view at all times).

The producer, in essence, is the quintessential entrepreneur who takes an idea and makes it happen.

No film is ever going to get made without someone waking up one morning with a can-do attitude and announcing that he's producing a film. 🧳 ***Nine words is all that's needed to be a producer: no degree, no license, no certification.***

Stop saying you're a filmmaker. When you tell someone you're a film-maker all you do is let them know that you're broke and out of work. Have you ever seen the word "filmmaker" as an opening title credit? The answer is no. So stop announcing that you're something that doesn't exist. So when asked, "What do you do?" state, "I'm a producer!" Act like a duck. Talk like a duck. People might think you're a duck.

You're scared to say you're a producer because of the question that follows. But when asked, "What have you produced?" or "What are you producing?" you'll now answer with the nine words, which are; (1) *I* . . . (2) *HAVE* . . . (3) *NUMEROUS* . . . (4) *PROJECTS* . . . (5) *IN* . . . (6) *VARIOUS* . . . (7) *STAGES* . . . (8) *OF* . . . (9) *DEVELOPMENT.* These are the nine magical words that proclaim you are a professional.

You aren't lying. You are a producer. You do have ideas. Your ideas are projects. Projects that are in various stages of development. And the stage of development they're in is pre-production and script development. See? You are a producer with numerous projects (ideas) in various stages of development.

EXECUTIVE PRODUCER: *"I'll get the money."*

The executive producer has access to "other people's money." It is his job to get that money. Once you own a script, you must find an investor. If you don't know anyone who is wealthy, then partner with someone who knows wealthy people. This person, your partner or associate, will be called the executive producer. He could be a banker, a tax attorney, a local real estate magnate, a money-laundering cocaine trafficker, a "sugar daddy," a hip-hop record mogul, or merely Mom and Dad.

Since there are no directories or mailing lists for executive producers, how do you find one? Let me cut your search from two years to two weeks. There is an excellent list of wealthy people who like to invest in films. Pick up the Yellow Pages. Yes, the phone book. Turn to the letter "D" and look under dentists. 🧳 ***Dentists are the wealthiest group of stupid investors*** *in North America.* Scoff, but the next time a low-budget film is reviewed in your local newspaper, the odds are five to one that in the article there will be a single line about how the filmmaker, after a five-year search for a studio deal, met a doctor or dentist and the financing happened.

IMPORTANT POINT   All dentists and doctors have $250/hour accountants. Only accountants know how wealthy a person is. My wife, God bless her, has access to all our funds, but she really doesn't know what our net worth is. Only my accountant knows. Find an accountant or insurance agent who specializes in the medical practice and knows dentists. Partner with that accountant and let him become your executive producer.

Here's another place to find an executive producer. Every decent-sized city has a sports (NBA, NFL, MLB, even hockey) franchise whose players are multimillionaires. Each one of these toddler-millionaires has an attorney. So find the law firm in your city that specializes in professional athletes and approach one of those attorneys with the opportunity to be your executive producer and his athlete-investor to be your co-producer. "Yo, Kobe. Yo, Shaq. Wanna go to the Oscars?"

CO-PRODUCER: *"I've got the money!"*

There are two types of co-producers. The first is the hands-on. While you, the producer, may be in the recording studio working on the final touches for sound, the co-producer can be meeting with a publicist or phoning around to check rental rates for a cast and crew screening. When you run out of steam or are overbooked, the co-producer can take over. If you can't resolve a personality issue, the co-producer can see if a different solution might work.

The second type of co-producer is one in title only; he's wealthy (i.e., a professional athlete, real estate magnate, hip-hop artist) and has provided a majority of the film's financing. When raising money, you'll start with the 50–50 deal. Which is, if the investor gives you 100 percent of the financing, he gets 50 percent of the profits. That is, if he doesn't assume business's golden rule.

The golden rule is: 🗄 *He who has the gold makes the rules.* Therefore, if you find someone who has the money to make your first film, but wants more than the 50 percent you are offering, then don't be a fool. The dude's got the gold. Take the money. Don't kill the golden goose. Give him whatever he wants—60 percent, 70 percent, 80 percent. Further, if he wants a title credit, which he will, give it to him. Take his money, and let him be the co-producer.

ASSOCIATE PRODUCER: *"I know where the money is!"*

The associate producer literally does nothing. He knows little about film-making, donates no money, and offers little more than moral support. However, associate producers are vital in that they help you to find the monies needed by introducing you to wealthy people. I call them the "I know" people, as in "I know where the money is," "I know this guy," "I know this company," or "I know Guido and Carmen . . ."

Basically, this person is a middleman, and will expect a finder's fee of 3–5 percent of the funding he secures for your project. Many times, that middleman also desires a title on the film. The usual credit given this person—only if he succeeds in introducing you to people who invest—is associate producer.

> **AUTHOR'S NOTE**   A thin line separates an executive producer from an associate producer. Usually the executive producer pays for the legal work and gets the investors to invest in the project. The associate producer pays for nothing (maybe a lunch or two, if you're lucky) and just introduces you to wealthy persons.

LINE PRODUCER: *"I'll allocate the money."*

A line producer is someone who knows how to mechanically make a film. He has relationships with camera rental houses, film labs, film stock suppliers, unions, etc. He knows how to get a crew and how to keep the shoot on schedule and on budget.

The best way to find a line producer is to hire an experienced production manager (PM) who's seeking a more visible title card to boost his career. Line producers receive an opening title credit where production manager is a rear title credit. When you see a movie, the last thing you view are the rear title credits. The next time you see a movie, watch how 90 percent of the audience leaves when the end credits start. There is little likelihood that the audience will remember anyone's name, especially with 70–80 other names spiraling by, in the rear title crawl.

Opening title credits appear when 100 percent of the audience is seated. Everyone sees them one at a time. Rear title credits are viewed by 10 percent of the audience and are never remembered. Power, in Hollywood, is achieved with opening title credits. Thus, the next film can be marketed as "From the Producer of . . . ," "The writer of . . . ," "The director of . . ." This has cash value. Line producers are production managers who also want to achieve marquee value by getting an opening title credit.

PRODUCTION MANAGER: *"I work for the money!"*

The production manager (PM) secures locations, hires crew, obtains equipment, gets the cameras rolling, and makes sure everything and everyone is on the set when needed. Then the job shifts into preparing for the next day's shoot. At the end of each day, the production manager coordinates the evening film drop to the lab, the lab work, and the reviewing of the dailies. He is the person who keeps the film on schedule, on time, and within the budget.

> **AUTHOR'S NOTE**   The production manager and line producer perform the same function during your shoot. You need only one.

EXECUTIVE IN CHARGE OF PRODUCTION: *"I account for the money."*

This person is hired by the company funding the film, and serves as an accountant. He/she writes the checks on an as-needed basis as the production progresses. Do you think that when a studio "greenlights" your project, they simply give you a check and say, "Please come back with the movie in four months"? Hardly. They approve a budget and then assign someone to dole out the money needed week-by-week according to an approved cash-flow analysis. The person they assign is eventually titled the executive in charge of production.

Now, armed with an understanding of the differences between a producer, an executive producer, a co-producer, an associate producer, a line producer, and a production manager, let's proceed to what a producer needs to succeed and see if you qualify.

———————

TO DO:

1. Watch theatrical movies and count producer credits.
2. Write down the traits you feel you have to be successful as a producer. Then proceed to the next chapter and compare.

Trait #1: _____

Trait #2: _____

Trait #3: _____

Trait #4: _____

 BOOKS

How to Make It in Hollywood
L. Buzzell, 401 pp., $16.00
Described as a must-own for any wannabe considering a career in Hollywood.

The Film Producer
P. Lazarus, 213 pp., $14.95
An industry veteran reveals what it takes to be a producer in today's Hollywood.

What a Producer Does
B. Houghton, 200 pp., $14.95
A detailed book on what a producer does from pre-production to distribution.

Reel Power
M. Litwak, 336 pp., $14.95
An accurate and exhaustive breakdown of today's movie industry for first-time producers.

Movie and TV Business
G. Resnik, 335 pp., $13.00

The book that explains the rules of the game in Hollywood.

The Beginning Filmmaker's Business Guide
R. Harmon, 199 pp., $15.95
A basic business primer to get your movie made and into theaters.

The Independent Filmmaker's Law and Business Guide
J. Garon, 288 pp., $24.95
Answers the legal, financial, and organizational questions an independent filmmaker will have.

Producers
HCD staff, 399 pp., $59.95
The Hollywood bible that lists, with contact info, production companies that have deals with the studios and networks.

Producers 411
Variety staff, 400 pp., $49.00
An entertainment directory with over 1,000 companies who either finance, produce, or distribute films and TV shows.

GLOBAL PRODUCER ASSOCIATIONS

Producers Guild of America (USA)
8530 Wilshire Blvd, Suite 450
Beverly Hills, CA 90211
Ph: 310-358-9020
Web: www.producersguild.org

Academy of Motion Picture Arts and
   Sciences (USA)
8949 Wilshire Blvd
Beverly Hills, CA 90211
Ph: 310-247-3000

Motion Picture Association of
   America (USA)
15503 Ventura Blvd
Encino, CA 91436
Ph: 818-995-6600
Web: www.mpaa.org

British Academy of Film and Television
   Arts (UK)
195 Piccadilly
London W1V 0LN England
Ph: 44-207-734-0022
Web: www.bafta.org

Producers Alliance for Cinema &
   Television (UK)
45 Mortimer St
London W1W 7TD England
Ph: 44-207-331-6000
E-mail: inquires@pact.co.uk

Academy of Canadian Cinema and
   Television (Canada)
172 King St East
Toronto, ONT M5A 1J3 Canada

Ph: 416-366-2227
Web: www.academy.ca

Motion Picture Theatre Associations
   (Canada)
146 Bloor St West
Toronto, ONT M5S 1P3 Canada
Ph: 416-969-7057
E-mail: mptac.ca@ca.inter.net

Canadian Film and Television
   Production Association (Canada)
20 Toronto St, Suite 830
Toronto, ONT M5C 2B8 Canada
Ph: 416-304-0280
Web: www.cftpa.ca

Verband der Filmverleiher e.V.
   (Germany)
Kreuzberger Ring 56
65205 Wiesbaden, Germany
Ph: 49-611-778-920

Centre National de la
   Cinematographie (France)
12 Rue de Lubeck
75116 Paris, France
Ph: 33-1-4434-3440

Israeli Film & TV Producers
   Association (Israel)
PO Box 20486
Jerusalem, Israel
Ph: 972-3-561-3919

Anica (Italy)
Viale Regina Margherita, 286
00198 Roma, Italy
Ph: 39-06-442-5961

Australian Film Commission
  (Australia)
150 William St
Wooloomooloo, NSW 2011 Australia
Ph: 61-2-9321-6444
Web: www.afc.gov.au

Australian Film Finance
  (Australia)
130 Elizabeth St
Sydney, NSW 2000 Australia
Ph: 61-2-9805-6611
Web: www.ffc.gov.au

PRODUCING

"What It Takes"

From experience, I've discovered that all successful producers possess the following seven traits or qualities, in descending order of importance. They are:

1. **Script** (absolute most important): The ability to read and write.
2. **Money** (also most important): The ability to be a salesman.
3. **Contacts** (very important): The ability to communicate.
4. **Organization** (very important): The ability to plan and coordinate.
5. **Authority** (very important): The ability to stay on budget.
6. **Energy** (very important): The ability to finish what you start.
7. **Talent** (imperative but useless without #1–6): The ability to create.

Did you notice that talent is at the bottom of the ladder? 🎬 **_Talent is the least important trait needed to succeed as a producer._** I know that sounds shocking, but without a doubt, the script is the most important element in the success of the movie. I don't care how much talent God blessed you with, if you don't have the great script then all your talent is useless. The saying is, "If it ain't on the page, it ain't on the stage."

But not just any script. The great script. Don't fall in love with typing. Be very careful about liking the first script that comes your way—especially if you wrote it. The ability to get the great script—not just any script but the great script—is extremely important. And the three ways (none guaranteed) to secure it are by either optioning (chapter 8) an already written "spec script" (written on speculation that someone will buy it); or by hiring a writer (chapter 8) to write it for you (writer-for-hire); or by writing it (chapters 9–10) yourself.

Keep in mind, 🧳 *there are only two types of scripts. It's either great ... or it sucks.* There is no middle ground. Don't brag that so-and-so has read your script and given you good feedback. There is no such thing as good feedback; if the person or company who read it didn't buy it or finance it . . . it sucks! The ability to obtain the great script, by whatever means, is by far the most important quality to possess to be a successful producer.

After obtaining the great script, your skills turn to securing MONEY. Trying to make a movie without money is impossible. Now can you see why I put talent as the least important? Because no matter how much talent you have, if the script isn't great and you have no money, your talent is useless.

If you don't have the money to invest in your own film, your job is to find an executive producer (chapter 2) who has access to OPM (other people's money). Bring him the script and the budget. Partner with him. He does the legal work (business license, incorporating, contracts, offering memoranda, etc.) and secures the investors. You make the film.

Assuming you have the money and the great script, the next quality you need is the ability to CONTACT crew and vendors from your local production directory (chapter 2). You must project authority. Remember—you are a producer with numerous projects in development. Act like one! Don't sound like a wannabe! Practice talking in front of the mirror, phone in hand. Specifically practice the line, "Hello. This is [fill in your name], and I'm a producer. Yadda yadda, yadda yadda."

Salesmanship will get crews and vendors to give you their time, talent, equipment, services, and creative energies at reduced fees. 🧳 *Salesmen make great producers.* When negotiating for lab time, or a camera rental, or hiring a writer, you'll become a salesman. Admit it now, perfect it later, and your producing career will go a lot smoother.

If you're not comfortable with haggling and it's not in your nature to confront, then use the non-confrontational line of, "But I'm just a student filmmaker!" Then bite your bottom lip, look cute, and shut up. Using the student filmmaker routine, you'll always hear the reply, "Student filmmaker? Hmmm. Okay, 10 percent off." WOW! On a $15,000 film purchase, you just saved $1,500. On a $30,000 lab bill you've saved $3,000. On a $40,000 editing fee you've saved $4,000. And it only took 10 seconds to say, "But I'm just a student filmmaker!" and create silence.

ORGANIZATION is needed to stay "on schedule" and "on budget." If not on schedule and on budget, you won't finish! If you don't finish, there's nothing to sell! If there's nothing to sell, you failed!

Getting organized consists of paperwork, paperwork, and more paperwork. When you prepare and oversee the following forms, you'll create a system of checks and balances that will keep your shoot on budget and on schedule.

The pre-production forms and contracts are:

1. Budget
2. Shooting Schedule
3. Storyboards
4. Script Breakdown Notes
5. Actors' Contracts
6. Crew Contracts
7. Camera/Lighting Checklist
8. Location/Prop Checklist
9. Production Manager Checklist

The production paperwork consists of:

1. Camera Reports
2. Sound Reports
3. Script Notes
4. Call Sheets
5. Production Reports
6. Actor Releases
7. Group Releases
8. Location Releases

The next trait a producer must possess is AUTHORITY. This translates into the ability to say no and stay on budget. "No" is the word that isn't taught in film school. Crew, actors, and vendors know your budget but still say they need more money after you hired them. The buck stops with you. You'll have a budget—now stick to it!

SHOOTING TRICK   Never say "no" during your shoot when someone needs money, for an argument instantly ensues, disrupts your production, and you've fallen behind schedule. Thus, simply listen to their request, nod your head, and say, "That's a great point." Pause, then say, "Let me see what I can do," and walk away. Never write an extra check. You have stayed "on budget." You won't get back to this person, who is usually a crew member—they'll dislike you, but they won't quit, and you stayed "on budget."

ENERGY is a trait never mentioned at film schools. There are no eight-hour days when shooting a low-budget film. You can't manufacture daylight. You are putting in 18-hour, tension-filled days. You better be in shape. Once the shoot starts, you never fall asleep or wake up. You "pass out" and "come to." The sun rises at 6:00 A.M., you awake at 5:00 A.M. You shoot until 7:00 P.M., when the sun sets. That's 12–14 hours. Wait, there's more. After each day's wrap (the final shot), there are hours spent preparing for tomorrow, and then watching dailies. You finish at 11:00 P.M. and awake again at 5:00 A.M. That's an 18-hour workday. After three days of this, talk to me about art.

After all of this comes TALENT. Don't get me wrong. I never said talent isn't important. Talent is important—it's extremely important, but just put it in its proper perspective. For if you don't possess the other six traits, your talent is worthless.

TO DO: Take this Producer's Quiz:

1. Would you know the great script if you read it? Yes ___ No ___
2. Have you ever raised money for a dream? Yes ___ No ___
3. Can you make people believe in you? Yes ___ No ___
4. Are you anal and meticulous? Yes ___ No ___
5. Is saying no easy for you? Yes ___ No ___
6. Are you ready for an emotional marathon? Yes ___ No ___
7. Are you really creative? Yes ___ No ___

If you answered no to any of these questions, think seriously about producing or directing.

BOOKS

Shoot Out
P. Bart and P. Guber, 320 pp., $26.95
The editor of *Variety* and a studio
head take you step-by-step through
the producing process.

You're Only As Good As Your Next One
M. Medavoy, 400 pp., $27.00
Learn the ins and outs of the Hollywood rat race system from a studio
head.

Filmmaker's Resource
J. Mackaman, 224 pp., $19.95
A superb guide to filmmaking
workshops, conferences, and academic
programs.

American Film School
E. Pintoff, 486 pp., $19.00
The most comprehensive listing of
schools offering cinema, television,
and video studies.

Film School Confidential
K. Kelly, 269 pp., $14.95
The book to read before applying to
any film school. Know what happens!

*Technical Film and TV for
   Nontechnical People*
D. Campbell, 256 pp., $19.95
An explanation of the technical skills,
crafts, and buzzwords needed to be a
filmmaker.

Hollywood 101
F. Levy, 303 pp., $19.95
How to succeed in Hollywood without
any connections.

Creative Careers in Hollywood
L. Scheer, 240 pp., $19.95
A how-to guide that focuses on the
more offbeat jobs in the film industry:
agents, editors, publicists, etc.

Breaking into Film
K. McHugh, 185 pp., $14.95
Industry experts explain how to
network and break into the industry.

Lights, Camera, Action!
J. Lanham, 276 pp., $19.95
Practical advice on how to break into
the film industry for each below-the-
line filmmaking skill and craft.

 AUDIOS

Shoot Out
Three audios, 220 minutes, $39.95
A studio head and the editor of *Vari-
ety* take you step-by-step through the
Hollywood system.

 SOFTWARE

Automated Contracts for the Film and
   Television Industry
M. Litwak, Windows or Macintosh,
$199.95
A $550/hour entertainment attorney in
a disc. Over 60 "fill in the blanks" contracts from distribution agreements to
writer and talent-for-hire forms needed
by a producer. A must!

TRADE ASSOCIATIONS

Academy of Motion Picture Arts and
  Sciences
(AMPAS . . . vote for Oscars)
8949 Wilshire Blvd
Beverly Hills, CA 90211
Ph: 310-247-3000
Web: www.Oscars.org

Academy of Television Arts & Sciences
(ATAS . . . vote for Emmys)
5220 Lankershim Blvd
North Hollywood, CA 91601
Ph: 818-754-2800
Web: www.Emmys.org

Actors' Equity Association
(AEA . . . actors for theater/stage)
5757 Wilshire Blvd, Suite 1
Los Angeles, CA 90036
Ph: 323-634-1750
Web: www.actorsequity.org

American Film Market Association
(AFMA . . . foreign film sales)
10850 Wilshire Blvd, 9th Floor
Los Angeles, CA 90024
Ph: 310-446-1000
Web: www.afma.com

Alliance of Motion Picture and
  Television Producers
(AMPTP . . . producers lobbying group)
15503 Ventura Blvd
Encino, CA 91436
Ph: 818-995-3600

American Cinema Editors
(ACE . . . film and video editors)
100 Universal City Plz, Bldg 2352B,
  Room 203
Universal City, CA 91608

Ph: 818-777-2900
Web: www.ace-filmeditors.org

American Society of Composers,
  Authors and Publishers
(ASCAP . . . music clearance and
  musicians)
7920 Sunset Blvd, Suite 300
Los Angeles, CA 90046
Ph: 323-883-1000
Web: www.ascap.com

Association of Film Commissioners
  International
(AFCI . . . global film commissioners)
314 N Main St
Helena, MT 59601
Ph: 406-495-8040
Web: www.afci.org

Association of Independent
  Commercial Producers
(AICP . . . commercial production
  companies)
650 N Bronson Ave, Suite 223B
Los Angeles, CA 90004
Ph: 323-960-4763
Web: www.aicp.com

Association of Talent Agents
(ATA . . . actors' agents)
9255 Sunset Blvd, Suite 930
Los Angeles, CA 90069
Ph: 310-274-0628
Web: www.agentassociation.com

Broadcast Music Inc.
(BMI . . . music monitoring
  organization)
8730 Sunset Blvd, 3rd Floor West
West Hollywood, CA 90069
Ph: 310-659-9109
Web: www.bmi.com

Casting Society of America
(CSA . . . casting agents)
606 N Larchmont Blvd, Suite 4B
Los Angeles, CA 90004
Ph: 323-463-1925

International Documentary Association
(IDA . . . documentary filmmakers)
1201 W 5th St, Suite M320
Los Angeles, CA 90017
Ph: 213-534-3600
Web: www.documentary.org

Motion Picture Association of
    America
(MPAA . . . movie rating organization)
15503 Ventura Blvd
Encino, CA 91436
Ph: 818-995-6600
Web: www.mpaa.org

National Association of Broadcasters
(NAB . . . television stations)
1771 N St, NW
Washington, DC 20036
Ph: 202-429-5300
Web: www.nab.org

National Association of Television
    Program Executives
(NATPE . . . television production and
    distribution companies)
2425 Olympic Blvd, Suite 600E
Santa Monica, CA 90404
Ph: 310-453-4440
Web: www.natpe.org

National Association of Theatre
    Owners
(NATO . . . theater circuits)
4605 Lankershim Blvd, Suite 340
North Hollywood, CA 91602
Ph: 818-506-1778
Web: www.natoonline.org

National Association of Video
    Distributors
(NAVD . . . video distributors)
700 Frederick St
Owensboro, KY 42301
Ph: 270-926-6002
E-mail: bpburton@bellsouth.net

National Cable Television Association
(NCTA . . . cable networks)
1724 Massachusetts Ave, NW
Washington, DC 20036
Ph: 202-775-3550
Web: www.ncta.com

Production Equipment Rental
    Association
(PERA . . . film and video equipment
    facilities)
PO Box 55515
Sherman Oaks, CA 91413
Ph: 818-906-2467
Web: www.productionequipment.com

Video Software Dealers Association
(VSDA . . . video distributors and
    stores)
16530 Ventura Blvd, Suite 400
Encino, CA 91436
Ph: 818-385-1500
Web: www.vsda.org

INDEPENDENT VS. STUDIO

"Don't Be Tricked"

Before embarking on your filmmaking journey, ask yourself, "Am I a producer-filmmaker or am I a producer-dealmaker?" There is a difference.

The producer-dealmaker is exotic. He puts together mega-million-dollar deals, hires people with large salaries, and makes big-budget studio features. On the other hand, the producer-filmmaker gets a script, moves the decimal point two spaces to the left on a studio budget, purchases some unexposed film stock, gets some friends, and makes a low-budget film.

This book focuses on the producer-filmmaker approach used by people like John Sayles, Quentin Tarantino, Spike Lee, Kevin Smith, and Robert Rodriguez, who've launched amazing careers. But first I'll address the producer-dealmaker approach, if only to acquaint you with the seduction of the big-dollar studio deals that almost always lead to a dead end.

The producer-dealmaker approach has glamour, is expensive to play, and is fraught with dangling golden carrots. And, 999 times out of 1,000, the beginner who pursues these carrots gets tied up in a costly web of pre-payments, pay-or-play checks, and attorney fees that he can't afford, and gets detoured from the goal of making his first film.

A classic dealmaking "golden carrot" is: You've pitched your project to either a foreign sales company or theatrical distributor for funding, and they state, "We're in for half the budget." They're lying. If a company ever gives you the "50 percent of the budget" line when pitching, respond, "Wonderful! Let's cut the budget in half and start shooting tomorrow." Now, watch how they wiggle. What they're really saying is, if you can raise the first half (used for the physical production), then their contract (not cash) will finance the marketing and promotion (after they see the finished project), guaranteeing them first position on recouping funds, and the ability to cancel the deal if the film you make doesn't meet their standards.

Another "golden carrot" is, "We're in if you can get a name attached." Sounds simple. All you have to do is get an actor with a credit or two to give you a "letter of intent" showing interest and you'll secure financing. The point, however, is that anyone can get a letter from an actor declaring that he/she is interested. 🔒 ***Every actor is interested in every single part as long as he/she gets paid.*** So what? That letter, which is not a contract, is absolute garbage in Hollywood.

What you want is a "firm commitment," a contract from an actor that states he/she will set aside X number of days, 4 to 12 months from now, to be in your film and will work nowhere else in the world during those days, for which he is to be paid Y salary. The salary will be large, and the actor, through his agent, wants a 30–50 percent deposit of it up front. If you want to shop an actor's name, you have to pay for that privilege. Otherwise, you're pissing in the wind; no distributor, or foreign buyer, will give a hoot about your "interested stars." They want guarantees (aka firm commitments). And guarantees cost money.

To get this guarantee in writing is called a "pay-or-play" agreement. You PAY the actor a percentage of his/her promised salary, up front, for the actor to commit the days needed for him/her to PLAY the part in your film, and make his/her name available to market and sell to secure project financing.

Therefore, if you can't write $300,000–$5 million checks (30–50 percent of $1–$10 million salaries) to commit name actors to finance a $20–$50 million feature, stop fantasizing. Unless you're wealthy, and your name is Steve Bing (inside Hollywood joke), and are willing to play Hollywood Vegas, with large pay-or-play checks. Then stop pretending that you're a producer-dealmaker and approach the industry from the producer-filmmaker route—which is to first make a film, then make the deal.

Here's the magic formula on how to get $20–$50 million to finance a feature film. First, there only six to seven distributors (Paramount, Fox, Warner Bros., Sony, etc.) that can write $20–$50 million checks. And they won't consider giving you this type of money until you've first made a $2–$5 million feature film that's been distributed, with you getting an opening title credit and the film making a lot of money. Then, and only then, are you marketable and bankable enough for a studio to gamble $20–$50 million on your next project.

So how do you get $2–$5 million, to eventually make your $20–$50 million film? Well, several medium-size distributors (Miramax, New Line, Artisan Entertainment, MGM/UA, etc.) write $2–$5 million checks. Here's all they ask you to do: Make an excellent $200,000–$500,000 feature film that's been distributed, with you getting an opening title credit and the film making a lot of money. Then, and only then, are you marketable and bankable enough to have a medium-size distributor gamble $2–$5 million on your next project.

Now, who has $200,000–$500,000? Well, to get that amount of money from small distributors, first make an excellent $20,000–$50,000 digital feature. If not, then you must start with $2,000–$5,000 and shoot a digital feature for the Web. Get the point? 🗎 *First make a film, then make a deal.*

The problem with filmmakers who never make a film is they spend their entire lives trying to make a deal. Hollywood doesn't finance first-timer nobodies. Here's the bottom line.

> Want $20,000,000? Make a $2,000,000 feature.
> Want $2,000,000? Make a $200,000 feature.
> Want $200,000? Make a $20,000 feature.
> Want $20,000? Make a $2,000 Web feature.

This is how Hollywood works. It's not complicated.

So where are you going to start? At the most, only 1 percent of the people reading this book are rich enough to gamble $200,000–$500,000 to shoot their first (35mm three-week shoot) feature. The other 99 percent probably had a hard time parting with the money to buy this book. Then you'll be shooting a $20,000–$50,000 digital feature or a $2,000–$5,000 feature for the Web.

Therefore, start from the bottom. Be a producer-filmmaker. Prove your talents. Forget about being a producer-dealmaker. Stop chasing the deal—just make a film, and if the film you made is great, you'll make a deal. But 🗎 *your first film must be great. Good is not good enough.* Only *great* will launch your career. And since you won't have money for name actors, exotic locations, stunts, and special effects, you will find yourself being totally story dependent. Thus, to succeed as a producer-filmmaker you will, on your first film, be totally script dependent and must prepare by first reading at least 20–30 screenplays of successful movies that you've seen. Don't read these 20–30 scripts and you are guaranteed to fail.

TO DO:

1. Read the trades. Go to your local library and read the past year of *Variety* and the *Hollywood Reporter,* especially the special edition issues (AFM, Cannes, MIFED, independent filmmaking, financing, etc.).

2. Read produced scripts (see chapter 2). You can also check the Internet for sources.

   A. Read three to five action-adventure scripts. (i.e., James Bond scripts, *Die Hard, Mission Impossible, Raiders of the Lost Ark,* etc.).

   B. Read three to five love stories (i.e., *When Harry Met Sally, Sleepless in Seattle, Casablanca, Pretty Woman,* etc.).

   C. Read three to five buddy scripts (i.e., *Lethal Weapon, Men in Black, Charlie's Angels, Thelma and Louise,* etc.).

   D. Read three to five family scripts (i.e. ,*Stuart Little, My Dog Skip, E.T., Miracle on 34th Street, It's a Wonderful Life,* etc.).

   E. Read three to five horror scripts (i.e., *The Exorcist, Scream, Friday the 13th, Halloween, Bride of Chucky,* etc.).

   F. Read three to five suspense-thriller scripts (i.e., *The Sixth Sense, The Manchurian Candidate, Fatal Attraction, Body Heat, Chinatown,* etc.).

   G. Read three to five against-all-odds scripts (i.e., *Rocky, Rudy, Chariots of Fire, Hoosiers,* etc.).

 BOOKS

Independent Feature Film Production
G. Goodell, 481 pp., $16.95
A must! A complete guide to independent filmmaking from concept to distribution.

Creative Producing from A–Z
M. Schreibman, 268 pp., $21.95
A practical step-by-step guide to producing an independent film.

Producing for Hollywood
P. Mason, 260 pp., $19.95
An excellent guide for the independent producer.

Making Independent Films
L. Stubbs and R. Rodriguez, 210 pp.,
$16.95
From first pitch to final cut, this
overview chronicles the first-time
filmmaker's journey.

Shoot Me
R. Simonelli, 240 pp., $19.95
Details dozens of real-life experiences
and worst-case scenarios for first-
timers, from developing an idea to
promoting your film.

Film Production
G. Merritt, 235 pp., $24.95
This uncensored guide to filmmaking
cuts through the fluff and provides
real-world producing facts.

Entertainment 101
R. Claire, 221 pp., $16.95
An industry primer for the film, television, music, new media, theater, and
radio industries.

 THE SEVEN MAJOR DISTRIBUTORS

Warner Bros.
4000 Warner Blvd
Burbank, CA 91522
Ph: 818-954-6000
Web: www.warnerbros.com

Fox Studios
10201 W Pico Blvd
Los Angeles, CA 90035
Ph: 310-369-1000
Web: www.fox.com

Paramount Pictures
5555 Melrose Ave
Los Angeles, CA 90038
Ph: 323-956-5000
Web: www.paramount.com

Sony/Columbia/Tri-Star
10202 W Washington Blvd, Plaza 4812
Culver City, CA 90232
Ph: 310-244-4000
Web: www.sony.com

The Walt Disney Co.
500 S Buena Vista St
Burbank, CA 91521
Ph: 818-560-1000
Web: www.disney.com

MCA/Universal Pictures
100 Universal City Plz
Universal City, CA 91608
Ph: 818-777-1000
Web: www.universalstudios.com

DreamWorks SKG
100 Universal Plz, Bldg 10
Universal City, CA 91608
Ph: 818-733-7000

LOW-BUDGET

"$5,000 to $500,000 Feature"

HOW LOW IS LOW?

When producing your first feature, it is important to be not just realistic but ultra-realistic. You perceive yourself as reality based when you say that your first feature will be low-budget. Then you instantly lose reality by assuming low-budget to be $1 million to $10 million. Get real! One million dollars is a lot of money. Don't be naive. Do you think anyone is going to give you that amount when you don't even know how to buy unexposed film?

POINT OF INTEREST Major studios think of "low-budget" as a film with no box-office stars (Mel Gibson, Bruce Willis, Julia Roberts, etc.) and a high-concept story. The film is shot over six to eight weeks with a guild cast and union crew, a decent producer's fee, five to seven licensed songs, a completion bond, and a 500–750 print release. These films (e.g., *The Big Chill, Ferris Bueller's Day Off, Heathers, Mortal Kombat, Groundhog Day,* etc.) are made with a budget of $5 million–$10 million.

Independent distributors think of "low-budget" as a dialogue-oriented film (black comedy, coming-of-age, or heist-gone-bad) with two or three TV actors, but not big-name movie stars, working for guild minimums. The shoot takes four to six weeks. The budget allows for two or three songs, a 300–500 print release, and the film is financed by foreign, cable, and video pre-sales at $3–$5 million (e.g., *The Big Easy, Body Heat, The Crying Game, Dirty Dancing, American Pie, Footloose,* etc.).

Small distributors think of "low-budget" as a genre-oriented feature (horror, action, T&A), starring one or two over-the-hill actors (names spared to protect anyone found in 12-step meetings) and shot on a three- to five-week schedule, with one guild, SAG, being used (*Reservoir Dogs, Halloween, Scream,* etc.). Minimal digital effects and a limited release of 50–100 prints are included in the budget of $1–$3 million.

Foreign sales agents and video distributors think of "low-budget" as a 90-minute movie with the words "Blood," "Zombie," "Slime," "Nightmare," "Warlord," "Massacre," "Revenge," "Warrior" (pick two and add a noun) in the title. It has SAG actors (Lorenzo Lamas, Andrew Stevens, Jeff Fahey, Eric Roberts, etc.), but is shot non-union, in 13–18 days (two or three weeks), with no U.S. theatrical release, on a budget of $500,000–$700,000.

Ten million dollars is not low-budget. Neither is $5 million nor $1 million. For you, low-budget is anything between $5,000 and $500,000—with $5,000–$75,000 classified as "no-budget," $75,000–$150,000 classified as "ultra-low-budget," and only $250,000–$500,000 being called "low-budget."

And, with the following amounts (cutting to the chase), here's what you can produce:

1. $5,000–$75,000: You can make a digital video feature (*The Blair Witch Project, The Cruise, Chuck & Buck,* etc.) shot in one or two weeks with a three-chip mini-DV camera and a five- to eight-person crew.

2. $75,000–$150,000: You can produce a 16mm feature film (*She's Gotta Have It, Stranger Than Paradise, Return of the Secaucus 7, In the Company of Men,* etc.) shot in nine days with an Arriflex SR2 camera and a 10–12 person crew or a digital feature utilizing two cameras (mini-DV) and a 12–15 person crew.

3. $150,000–$250,000: You can make a 16mm film shooting for two or three weeks with a small name, or a 35mm film shooting for two or three weeks with no names, or a digital feature utilizing three cameras (DVCAM or DVPRO) and a 15–20 person crew over three to four weeks.

4. $250,000–$500,000: You can produce a 35mm feature film on a three-week shoot with a name and a 15–20 person crew that you will market as a "just under" $1 million feature film with the possibility of one to two names attached.

WHAT IS A LOW-BUDGET SCRIPT?

What is the formula, the formula script, that all filmmakers, like John Sayles, Spike Lee, Kevin Smith, and Quentin Tarantino, used to launch their careers when all they had was enough money to be a no-, ultra-low-, or micro-budget feature?

First, you must realize that the present idea/script you have, although possibly great, will be either too expensive to make or, even if you could get the cash, too difficult to make when you truthfully don't know what you're doing.

Thus, put this idea/script aside for your second project. Now, come up with an idea/script that you can handle when you don't know what you're doing (you don't) and you don't have a lot of money (you won't). The answer is: *KISS—Keep It Simple, Stupid.* Let me explain. Let's talk formula.

Almost all movies are 90–120 minutes in running time. The rule of thumb is that one page of properly typed script becomes one minute of running time. Therefore, when applying the rule that one page of script typed (formatted) properly is one minute of running time, then you'll want a 90-page script. Why?

All movies have the same ticket price. The price of admission has nothing to do with the film's budget or running time and 🛄 *The movie industry is about renting seats and selling sugar.* Give a theater owner a 90-minute movie and he rents the seat at 12:00, 1:30, 3:00, 4:30, 6:00, 7:30, 9:00, and 10:30—eight times in a day. Allow breaks between shows to clean the theater and sell candy, and he'll screen the film (rent the seat) five or six times a day.

Now, give the theater owner a 120-minute movie. Watch what happens. He can screen that film at 12:00, 2:00, 4:00, 6:00, 8:00, and 10:00—six times in a day. Then allow the theater owner breaks between shows, and he'll show the film only four times. A 90-minute film screens five or six times a day, while a 120-minute film screens four times a day—and the price of admission is always the same, no matter what the film's budget is. This is not rocket science.

Common sense (Hollywood, believe it or not, is based on common sense) tells you that theater owners prefer 90-minute movies. They have more profit potential. And if theater owners like it, distributors like it. And if distributors like it, you should produce for it. Thus, for your first feature film get a great 90-page script. Plus, a 90-page script has 25 percent fewer problems than a 120-page script—25 percent fewer pages.

Now, what do you write in those 90 pages? What's the magic formula that launched hundreds of careers, from John Carpenter to John Sayles to Steven Soderbergh to Quentin Tarantino to the kids that made *The Blair Witch Project*? The script that everyone uses to launch their career is— 🧰 *in 90 pages, take 12 kids to a house and chop them up.*

Stop! I'm not suggesting you make a slasher film. I'm just using it as an example, but think about *Halloween, I Know What You Did Last Summer, Scream, Friday the 13th, Blair Witch,* etc. They all made money and launched careers. What I am really saying is, take 12 actors to one location—a house, an apartment building, a courtroom, a restaurant, a police station—and shoot a stage play. 🧰 *Hollywood loves courtroom dramas—they're one-room, cheap-to-shoot dramas.*

Spike Lee started his career with *She's Gotta Have It,* shot in an apartment building. John Sayles's first feature, *Return of the Secaucus 7,* was shot at a friend's house in the country. Henry Jaglom shot *Always* at his house in the Hollywood Hills, and *New Year's Day* was shot in a two-bedroom apartment. Kevin Smith's *Clerks* used a convenience store. Quentin Tarantino's *Reservoir Dogs* was shot in a warehouse. Roger Corman (the king of B movies) has shot and produced hundreds of low-budget features using very few locations, often at isolated motels. Steven Soderbergh's *sex, lies and videotape* used three houses, a restaurant, and an office as building locations.

Even Kevin Spacey. An Oscar-winning actor who has been on many shoots, he knew the magic formula when he decided to launch his career as a director. His first project, *The Big Kahuna,* starring himself, Danny De Vito, and an unknown, was a stage play that took place in literally one room. Ethan Hawke launched his directing career with *Tape,* a no-budget digital feature shot in one week, in one room, with three actors, as did Alan Cumming and Jennifer Jason Leigh with their first film *Anniversary Party.*

Get the point? Your first feature film, when you have limited funds, is going to be a dressed-up, dialogue-oriented stage play. Alfred Hitchcock, the directing genius, should also be known as the first king of low-budget. Think of *Rope* (shot in one take in a small apartment), *Rear Window* (two sets with James Stewart in a wheelchair), or *Lifeboat,* a mini-mini-budgeted *Titanic* with more drama.

Ninety pages, one room, a stage play. Keep It Simple, Stupid!

TO DO:

1. Rent and view *She's Gotta Have It, Return of the Secaucus 7, Always, New Year's Day, Metropolitan, Clerks, Reservoir Dogs, Bound, Two Girls and a Guy, The Blair Witch Project, The Big Kahuna, Anniversary Party,* or any video with the words "Blood," "Zombie," "Slime," "Horror," "Hell," "Nightmare," or "Haunted" in the title.

 BOOKS

Low-Budget Films That Sell
R. Harmon, 153 pp., $12.95
An introduction to the ins and outs of successful low-budget production.

Feature Filmmaking at Used-Car Prices
R. Schmidt, 409 pp., $16.95
A must! How to write, produce, direct, shoot, edit, and promote a feature film for under $15,000.

How to Shoot a Feature for Under $10,000
B. Stern, 304 pp., $14.95
An excellent book on no-budget film-making from A to Z from the producer of three independent features.

Rebel Without a Crew
R. Rodriguez, 285 pp., $15.00
How a 23-year-old produced *El Mariachi* for $7,000 and became a Hollywood player.

Hollywood on $5,000, $10,000 or $25,000 a Day
P. Gaines and D. Rhodes, 147 pp., $11.95
The survival guide for low-budget filmmakers.

The Guerilla Film Maker's Handbook
C. Jones and G. Jolliffe, 640 pp., $34.95
The ultimate guide to independent filmmaking. Comes with free filmmaking software, forms, and contracts. An absolute must!

Persistence of Vision
J. Gaspard and D. Newton, 431 pp., $26.95
A must-read. An excellent guide on how to step-by-step produce a feature film for under $30,000.

Make Your Own Damn Movie
L. Kaufman, 268 pp., $14.95
Low-budget manual for the first-timer from Troma Studios, the makers of *Toxic Avenger* and *Nuke Em High*.

 VIDEOS

Video School
Six 30-minute VHS instructional videos, $134.95
   1. *Basic Shooting*, $22.95
      The very basics for production.
   2. *Advanced Shooting*, $22.95
      The A–Z of camera moves to composition.

3. *Light It Right,* $22.95
   An essential guide to lighting techniques.
4. *Sound Success,* $22.95
   The audio basics from miking to post-production.
5. *Video Editing,* $22.95
   Basic editing techniques and more.
6. *Computer Video,* $22.95
   Computer video tips and techniques.

Videomaker/DVD
DVD/DVD-ROM, three instructionals, $99.00
Learn on your computer with three filmmaking how-tos on "Basic Shooting," "Lighting," and "Sound Techniques."

 SOFTWARE

How to Make Your Movie
Three CD-ROMs plus a production notebook
Windows or Macintosh, $89.95
An interactive film school that takes you through the steps of production from screenwriting to striking the final print.

Movie Magic Budgeting
Windows or Macintosh, $699.00
Create budgets from $50,000 to $300 million with this dynamic tool used by 80 percent of the industry professionals.

Movie Magic Scheduling
Windows 95/98/NT or Macintosh, $699.00
Construct an efficient and cost-effective shooting schedule for your production.

Turbo Budget
Windows or Macintosh, $99 to $699
A Web download program that is on a pay-per-use basis.

Easy Budgets for Features
Windows or Macintosh (with a spreadsheet program), $189.95
The best inexpensive program. With any full-function spreadsheet program you can create accurate, good-looking budgets in half the time.

Easy Budgets for Commercials
Windows or Macintosh (with a spreadsheet program), $189.95
Budgeting for commercials is different than features. With any full-function spreadsheet this program will create precise, good-looking budgets quickly.

Cinergy 2000 Budgeting
Windows or Macintosh, $399.00

Cinergy 2000 Scheduling
Windows or Macintosh, $499.00

Cinergy 2000 Producers Package
Windows or Macintosh, $699.00
The Cinergy budgeting and scheduling programs are combined into one package at half the cost of the *Movie Magic* programs.

FILMMAKING WORKSHOPS

Independent Feature Project/West
8750 Wilshire Blvd, 2nd Floor
Beverly Hills, CA 90211
Ph: 310-432-1200
Web: www.ifpwest.org

International Documentary Association
1201 W 5th St, Suite 4320
Los Angeles, CA 90017
Ph: 213-534-3600
E-mail: idf@netcom.com
Web: www.documentary.org

Women In Film
8857 W Olympic Blvd, Suite 201
Beverly Hills, CA 90211
Ph: 310-657-5144
Web: www.wfi.org

Writers Boot Camp
2525 Michigan Ave, Bldg I
Santa Monica, CA 90404
Ph: 310-998-1199

Bay Area Video Coalition
2727 Mariposa St, 2nd Floor
San Francisco, CA 94110
Ph: 415-861-3282
Web: www.bavc.org

Film Arts Foundation
145 9th St
San Francisco, CA 94103
Ph: 415-552-8760
Web: www.filmarts.org

American University Summer Film
    Program
4400 Massachusetts Ave, NW
Washington, DC 20016

Ph: 202-885-2061
Web: www.soc.american.edu

Image Film Video
75 Bennett St NW
Atlanta, GA 30309
Ph: 404-352-4225
Web: www.imagefv.org

Chicago Filmmakers
5243 N Clark St
Chicago, IL 60640
Ph: 773-293-1447
Web: www.Chicagofilmmakers.org

Community Film Workshops
1130 S Wabash Ave, Suite 302
Chicago, IL 60605
Ph: 312-427-1245
E-mail: cfwChicago@aol.com

New Orleans Video Access Center
4840 Bank St
New Orleans, LA 70119
Ph: 504-486-9192

International Film & Television
    Workshops
PO Box 200
2 Central St
Rockport, ME 04856
Ph: 207-236-8581
Web: www.meworkshops.com

Boston Film & Video Foundation
119 Braintree St
Boston, MA 02215
Ph: 617-783-9241
Web: www.bfvf.org

Independent Feature Project/North
401 N 3rd St, Suite 450
Minneapolis, MN 55401
Ph: 612-338-0871

Film Video Arts
462 Broadway, Suite 420
New York, NY 10046
Ph: 212-941-8787
Web: www.fva.com

Independent Feature Project/New York
104 W 29th St, 12th Floor
New York, NY 10001
Ph: 212-465-8200
Web: www.ifp.org

Millennium Film Workshops
66 E 4th St
New York, NY 10003
Ph: 212-673-0090

The New School
66 W 12th St
New York, NY 10011
Ph: 212-229-8903
Web: www.newschool.edu/
  mediastudies

Cleveland Film Society
2510 Market Ave
Cleveland, OH 44113
Ph: 216-623-3456
Web: www.clevelandfilm.org

Northwest Film Center
1219 SW Park Ave
Portland, OR 97205
Ph: 503-221-1156
Web: www.nfw.org

Philadelphia Independent Film &
  Video Association
International House
3701 Chestnut St
Philadelphia, PA 19104
Ph: 215-895-6594

Pittsburgh Filmmakers
477 Melwood Ave
Pittsburgh, PA 15213
Ph: 412-681-5449
Web: pghfilmmakers.org

Watkins Film Center
601 Church St
Nashville, TN 37219
Ph: 615-242-1851

IndieU
10134 Hammerly, Suite 178
Houston, TX 77080
Ph: 877-463-4375
Web: www.indieslate.com

Southwest Alternative Media Project
1519 W Main
Houston, TX 77006
Ph: 713-522-8592
Web: www.swamp.org

911 Media Arts Center
117 Yale Ave North
Seattle, WA 98109
Ph: 206-682-6552
Web: www.911media.org

THE SCRIPT

"Only Great Will Do"

To launch your career, it starts with the script, and 📰 *"good is not good enough."* Your script must be great. Ideas are a dime a dozen. Everyone has one. Your job is to get the great script, which is based on a great idea. There is nothing easy about this. Don't be lazy.

I know you've read that Hollywood buys ideas. This is true, but only for celebrities like Mel Gibson, Kevin Costner, or Quentin Tarantino because the purchasing studio wants the name of that celebrity on the project's poster. Don't be naive and think that a movie studio is going to buy a thought (idea) from you, a person with no marquee value. You are not Mel. You are not Kevin. You are not Quentin.

SO WHAT DO YOU DO?

You're the producer. Get into action. If you want to make a movie, then your first step is to take your great idea and make it into a great script!

There are three ways to get a great script. The first, obviously, is to WRITE IT (chapters 9–10). This is not expensive. But if you're not a great writer, then you look for an already written script that is great and OPTION IT (chapter 8) or HIRE A WRITER (chapter 8) to start from scratch and write one for you.

But remember: Without a great script you have nothing. The greatest shortcoming of first-timers is their inability to tell the difference between a good script and a great script. And the only way to gain this vital skill is to read scripts, read more scripts, then read still more scripts, which you'll find at either your local library, at script stores, or on Web sites. And it's important to read only scripts of movies you've seen. You saw the movie. You viewed the visual image. Now let's see what the typing looks like. Get your eyes educated. To do this you should repeat the "To Do" exercise 2 of chapter 5.

HOW TO TELL IF YOUR SCRIPT IS GREAT

Here are three tests to determine whether your script is great:

Wallet test: Give it to an industry executive to read. If he/she wants to purchase, option, finance, or, at the least, co-produce it with you, then your wallet will tell you. You'll get a check. But don't get your hopes up if they tell you it's good but it needs a little work. Bullshit! No check! No good! If it was so good, then why didn't they option it and pay you to rewrite it? The answer is because it really wasn't that good.

> **AUTHOR'S NOTE**   Get ready for the fact that no one in Hollywood will ever say no to you. The reason is fear. They know that if you persevere, accumulate knowledge, and someday make a "hit," you will always remember the asshole who said no to you 10 years ago and will never work with him.

Mind test: Your mind is also a great test. **If it ain't on the page it ain't on the stage.** Think you have a comedy script? Then when you read it, you should be laughing out loud. If you're not laughing out loud, but thinking, "That's cute," then it's not funny—it's cute. If you have a horror picture, you should be reading it and saying, "Yuck, gross." If just reading it repulses you, imagine how horrible it will be when an audience sees it.

Head test: When you're reading something boring, your head moves from left to right. When you're reading something that is great, notice how your head moves: down the page. Time flies. You can't wait to get to the next page to find out what happens next. If you're reading and you feel your eyes and head going left to right, it's labor. If, however, your eyes go down the page (a page-turner), not left to right, then what you're reading could be great.

LET'S GET STORY EDUCATED

Next you must understand what makes a story good. Learn structure. Before searching for a great script, read several how-to books (see "Books," chapters 9 and 10) and attend weekend writing workshops to learn what story structure (conflicts, plot points, crisis, etc.) is. Discover where clearly defined plot points in a well-structured script are. I call it the "Hollywood Formula." All the books and courses teach the same information, they just label it differently. Because writing instructors are elitists, they are paranoid about being categorized as not teaching art but formula. Well, I don't give a damn. It's a frickin' formula. It's called the "Hollywood Formula." Learn it! Anyway, I'll teach it to you in chapters 9 and 10.

WHAT ABOUT DIALOGUE?

A screenwriting course can't teach how to write great dialogue. You either have a "good ear" or not. You can learn how to type properly and how to structure your script, but if the dialogue isn't great, the script becomes boring. No one can teach how to write great dialogue. It's a skill God either gifted you with or you don't have it.

To see if you have it, try this test. Pick up the last script you wrote. Turn to a page that has a man (John) and woman (Mary) conversing. Put your thumb over the word "John," to pretend you now don't know who's talking, and see, by reading 5 to 15 words of dialogue, if that is a man talking. Then put your thumb over the word "Mary" and see, from the 5 to 15 words, if you can tell if that's a woman. I bet your dialogue is so one-dimensional that you can't differentiate between a man and woman, much less between Man #1 and Man #2.

> **AUTHOR'S NOTE**   To see what true dialogue looks like, in typed form, read attorney depositions. These are typed transcripts, word for word, of two people when they are in conflict.

Be cautious and resist the urge to fall in love with the first script that comes your way, especially if you've written it yourself. Be patient. Learn what a great script looks like. Read 20 to 30 previously made scripts and a couple of screenwriting books, take a couple of writing workshops, understand dialogue, and write a sample script. Then, and only then, you will be ready to recognize the great script if it comes your way.

The next three chapters will cover the three ways to get a great script. But first, a word of caution. Never overpay! It's not necessary. Although **the script is the most important thing, it doesn't mean it's the most expensive thing.** Writers are the biggest hypocrites I've ever met. They love whining about how they don't get enough respect. Aristotle complained about it.

Shakespeare complained about it. And every contemporary screenwriter complains about it. Respect, ha! They don't want more respect. You know what they want. They want more money. And the studios and networks aren't going to give it to them. You know why? Because they just don't want to. Point. Period. End sentence. And if you think you're going to get better typing or more respect by paying a writer more, and thus giving them control over how you can spend your money, then you're a fool who is going to go broke.

TO DO:

1. Read 20 to 30 scripts of movies you've seen, and books on the structure of screenplays.
2. Attend one or two screenwriting workshops that detail structure.
3. Read attorney depositions to discover what dialogue looks like when typed.

 BOOKS

The Screenwriter's Guide to Agents and Managers
J. Lewinski, 236 pp., $18.95
A directory for the first-timer that covers all aspects of representation.

The Script Is Finished, Now What Do I Do?
K. Callan, 302 pp., $18.95
Discover the truth on how Hollywood works with first-time screenwriters and succeed.

500 Ways to Beat the Hollywood Script Reader
J. Lerch, 170 pp., $12.00
An excellent book. If your script can't get past the Hollywood reader, it will never get sold. A must!

The Big Deal
T. Taylor, 317 pp., $16.00
Discover the inside story on all those million-dollar screenplay sales in the spec script market. Good info!

Selling Scripts to Hollywood
K. Herbert, 157 pp., $12.95
Outlines the hard facts about writing for Hollywood. The nuts and bolts!

Selling Your Screenplay
C. Whitcomb, 200 pp., $16.95
The screenplay columnist for *Writer's Digest* outlines how to succeed in Hollywood as a writer.

Crafty Screenwriting
A. Epstein, 288 pp., $15.00
A development executives' real-world approach to writing scripts that get optioned, bought, and produced.

Opening the Doors to Hollywood
C. Abreau and H. Smith, 428 pp.,
$17.00
How to sell your idea, story,
screenplay, and/or manuscript.

The Screenwriter's Survival Guide
M. Adams, 301 pp., $13.95
The dos and don'ts to getting your
feature screenplay read, sold, and
produced.

How to Sell Your Screenplay
L. and J. Wilen, 301 pp., $17.95
A very realistic guide to getting a tele-
vision or film deal.

The Complete Book of Scriptwriting
J. Straczynski, 416 pp., $22.95
A must! An all-in-one guide to selling
screenplays, teleplays, plays, and radio
and animation scripts.

*How to Enter a Screenplay Contest
    and Win*
E. Joseph, 247 pp., $19.95
Screenplay contest awards will open
doors to lucrative Hollywood writing
assignments.

 VIDEOS

Writing a Screenplay That Sells
VHS, 125 minutes, $39.95
Syd Field's screenwriting workshop is
an invaluable tool for first-timers and
seasoned professionals.

Making a Good Script Great
VHS, three videos and workbook,
$95.00
Linda Seger's master class on how to
make your script great with story,
theme, and character.

 AUDIOS

Story
Four audio cassettes, 6 hours, $29.95
Robert McKee's acclaimed $495
screenwriting seminar is condensed in
these cassettes.

Screenwriting for Hollywood
Two audio cassettes, 180 minutes,
$17.95
Michael Hauge teaches how to step
right up and write the great American
screenplay.

Screenwriting: How to Move Your Tale
Audio cassette, 90 minutes, $14.95
Richard Walter, UCLA's dean of
screenwriting, details the creation and
importance of story.

Screenwriting: Tricks of the Trade
Audio cassette, 90 minutes, $14.95
William Froug, the founder of UCLA's
writing program, describes how to
write from the gut.

Making a Good Script Great
Three audio cassettes, 180 minutes,
$24.95
Nothing is written, it's rewritten. Linda
Seger teaches the craft of the rewrite.

Whose Story
Two audio cassettes, 150 minutes,
$17.95
Deciding on a point of view is the
hardest task for a screenwriter. Made-
line Dimaggio teaches how.

Using Myth to Power Your Story
Two audio cassettes, 190 minutes,
$17.95

Discover how to create great scripts, with Chris Vogler using the powerful storytelling myths that link us all.

 SOFTWARE

Final Draft
Dual platform for Windows or
Macintosh, $199.95
Makes writing easy. One of the top
two formatting programs for writing a
screenplay, sitcom, or stage play.

Movie Magic Screenwriter 2000
CD-ROM for Windows or Macintosh,
$199.95
The other top formatting program
that makes typing and retyping your
screenplay as easy as possible.

 WRITERS COMPETITIONS

Carl Sautter Memorial Competition
c/o Screenwriters Network
11684 Ventura Blvd, Suite 508
Studio City, CA 91604
Ph: 323-848-9477

Chanticleer Award
c/o Discovery Program
1680 N Vine St, Suite 1212
Hollywood, CA 90028
Ph: 213-462-4705

Christopher Columbus Discovery
   Awards
433 N Camden Dr, Suite 600
Beverly Hills, CA 90210
Ph: 310-288-1988

Disney Fellowship
c/o Walt Disney Studios
500 S Buena Vista St
Burbank, CA 91521
Ph: 818-560-6894

Guy Hanks & Marvin Miller
   Screenwriting Program
c/o USC School of Cinema-
   Television
Lucas Building, Room 400
University Park
Los Angeles, CA 90089
Ph: 213-740-4432

Beigel Screenplay Award
c/o IFP/East
104 W 29th St, 12th Floor
New York, NY 10001
Ph: 212-465-8200 ext. 221

Nicholl Screenwriting Fellowship
c/o Academy Foundation
8949 Wilshire Blvd
Beverly Hills, CA 90211
Ph: 310-247-3000

Sundance Writers Award
c/o Sundance Institute
8857 W Olympic Blvd
Beverly Hills, CA 90211
Ph: 310-360-1981
Web: www.sundance.org

Diane Thomas Awards
c/o UCLA Writers Program
UCLA Extension
10995 Le Conte Ave, Suite 440
Los Angeles, CA 90024
Ph: 310-206-1542

Chesterfield Writers Award
1158 26th St
PO Box 544
Santa Monica, CA 90403
Ph: 213-683-3977

DGA/WGA Women Filmmakers
   Program
c/o Writers Guild of America/West
7000 W 3rd St
West Hollywood, CA 90048
Ph: 323-951-4000

Writer's Digest Writing Competition
4700 Galbraith Rd
Cincinnati, OH 45236
Ph: 513-531-2222

OPTIONING AND HIRING

"Purchase the Great Story"

Other than writing the screenplay yourself (chapters 9–10), there are only two other ways to obtain the great script. One is to purchase (i.e., option) an already written one. And the other is to hire someone (a writer-for-hire) to write it for you. Let's learn how to do each of the latter two cost-effectively.

OPTION PROPERTIES

To succeed in Hollywood, you must own something. A real estate developer "ties up" the land. A film producer "ties up" the script. Does a real estate developer pay the full amount for land when he doesn't know what zoning laws will permit? No way. Instead, he makes a nominal down payment, and if things don't work out, he only loses the 5–10 percent instead of 100 percent. Take the same approach with filmmaking. Option properties, be they scripts, real-life stories, or books. But, don't buy them outright. **Nobody in Hollywood buys scripts—they option them.**

Let's assume you've read a script that is great. Option it! You've heard an amazing true story (Amy Fisher, JonBenet Ramsey, Ted Bundy, Monica Lewinsky, etc.) on the news. Option it! You've read a great book. Option it!

The first step in optioning a property is to trace the source. If it's a script, find out who registered or copyrighted it. If it's a true-life story, find the person (or next of kin). They're probably in the phone book. If it's a book, call the publisher and ask for an employee who has the word "rights" somewhere in his/her job title ("rights and permissions," "subsidiary rights," or "ancillary rights") and ask, "Are the movie rights to X book available?" Publishers won't be secretive. They'd love you to make the book into a movie—it'll sell more books. They will gladly tell you who owns the rights.

Now, when you call you must be ready to make an offer. But what do you say? Well, first make the property owner comfortable with you. Tell him, "I'm a producer with numerous projects in development." Tell him how excited you are about his book, script, or story. Then appeal to his ego and ask, "Who do you think should star in your [emphasize 'your'] movie?" or "Who should play your part?" No matter which actor he names, agree and say, "Amazing. I was thinking of the same person and I have strong contacts with his/her production company."

He'll go ga-ga for you, but it still comes down to business. Put on your salesman hat and remember: *He who says the first number loses* is the first rule of salesmanship. Ask the person, "What do you want?" or "Give me a number to work with." Make him say a number, a dollar amount, first. Then, no matter what number he chooses (unless ridiculously high), say "Okay." You've just agreed on the purchase price and negotiated the first of the seven major deal memo points (see below) in an option agreement.

1. Purchase price: This is the dollar amount the author/owner wants. If the amount is small, then buy it. Ninety-nine percent of the time, however, the seller wants a large sum. Unless it is outrageously high, just agree with him. This is the purchase price, but this is not the dollar amount that you will give him now.

2. Option price: This is the partial amount (down payment) you give the seller to obtain exclusive rights to purchase the property (purchase price) at a later date. If the seller wants $50,000, maybe you give him 10 percent (the most commonly used figure) and option it for $5,000 with a written promise to pay the purchase price at a later time. Maybe he'll take $500 (who knows?), which is only 1 percent. Or, maybe he believes in you so much he'll take less. **One dollar and a good line might be all you need to become a Hollywood player.**

> **AUTHOR'S NOTE**   Never option anything for zero down. You must always give someone at least $1 (in a check that gets deposited, not a dollar bill) to make it an enforceable contract.

3. Option period: Now determine how long your option price ties up the property. Never option anything for less than one year. It takes at least three or four months before you figure out what to do and another three or four months before you get to the person who can greenlight the project. And if you go to a Hollywood Shark (aka studio executive), who discovers there are only three weeks left in your option, he'll take good meetings, let your option expire, and do an end run to the author/writer and cut you out of the deal. But if you option the property for 18 months (never less than 12), and get to the Hollywood Shark with 14–16 months remaining, he's stuck with you because too much time is left on the option. Now you can become a co-producer.

4. *Renewal periods:* Put in a paragraph to extend (renew) the option by two 12-month (extensions) periods, that can be activated anytime during the initial 18-month option period with an additional payment or two. (Negotiate amounts, like $500, $1,000, or $2,000.) This allows you to control the property for up to three and a half years.

5. *Payment schedule:* The purchase price is usually due on commencement of principal photography. If you option a property for $5,000, against a purchase price of $50,000, on commencement of principal photography what do you owe, $50,000 or $45,000? If the statement "option price is applied to the purchase price" is in your contract you owe only $45,000. If that statement isn't in the contract, you owe $50,000. Obviously, always put in the contract, "option price to be applied to purchase."

6. *Writing assignment:* More than likely, if you option a book the author, if alive, will want to write the screenplay. Just say yes and tell him he'll be paid according to "suggested Writers Guild minimums" for two drafts. The author will now get (a) the option payment, (b) the purchase payment, and (c) screenwriting payments. Three to four checks. How could he say no?

7. *Profit participation:* If the seller hesitates, your final incentive is to give him a percentage of profits—but never a percentage of the gross. Since there probably won't be any profits (chapter 48), and very probably won't be any "net profits," sweeten the offer with 5 percent or even 10 percent (5–10 percent of nothing is nothing) of "net producer's profits" and secure the property.

The bottom line is that unless you have a binding contract (option agreement) that secures that script/book/story in your name, you have nothing. So look for the hot property. Tell the owner you're a Hollywood producer. Ask how much he wants (purchase price). Agree with him. Ask who should act in it. Agree again and give him a small amount down (option price), with a possible writing credit, a promise of profits, and tie up the property for at least three and a half years, and you're on the road to becoming a producer.

WRITER-FOR-HIRE

If you're not writing, then, after optioning, the only other way to own the great script is to hire a talented but undiscovered writer. Caution! There are a lot of people out there claiming to be writers. 📁 *Everyone can type, everyone can write, but very few can write great.*

Let's run some numbers. More than 300,000 screenplays are written annually, 50,000 are registered with the Writers Guild, and less than 1,000 a year get turned into a film. Simple math shows that over 299,000 scripts per year die on the shelf.

The point is that there are a lot of people who type and call themselves writers. But very very few have ever written a screenplay that gets made. People who call themselves writers are everywhere. They're a dime a dozen. The situation for you, the first-time producer, who is not a writer, is to discover the as yet undiscovered writer who is truly talented.

WHAT TO PAY A WRITER?

The WGA establishes these minimum wages that major studios and big-name producers must pay:

WGA Minimums

	Low-Budget	*High-Budget*
Treatment	$23,540	$38,981
First Draft	$20,460	$38,981
Rewrite	$17,047	$25,989
Polish	$8,528	$12,992

If all you have is a thought bouncing around in your head and you hire a Writers Guild member, you're going to spend a lot of money, even if the WGA deems it as low-budget. A treatment ($23,540) based on your thought, along with a first draft ($20,460) and a rewrite ($17,047), will cost over $60,000. When you include an agent's fee (10–15 percent) along with guild pension and health fees, hiring this writer will cost more than $70,000. This is not affordable.

There is a better way to proceed. Don't merely go to a writer with just a thought. First, put that thought on paper (chapter 9) into a three- to five-page treatment and save $21,387. Next, register that treatment with the WGA (www.wga.org) in your name for $20. Now, approach a writer, not with just a thought, but with a *treatment for a feature film* that you want him/her to flesh out, with two drafts, into a screenplay. What you pay the writer will be contingent on whether he/she is a member of the Writers Guild or not.

WORKING WITH A WGA WRITER

Whom do you hire? One option is to hire an episodic TV writer and pay only WGA minimums. Why would an established TV writer want to work for you, a first-time film producer? The answer is: Money! First, the pay, even at WGA low-budget minimum, is not bad. Second, and more important, if a TV writer writes a successful, low-budget feature that "hits," he becomes a feature film writer and will command $300,000–$600,000 for his next script. Hiring established TV writers is not difficult, if you're paying guild minimums. *Ninety-five percent of WGA writers write for 110 percent of scale—100 percent for the writer, and 10 percent for his agent.*

WORKING WITH NON-WGA WRITERS

Just because a writer is in the WGA doesn't mean that the script he's about to write is guaranteed to be great. Hiring a writer is a gamble. And writers don't refund money. Instead of hiring an established TV writer, if you can't afford it, which you probably can't, you might want to hire a writer who isn't a WGA member, who hasn't had a script produced, but is still talented.

Where can you discover this talented but undiscovered writer? Where do these aspiring writers hang out? The answer is, they can always be found in writing classes and writing groups because they're seminar junkies and network freaks. Thus, attend several writing workshops, where you'll not only learn more about writing but hopefully discover the undiscovered writing talent.

AUTHOR'S NOTE I repeat this point due to its importance. Anyone can type and call themselves a writer. Your job is to be sure that the writer you've discovered has the talent to write great dialogue. Dialogue can't be taught. Certain people are gifted with it. Most aren't. Professional readers call it a person who has a "good ear." You must find the undiscovered writer who has a good ear and a gift for dialogue.

What should you pay this undiscovered writer that you've just discovered in the writing class? Remember, 🔲 *every first-time writer thinks he/she should get mid-six-figures but will be happy with $3,000–$5,000 and an opening title credit.* Don't worry about him/her demanding creative control and big dollars. Remember, this is a nobody, someone who is paying to be in the class. This is your deal. Hire him/her for two drafts, paying $500 to $700 per week, for five weeks for a first draft, and three weeks for the second draft. When someone who has never been paid to write gets that first check, he/she will turn into a typing whirlwind. You've now hired an undiscovered writer with a shot at getting a great script, and you're only paying $4,000–$6,000 for two drafts rather than $50,000–$60,000 for a Writers Guild member.

After the first draft is delivered, get "coverage" (script reports) from script consultants. Then give the coverage notes to your undiscovered writer for a second draft, to be delivered in three weeks. Always hire a writer for two drafts but no more. The rule of thumb is that after the second draft, they're brain-dead and don't know what to do anymore to improve the script. Now, for the third draft, if needed, pay a second, fresh writer $1,000–$2,000.

You have now paid only $5,000–$8,000 and hired two writers to give you three drafts of your registered treatment, which is based on your great idea. Although there are no guarantees, this will give you a fair shot at a great script.

Finally, the third, and by far the cheapest, way to obtain the great script is to write it—yourself. So let's proceed to the next two chapters, budget $8.00 for two reams of paper, and obtain the ultimate screenwriting crash course.

TO DO:

1. Practice optioning books. Pick any book. Call the publisher and ask if the motion picture rights are available. It doesn't hurt to ask.

2. Practice optioning true stories. Watch the news for an interesting story about a person. Nine out of ten times they will be in the phone book. Call and say you're a Hollywood producer. Watch what happens.
3. Call the Writers Guild (323-951-4000) and ask for their "Schedule of Minimums."
4. Watch a TV show that you like, and look for the writer's name. Then get his agent's phone number from the Writers Guild and offer 110 percent of scale.
5. Attend night writing classes to find the undiscovered talented writer.

 BOOKS

The Screenwriter's Legal Guide
S. Breimer, 320 pp., $19.95
An illuminating overview of the legal aspects that are an everyday part of the writer's vocabulary.

This Business of Screenwriting
R. Suppa, 225 pp., $19.95
How to protect yourself as a screenwriter.

The Writer Got Screwed
B. Wharton, 276 pp., $14.00
A guide for the legal and business practices that a screenwriter must know.

The Art of Adaption
L. Seger, 232 pp., $16.00
How to transform novels, plays, and true-life stories into screenplays.

Write for Television
M. Dimaggio, 256 pp., $14.00
Learn writing for the TV industry from a successful TV writer. Sample scripts included.

TV Scriptwriter's Handbook
A. Brenner, 326 pp., $15.95
Eighty-five percent of all writing jobs are in television. This book teaches how to succeed in this medium.

Writing Television Sitcoms
E. Smith, 279 pp., $14.95
The insider's guide to writing and selling a half hour sitcom.

Writer's Guide to Hollywood
S. Press, 432 pp., $24.95
A treatise on how to market screenplays and get the best agent, with thousands of contacts.

 WRITER'S LEGAL AID

Beverly Hills Bar Association
300 S Beverly Drive, Suite 201
Beverly Hills, CA 90212
Ph: 310-553-6644

Georgia Lawyers for the Arts
City Hall East, 5th Floor
675 Ponce de Leon Ave
Atlanta, GA 30308
Ph: 404-873-3911

Southern California Lawyers for
  the Arts
1549 11th St, Suite 200
Santa Monica, CA 90401
Ph: 310-395-8893

Northern California Lawyers for
  the Arts
Fort Mason Center
Bldg C, Room 255
San Francisco, CA 94123
Ph: 415-775-7200

Colorado Lawyers for the Arts
PO Box 48148
Denver, CO 80204
Ph: 303-722-7994

Lawyers for the Creative Arts
213 W Institute Pl, Suite 411
Chicago, IL 60610
Ph: 312-944-2787

Texas Accountants & Lawyers for
  the Arts
1540 Sul Ross
Houston, TX 77006
Ph: 713-526-4876
Web: www.talarts.org

St. Louis Volunteer Lawyers for
  the Arts
3540 Washington
St. Louis, MO 63103
Ph: 314-652-2410

Volunteer Lawyers for the Arts
1 E 53rd St, 6th Floor
New York, NY 10022
Ph: 212-319-2787

Washington Lawyers for the Arts
Stables Art Center
410 8th St, NW
Washington, DC 20004
Ph: 202-393-2826

SCREENWRITING, PART I

"Writing the Script"

You looked for the great script to option. You couldn't find it. You thought about hiring a writer. You didn't have the money. What's left? The answer is obvious: You must write it yourself. So schedule three weeks and you'll have it written. Yes, three weeks is all it will take to write a 90–120 page script, by typing only 5–10 minutes per day, if you follow these six easy steps.

1. Write the TITLE
2. Write the THEME
3. Write the LOGLINE
4. Write the TREATMENT
5. Write the OUTLINE
6. Write the SCRIPT

Professionals know that 🗄 *"nothing is written, it's rewritten."* So stop worrying that your first draft must be great. You're only creating writer's block. Move your fingers and type. Shakespeare didn't just pick up a quill and *Macbeth* poured out. I'm sure Willie wrote and rewrote as did Tennessee Williams and every great writer. Your first draft won't be great. Matter of fact, it will probably stink. But it's written. Just get that first draft onto paper. Have it registered and copyrighted (chapter 11) for protection. Then do the rewrite and, if you're gifted with a sense of dialogue, it will be great. Now, let's proceed with the six steps.

3 WEEKS! 6 STEPS! 1 SCRIPT!

Step 1 (Monday, week 1). Write the title: Type one to three words. Nothing more. You can handle that. Keep it simple. Make it visual if you can. If the audience can envision the film from just the title (aka high concept) then that's a marketing plus.

Step 2 (Tuesday, week 1). Write the theme: Type five to nine words. This is a 300 percent increase in writing over yesterday. The theme is emotional. This is the heart of your movie. Squeeze it into a few words ("men are truly evil"—four words; "men and women can't be buddies, sex always interferes"—nine words; "siblings are born to be rivals"—six words). Then with scissors, cut it out and tape it to your keyboard or monitor. When you hit a snag in writing, look at the five- to nine-word theme taped on your keyboard, keep typing, and create a new scene emphasizing the theme by either dialogue or action.

Step 3 (Wednesday, week 1). Write the logline: This is another 300 percent increase, but it's only 18–25 words. Condense your story into a synopsis (protagonist, antagonist, setting situation, and problem) that will fit into a *TV Guide* listing, which is now called a "logline." The bottom line is, if you can't get the story down to 18–25 words, you can't create buzz through word of mouth.

To write your logline start with the words "This is the story of . . ." and fill in the following categories:

1. Project's title: _____
2. Hero/protagonist: _____
3. Desired goal of #2: _____
4. Situation: _____
5. Dilemma facing #2: _____
6. Villain/antagonist: _____
7. Desired goal of #6: _____
8. Complications arise when: _____

Here is an example of a logline: "A Hollywood star returns to her small-town roots and high school lover. Complications arise when she discovers that . . ." Make up the complications. That's your job as a storyteller. Until now, your idea, although you thought it was great, was probably no more than a setting or an atmosphere. However, once you insert the phrase "complications arise when," along with the complication, your idea instantly evolves into a story with drama and tension built in to each scene. Watch: End with "complications arise when . . . ," such as "she discovers that her high school boyfriend is gay," or "her high school boyfriend and she, unbeknownst to either of them, have the same mother and are actually brother and sister," or "her high school boyfriend is actually the murderer of their best friend who she assumed drowned," etc. and you have a logline.

Step 4 (Thursday, week 1). Write the treatment: Start by telling yourself that you are about to write a terrible treatment. Now there won't be pressure. Commence with typing three to five pages in length. Treatments are double-spaced, so you're really only writing one and a half to two and a half pages. Start with "the Five W's and the H":

Who: The main characters
What: The action taking place
Where: The location(s) where the story takes place
When: The time period, which includes era and year, as well as time of day
Why: The central character's main motives, and obstacles he/she encounters
How: How the character sets out to achieve his/her goal(s)

Here's how to do it. Take three pieces of blank paper. Number them 1, 2, and 3. All movies have a beginning, a middle, and an end. Make page 1 the BEGINNING, page 2 the MIDDLE, and page 3 the ENDING.

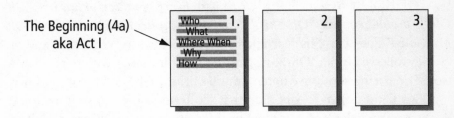

**The Beginning (4a)
aka Act I**

Step 4a (Friday, week 1). Write the beginning: Write one or two paragraphs on the top half of page 1, double-spaced, with the Five W's and the H. Describe *who's* in the story, *what's* happening, *where* it's happening, *when* it's happening, *why* it's happening, and *how* it's happening.

Step 4b (Saturday, week 1). Write the Ending: Skip the bottom half of page 1 and all of page 2. Leave it blank. Go to the bottom half of page 3 and write the ending.

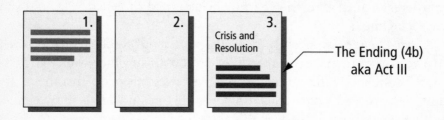

Step 4c (Saturday, week 1). Write the Middle: The middle, or act II, is the tough part. The first 5–10 minutes (the beginning) and the last 5–7 minutes (the ending) of every movie I've ever seen is good, even great. It's just those 70–80 minutes in the middle, the story (the bottom of page 1, all of page 2, and the top of page 3), when I get bored. This middle is the key to storytelling.

Now, let's get into the Hollywood Formula. You know—that thing that every writing instructor swears doesn't exist and then they proceed to teach it. Writing instructors call the events that occur during acts I, II, and III "plot points," "inciting moments," "turning points," "antagonistic complications," "protagonistic detours," etc. I keep it simple. I call them the "Uh-Ohs," "Oh-Shits," and the "Oh-My-Gods," and they are plotted in the story with highs (peaks or victories) and lows (valleys or tragedies).

THE HOLLYWOOD FORMULA: 🧰 ***Every great script has five "Uh-Ohs" (problems), five "Oh-Shits" (further complications), and two "Oh-My-Gods."*** The "Uh-Ohs" (problems) occur every 10–12 minutes and are quickly followed by an "Oh-Shit" (further complication), with the "Oh-My-Gods" occurring about five to ten minutes prior to the ending of the story.

This is the roller-coaster ride that Hollywood uses so well. In *Rocky*, Rocky realizes he's a nobody when he loses a fight ("Uh-Oh") and can't use his gym locker ("Oh-Shit"), then gets a fight with Apollo Creed ("Uh-Oh") but can't get a manager ("Oh-Shit"), then gets a crusty old manager ("Uh-Oh") and a pacifist girlfriend ("Oh-Shit") who doesn't want him to fight. All these "Uh-Ohs" and "Oh-Shits" eventually lead to the final fight with ("Oh-My-God") Apollo Creed.

The Hollywood Formula

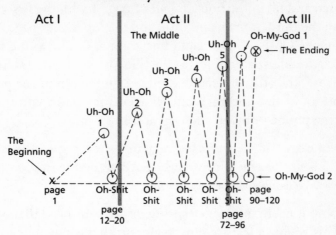

It is your job to come up with interesting "Uh-Ohs" and "Oh-Shits," spaced every 10–12 scenes, and the near-cataclysmic "Oh-My-God" obstacles that occur five to ten pages before the script ends.

Suppose you're doing a boy-meets-girl story. The story starts with scene 1, introduction of boy; and scene 2, introduction of girl. They meet in scene 3 and go on a date in scene 4. In scene 5, they fall in love. In scene 6, they decide to run away and elope. They steal a car to run away in scene 7. In scene 8, they get into a car accident. In scene 9 they discover the car they've stolen is owned—"Uh-Oh"—by the Mafia, and 40 pounds of cocaine—"Oh-Shit"—is hidden in the tires. In scene 10 the Mafia is after them.

Come up with five "Uh-Ohs" and "Oh-Shits" (aka scenes) as the boy and girl are on the road to happiness and you are 80 percent (72–96 pages) into the story. Just after the fifth "Uh-Oh/Oh-Shit," act III, the ending, commences, with a massive "Oh-My-God 1" insurmountable roadblock (Rocky walks into the ring with Apollo Creed). That is further complicated with an even worse "Oh-My-God 2" . . . But somehow the story gets resolved and "they live happily ever after."

**The Middle (4c)
aka Act II**

Type each pair of "Uh-Oh"/"Oh-Shits" into a paragraph, in chronological order, and fill in the bottom half of page 1 with the first two; all of page 2 with the third, fourth, and fifth; and the top half of page 3 with the final "Uh-Oh"/"Oh-Shit." Do some fine-tuning. Create a title sheet that lists on each double-spaced line: (a) the title, (b) "A Treatment for Feature Film," (c) "by," and (d) your name centered on the top of the page. Then on the bottom of the title page put "For Further Information" and give your address, phone number, and e-mail contact info.

AUTHOR'S NOTE If the treatment becomes seven pages, 10 pages, 20 pages, it's better than three to five pages. But don't bore the reader or think he/she will be dazzled with a lot of typing.

This is no longer a mere idea sitting inside your head that is not protectable. This is now a feature film treatment that is possibly protectable. It will take no more than one week. But, before celebrating, send a photocopy to the Writers Guild of America (chapter 11) and you now have a registered treatment that you own.

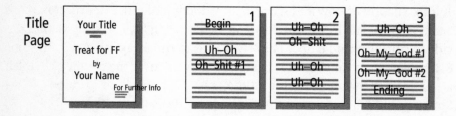

Step 5 (Monday, week 2). Create an outline: Next, flesh out your treatment into a story. Great writers say there are 40–60 scenes in a movie. There is no definitive number. What's a scene? I don't know! All I know is that there are 40–60 of them in a movie. Thus, rent a couple of movies you enjoyed and, with a pencil, count the scenes that include "Uh-Ohs, "Oh-Shits," and the "Oh-My-Gods," and you'll come up with 40–60.

Suppose 50 scenes appear to be the number that you like in movies. Then, on a long piece of paper write the numbers 1–50 down the left side. Next, fill in each scene with 7–10 descriptive words. Start with scene 1 and a situation. In scene 2, introduce the protagonist. Scene 3 introduces the antagonist. Scene 4 introduces the problem. In scene 5, have the antagonist make a decision. Etcetera. You don't have to write them in order. Skip around. Go to scene 50 and write the ending. Write the great car chase in scene 49. In scene 48, tell why the car chase is about to happen. Then go to your "Uh-Ohs" and "Oh-Shits" and put them in the various scenes. Fill in the remaining scene numbers with what are called B stories or subplots.

Flesh out the remaining scenes with subplots, B stories, character development scenes, all coming to a junction at about five scenes before the movie ends, which coincides with the final "Oh-My-God" and gets resolved. In just a few days you have created a detailed story, with a beginning, middle, and end, with four to six major crises and several backstories. Your idea will now be a fully fleshed-out story.

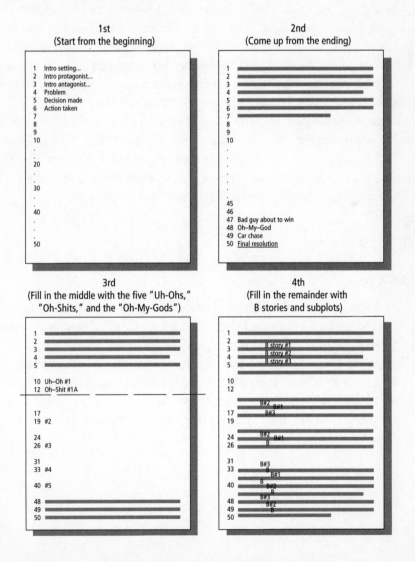

1st (Start from the beginning)	
1	Intro setting...
2	Intro protagonist...
3	Intro antagonist...
4	Problem
5	Decision made
6	Action taken
7	
8	
9	
10	
20	
30	
40	
50	

2nd (Come up from the ending)	
45	
46	
47	Bad guy about to win
48	Oh–My–God
49	Car chase
50	Final resolution

3rd
(Fill in the middle with the five "Uh-Ohs,"
"Oh-Shits," and the "Oh-My-Gods")

10 Uh–Oh #1
12 Oh–Shit #1A
19 #2
26 #3
33 #4
40 #5

4th
(Fill in the remainder with
B stories and subplots)

B story #1
B story #2
B story #3

B#2 B#1
B#3

B#2 B#1
B

B#3
B#1
B#2
B

B#3
B#2
B

Step 6 (weeks 2–3). Write the first draft: Now, after your treatment is written and registered and you fleshed out 40–60 scenes, you are finally ready to write your script.

On Tuesday, write *only* scene 1. Spend no more than 5–10 minutes, and plan to write only one scene per day. If scene 1 ends up being half a page, two pages, or three pages, it doesn't matter. On Wednesday, write *only* scene 2, no more. Spend 5–10 minutes. On Thursday, write *only* scene 3. Spend 10–15 minutes. Write half a page, a page, two pages—it doesn't matter. Just write scene 3.

On Friday, now that you're structured, I bet you're pissed that I told you to only write one scene a day, and I bet you call in sick at work, stay home, and type 15–20 scenes of 30–40 pages. On Saturday, do another 10–15 scenes and 20–30 pages. On Sunday, go to church and say thank you to God, and ask for the ability to write great dialogue. Then on Monday through Friday (week 3), you'll finish your first draft.

A first draft written, step-by-step, in three weeks, in six easy-to-follow steps. Now remember, "Nothing is written, it's rewritten." All you have is a first draft. It will be good. It might even be very good. But it won't be great! And only great is good enough. Then, like your treatment, send it with $20 to the Writers Guild to register it. Then start your rewrite.

TO DO:

1. Look at movie directories (*Leonard Maltin's Movie and Video Guide* or *Halliwell's Film and Video Guide*) or *TV Guide* and see how stories (loglines) are written in two sentences.
2. Write your treatment and register it with the Writers Guild.
3. Learn structure. Rent videos you love and count the scenes.
4. Plot the 40–60 scenes of your movie.
5. Write the first draft and register and copyright it.

BOOKS

*The Complete Guide to Standard Script
    Formats, Part I: Film Format*
H. Cole and J. Haag, 170 pp., $19.95
The only book totally dedicated to
how to correctly type your screenplay
for movies. A must!

*The Complete Guide to Standard Script
    Formats, Part II: Television Format*
H. Cole and J. Haag, 170 pp., $19.95
The only book totally dedicated to
how to properly type your teleplay for
television.

Screenplay
S. Field, 263 pp., $13.95
The first book to teach the craft of
screenwriting in simple-to-
understand terms.

The Screenwriter's Bible
D. Trottier, 310 pp., $14.95
If you're only getting one book about
screenwriting, this is the book to get.

Story
R. McKee, 456 pp., $35.00
Why take McKee's $500 seminar when
everything he says is in this book?

The Writer's Journey
C. Vogler, 326 pp., $24.95
A script consultant who has read over
10,000 scripts outlines how to write a
successful script.

Plots Unlimited
T. Sawyer and A. Weingarten, 295 pp.,
$25.00
Details over 200,000 plot possibilities.
It's like owning a writer's idea factory.

20 Master Plots
R. Tobias, 236 pp., $14.99
Outlines the 20 basic plots that all
stories, even yours, are boiled down to.

*The Complete Idiot's Guide to
    Screenwriting*
S. Press, 365 pp., $16.95
A simple, easy-to-understand book for
the first-timer. It's a very good book.

How to Write a Movie in 21 Days
V. King, 189 pp., $15.00
A simple method to get the movie in
your heart onto the page.

 SOFTWARE

Truby's Blockbuster
Windows or Macintosh, $259.95
Storytelling software whose
brainstorming features enable you to
develop your story, character, and plot
according to Hollywood standards.

Dramatica Pro: Writing Partner
Windows or Macintosh CD, $199.95
Got an idea for a script or novel? This
program will have you flesh out your
theme, plot, and characters step-by-
step into a successful screenplay.

Plots Unlimited
DOS (Windows compatible) or
Macintosh, $189.95
Literally an idea factory. Over 13,000
master plots and 5,600 story-moves
guide you in creating an excellent story.

Truby's Master Genre Classes
Add-on to Truby's Blockbuster
Windows or Macintosh, $99.00 each

   A. "Action"
   B. "Comedy"
   C. "Crime"
   D. "Detective"
   E. "Fantasy"
   F. "Horror"
   G. "Love"
   H. "World Myth"
   I. "Science Fiction"
   J. "Thriller"
   K. "TV Drama"

 AUDIOS

Great Screenwriting
12 audio cassettes, 15 hours, $295.00
John Truby's superb screenwriting
class dispenses all the elements of
and the how-to information to writing the great script. Workbook
included.

THE HIT GENRE SERIES

1. *Comedy Writing*
   Four audios, 6 hours, $99.00
   How to get the comedy on the
   page and sustain the laughs for
   two hours.

2. *The Love Story*
   Four audios, 6 hours, $99.00
   How to choreograph a story that
   moves your audience to care deeply
   for your two characters.

3. *Horror, Fantasy, Sci-Fi*
   Four audios, 6 hours, $99.00
   Learn how to keep your audience on
   the edge of their seats with each of
   these genres.

4. *Sitcom Writing*
   Four audios, 6 hours, $99.00
   Discover how to write a complete,
   laugh-filled comic story in
   22 minutes.

5. *Dramatic Television*
   Four audios, 6 hours, $99.00
   Learn how to succeed in the world
   of dramatic one-hour television by
   writing the great script.

6. *The Action Story*
   Four audios, 6 hours, $99.00
   Don't underestimate this tricky
   form. Learn how to create unique
   characters, plot, structure, and
   pacing for this popular Hollywood
   genre.

7. *Advanced Screenwriting*
   Four audios, 6 hours, $99.00
   The information needed to make
   your good script a great script.

 SCREENWRITING SITES

www.Wga.org
www.CreativeScreenwriting.com
www.ScriptMag.com

www.HollywoodScript.com
www.HollywoodScriptwriter.com
www.WriteMovies.com
www.WritersScriptNetwork.com
www.Screenwritersutopia.com
www.ASAScreenwriters.com
www.Wordplayer.com
www.FadeInMag.com
www.Stories.com
www.TheScript.com
www.ScriptSales.com
www.GoCoverage.com
www.GoodStory.com
www.HollywoodLitSales.com
www.Inzide.com
www.NYScreenwriter.com
www.StudioNotes.com
www.Writerswrite.com/screenwriter
www.ScriptSeeker.com
www.ScriptShark.com
www.ScreenwritersGuild.com

 SCREENWRITING INSTRUCTORS

Robert McKee
Two Arts Inc.
PO Box 452930
Los Angeles, CA 90045
Ph: 888-676-2533
Web: www.McKeeStory.com

Syd Field
Screenwriters Inc.
270 N Canon Dr, Suite 1355
Beverly Hills, CA 90210
Ph: 310-477-5425

John Truby
Truby's Writers Studio
751 Hartzell St

Pacific Palisades, CA 90272
Ph: 310-573-9630

Michael Hauge
Hilltop Productions
PO Box 55728
Sherman Oaks, CA 91413
Ph: 818-995-8118

Linda Seger
2038 Louella Ave
Venice, CA 90291
Ph: 719-684-0405

Vicki King
PO Box 563
Malibu, CA 90265
Ph: 310-457-6691

James Bonnet
Astoria Filmwrights
PO Box 841
Burbank, CA 91503
Ph: 818-567-0521
Web: www.StoryMaking.com

Jeff Gordon
Writers Boot Camp
1525 S Sepulveda, Suite A
Los Angeles, CA 90025
Ph: 800-800-1733

Leslie Kallen
15303 Venture Blvd, Suite 900
Sherman Oaks, CA 91403
Ph: 818-906-2785

Richard Walter
UCLA, Department of Film and TV
Box 951622
Los Angeles, CA 90095
Ph: 310-825-5761

David Freeman
2118 Wilshire Blvd, Suite 274
Santa Monica, CA 90403
Ph: 310-394-6556
Web: www.BeyondStructure.com

Richard Krevolin
Ph: 310-288-0946
E-mail: krevolin@almaak.usc.edu

Elliot Grove
81 Berwick St, Soho
London W1V 3PF England
Ph: 44-207-287-3833
Web: www.raindance.co.uk

 PITCHING CONFERENCES

Writers Connection
Selling to Hollywood
PO Box 24770
San Jose, CA 95154
Ph: 408-445-3600

The Writers Network
Hollywood Screenwriters Conference
289 S Robertson Blvd, Suite 465
Beverly Hills, CA 90211
Ph: 310-275-0287

IFP/West
Screenwriters Conference
8750 Wilshire Blvd, 2nd floor
Beverly Hills, CA 90211
Ph: 310-475-4379

American Screenwriters Association
269 S Beverly Dr, Suite 2608
Beverly Hills, CA 90212-3807
Ph: 866-265-9091

Hollywood Film Festival
433 N Camden Dr, Suite 600
Beverly Hills, CA 90210
Ph: 310-288-1882
E-mail: awards@hollywood
  awards.com

SCREENWRITING, PART II

"Make the Script Great"

Your first draft is done. I beg you, don't fall in love with it. A first draft is like your first child. When it's born you are ecstatic. You fall in love. You count toes and body parts and fall further in love. But, your newborn is probably only average-looking and maybe even ugly (but no one will dare tell you), and your first draft is probably mediocre, and it may even suck (but no one will dare tell you). Remember, "Nothing is written, it's rewritten." So now let's make this first draft, which is probably good but not great, into a final draft that is great.

First, try this test to discern if your script is great. When scoring, 1 stands for very poor, 5 for adequate, 8 for good, 9 for very good, and 10 for excellent.

WRITING TEST

A. **EYE QUIZ:** When reading your script, do your eyes flow down the page, instead of moving left to right, line-by-line?

SCORE: 1–10 _____

B. **LINE 7 QUIZ:** You must hook readers/viewers in the first 15–20 seconds. Does something happen on line 7 or 8 of page one to grab the reader?

SCORE: 1–10 _____

C. **PAGE 1 QUIZ:** Does something happen at the bottom of page one (one minute into the film) or top of page two to hold the TV viewer through two minutes of commercials so he won't hit his remote?

SCORE: 1–10 _____

D. **10-PAGE QUIZ:** Do your first 10 pages make the reader want more?

SCORE: 1–10 _____

E. **PLOT QUIZ:** Do you manipulate the reader every 10–15 pages (or minutes) to expect something to happen, and then throw in a sudden twist?

SCORE: 1–10 _____

F. **CHARACTER QUIZ:** Can you sit down and outline three reasons why each of the major characters is unique?

SCORE: 1–10 _____

G. **DIALOGUE QUIZ:** Pick any page in your script. Put your thumb over the character's name above a line of dialogue. Can you tell from the dialogue which character is speaking? Can you even tell if it is a man or a woman?

SCORE: 1–10 _____

TOTAL SCORE _____

Add up your score, and it will be between 7 and 70. What did you come up with? 32? 49? 65? 67? If your score is anything other than 70—yes, perfect—your script sucks! 50–60 is horrendous; 65 or 67 isn't good enough. Even 69 means there is something you can do to make it better. *Hollywood can get away with mediocrity. You can't.* You have one shot. And the script had better be great. Since it isn't perfect, rewrite and rewrite until you score 70! Then, and only then, can you proceed.

Now you must get your script to score 70. After taking three weeks to write your first draft, take a week off. You're much too close to it. You can't see the forest from the trees. After the week off, hire two professional readers and have them do "coverage."

AUTHOR'S NOTE   Do you have the guts to get a real opinion? When hiring a reader to evaluate, never let him/her know that you wrote the script. For they will be polite, tell you the story is good but the second act is a little weak, and want to be hired to advise on the rewrite. Always, change the title page (just temporarily) to make it appear as if someone else wrote the script. And tell the reader that you, a producer, are thinking of optioning it. Now the reader will be ruthlessly honest, which is what you want.

HOW TO FIND A READER

There is no category in the phone book for "Readers." Get a film directory from either New York or Los Angeles that lists production companies. The smaller, but established, companies don't have an on-staff reader (aka junior development executive), so they hire independent readers. I did this job for two years. Call a couple of companies and ask for referrals. Readers also advertise in the back of screenwriting trades.

Readers evaluate 400–700 scripts a year for $45–$75 each. Your script will have to be quite extraordinary to get a good rating. This will be a superb test of how good your script really is. Your fee, since you aren't giving the reader 5–10 scripts a week as production companies do, will be $125–$250.

After you have several coverages, read them (don't get defensive) and let their opinions sink in. Then peruse a couple of books on rewriting, story, structure, character development, and dialogue, and you are ready to commence the rewrite.

Now, outline these 10 points and think them through, keeping the readers' coverages in mind.

1. Three-act Structure: Where do the "setup," the "development," and the "resolution" start and end?
2. The Opening: Does the script start with a visual image like *West Side Story*'s (gang fight), *Star War*'s (space battle), or *The Sound of Music*'s (singing in Alps) that introduces the atmosphere and tone?
3. First 10 Pages: Are the major storytelling points (characters, desires, objectives, conflicts, etc.) introduced within the first 10 pages?
4. Plot Points: Can you list the times when the story, usually through a character's decision or revelation, takes a twist?
5. Subplots: How many do you have? Is there a clear structure (setup, turning point, and climax) for each one? Do your subplots add to the story or just take up space?

6. Scene Structure: Do each of the 40–60 scenes have a beginning, middle, and end?

7. Characters: Can you list three unique traits of each character in the script and state on what page and line that trait is announced and/or demonstrated?

8. Dialogue: Is each line of dialogue believable? When in doubt, delete the first two words of each sentence. People always interrupt each other and don't talk in grammatically correct sentences.

9. Conflict: When two people want the same thing and only one can have it, there is conflict. Can you list where the internal and external conflicts arise in your script? If not, create scenes that depict the conflict while simultaneously move the plot.

10. Resolution: Do your major plot and your subplots come together for the "big finish"? Does Marty get "Back to the Future"? Does Tootsie get unmasked and get the girl?

After outlining, rethinking, and refining, you are ready to rewrite. Allocate as much time to the rewrite as you spent on the first draft. Give yourself a schedule of two to five pages per day, work page-by-page, scene-by-scene, line-by-line (exposition and dialogue), and make the script great.

TO DO:

1. Give your script to three professional readers for analysis.
2. Learn dialogue. Get depositions from court stenographers and see how people in conflict really talk.
3. Rewrite until you get a score of 70 on the writing test.

 BOOKS

Making a Good Script Great
L. Seger, 240 pp., $13.95
Nothing is written, it's rewritten. This book takes you through the rewriting process. It is excellent!

Making a Good Writer Great
L. Seger, 233 pp., $14.95
Outlines a bold, but successful, new approach to screenwriting and creativity.

Writing the Second Act
M. Halperin, 159 pp., $19.95
The second act is the story. Learn how to make yours great.

Secrets of Screenplay Structure
L. Cowgill, 313 pp., $16.95
Allows you to understand why great films work and how to get your script to the level of great.

The Art of Dramatic Writing
L. Egri, 303 pp., $12.95
A dramatist's classic! The book recommended by every writing instructor.

Creating Unforgettable Characters
L. Seger, 237 pp., $15.00
Without great characters a great story becomes very bland.

Writing Great Characters
M. Halperin, 194 pp., $19.95
A step-by-step guide to creating emotionally complex characters.

Creating Character Emotions
A. Hood, 169 pp., $14.99
A how-to for writing fresh approaches that express your characters' feelings.

Writing Dialogue
T. Chiarella, 170 pp., $14.99
Without believable dialogue your script's great characters become flat and uninteresting.

Dialogue
L. Turco, 118 pp., $13.95
Another excellent book explaining how to write the way people talk.

 SOFTWARE

Storyview
CD-ROM for Windows only, $119.95
Permits you to see what pieces/scenes make up your story and the timelines for each. Great for the rewrite.

Writer's Blocks
Windows 95/NT only, $119.95
You enter scenes and characters into blocks. Then arrange them with drag and drop and quickly create an effective and marketable story.

Story-Builder
Windows CD-ROM, $99.95
With over 100 story element templates, this program aids in mapping out your story into a solid three-act structure.

 SCRIPT ANALYSTS

Dara Marks
513 Pleasant Ave
Ojai, CA 93023
Ph: 805-640-1307
E-mail: dara@ojai.net

Michael Hauge
Hilltop Productions
PO Box 55728
Sherman Oaks, CA 91413
Ph: 818-995-8118
Web: www.screenplaymastery.com

Sandi Steinberg
Script Surgeon
17968 Boris Dr
Encino, CA 91316
Ph: 818-342-9794

Marlene Swartz
Story Conference
95 6th Ave, Suite 202
Brooklyn, NY 11217
Ph: 718-638-5570
E-mail: storyconf@iname.com

Paul Young
22647 Ventura Blvd, Suite 524
Woodland Hills, CA 91364
Ph: 818-887-6554
Web: www.scriptzone.com

Hank Searls
Screenwriters Workshop
PO Box 1877, Suite 1C
Gig Harbor, WA 98335
Ph: 253-851-9897
E-mail: hanksearls@harbornet.com

Jeff Newman
Story Notes
15721 Brighton Ave, Suite D
Gardena, CA 90247
Ph: 310-715-6455
Web: www.storynotes.com

Peter Mellencamp
3668 Motor Ave, Suite 312
Los Angeles, CA 90034
Ph: 310-204-4561
E-mail: petemcllen@aol.com

David Trottier
The Screenwriting Center
4456 Manchester St
Cedar Hills, UT 84062
Ph: 800-264-4900
E-mail: dave@davetrottier.com

David Hagan
Hollywood Screenplay Consultants
17216 Saticoy St, Suite 303
Van Nuys, CA 91406
Ph: 818-994-5977

Melody Jackson
Smart Girl Productions
15030 Ventura Blvd
Sherman Oaks, CA 91403
Ph: 818-907-6511
E-mail: smartgirls@smartgirls
   prod.com

Craig Kellem
HollywoodScript.Com
11 Dorchester Rd
Lyme, NH 03768
Ph: 603-795-9424
E-mail: craig.kellem@valley.net

Barbara Schiffman
Script Consulting
2308 Clark Ave
Burbank, CA 91506
Ph: 818-848-9040

Natalie Rothenberg
The Insiders System
1223 Wilshire Blvd, Suite 336
Santa Monica, CA 90403
Ph: 800-397-2615
E-mail: InsidersSystem@msn.com

Jim Mercurio
Script Consultant
5216 Corteen Pl, Suite 14
North Hollywood, CA 91607
Ph: 818-509-5868

Howard Allen
The Script Doctor
200 E Roger Rd, Suite B-1
Tucson, AZ 85719
Ph: 520-795-3727
E-mail: thedoc@scriptdoctor.com

Michael Ray Brown
Story Sense
PO Box 3757
Santa Monica, CA 90408
Ph: 310-394-0994
E-mail: info@storysense.com

Suzanne Ballantyne
Raindance Consulting
81 Berwick St, Soho
London W1V 3PF England
Ph: 44-207-287-3833
Web: www.raindance.co.uk

PROTECTION

"CYA. Register and Copyright"

You now own the great script. In Hollywood this is power. You're on your way to fame and fortune. Be careful. You better protect it! Some over-the-hill industry sleazeball who has failed numerous 12-step programs and who you showed it to could tear off the title page, put his name on it, claim it as his own, and register it. That's why "copyright infringement" attorneys make big bucks.

I truly doubt that this will happen, but the steps to protect yourself are so simple that it is foolish not to take them. Cover Your Ass (CYA), but keep in mind that *paranoia will never sell anything*. You can't sell your script unless you let someone read it.

Protect yourself by establishing a paper trail (attorneys love this) documenting the history of the project, depicting the dates that you registered the treatment, the first draft, and the final draft. There are three ways to do this. Don't depend on just one. Do all three.

1. WGA registration
2. Copyright
3. Historical chronicle

WGA REGISTRATION

What does protection cost? Sixty to one hundred dollars is the answer! The WGA (Writers Guild of America) registers treatments, drafts, outlines, and screenplays. If it's written, it can be registered. 🗄 *Anyone* *with $20 can register his or her property with the WGA.* Members pay only $10.

The WGA does not provide protection against theft and will never have anyone testify that they have read your script and that, in their belief, the concept has been infringed or stolen. All the WGA does is state the date (registration date) they received your typing.

There are three to five stages in script development when you should register your work: (1) the preliminary 3–5 page treatment, (2) the expanded 7–20 page treatment, (3) the first draft, (4) the rewrite, and (5) the final draft. Register at each stage ($20 each time), get three to five dated receipts, and you created a verifiable documentation (three to five registration slips) of your project's creation for only $60 to $100.

> IMPORTANT POINT   It is so cheap to register with the Writers Guild that I demand you do it each and every time you type, retype, change, or adapt your project. Don't argue—just do it.

COPYRIGHTING

Let's bolster your Writers Guild registration slips with a second tier of protection called copyrighting. To copyright your screenplay (only completed works are copyrightable), request "Form PA" from the Copyright Office in Washington, D.C. The cost is only $30. But remember, copyrighting, like registering, does not protect ideas, concepts, or marketing plans. It merely creates a verifiable date of when your alleged project was created.

Register and copyright. Do both! It costs only $90–$150 for you to register your project three to five times, at various stages of development, and copyright it. There's no such thing as too much protection.

HISTORICAL CHRONICLE

Besides the registration slips and copyright notice, create a paper trail proving who has read or received the script. Each time you submit your script to a production company, studio, or network, send it with a cover letter that includes (1) who you're sending it to, (2) his/her title, (3) the company's name, (4) the date, (5) the project's title, and (6) a short, two-line synopsis of the story. End the letter with a sentence like, "Looking forward to making my project, tentatively titled ————, a reality with your company," and (7) sign and (8) date it.

Next, get a three-ring binder. Every time you register and copyright what you've written or rewritten, place the forms and receipts into the binder with copies of each cover letter. Put in copies of all submission releases, confidentiality agreements, phone logs—anything and everything that has to do with the development of your project. Over a one- or two-year period, this notebook—if you're actively shopping your script—will consist of 50–70 documents, dated and arranged in an order, that chronicle the complete history of your project while detailing every person and company that has received it.

WHAT NOT TO DO

Many screenwriting books, written with little business common sense, advise you to get a "poor man's copyright," which will only serve to give you a false sense of security. This is how it's done: Take a 9-by-12 envelope, place a photocopy of your script in it, address and mail it to yourself. The next day the postmarked package will come to your house. Don't open it. Store it as proof (date of postmark) of creation. It is very cheap ($3 for postage) to do, but it has little to no credibility in court.

Watch, let me show you how sleazeballs make $50,000–$100,000 by investing $200. But remember, sleazeballs don't go to heaven, and if you attempt this you are a sleazeball who will not go to heaven. I don't know about you, but my life on earth is all about going to heaven. I'll push the envelope as far as possible, but my bottom line is, I want to go to heaven.

Buy 100 9-by-12 envelopes at Office Depot or Staples. This costs four bucks. Then every Monday, for the next two years, mail yourself an empty unsealed (the post office doesn't care if it is licked) one that you store after it's returned postmarked. Over two years you'll get 100 postmarked 9-by-12 unsealed envelopes. Somewhere during those two years a movie will gross almost $500 million. Type into the Web to a script storage site and get the original script. Take the title page off and sleazily put on your title page. Then take the script with your title page and seal it in one of the empty postmarked envelopes from about a year ago, lick it, and get a scumball copyright infringement attorney to attack.

You will never win the lawsuit in court, but will likely be paid off ($50,000–$100,000) by the studio's insurance company to settle out of court because it's cheaper than to pay for attorneys and fight. If you ever try this all that I can say is, you'll probably succeed. "Congratulations, you scumball, you ain't goin' to heaven."

The real point of my giving you this short disquisition is to demonstrate that there is little credibility to the "poor man's copyright." Please don't do it. For what I have discovered is that people who do the "poor man's copyright" get lazy and invariably never register and copyright their project.

WHY YOU PROTECT

This is from firsthand experience. Once a written (registered and copyrighted) idea for a TV show was stolen from me and I went in search of a copyright infringement attorney. When I interviewed attorneys (actually, they were interviewing me) they always asked for three things.

1. ORIGINATION: Proof of copyright and registration.
2. SIMILARITY: Proof of project's similarity.
3. SUBMISSION: Proof of who saw the material.

By asking for "origination," they wanted to see proof that I was the original creator or owner of the allegedly pirated show. This is when my registration slips and copyright confirmations come in handy. They all told me that my "poor man's copyright" envelope was useless. Then they wanted proof of "similarity," which is obtained by getting a tape of the show or movie (the actual shooting script would be better) that you claim was pirated from your script. Hire a transcriber to type a script from that tape, then compare scripts by literally counting lines.

Finally, the attorneys wanted me to prove that the alleged pirating company received the project. This is known as either "prior access" or "proof of submission," which is difficult to prove unless you've maintained a detailed historical chronicle.

Now pull out your three-ring binder, with the 50–70 documents accumulated over the two years that you've been hustling, and you should have a letter or two or three showing you submitted your project to that company. Armed with this proof, you will get a pit bull attorney to attack, and if their movie infringed on your submitted property (approximately 20 percent or more of the lines are identical) then you are probably going to receive a huge settlement . . . and still go to heaven.

In any industry that has opportunities for quick wealth, there are always uncreative vermin who take advantage of first-timers. Be aware but don't be paranoid. Write, create, and at all times be a mature businessperson and protect yourself.

TO DO:

1. Register your treatment(s) and script(s) with the Writers Guild, get "Form PA" from the Copyright Office, and copyright each draft.
2. Purchase a three-ring notebook and create a historical chronicle of your project.

 BOOKS

 REGISTER AND COPYRIGHT

Clearance and Copyright
M. Donaldson, 275 pp., $26.95
Everything the screenwriter and film-maker need to know for protection.

This Business of Screenwriting
R. Suppa, 225 pp., $19.95
Chapters on copyright registration and protection as well as how to sell.

The Screenwriter's Legal Guide
S. Breimer, 320 pp., $19.95
Chapters with contracts on option-purchase agreements, writer-for-hire assignments, and much more.

Writers Guild of America/East
  (WGA/E)
555 W 57th St, 12th Floor
New York, NY 10019
Ph: 212-767-7800
Web: www.WGAEast.org

Writers Guild of America/West
  (WGA/W)
7000 W 3rd St
Los Angeles, CA 90048
Ph: 323-951-4000
Web: www.wga.org

Copyright Office
Library of Congress
Washington, DC 20599
Ph: 800-688-9889
    202-707-3000
Web: www.loc.gov/copyright/forms

FORM YOUR PRODUCTION COMPANY

"Do Your Legal Work"

There is nothing magical about forming a production company. Anyone can do it. It is simple. There are no exams, licenses, or degrees necessary. 📁 *You don't need an attorney to form your production company.* All you need is a company name, a trip downtown for a business license, and $19.95 for a box of business cards.

First, go to your respective city hall and get a business license application. The only question it asks, other than name, address, etc., is "Are you (A) a Sole Proprietorship, or (B) a Partnership, or (C) a Corporation?"

If the company is solely yours, then it is a "Sole Proprietorship." If other people have an ownership in the company with you, then check the box that reads "Partnership" and write the name, address, and Social Security number of each partner. If you have a large personal net worth, and have incorporated to create a shield to protect your assets, then check the box indicating "Corporation" and use your corporation's tax ID number instead of your social security number. Depending on the city, obtaining a business license takes 30 to 60 minutes and costs $25–$175.

The next step is to display a "fictitious business statement" notice, announcing the name of your company, in the legal section of a local newspaper. This costs an additional $50–$75. When applying for your business license, you'll notice people passing out flyers, saying that they will post your fictitious business statement for you. Pay their nominal fee. Once done, you'll be mailed a DBA (doing business as) statement that proclaims you are operating under your business's "assumed name."

I also suggest that you register your company's name as a Web domain by placing a .com, .net, or .tv after it. Even if you don't have plans for putting up a Web site now, you may want to later, so secure the name. If you have access to the Internet, type www.networksolutions.com (the most commonly used Web registration site) and see if your movie's name is available. Registration costs $50–$70 for two years.

The final steps, after your DBA statement, is to open a business checking account (deposit $100–$200) and establish an escrow account (chapter 14) where your investors, when you have them, will place their money. All told, it should cost no more than $450, plus the cost of incorporating (if you desire), to start a production company.

PICKING AN ATTORNEY

You do not need an expensive entertainment attorney. You should pick an attorney who believes in you and your project and whom you can trust.

To do this, interview attorneys and ask, "What are the specific filing costs to get a business license and what will you charge to do it for me?" If the attorney hems and haws without telling you the exact amount but says it shouldn't cost more than $2,000 to handle what you can do for $150–$450 by going to city hall (filing fees and fictitious statement filing), then walk out of his office. Also, ask the prospective attorney, "What's the cost of incorporating in this state?" If he replies anything other than the exact amount, run—don't walk—out of his office.

Additional work you'll want the attorney to do is to prepare the paperwork to properly solicit funds (chapter 14) from investors. This will include creating a limited partnership (LP) or a limited liability company (LLC); establishing an escrow account with your bank; and preparing an "offering memorandum." He should charge no more than $2,000 for this.

If the attorney you are about to hire has experience in preparing limited partnership papers for investor solicitation, *if* he says he will charge you $2,000–$3,000 (to include filing fees) for everything, *if* you have a good feeling about him and he gives you verifiable references, then he is the one.

> **IMPORTANT POINT**   Only hire an attorney who believes in your project enough to introduce you to investors. If he won't help you meet investors then he doesn't believe in you and is just another scum-sucking attorney who says anything to get a retainer.

Two or three thousand dollars is what it should cost to contract with an attorney to set up your production company to solicit investors (and that's in a state like California, where it's expensive to incorporate). And you can get this done for nothing if you partner with an attorney and make him executive producer. His job will be to do the legal work, pay for the hard costs (filing fees, photocopying, postage, etc.), and take his fee from either profits or upon raising finances. Your job will be to make the film, and take your fee during production. Welcome to Hollywood.

TO DO:

1. Go to city hall and get your business license.
2. Call your state's department of incorporations and find out the filing fees to incorporate.
3. Interview attorneys about their fees. Ask what they can accomplish for $2,000.

 BOOKS

How to Form Your Own Corporation Without a Lawyer
T. Nicholas, 263 pp., $19.95
Includes state-specific how-to information. Do it yourself!

How to Form Your Own "S" Corporation
T. Nicholas, 213 pp., $23.95
Save on double taxation by forming an "S" corporation.

The Partnership Book
D. Clifford & R. Warner, 305 pp., $39.95
Written in plain English, with a CD-ROM; gives you the info needed to form a business with a partner.

How to Form a Non-Profit Corporation
A. Mancuso, 310 pp., $44.95
Obtain your IRS 501(c)(3) tax exemption. Comes with a CD-ROM.

Form Your Limited Liability Company
A. Mancuso, 304 pp., $44.95
Learn how to form the most common legal entity used by filmmakers to solicit investors. CD-ROM.

 SOFTWARE

Automated Contracts for the Film and Television Industry
M. Litwak, Windows or Macintosh, $199.95

A $550/hour entertainment attorney on a disc. Over 60 "fill in the blanks" contracts needed by a producer, from distribution agreements to writer- and talent-for-hire forms.

LEGAL INFORMATION

Barab & Assoc.
9606 Santa Monica Blvd, 3rd Floor
Beverly Hills, CA 90210
Attn: Sean Fawcett, Esq.
Ph: 310-859-6644

Sloss Law Office, PLC
555 W 25th St, 4th Floor
New York, NY 10001
Attn: John Sloss, Esq.
Ph: 212-627-9898
Web: www.SlossLaw.com

Fredericks and Vonderhorst
12121 Wilshire Blvd, Suite 900
Los Angeles, CA 90025
Attn: Dennis Fredricks, Esq.
Ph: 310-472-1122
E-mail: FredricksLaw@Earthlink.com

Harris Tulchin Law Offices
11377 W Olympic Blvd, 2nd Floor
Los Angeles, CA 90064
Attn: Harris Tulchin, Esq.
Ph: 310-914-7979
Web: www.MediaLawyers.com

Mark Litwak Law Firm
433 N Camden Dr, Suite 1010
Beverly Hills, CA 90210
Ph: 310-859-9595
E-mail: atty@MarkLitwak.com

John Tormey III, PLC
217 E 86th St, PMB 221
New York, NY 10028
Attn: John Tormey
Ph: 212-410-4142
Web: www.tormey.net

Surpin, Mayersohn and Edelstone
1880 Century Park East, Suite 618
Los Angeles, CA 90067
Attn: Shelly Surpin, Esq.
Ph: 310-552-1808

The Firm
19 W 21st St, 6th Floor
New York, NY 10010
Attn: Jeffrey Jacobson
     Bruce Colfin
Ph: 212-691-5630
Web: www.TheFirm.com

Pierce & Gorman
9100 Wilshire Blvd, Suite 225
East Tower
Beverly Hills, CA 90212
Attn: David Pierce, Esq.
     Patrick Gorman, Esq.
Ph: 310-274-9191
Web: www.PierceGorman.com

Frankfurt Kurnit Klein & Selz
488 Madison Ave
New York, NY 10022
Attn: Michael Frankfurt
     Stuart Kleinman
Ph: 212-980-0120
Web: www.fkkslaw.com

Donaldson & Hart
9220 Sunset Blvd, Suite 224
Los Angeles, CA 90069
Attn: Michael Donaldson, Esq.
Ph: 310-273-8394
Web: www.DonaldsonHart.com

Weissman & Wolff
9665 Wilshire Blvd, Suite 900
Beverly Hills, CA 90212
Attn: Eric Weissman, Esq.
Ph: 310-858-7532
Fax: 310-550-7191
E-mail: wwllp@wwllp.com

FINANCING, PART I

"The Studio Method"

Every film funding process that you can imagine eventually boils down to a combination of the following seven routes. Try them all.  **Which one is best? The one that gets you the first bank check.**

The seven financing routes are:

1. Development route
2. Packaging route
3. Gap financing and pre-sell route
4. Actor-partner route
5. Co-production route
6. Dealmaker route
7. Independent route

Although 99.9 percent of first-time filmmakers take the independent route (#7), they are initially seduced by the other six routes, which on the surface appear easier, faster, and more glamorous.

Let's take a quick look at each of the seven routes and decide which is for you.

1. DEVELOPMENT ROUTE

Hollywood is always announcing that it is seeking fresh talent. What a crock! So, here you are, that fresh talent. Watch how quickly you discover that even though you qualify as fresh talent no one is seeking you.

You want to be a "player." You're loaded with original ideas. You want to sell them. You need to set up meetings with studio executives, "pitch" (orally present) projects, and have the executives give you money to go into development.

Let's assume you're successful and an executive you pitch to, for whatever reason, loves your idea. He won't merely say, "Here's the money. Could you come back with the film in six months, please?" That's naive. He'll dole it out, step-by-step, as you develop your project. First, you receive just enough money to hire a writer (usually 110 percent of scale—100 percent for the writer and 10 percent for his/her agent) for two drafts, and I doubt you'll even get a penny to pay for your expenses. Now get ready for Development Hell.

What seems simple gets complicated, because every executive who reads your first draft to justify his existence is going to put in his two cents, and you now commence the rewrite. If the second draft is great, which is doubtful, you'll get more money to make pay-or-play offers and attach an A-list actor, who wants the script rewritten.

Several months and rewrites later, your pay-or-play actor's three-week availability window is gone and he drops out of the project. Back to the development executive who approved the actor, if he/she is still working for the company, and you get approval for another A-list actor (more pay-or-play money), who likes the concept but not the script, which was tailored to the first actor. He has the power to demand and get a rewrite of the rewrite of the once great script.

Now, factor in co-star availabilities, pre-production ego clashes with directors, revolving door executives, and you understand the phrase "development hell"—this could take three to five years. And your nice, simple suburban love story, thanks to the development process, has become a musical epic set in heaven, with the American Civil War as a backdrop, starring a cat as the woman, an elephant as the man, and Ted Turner as Ulysses S. Grant.

> **REALITY CHECK**   Unless you're a great writer, an amazing corporate politician, or have access to pay-or-play money, don't try the development route to launch your career.

2. PACKAGING ROUTE

In this case you associate with a large agency (William Morris, ICM, CAA, Endeavor, UTA, etc.) that has a "packaging" division.

Agents normally get 10 percent of the talent's (writer, actor, director) revenues. On a $10–$20 million film, assuming the writer gets $100,000–$250,000 ($10,000–$25,000 for agent); the star gets $2–$3 million ($200,000–$300,000 for agent); the co-star gets $300,000–$500,000 ($30,000–$50,000 for agent); and the director gets $200,000–$300,000 ($20,000–$30,000 for agent), the agent and his/her respective agency will split $260,000–$405,000 in commissions.

But if the agency creates the entire package (writer, director, and actors) and sells it as a whole, besides receiving the $260,000–$405,000 10 percent agent fee they'll also make 3–5 percent (a packaging fee) of the entire $10–$20 million budget, or $300,000–$1 million. Plus, they'll participate in profits.

REALITY CHECK   Powerful packaging agencies don't need novice filmmakers, so good luck trying to get a meeting.

3. GAP FINANCING AND PRE-SELL ROUTE

This requires the ability to hustle international buyers, bankers, and insurance executives and sell, sell, sell. Gap financing involves a lot of contracts and paperwork. But on the bright side, you might go to Cannes or Milan.

The process entails taking your package (script, budget, director, and actor commitments) and attending a film market (AFM, Cannes, and MIFED), where you pre-sell your project nation-by-nation (Germany, Japan, India, Korea, Brazil, etc.) at about a 50 percent discount of what those foreign buyers would have paid if the film was finished.

When pre-selling you don't receive cash. You obtain financial guarantees (pre-sell contracts) committed to your project, which will be paid to you once that foreign buyer receives the finished film's negative. You then bring those pre-sell guarantees (three suitcases of paperwork) to a bank with an entertainment division, which loans you production dollars utilizing the pre-sell contracts as collateral.

If you've raised most (say, 80 percent), but not all, of the funds via pre-selling only 5 of the 35 nations and territories from around the world, then a bank might loan the final 20 percent or so based on the value assigned to the 25 countries or territories that you've yet to pre-sell to. This is "gap financing," where the bank loans you production monies based on the gap (unsold nations or territories).

This route requires a lot of foreign travel, a fair amount of money to secure actor commitments, and a lot of legal work, which burns up more money. Distributors like Miramax and New Line do this all the time. So do low-budget producers like Roger Corman, Steve Stabler, or Michael Curb ... but, sad to say, not you.

> **REALITY CHECK**   Forget this route for your first project. For although it is not as expensive as pay-or-play deals, it is fraught with tons of contracts, completion guarantees, and bank commitments.

4. ACTOR-PARTNER ROUTE

Instead of approaching actors as employees and writing big pay-or-play checks, you think of the actor more as a partner than as an employee. Find an A-list actor whose production company has a studio development deal and is looking for new projects and scripts to purchase. Send that powerful actor your script and, if you get an offer, you refuse it unless you also come along as the co-producer. This is nicknamed, "Get the great script and hold it hostage."

Each studio has A-list actors' companies with development and production financing. (*Variety* publishes "Facts on pacts," a chart that lists studio development deals, in late June.) Disney has Tim Allen ("Boxing Cat"), Bruce Willis ("Flying Heart"), and Glenn Close ("Trillium Entertainment"). Paramount has Tom Cruise ("C/W"), Mel Gibson ("Icon Films"), and Jodie Foster ("Egg Pictures"). Warner Bros. has George Clooney ("Section Eight"), Clint Eastwood ("Malpaso"), and Sandra Bullock ("Fortis Films").

Get the chart. Itemize actors with development deals. Get the names of their respective development executives and send that person your script. Wait for it to be read, and if an offer ensues (usually an option agreement), say no and counter with a co-production arrangement. But don't expect to have any creative control. The name actor will have all the power.

> **REALITY CHECK**   It's doable, but doubtful, and totally depends on owning the great script and holding it literally hostage.

5. CO-PRODUCTION ROUTE

You pay the above-the-line costs (writer/actor/director salaries) and partner with a company in a nation whose government covers all the below-the-line costs (crew/equipment/food/labor). Your foreign partner/co-producer keeps the film rights for his nation. You keep the North American (USA/Canada) rights and argue about how to split revenues from the rest of the world.

Examples of nations with government financing plans are England, which has distributed over $50 million thanks to the British lottery via its British Film Council. Canadian production companies can get funding from the National Film Board and respective rebates from the province in which the movie is shot. Germany taxes TV viewing and disseminates millions of dollars through its respective regional film funds. Australia, Ireland, and France also have government-sponsored film funds.

As an American, to tap into these foreign film funds you must co-produce with a production company from that nation. The deal will probably entail you attaching an A-list American actor. That's why Toronto, London, and Berlin have become such production hotbeds. However, can you get the cash to make the deal, convince a name talent to commit (pay-or-play), and wrangle a North American distribution deal?

> **REALITY CHECK**   Forget it. You don't have the money to attach a large enough actor to the project, or even the cash to make the numerous trips to the corresponding nation.

6. DEALMAKER ROUTE

Play like the big boys. Producers write checks. If you are a producer without a checkbook, you're a canoeist without a paddle drifting in the River of No Production.

Write two large checks. The first to buy or option the great script, and the second to get an A-list actor committed. Then travel the world raising 100 percent of the financing from the different revenues sources (video, cable, broadcast, theatrical, merchandise, etc.) in each of the nations where the film will be projected.

This is done by producers like Arnold Kopelson, Brian Grazer, Peter Guber, Arnon Milchan, and Joe Roth. Do you think you can join this group of producers with your very first film?

> **REALITY CHECK**   Forget it. This route will occur, but not on your first or second film but on your third film, and that assumes that your first two films were widely successful.

7. INDEPENDENT ROUTE

This is the most common route used by the first-timer, especially if you want to maintain control. It entails financing your film by securing OPM (other people's money). Sometimes it's referred to as, "First make a film . . . then you'll make a deal."

Want $20 million to finance a feature? First make a $2 million feature that makes money. But you don't have $2 million. Thus, make a $200,000 feature that makes money. And if you don't have the $200,000 then you must first make an excellent $20,000 feature.

First make a film. Then, if that film is successful, you'll make a deal. This is the independent route. It works!

To get "OPM" (chapter 14), form a limited partnership or a limited liability company, with you or your company (incorporated) operating as the general partner, and sell shares or units. For example, raise $1 million by selling 50 percent of your project's projected profits to 10 investors for $100,000 each, with each investor receiving a 5 percent interest (one-tenth of 50 percent) in the profits. If you're trying to raise $200,000, you might sell 75 percent (you keep 25 percent) of the potential profits, if any (always put in "if any"), by selling 25 units ($8,000 each), with each unit to receive 3 percent of the profits.

> **REALITY CHECK**   The independent route is the most realistic approach. Use OPM and first make a film. If your film is profitable you'll climb the ladder and implement the other six financing routes for your follow-up projects—but first, make a film.

————————

TO DO:

1. Try dealmaking. Try the development route. Try to get a meeting with a development exec.
2. Try dealmaking again, this time the packaging route. Try to get an agent to package your project.
3. Try dealmaking again, this time the pre-sell route. Try to get a foreign sales agent to get you international pre-sales.

BOOKS

 SOFTWARE

The Movie Business Book
J. Squire, 479 pp., $15.95
The inside story of how studios
finance, market, and sell feature films.

*The Independent Filmmaker's Law and
    Business Guide*
J. Garon, 288 pp., $24.95
Takes you step-by-step through the
contracts needed for an independent
or digital filmmaker.

Film Finance and Distribution
J. Cones, 558 pp., $24.95
A superb dictionary of terms explaining dealmaking, financing, and distribution. Solid information!

The Biz
S. Moore, 365 pp., $27.95
A thorough explanation of the
business, legal, and financial aspects
of the film industry.

Movie Money
B. Daniels and S. Sills, 380 pp., $19.95
Understand accounting practices and
you'll become a Hollywood pro—
instantly.

*Dealmaking in the Film and Television
    Industry*
M. Litwak, 340 pp., $29.95
Considered the best overall guide to
dealmaking. A must-have!

Reel Power
M. Litwak, 336 pp., $14.95
A comprehensive look at how today's
Hollywood works.

Film Profit
Windows or Macintosh, $99.95
Excellent for investor presentations.
Designed to develop a solid business
plan and calculate net and gross profit
projections for your project.

 **PRODUCER-
DEALMAKERS**

Armyan Bernstein
c/o Beacon Communications
120 Broadway, Suite 200
Santa Monica, CA 90401
Ph: 310-260-7000
Web: www.beaconpictures.com

Steven Reuther
c/o Bel-Air Entertainment
4000 Warner Blvd, Bldg 66, Suite 100
Burbank, CA 90046
Ph: 818-954-4040

Andrew Vajna
c/o Cinergi Pictures Entertainment
2308 Broadway
Santa Monica, CA 90404
Ph: 310-315-6000

Ed Feldman
c/o Feldman Co.
520 Evelyn Pl
Beverly Hills, CA 90210
Ph: 416-761-0123

Elie Samaha
Franchise Pictures
8228 Sunset Blvd
Los Angeles, CA 90046
Ph: 323-848-3444

Bruce Davey
c/o Icon Productions
808 Wilshire Blvd, 4th Floor
Santa Monica, CA 90401
Ph: 310-434-7400

Brian Grazer
c/o Imagine Entertainment
9465 Wilshire Blvd, 7th Floor
Beverly Hills, CA 90212
Ph: 310-858-2000
Web: www.imagine-
    entertainment.com

Arnold Kopelson
c/o Kopelson Entertainment
8560 Sunset Blvd, Suite 600
West Hollywood, CA 90069
Ph: 310-360-3200

Ted Tannenbaum
c/o Lakeshore Entertainment
5555 Melrose Ave
Gloria Swanson Building
Los Angeles, CA 90038
Ph: 323-956-4222

Peter Guber
c/o Mandalay Pictures
4751 Wilshire Blvd, 3rd Floor
Los Angeles, CA 90010
Ph: 323-549-4342

James Robinson
c/o Morgan Creek
4000 Warner Blvd, Bldg 76

Burbank, CA 91522
Ph: 818-954-4800

Gary Levinsohn
c/o Mutual Film
Raleigh Studios
650 N Bronson Ave
Clinton Building
Los Angeles, CA 90004
Ph: 323-871-5690

Arnon Milchan
c/o New Regency
10201 W Pico Blvd, Bldg 12
Los Angeles, CA 90035
Ph: 310-369-8300
Web: www.newregency.com

Mike Medavoy
c/o Phoenix Pictures
10202 W Washington Blvd
Frankovich Building
Culver City, CA 90232
Ph: 310-244-6100

Joe Roth
c/o Revolution Studios
2900 W Olympic Blvd
Santa Monica, CA 90404
Ph: 310-255-7000

Roger Birnbaum
c/o Spyglass
500 S Buena Vista St
Burbank, CA 91521
Ph: 818-560-3458

Bruce Berman
c/o Village Roadshow
3400 Riverside Dr, Suite 900
Burbank, CA 91505
Ph: 818-260-6000

FINANCING, PART II

"The Independent Method"

You tried being a dealmaker (chapter 13). Dead end! All those glamorous financing methods like pre-selling, gap financing, international co-productions, and packaging agencies didn't work, did they? Now try the unglamorous independent route. It works. Simply put, you get your script, form a limited liability company, and sell units. Let me explain.

> **IMPORTANT POINT** When raising money from private investors, you must get the money on the very first meeting. Attempt a second meeting after you've told him/her everything you know in the first meeting, and they'll discover that they know as much as you do.

Here's how to get the money from an investor the first time you see his/her face, by applying these 10 steps:

1. Get the script.
2. Prepare your paperwork.
3. Write a business plan.
4. Do your legal work.
5. Select a cinematographer.
6. Get ready to sell.
7. Phone the investor(s).
8. Send the paperwork.
9. Sell the sizzle.
10. Ask the closing statement.

1. Get the script: Don't fall in love with typing. You are going to raise the money. You are going to make the film. But if the script ain't great, the film ain't gonna be great, and you've wasted 18 months. Make sure your script is great.

2. Prepare your paperwork: Get a budget, a shooting schedule, a production board, talent and crew lists, and storyboard panels to impress the investors.

3. Write a business plan: Prepare a 13–15 page business plan that contains:

Synopsis (page 1): Outline the film and your company's mission.

Top sheet (page 2): The first page (aka "top sheet") of the budget.

Box-office chart (page 3): A list detailing what other independent films cost and grossed.

Game plan (page 4): Outline how you plan to make and market the film.

Film festivals (page 5): Present a list of those you intend to attend.

Distributors (page 6): Prepare a list of distributors that you intend to approach.

Film markets (page 7): Make a list of film markets where you intend to generate foreign revenues.

Résumés (pages 8–12): Details of your key management team and talent.

Window dressing (pages 13–?): Photos, poster artwork, production schedules, and storyboard panels are always helpful to impress investors.

4. Do your legal work: Form your production company. Get (a) a business license. Prepare (b) the limited partnership or limited liability company papers, to include (c) an "offering memorandum" that outlines what each (d) "unit" (share) that you are offering represents and costs.

A. Business license: You're conducting a business—a film production company. Go to city hall and get a business license either as a sole proprietorship (you're by yourself), a partnership (if you're with another person[s]), or an incorporation (if you're wealthy and want to protect your personal assets).

B. Limited partnership: This is the most common form of motion picture partnership. You (your production company) are the general partner and your investors (the wealthy but bored dentists) will become the limited partners. This means that they have no say in how to run the business and they can make an unlimited amount of money but can only lose what they invested, no more.

To do this (a) you'll file a certificate with the secretary of the state you're conducting business in, (b) you'll file a list of all partners' names, and (c) you'll adhere to minor requirements for holding and conducting meetings.

In recent years a limited liability company (LLC), a slight variation of the limited partnership (LP), is most commonly used.

C. Offering memorandum: This sounds exotic but is merely a paragraph of typing in the LP or LLC papers that states how much money you're raising; then how many "units" you're offering to raise that money; what each "unit" costs; and finally what each "unit" represents in percentage of profits, if any.

D. Units: Units are partnership shares that are mentioned in the offering memorandum paragraph. For instance, if your budget is $400,000 you might be offering investors 50 percent of profits by selling 4 "units" at $100,000 each, with each unit equaling 12.5 percent (50 percent divided by 4) of the profits.

However, if you're not comfortable asking people for $100,000, but can feel comfortable asking for $20,000, then sell 20 units, with each unit representing 2.5 percent (50 percent divided by 20) of the profits.

5. Select a cinematographer: A cinematographer (aka DP or director of photography) is the most important person you will hire. Never, ever hire someone fresh out of film school—these are kids that barely know how to make a bed. Hire only a professional and don't even think about approaching investors until you know who your cinematographer is.

To find a professional DP, call your local film lab, camera rental facility, and film commissioner for referrals. Once you have a list of potential DPs, phone and tell them you're producing a feature (just assume that they want the job) and ask if they have a 35mm demo reel, a sample reel of footage they've shot (all DPs do). Screen their reels and pick the DP whose style visually excites you—but only if you feel that there won't be any personality conflicts with him/her.

Now armed with your script, paperwork, business plan, legal work, and cinematographer-with-demo-reel, you are ready to solicit investors.

6. Get ready to sell: Successful producers are salesmen. To raise money you must sell. Car and garment salesmen have the trait (pushy, pushy) to become (if they want to) excellent producers. So let's take a moment to learn the three rules of salesmanship:

Rule 1: Bring them to the track!
Rule 2: He who says the first number loses!
Rule 3: Ask the closing statement and shut up!

Rule 1. Bring them to the track: When raising money, never go to money—make money come to you. What I mean by this is, never physically go to a potential investor's house or office with a business proposal. They must come to you.

If you can't even get them to leave their office and come to your office, then you are not going to get any money from them. I have a friend who raises money from doctors and dentists who invest in racehorses. He never goes to their offices/homes. He meets them at the track—the racetrack. The racetrack is glamorous. At the racetrack is where he makes the investment proposal.

Never go to an investor, they must travel to you. That's why Hollywood "does lunch." Executive A doesn't want to go to Executive B's office, and B doesn't want to go to A's office. So they do lunch and meet at an equal track.

You have no track? Yes, you do. Your track is a movie theater, a cinema. You will meet each and every investor at a movie theater for a 15-minute presentation (this will be explained in depth further in the chapter). There is something glamorous about this. Remember, Sell the Sizzle.

Rule 2. He who says the first number loses: Car salesmen are great at this. They never say the first number. Ask one, "What's the best price you'll give me?" He'll reply with, "What can you afford?" "What's your weekly take-home?" But he won't say the first number. If he does, he'll get fired.

When investors ask, "What's your budget?" and you tell them, you've just given them a number (the first number) and you've lost. You must first ask investors (it's called "qualifying"), "Can you afford to invest in the arts?" If they say yes, then ask, "What can you afford?" 🛄 ***Never, ever say the first number. They must say a number first. Or you'll lose.***

Rule 3. Ask the closing statement, and shut up: The loudest noise in the world is silence. 🛄 ***You won't get the money if you don't ask for it.*** Find a way to get in front of a wealthy individual, qualify him, titillate him, ask the closing statement (i.e., "How many units may I put you down for?"), and bite your bottom lip. Don't break the silence. Stare at him. Watch him squirm—just don't break the silence. Ask for the money, shut up, and you just might get it.

7. *Phone investor(s):* Where do you find investors? If your friends or relatives are wealthy, hit 'em up. If not, where do you go for a list of wealthy dudes? The answer is simple. I already told you, and this is where nine out of ten first-time filmmakers get their investors. Pick up the Yellow Pages, turn to the letter D, and start calling doctors and dentists (the wealthiest group of stupid people in North America). It's just a phone call. Turn to the letter D. Phone Dr. Abramson and start with, "Dr. Abramson, I don't know how I got your name. I was wondering if you're interested in the arts?" If Dr. Abramson says no, dial Dr. Bernstein. If Dr. Bernstein says no, dial Dr. Cohen. Nineteen out of twenty dentists will hang up before you finish your sentence. Just smile and dial, for it only takes one dentist.

8. *Send the paperwork:* Once someone is interested, send him the paperwork (budget, script, storyboards, limited partnership papers, offering memorandum). Tell him to do his due diligence (legalese for "homework") with his attorney and accountant and ask if his/her spouse's permission is needed to invest. Let him know that you will make one follow-up phone call. If his secretary says he's in a meeting, you won't call again.

Let's assume you send the paperwork, he reads the script, looks at the storyboards, peruses the budget, goes ga-ga over the actors' headshots and storyboards. You phone a week later and he takes the call. You have a mark. Now start to close. Ask what he thinks of the script, and no matter what he says, respond with, "Amazing. We're working on that right now." Then compliment him on his filmmaking insight and offer, "Would you like a demonstration of the production company?" He'll say yes, and now you "bring him to the track" which in your case is a movie theater.

9. *Sell the sizzle:* Wealthy people invest in movies because Hollywood is glamorous. Dentistry is not. Now, I know you're disagreeing with me, because investors want to make money. True. But, 🧰 *glamour induces investors to invest in movies more than the profit potential. Sell the sizzle.*

IMPORTANT POINT #1   It is important that you appear glamorous to a dentist or doctor who wants glamour in his life. Here's how to do it:

Pick the loveliest art deco movie theater in your city. Introduce yourself to the manager. Tell him you're an independent filmmaker raising money for a project and ask, "Next Thursday morning, before the daily shows start, could the projectionist come in a half-hour early and screen a 10-minute, 35mm demo reel for an investor?"

IMPORTANT POINT #2 You will screen your prospective DP's demo reel, which will look 10 times better, and more impressive, than any short you're thinking of making.

Theater managers love being asked this and treated as part of the movie industry, rather than merely someone who cleans up popcorn and Goobers. You might be asked to tip the projectionist $100, but that's a small price to pay.

Remember, you must get the money on the very first meeting and you have yet to physically meet the dentist. When the dentist says he'd like a demonstration of your production company, make plans to meet him at the movie theater 30 minutes before the projectionist starts the theater's normal show—this will be 11:30 A.M.

At 10:30 A.M. Dr. Abramson takes his hand out of a patient's mouth, gets in his car (usually a Lexus), and drives excitedly to the movie theater, where he is about to meet you and your cinematographer for the first time. Dr. Abramson parks his Lexus, walks to the theater, and waits by the empty ticket booth. Let him stand by himself (you are with your DP in the theater's auditorium). After a few moments he gathers enough nerve to walk into the gorgeous art deco lobby. This is glamorous. After a short wait, you and your cinematographer come from the auditorium and meet the dentist in the lobby. Make your introductions and proceed into the empty theater. Once seated, the projectionist, upon your cue, opens the curtains, lowers the theater lights, and runs the DP's demo reel.

This is exciting—you, your cinematographer, and an investor in an empty theater. Don't mislead. Tell the investor that what he is viewing was shot not by you, but by your cinematographer, and that most of your crew will come from those shoots. Honesty works. The dentist likes this. Now, let's get the money.

10. Ask the closing statement: After screening the demo reel, wait 10–15 seconds, turn to the investor, and ask the closing statement: "How many units may I put you down for?" Then shut up. Create silence. Just stare. The dentist will break the silence. He might say no, and he just might say, "How many units are available?" or "Put me down for three" or "I'll take one." If the investor hesitates, hems and haws, then firmly proclaim (pushy, pushy), "Let me put you down for a half."

If you're selling 20 units at $20,000 each trying to raise $400,000 and you have just closed on half a unit—you have just raised $10,000! This is a start.

ONE INVESTOR OR MANY?

Let's say you want to raise $500,000 by selling 10 units at $50,000 a unit, the question becomes: Is it better to present to one investor at a time or a group? Both have pros and cons. However, it is usually better to bring in a group. It is easier to raise money from a group (peer pressure and mob psychology take over) than from an individual. If one dentist wants a unit, ego provokes another dentist to want two or three units, or, at least, he doesn't want to be left out, and takes one unit.

The difficulty, however, in presenting to a group lies in getting 15 to 20 wealthy people with limited availability schedules in a room at one time. The only way to do this is to create an event, a fund-raiser or a party. That's how civic groups (wealthy beggars) raise money for the opera, symphony, or ballet. And people who donate to the opera or symphony don't even have an opportunity to make a profit.

To get a group of wealthy people together at one time you must create a social function. A party. Thus, qualify 15–20 investors. Send them the paperwork (script, budget, legal, etc.) and rent a screening room or theater for a night. Have a buffet—wine and cheese. Alcohol works. Thank them for coming. Introduce your cinematographer. Project his/her demo reel. This will dazzle them. Then give each potential investor several two-page scenes from the script and bring in four to five actors. This is more sizzle.

IMPORTANT POINT   Wealthy people get super stupid when they are within five feet of an actor who is acting. This same actor, one hour prior, was a waiter whom the wealthy person was probably rude to. But once the waiter puts on his/her acting persona the wealthy person gets dumbfounded.

After the actors do their reading, thank everyone for supporting the arts and give each investor the offering memorandum, with a pen, that you would appreciate it if they filled in with either the dollar amount or the number of units they want to purchase. Then tell them that on the way out they can hand their filled-in offering memoranda to your assistants who, along with the actors, are strategically placed at each exit.

Ten minutes later, after everyone has left, open the envelopes with the filled-in offering memoranda and count the money.

It is never as simple as this. But it is not as difficult as you think.

WHAT TO OFFER INVESTORS

If an investor wants to know how much he can make, tell him what he wants to hear. Tell him that *The Blair Witch Project* was shot for $20,000–$30,000 and grossed over $150 million. Tell investors what they can make. But emphasize the "can make." Say, "It is possible to get a tenfold return on your money in 18 months." You haven't lied. It is possible— but it is doubtful.

The business plan that you give investors should include a chart (taken from *Variety* or the *Hollywood Reporter*) of independent films, indicating what they cost to make and what they grossed. It will look something like this:

Film	Budget	Gross
sex, lies and videotape	$1,000,000	$50,000,000
Clerks	$22,000	$15,000,000
In the Company of Men	$25,000	$5,000,000
Sliding Doors	$3,000,000	$60,000,000
The Full Monty	$2,000,000	$70,000,000
The Blair Witch Project	$20,000	$150,000,000
My Big Fat Greek Wedding	$1,000,000+	$220,000,000

Everyone loves to talk about what a film grossed. The key word here is "gross," which is not the same as profit. In every business, investors understand the difference between gross and profit. Yet it is amazing how many smart businessmen come to the film industry with their money and instantly get stupid. Hollywood likes this. You will like this. And, if wealthy individuals turn ignorant and misconstrue what "gross" means, don't educate them. Sell the sizzle. Show them the charts in the Hollywood trades that state grosses.

After you show them the chart(s), there are three things that you offer them:

1. Profit participation
2. First position
3. Interest return

PROFIT PARTICIPATION

Let's assume you have a 50–50 profit split—commonly known as a "50–50 net deal." Investors get 50 percent of net profits and the production company (you) gets 50 percent. 🗄 *You can guarantee that the investors will get 50 percent of profits.* What you can't guarantee is that there will be profits.

Assume the film's budget is $400,000 and the film makes $2 million in profits. How do you split? Do you give $1 million to the investors and keep $1 million for yourself or your production company? No, because that's not fair to investors. Here's why.

First Position

Shouldn't investors, who gave you $400,000 get their $400,000 back before you split 50–50? Absolutely! The investors will think so.

Thus, tell investors that they'll be in "first position" to recoup their investment. If the film is made for $400,000 and profited $2 million, the investors will first recoup their $400,000 investment. Then, what's left over ($2 million – $400,000 = $1.6 million) is split 50–50.

Thus, the investor first gets his $400,000 back and then earns an additional $800,000 (50 percent of $1.6 million), totaling $1.2 million. The production company (you) receives $800,000. This is fair. However, a way to make it an even better deal is to sweeten the pot with interest.

Interest Return

If your investors hadn't given you $400,000, they would have had that money in a bank or a bond or a mutual fund collecting 3–7 percent interest. Thus, offer them 15 percent, 25 percent, or 125 percent interest, which is much more attractive than 3–7 percent.

First, you can offer 15 percent compounded daily. And, since it takes about 18 months until profits (if any) are determined, when you compound 15 percent daily, over 18 months, it is about 25 percent at payout. Finally, if you present the offer by combining first position (100 percent) and interest return (25 percent), you can phrase it more glamorously by stating 💼 *you can guarantee a 125 percent return of their investment to be paid out of profits,* plus 50 percent of remaining profits—if there are any.

Running the numbers: If an investor puts in $400,000, the film profits $2 million, and you promised him (a) first position recoup, plus (b) 25 percent interest and (c) 50 percent profits, this will result in the investor(s) receiving $1,250,000 and you, or your production company, receiving $750,000.

First, first position recoup is $400,000. Then 25 percent interest on $400,000 is $100,000. This now totals $500,000. Finally, add the 50 percent of the remaining $1.5 million ($2 million − $500,000 = $1.5 million) net profit, which is $750,000. Totaling ($400,000 + $100,000 + $750,000) gives $1.25 million for the investors.

Find some fat cats who want to play with Hollywood. Meet them at a movie theater, dazzle them with glamour (the cinematographer's reel and actors' recital), offer them first position, 25 percent interest, and 50 percent of profits, ask how much can they afford, create silence, and voilà!

––––––––––

TO DO:

1. Compile a list of potential investors.
2. Call attorneys and peruse sample limited partnerships, limited liability companies, and offering memorandum forms.
3. Call a wealthy person and offer him 50 percent of profits.
4. Call another wealthy person and offer him 50 percent of profits plus 25 percent interest on his investment.
5. Call another wealthy person and guarantee that he will get his money back before any split, and offer an additional 25 percent interest and 50 percent of profits.

BOOKS

 PRODUCER-FILMMAKERS

Entertainment Industry Economics
H. Vogel, 557 pp., $44.95
Looking for dollar statistics for your
business plan? This is the bible.

Spike Lee
40 Acres & a Mule
75 S Elliot Pl, 3rd Floor
Brooklyn, New York 11217
Ph: 718-624-2974

Film and Video Financing
M. Wiese, 294 pp., $22.95
The toughest thing is getting the
money. This book is a guidebook for
financing independent films.

Martin Scorsese
Cappa Productions
445 Park Ave, 7th Floor
New York, NY 10022
Ph: 212-906-8800

*The Beginning Filmmaker's
    Business Guide*
R. Harmon, 200 pp., $15.95
Financial basics for the beginner.
Financing A–Z!

Ted Hope and James Schamus
Focus Features
417 Canal St, 4th Floor
New York, NY 10013
Ph: 212-343-9230

43 Ways to Finance Your Feature Film
J. Cones, 192 pp., $18.00
Details the four areas of finance—
industry, lender, investor, and
foreign—and all their derivatives.

Christine Vachon
Killer Films
380 Lafayette St, Suite 302
New York, NY 10019
Ph: 212-473-9350

Filmmakers and Financing
L. Levison, 216 pp., $29.95
Shows how to prepare business plans
for independent filmmakers.

Ismael Merchant and James Ivory
Merchant Ivory Productions
250 W 57th St, Suite 1825
New York, NY 10107
Ph: 212-582-8049

Fundraising Houseparty
M. Warshawski, 168 pp., $15.95
A must! Dispenses the nuts and
bolts of doing a presentation at
home to raise film funds from
investors and corporations. Very
important!

Kevin Smith
View Askew Productions, Inc.
3 Harding Rd
Red Bank, NJ 07701
Ph: 732-842-6933

John Sayles
Paradigm (Agent)
10100 Santa Monica Blvd, 25th Floor
Los Angeles, CA 90067
Ph: 310-277-4400

Barry Levinson
Baltimore/Spring Creek LLC
335 N Maple Dr, Suite 209
Beverly Hills, CA 90210
Ph: 310-270-9000

Roger Corman
Concorde-New Horizons
11600 San Vicente Blvd
Los Angeles, CA 90049
Ph: 310-820-6733

Wes Craven
Craven Films
11846 Ventura Blvd, Suite 208
Studio City, CA 91604
Ph: 818-752-0197

Todd Harris
Davis Entertainment Classics
2121 Ave of the Stars, Suite 2900
Los Angeles, CA 90067
Ph: 310-551-2266

Gregory Nava
El Norte Productions
8701 W Olympic Blvd
Los Angeles, CA 90035
Ph: 310-360-1194

John Woo
2450 Broadway, Suite E590
Santa Monica, CA 90404
Ph: 310-449-3205

Anthony Minghella
Mirage Enterprises
233 S Beverly Dr, Suite 200
Beverly Hills, CA 90212
Ph: 310-888-2830

Neil Labute
Pretty Pictures
100 N Crescent Dr
Beverly Hills, CA 90210
Ph: 310-385-6611

Henry Jaglom
Rainbow Film Company
9165 Sunset Blvd, Suite 300
Los Angeles, CA 90069
Ph: 310-271-0202

John Hughes
Rhythm & Hues Studios
5404 Jandy Pl
Los Angeles, CA 90066
Ph: 310-448-7500

Steven Soderbergh
Section Eight Films
4000 Warner Blvd, Bldg 15
Burbank, CA 91522
Ph: 818-954-4840

Clive Barker
Seraphim Films
9326 Readcrest Dr
Beverly Hills, CA 90210
Ph: 310-246-0050

 FILM FINANCE BANKS

Bank of America NT
2049 Century Park East, Suite 200
Los Angeles, CA 90067
Attn: Kapil Sharma
Ph: 310-785-6015
Fax: 310-785-6100

California Trust Bank
16130 Ventura Blvd
Encino, CA 91436
Attn: Gwen Miller
Ph: 213-625-2628
Fax: 310-446-3101

City National Bank
400 N Roxbury Dr, 4th Floor
Beverly Hills, CA 90210
Attn: Daniel Zbojniewicz
Ph: 310-888-6183
Fax: 310-888-6159

Comerica Bank
9777 Wilshire Blvd, 4th Floor
Beverly Hills, CA 90212
Attn: Morgan Rector
Ph: 310-338-3100
Fax: 310-338-3171

Mercantile National Bank
1840 Century Park East
Los Angeles, CA 90067
Attn: Melanie Krinsky
Ph: 310-282-6708
Fax: 310-788-0669

Natexis Banque
1901 Ave of the Stars, Suite 1901
Los Angeles, CA 90067
Attn: Bennett Poxil
Ph: 310-203-8710
Fax: 310-203-8720

Pacific Century Bank
16030 Ventura Blvd
Encino, CA 91436
Attn: David Henry
Ph: 818-907-9122
Fax: 818-379-1620

Union Bank of California
445 S Figueroa St, 16th Floor
Los Angeles, CA 90071

Attn: Joseph Woolf
Ph: 213-236-5827
Fax: 213-236-5852

US Bank
1888 Century Park East, Suite 915
Los Angeles, CA 90067
Attn: Ken Whiting
Ph: 310-407-4413
Fax: 310-286-1030

 INDEPENDENT FILM FINANCE COMPANIES

Film Finances
9000 Sunset Blvd, Suite 1400
Los Angeles, CA 90069
Attn: Steve Ransohoff
Ph: 310-275-7323
Fax: 310-275-1706

JPMorgan Entertainment
1800 Century Park East, Suite 400
Los Angeles, CA 90067
Attn: John Miller
Ph: 310-788-5600
Fax: 310-788-5629

Kramer & Kaslow
2029 Century Park East, Suite 1700
Los Angeles, CA 90067
Attn: Harmon Kaslow
Ph: 310-553-3838
Fax: 310-553-3939

Lewis Horwitz Organization
c/o Imperial Capital Bank
1840 Century Park East, Suite 1000
Los Angeles, CA 90067
Attn: Art Stribley
Ph: 310-275-7171
Fax: 310-275-8055

Mark Litwak & Assoc.
9595 Wilshire Blvd, Suite 711
Beverly Hills, CA 90212
Attn: Cole Martin
Ph: 310-859-9595
Fax: 310-859-0806

Newmarket Capitol Group
202 N Canon Dr
Beverly Hills, CA 90210

Attn: William Tyrer
Ph: 310-858-7472
Fax: 310-858-7473

Paribas Entertainment Finance Group
2029 Century Park East, Suite 3900
Los Angeles, CA 90067
Attn: Michael Mendelsohn
Ph: 310-551-7340
Fax: 310-556-3145

BUDGETS

"The Real Numbers"

In order to raise production money you must first have your script. It should be great. And then you must prepare a budget. So let's talk budgets. **There are only four budgets in Hollywood.** And the budget of your film is going to be one of them. The four budgets are:

1. The Mega-budget
2. The Hyphen-budget
3. The Million-dollar budget
4. The Micro-budget

1. THE MEGA-BUDGET

Every year feature film budgets get bigger and bigger. Every year studios swear they'll never pay outrageous star salaries. They lie! They lie! They lie! Every year studios swear they'll make high-quality, story-driven products. They lie! They lie! They lie! Studios are always going to make star-studded, visually oriented, mind-numbing films with casts of 1,000s (now digitally enhanced), with outrageous budgets.

From *Wings,* to *The Birth of a Nation,* to *Gone With the Wind,* to *Cleopatra,* to *Heaven's Gate,* to *Superman,* to *Jurassic Park,* to *Waterworld,* to *Titanic,* to *Pearl Harbor,* the budgets just grow and grow. And you know that by the end of the twenty-first century's second decade there will be a feature film with a $500 million budget!

There is logic to it. A large percentage of a distributor's revenues come from foreign, TV, and cable sales. Studios don't sell films one at a time to nations and networks. They sell (actually license) packages of 6 to 10 films. So they need what they call a single "locomotive" title, which drives the sale of the package. If you're a foreign TV buyer and want *Pearl Harbor, Titanic, Gladiator,* or even *The Sixth Sense* or *American Beauty,* you have to buy the entire package of 6 to 10 films. Hollywood isn't dumb.

Next, a $100 million or $200 million budget? Have you ever wondered why the dollar amount is exact? The answer is simple. They (the distributors) literally pick the number out of thin air and create a marketing campaign. *Jurassic Park,* when it was released, was marketed as having a budget of $100 million. Give me a break. Think for a moment, *Jurassic Park* was a one-location shoot—a park. It didn't have a cast of thousands. It had about eight actors. Sam Neill, Laura Dern, and Jeff Goldblum are excellent actors with a little name power. They aren't cheap. But they are not $20 million A-list stars.

So what made *Jurassic Park* so expensive? Did I hear you say "special effects"? Hollywood has such a scam going with this special effects stuff. I'm not saying that special effects aren't expensive, but I am saying that Hollywood uses the words "special effects" as a marketing smokescreen.

The dinosaurs in *Jurassic Park* were great. But did you see Roger Corman's feature *Carnosaurus,* which he made for $400,000? If you didn't, rent it. The dinosaurs were quite good. Were they as good as Spielberg's alleged $100 million ones? No. But was there a $99.6 million difference? No way. *Jurassic Park* was marketed as having cost $100 million so you would say, "I gotta see what $100 million looks like."

Two years later Hollywood made *Waterworld,* for supposedly $200 million. Once again, a one-location shoot. It was shot on water, which is difficult, and they built the set twice (it fell down once due to a tropical storm), but it still was just one location. Think it through. If you pay 1,000 employees $1,000 a week it will take almost four years before you spend $200 million. Oh, but it starred Kevin Costner. Whoa, Nellie, let's step back a moment. He produced it, and when you produce a studio-financed film, you get most of your salary when the film is delivered on-budget and on-schedule. *Waterworld* was neither and Costner had to dig into his pocket to help with finishing funds. So Costner cost close to nothing.

Who else was in it? Dennis Hopper. How expensive do you think he is? The rest of the cast was basically a bunch of Australian unknowns being paid actor's ("SAG") minimums. So how did *Waterworld* cost $200 million? The answer is, it didn't! It was expensive, it went over budget, but it did not cost $200 million. I guesstimate the actual "negative cost" of the film to be less than $20 million.

However, by saying it cost $200 million the studio created a marketing event and audiences wanted to see what the most expensive film ever made looks like. *Waterworld* piqued interest, but it bombed. It stunk! It was a piece of crap! *Waterworld* was one of the worst films (*Showgirls* and *Battlefield Earth* knocked it out of its #1 slot) ever made.

Several years later came *Titanic.* Again, it was marketed as the most expensive film ever made. Do you think anyone went to see the story? Everyone knew the boat sinks. It's history. Audiences went to see what all that money looks like. And for once, James Cameron—who knows how to handle special effects—also told a nice love story. Poor boy meets rich girl. Boy wants girl. Girl snubs boy. Boy gets girl. Boy dies. How many times have you seen that movie? I just described *King Kong,* or *Love Story* in reverse, didn't I? . . . Welcome to Hollywood.

Reality Check

What are the odds of your first film being a mega-budget feature? Zero! You'll reach this budget on your fifth or sixth film only if your first four or five films, as you go up in budget, are each highly profitable.

2. THE HYPHEN-BUDGET

If the mega-budget is your fifth or sixth film, then the hyphen-budget will be your second, third, fourth, and possibly fifth films. This is the budget that's always reported with two numbers and a hyphen (–). Examples are:

1. The $50–$70 million feature
2. The $20–$30 million feature
3. The $10–$15 million feature
4. The $3–$5 million feature
5. The $1–$2 million feature

As you can see, they all have two numbers and a hyphen. 📼 *Every film has two budgets—the real budget and the grossly inflated marketing budget.* The only budget that you, the moviegoer, have ever heard of is the grossly inflated marketing budget. However, if you want to discern an actual shooting budget, or the negative cost of making the film, the rule of thumb is to take the lower of the two numbers, halve it, and go a million or two lower.

For instance a $7–$10 million budget, is really made for about $2.5 million (half of $7 million is $3.5 million; subtract $1 million and you have $2.5 million) in cash. If you had $2.5 million in cash, you'd be able to do a five-week shoot, paying your 50-person crew each $2,000 per week, with $100,000 for special effects, $100,000 for stunts. You'd hire a name actor with a $1 million check for three weeks and two other name actors with $100,000 checks for a week's work and still have almost $500,000 left over for music and post-production. The bottom line is, you'll have made a movie, with three names, that you're calling a $7–$10 million feature for only $2.5 million. Wow. Why not call it a $10–$12 million feature, or a $12–$15 million, or a $15–$20 million . . . Welcome to Hollywood.

3. THE MILLION-DOLLAR OR UNDER-A-MIL BUDGET

The million-dollar feature is the most common feature film made every year. It's usually a 35mm, three-week shoot, with SAG actors and limited locations. I worked on a lot of them as a production manager/line producer. They were all called $1 million budgets. Yet, while making the films, I never saw or spent more than $250,000–$500,000. I know, because I wrote the checks.

Although this is the most commonly produced feature film, only one out of ten first-time filmmakers can come up with $250,000–$500,000. But if they do and the first-timer spends his/her money cost-effectively, he/she will make a feature film that will be marketed as a million-dollar feature. And when queried, usually by press at a festival screening, as to the budget, he/she invariably responds with, "The budget is slightly under a million dollars." There are a lot of numbers under a million . . . Welcome to Hollywood.

4. THE MICRO-BUDGET

Ninety-five percent of all feature film budgets have been massively inflated; 300 to 700 percent when marketed to potential ticket buyers; the other 5 percent are grossly deflated 400 to 500 percent. This is due to the fact that the publicity for these films boasts not about how expensive they are but rather how cheaply they were made.

The phrase distributors always use when referring to these films is, "It was shot for . . ."

She's Gotta Have It was *shot for* $60,000.
In the Company of Men was *shot for* $25,000.
Clerks was *shot for* $22,000.
The Blair Witch Project was *shot for* $20,000.
El Mariachi was *shot for* $7,500.
pi was *shot for* $60,000.

For instance, with *El Mariachi* Robert Rodriguez rented a camera for a week, purchased some film and tape, paid for gas, got his friend to act, went across the border, bought some tacos, and shot the movie—he *shot it* for $7,500. He didn't pay the lab. It wasn't edited. He had no music. It wasn't even 35 mm. He didn't finish it. Likewise, Sanchez and Myrick shot *The Blair Witch Project* for $20,000, but the final, edited, color-corrected, blown-up-to-35mm print, with sound and proper music clearances, that you saw in a movie theater, cost at least $200,000–$300,000.

Decades ago, thanks to John Cassavetes (the godfather to independent filmmakers), it was discovered that it is possible to produce feature films for as little as $60,000. Now, if the distributor plays the inflate-the-budget game and increases the $60,000 feature by 700 percent, they'll market it as a film that cost $420,000. This is a marketing black hole. There's no uniqueness to a $420,000 feature. So the distributor, instead of inflating the budget, deflates it by 400–500 percent and claims the film was *shot for* $12,000–$15,000.

Now the film sounds like a little darling. Audiences will come to see what it looks like, and the micro-budget film (aka no-budget, ultra-low-budget, guerrilla film, mini-DV, or digital feature) is sometimes as marketable as the mega-budget film. Compare *The Blair Witch Project* revenues to those of Lucas's *Star Wars* prequel, *The Phantom Menace,* and Kubrick's *Eyes Wide Shut,* which were released almost at the same time.

PREPARE A REALISTIC BUDGET

There are only two ways to prepare a budget—the right way and the wrong way. ■ *The wrong way works and the right way doesn't.*
The right way, the method taught at those ridiculously expensive four-year film schools, is to analyze the script and break it down. Plug in guild

and union rates, get rate cards from vendors and suppliers, do location scouting, hire an excellent crew, add contingencies, add miscellaneous on top of contingencies, allow for legal and accounting fees, and fill in the budget line-by-line. This is good, but the problem is you'll have a budget between $3 million and $30 million when done. And, even though you prepared it the right way, it will get you nowhere because *who the heck is going to give you $3 million,* much less $30 million? Answer: Nobody!

Budgeting the right way looks good, gets you a diploma, and sounds correct, but it doesn't work! Now let's try it my way—the wrong way. Don't budget—"reverse-budget." Your odds of success are better. Spike Lee did it the wrong way. So did John Sayles, Robert Rodriguez, Kevin Smith, and the kids who made *The Blair Witch Project.* Here's what they did and you do: Just pick a dollar amount ($5,000, $18,000, $65,000, etc.) that you can get, and back into it.

What's in your bank account? Got any money in a shoebox? Gotten an inheritance lately? Any equity in your house? Now, I'm not saying go out and mortgage your house. In fact, I beg you not to. Don't go into debt to make your first film. It will put too much pressure on you. But you need to figure out how much money you are willing to invest in yourself.

Can you write a check for $500,000? I doubt it. $50,000? Maybe. $5,000? Probably. Everyone has a different lifestyle. But everyone has some money. Now, without lying, write the amount of money you are willing to invest in yourself. If you were rigorously honest, you probably wrote amounts like $7,500 (*El Mariachi*), or $22,000 (*Clerks*), or $60,000 (*She's Gotta Have It*), or, at the very most, $500,000 (*sex, lies and video- tape*). The number you wrote, be it $153,764 (from an inheritance), or $67,853 (from the sale of your AT&T stock), or $12,346 (sitting in your checking account), will become the budget of your first feature film. Now, reverse-budget!

> **IMPORTANT POINT**   Reverse-budgeting refers to what I call the "38 Steps of Filmmaking™," which are the 38 bank checks, that correspond to the 38 budget line items that you'll write while producing a feature film from beginning to end.

🔲 *There are only two budgets for first-timers—the million-dollar budget and the micro-budget.* Can you write a check for $1 million or $3 million? I think not. Thus, pick a dollar amount that you have access to. Obviously it will be very low. I beg you to be realistic. The dollar amount you picked is the budget for your first feature film, and 📰 *95 percent of all first-timers utilize the micro-budget.* Now, let's learn how to squeeze those 38 bank checks (aka 38 Steps of Filmmaking™) into that amount, make your first feature film, and launch your career.

———————

TO DO:

1. Write down the amount of money that friends and relatives might give you.
2. Write down the dollar amount that you have in bank accounts, stocks, etc.
3. Add up the two numbers and divide by three (because you exaggerated). This is the budget for your first feature film.

 BOOKS

Industry Labor Guide
Entertainment staff, 432 pp., $49.95
The bible for budgeting. This book lists all the film guilds' and union's rates and regulations.

Film Budgeting
R. Singleton, 465 pp., $22.95
The definitive work on motion picture budgeting. Budgeting nuts and bolts.

Film and Video Budgets
D. Simon and M. Wiese, 461 pp., $26.95
Includes budgets for digital projects, no-budget films, and video features.

Micro-Budget Hollywood
P. Gaines and D. Rhodes, 220 pp., $17.95
Step-by-step guide to budgeting—and making—feature films for over $50,000. Down 'n' dirty costs.

Production Budget Book
R. Koster, 209 pp., $29.95
An excellent guidebook for creating budgets on a computer. Movie Magic Budgeting CD-ROM included.

Film Scheduling and Budgeting Workbook
R. Singleton, 298 pp., $19.95
A sample script with sample production and budget forms for you to complete.

 SOFTWARE

Movie Magic Budgeting
Windows or Macintosh, $699.00
Create budgets from $50,000 to $300 million with this dynamic tool used by 80 percent of industry professionals.

Movie Magic Scheduling
Windows 95/98/NT or Macintosh,
$699.00
Construct an efficient and cost-
effective shooting schedule for your
production.

Easy Budgets for Features
Windows or Macintosh (with a
spreadsheet program), $189.95
With a full-function spreadsheet program you can create accurate, good-
looking budgets in half the time.

Easy Budgets for Commercials
Windows or Macintosh (with a
spreadsheet program), $189.95
Budgeting for commercials is different
than features. With a full-function
spreadsheet, this program will create
precise, good-looking budgets quickly.

Cinergy 2000 Budgeting
Windows or Macintosh, $389.000
Accurately create and track film, TV,
or video production expenses.

Cinergy 2000 Scheduling
Windows or Macintosh, $489.00
This is excellent for the creation of
script breakdowns and shooting
schedules for film and TV.

 **WALL STREET
FILM
FINANCIERS**

Herbert Allen
Allen & Co.
711 5th Ave, 8th Floor
New York, NY 10022
Ph: 212-832-8000
Fax: 212-832-8023

Gordon Crawford
Capital Research and Management
333 S Hope St
Los Angeles, CA 90071
Ph: 213-486-9000
Fax: 213-486-9217

Paul D'Addario
c/o Credit Suisse First Boston
2121 Ave of the Stars
Los Angeles, CA 90067
Ph: 310-282-5000
Fax: 310-282-6178

Michael Garin
ING Furman Selz, LLC
333 S Grand Ave, Suite 4200
Los Angeles, CA 90071
Ph: 213-346-3900
Fax: 213-346-3993

John Miller
J. P. Morgan
1800 Century Park East, Suite 400
Los Angeles, CA 90067
Ph: 310-788-5600
Fax: 310-788-5629

Alan Schwartz
Bear Stearns Securities Corp.
1 MetroTech Center N, Suite 1
Brooklyn, NY 11201
Ph: 212-272-1000
Fax: 212-881-9843

Garrett Curran
Dresdner, Kleinwort & Wasserstein
1301 Ave of the Americas
New York, NY 10019
Ph: 212-969-2700
Fax: 212-969-7836

Kapil Sharma
Bank of America
2049 Century Park East, Suite 200
Los Angeles, CA 90067

Ph: 310-785-6015
Fax: 310-785-6100

 FOREIGN PRE-SALE COMPANIES

Alliance Atlantis
121 Bloor St
Toronto, ONT M4W 3M5 Canada
Attn: Seaton McLean
Ph: 416-967-1174
Recent projects: *Stardom, Slackers, Five Senses*

Blow Up Pictures
198 Ave of the Americas
New York, NY 10013
Attn: Gretchen McGowan
Ph: 212-625-9090
Fax: 212-343-1849
Recent projects: *Chuck & Buck*

Capella Films
9200 Sunset Blvd, Suite 315
Los Angeles, CA 90069
Attn: David Korda
Ph: 310-247-4700
Fax: 310-247-4701
Recent projects: *Adventures of Rocky & Bullwinkle*

Fine Line Features
116 N Robertson Blvd
Los Angeles, CA 90048
Attn: Arianna Krikl
Ph: 310-854-5811
Fax: 310-659-1453
Recent projects: *Dancer in the Dark, Anniversary Party*

Fox Searchlight Pictures
10201 W Pico Blvd, Bldg 38
Los Angeles, CA 90035

Attn: Peter Rice
Ph: 310-369-3226
Fax: 310-369-2359
Recent projects: *Woman on Top, Quills*

Focus Features
417 Canal St, 4th Floor
New York, NY 10013
Attn: David Linde
Ph: 212-343-9230
Fax: 212-343-9645
Recent projects: *In the Bedroom, Ride with the Devil*

IFC Films
1111 Stewart Ave
Bethpage, NY 11714
Attn: Jonathan Sehring
Ph: 516-803-4511
Fax: 516-803-4506
Recent projects: *Boys Don't Cry, Mr. Death*

Interlight Partners
8981 Sunset Blvd, Suite 101
West Hollywood, CA 90069
Attn: Patrick Choi
Ph: 323-933-0312
Fax: 310-248-4494
Recent projects: *The Patriot, Resurrection*

Keystone Entertainment
23410 Civic Center Way, Suite E-9
Malibu, CA 90265
Attn: Anne Roberts
Ph: 310-317-4883
Fax: 310-317-4903
Recent projects: *Air Bud: Golden Receiver, Pillow Fight*

Lions Gate Films
4553 Glencoe Ave, Suite 200
Marina Del Rey, CA 90292
Attn: Sarah Lash

Ph: 310-314-2000
Fax: 310-392-0252
Recent projects: *Dogma, American Psycho, Red Violin, Perfume*

Overseas Film Group
8000 Sunset Blvd
Los Angeles, CA 90069
Attn: Ellen Little
Ph: 310-855-1199
Fax: 310-855-0719
Recent projects: *Titus, The Snow Walker*

Promark Entertainment Group
3599 Cahuenga Blvd West, 3rd Floor
Los Angeles, CA 90068
Attn: Eric Bernstein
Ph: 323-878-0404
Fax: 323-878-0486
Recent projects: *Styx, The Enemy*

Samuel Goldwyn Films
9570 W Pico Blvd, Suite 400
Los Angeles, CA 90035
Attn: Meyer Gottlieb
Ph: 310-860-3100
Fax: 310-860-3195
Recent projects: *Tortilla Soup, Big Blue*

Sony Pictures Classics
10000 W Washington Blvd, Suite 2072
Culver City, CA 90232
Attn: Clint Culpepper
Ph: 310-244-4266
Fax: 310-244-2037
Recent projects: *Time Code, Arlington Road*

Silver Lion Films
701 Santa Monica Blvd, Suite 240
Santa Monica, CA 90401
Attn: Conrad Hool
Ph: 310-393-9177
Fax: 310-458-9372
Recent projects: *Crocodile Dundee in Los Angeles*

Sony Pictures Classics
550 Madison Ave, 8th Floor
New York, NY 10022
Attn: Michael Barker
Ph: 212-833-8833
Fax: 212-833-8844
Recent projects: *Crouching Tiger, East West, Tao of Steve*

Storm Entertainment
127 Broadway, Suite 200
Santa Monica, CA 90401
Attn: Michael Heuser
Ph: 310-656-2500
Fax: 310-656-2510
Recent projects: *Hurlyburly, Modern Vampires*

Strand Releasing
1460 Fourth St, Suite 302
Santa Monica, CA 90401
Attn: Jon Gerrans
Ph: 310-395-5002
Fax: 310-395-2502
Recent projects: *Psycho Beach Party*

Artustry Home Entertainment
15910 Ventura Blvd, 9th Floor
Encino, CA 91436
Attn: Richard Abramowitz
Ph: 818-981-8592
Fax: 818-981-8653
Recent projects: *Chainsaw Massacre V, Urbania*

Focus Features West
100 Universal City Plz, Bldg 9128,
    2nd Floor
Universal City, CA 91608
Attn: Stephen Raphael
Ph: 818-777-7373
Fax: 818-733-5245
Recent Projects: *Nurse Betty, Traffic*

FILMMAKING

"The $1,000,000 Feature"

The first 15 chapters, hopefully, have gotten you to think of filmmaking more as a business than as an art form. Now the next 26 chapters (16–41) will show you (step-by-step) how to produce a $1 million feature film while you spend (check-by-check) only $250,000–$500,000.

Two hundred fifty thousand dollars to $500,000 is a lot of money. But if you have access to it, you'll be able to produce a three-week shoot (18 shooting days), working 12–18 hours a day, shooting a 90-page script (a dressed-up stage play with one to five locations) on a schedule (90-page script divided by 18 shooting days) of five pages per day.

Also, during the three weeks, you'll buy 50,000 feet of 35mm film stock (allowing for a 6:1 shooting ratio), rent cameras, lights, and sound equipment, and hire a professional, but non-union, crew to execute 25–30 shots a day. Your company will probably be a signatory to SAG on their lowest low-budget (limited exhibition or experimental filmmaker) agreement and possibly procure a name talent.

Finally, besides the three-week shoot, your budget permits a three-month post-production schedule, and from beginning (first day of principal photography) to end (striking your answer print) your film will be made in four to five months.

I have seen at least 20 different store-bought blank budgets, with the common factor being that each has a top sheet (a budget's first page summarizing all costs). When you are inside the industry (you are not inside) and want to pitch a project to a studio or network, they usually say, "Send me the script, a two-page synopsis, and the 'Top Sheet' of your budget" (the top sheet being the first page of the 30-page budget that summarizes all the costs). Studios or networks have no desire, during the initial stages, to see the detailed budget that will change 10 to 20 times. They just want to see the Top Sheet. Let's look at a Top Sheet!

Below is a typical Top Sheet, with the 38 line items (aka 38 Steps of Filmmaking™), that will be utilized throughout the book.

PRODUCTION BUDGET

Title: Your $1,000,000 Feature

Executive Producer: _____

Producer: _____

Writer: _____   **Director:** _____

ACCOUNT NUMBER	DESCRIPTION	BUDGET
01-00	Producer	
02-00	Writer/Script	
03-00	Director	
04-00	Cast/Actors	
TOTAL ABOVE-THE-LINE (Pre-Production)		
BELOW-THE-LINE		
5-00	Film Stock	
6-00	Film Lab (Shoot)	
7-00	Camera	
8-00	Expendables	
9-00	Sound Equipment	
10-00	Sound Transfer	
11-00	Light/Grip	
12-00	Dolly	
13-00	Cinematographer	
14-00	PM & AD	
15-00	Production Designer	
16-00	Film Crew	
17-00	Art & Props	
18-00	Wardrobe & Makeup	
19-00	Permits	
20-00	Insurance	
21-00	Dailies	
22-00	FX/Stunts/Cars	
23-00	Locations	
24-00	Office & Paperwork	
25-00	Publicity	
26-00	Food	
TOTAL PRODUCTION BUDGET (In-the-Can)		
THE SHOOT (Total Above & Below)		
27-00	Film Edit	
28-00	Film Lab (Edit)	
29-00	Sound Edit	
30-00	ADR	
31-00	Foley	
32-00	Music/Score	
33-00	Mix (Re-record)	
34-00	Optical Transfer	
35-00	M&E	
THE EDIT (Post-Production)		
36-00	Titles	
37-00	Negative Cutting	
38-00	Film Lab (Answer Print)	
TOTAL PRODUCTION COSTS		

For each line item, I will give two dollar amounts. The first is the lower rate that you will be able to negotiate after reading this book with the second figure being what the vendor or equipment supplier initially offers.

This will be done line item by line item, until we've gone through the 38 line items, budgeted $250,000–$500,000, and vicariously produced a feature film that will look like and will be marketed as a "million-dollar feature."

Next, I will show you (chapter 42) how to make a feature film for progressively lower amounts—for $150,000 . . . for $120,000 . . . for $80,000 . . . for $50,000 . . . for $20,000. Until last but not least, I will show you how to shoot a 35mm feature film for only $5,000.

That's correct, only $5,000. And, as the opening-page warning stated, "After reading this book, there are no excuses!" for you will have all the information needed to either produce or direct your first feature.

TO DO:

1. Peruse two books on budgeting.

 BOOKS

The Complete Film Production Handbook
E. Honthaner, 514 pp., $54.95
Indispensable. Almost all the paperwork, forms, and checklists you'll need to produce and direct your feature film. CD-ROM is included. A must-have!

Independent Filmmaker's Manual
N. Laloggia and E. Wurmfeld, 290 pp., $36.95
Walks you through the creative process of producing a feature film. CD-ROM includes interviews and valuable printable forms.

Pre-production Planning
S. Cartwright, 229 pp., $47.95
Details organization. Includes 30 planning, production, and post-production forms.

Surviving Production
D. Patz, 263 pp., $26.95
The art of production management for film and television.

Before You Shoot
H. Garvey, 296 pp., $14.00
Written in an easy-to-understand manner so the inexperienced filmmaker can prepare a low-budget feature.

Making Movies
J. Russo, 298 pp., $15.95
A street-smart guide to making an independent movie from scratch.

Film Production
S. Rosenstein, 321 pp., $44.95
The best of the college filmmaking
texts. Takes you through the mechanics of making a film.

 SOFTWARE

How to Make Your Movie
Three CD-ROMs plus a production
notebook
Windows or Macintosh, $89.95
An interactive film school that takes
you through the steps of production
from screenwriting to striking the
final print.

 **ACTORS WITH
STUDIO
FINANCING**

Tim Allen
Boxing Cat Productions
11500 Hart St
North Hollywood, CA 91608
Studio: Disney
Attn: Matt Carroll
Ph: 818-765-4870
Fax: 818-765-4975

Glenn Close
Trillium
9 Desbrosses St, 2nd Floor
New York, NY 10013
Studio: Disney
Attn: Suzette Porte
Ph: 212-343-8719
Fax: 212-343-0790

Denis Leary
Apostle
The Ed Sullivan Theater
1697 Broadway, Suite 906
New York, NY 10019
Studio: DreamWorks
Attn: Tom Sellitti
Ph: 212-541-4323
Fax: 212-541-4330

Bonnie Hunt
Bob & Alice Productions
2500 Broadway, Suite E-600
Santa Monica, CA 90404
Studio: MGM
Attn: Nady Ichinomiya
Ph: 310-449-3858
Fax: 310-586-8929

Pierce Brosnan
Irish Dreamtime
2450 Broadway, Suite E-5021
Santa Monica, CA 90404
Studio: MGM
Attn: Angelique Higgins
Ph: 310-449-3411
Fax: 310-586-8138

John Leguizamo
Lower East Side
375 Greenwich St
New York, NY 10013
Studio: Miramax
Attn: John Leguizamo
Ph: 212-941-4049
Fax: 212-375-0112

Ben Stiller
Red Hour Films
193 N Robertson Blvd
Beverly Hills, CA 90211
Studio: New Line
Attn: Rhoades Rader

Ph: 310-289-2565
Fax: 310-289-5988

Jodie Foster
Egg Pictures
5555 Melrose Ave
Jerry Lewis Building Annex
Los Angeles, CA 90038
Studio: Paramount
Attn: Lisa Buono
Ph: 323-956-8400
Fax: 323-862-1414

Mel Gibson
Icon Productions
808 Wilshire Blvd, 4th Floor
Santa Monica, CA 90401
Studio: Fox
Attn: Michael Wolkoff
Ph: 310-434-7300
Fax: 310-434-7377

Jennifer Love Hewitt
Love Spell
10202 W Washington Blvd, Suite 103
Culver City, CA 90232
Studio: Sony
Attn: Kim Kovac
Ph: 310-244-6040
Fax: 310-244-0740

Bruce Willis
Cheyenne Enterprises
406 Wilshire Blvd
Santa Monica, CA 90401
Studio: Sony
Attn: Arnold Rifkin
Ph: 310-455-5000

Julia Roberts
Red Om Films
16 W 19th St, 12th Floor
New York, NY 10011
Studio: Sony
Attn: Maggie Jones

Ph: 212-243-4035
Fax: 212-243-2973

Danny De Vito
Jersey Films
10351 Santa Monica Blvd, Suite 200
Los Angeles, CA 90025
Studio: Universal
Attn: Adrienne Biddle
Ph: 310-203-1000
Fax: 310-203-1010

Will Smith
Overbrook
450 N Roxbury Dr, 4th Floor
Beverly Hills, CA 90210
Studio: Universal
Attn: Rashad Liston
Ph: 310-432-2400
Fax: 310-432-2401

Tom Hanks
The Playtone Company
c/o Creative Artists Agency
9830 Wilshire Blvd
Beverly Hills, CA 90212
Studio: Universal
Attn: Rick Nicita
Ph: 310-288-4545

Robert De Niro
Tribeca
375 Greenwich St, 8th Floor
New York, NY 10013
Studio: Universal
Attn: Jane Rosenthal
Ph: 212-941-4000
Fax: 212-941-4044

Billy Crystal
Face
c/o Castle Rock Entertainment
335 N Maple Dr, Suite 175
Beverly Hills, CA 90210
Studio: Warner Bros.

Attn: Samantha Sprecher
Ph: 310-285-2300
Fax: 310-285-2386

Hugh Grant
Simian Films
c/o Castle Rock Entertainment
335 N Maple Dr, Suite 135
Beverly Hills, CA 90210
Studio: Warner Bros.
Attn: Meta Putt Kammer
Ph: 310-285-2371
Fax: 310-888-3540

Clint Eastwood
Malpaso
c/o Warner Bros.

4000 Warner Blvd, Bldg 81
Burbank, CA 91522
Studio: Warner Bros.
Attn: Joel Cox
Ph: 818-954-3367
Fax: 818-954-4803

George Clooney
Section Eight
c/o Warner Bros.
4000 Warner Blvd, Bldg 15,
   Suite 117
Burbank, CA 91522
Studio: Warner Bros.
Attn: Grant Heslov
Ph: 818-954-4840
Fax: 818-954-4860

FILM STOCK

"How Much?"

To make a feature film that can be projected in theaters, your final format must eventually be 35mm. Thus, you can shoot with either film or tape (digital or analog), but your final product must be 35mm film in order to be projected. And there are only three ways to get there. They are:

1. Shoot tape and transfer to 35mm.
2. Shoot 16mm and blow up to 35mm.
3. Shoot 35mm.

IMPORTANT NOTE   As of the writing of this book only 12 of the 13,000 screens in America have converted to digital projection. Film is slowly being phased out by the digital video format. However, until there are at least 9,750 (75 percent penetration) digital projectors in American theaters. The format for delivering movies to them will continue to be 35mm film.

1. Shoot tape and transfer to 35mm: This is not new. The film and television industries have shot on tape and transferred to film for half a century. Fifty years ago it was called kinescoping. But if you capture the image on tape, the end product, even though transferred to film, *will still look like tape.* And tape does not look like film. I'm not saying one looks better than the other. I'm just saying they look different.

Should your first feature be shot on film or tape? This is not an artistic decision. It is an economic decision. If your budget is less than $80,000—and definitely if it's under $20,000—all you can afford is tape. Film is not an option. And the best-quality tape format for ultra-low-budget first-timers is

PRODUCTION BUDGET

Title: "Your $1,000,000 Feature"   Executive Producer: _____

                                     Producer: _____

Writer: _____   Director: _____

ACCOUNT NUMBER	DESCRIPTION	BUDGET
01-00	Producer	
02-00	Writer/Script	
03-00	Director	
04-00	Cast/Actors	
TOTAL ABOVE-THE-LINE (Pre-Production)		
BELOW-THE-LINE		
5-00	**FILM STOCK**	**$20,000–$40,000**
6-00	Film Lab (Shoot)	
7-00	Camera	
8-00	Expendables	
9-00	Sound Equipment	
10-00	Sound Transfer	
11-00	Light/Grip	
12-00	Dolly	
13-00	Cinematographer	
14-00	PM & AD	
15-00	Production Designer	
16-00	Film Crew	
17-00	Art & Props	
18-00	Wardrobe & Makeup	
19-00	Permits	
20-00	Insurance	
21-00	Dailies	
22-00	FX/Stunts/Cars	
23-00	Locations	
24-00	Office & Paperwork	
25-00	Publicity	
26-00	Food	
TOTAL PRODUCTION BUDGET (In-the-Can)		
THE SHOOT (Total Above & Below)		
27-00	Film Edit	
28-00	Film Lab (Edit)	
29-00	Sound Edit	
30-00	ADR	
31-00	Foley	
32-00	Music/Score	
33-00	Mix (Re-record)	
34-00	Optical Transfer	
35-00	M&E	
THE EDIT (Post-Production)		
36-00	Titles	
37-00	Negative Cutting	
38-00	Film Lab (Answer Print)	
TOTAL PRODUCTION COSTS		

mini-DV (mini–digital video). When you are finished, you will have a feature tape (notice I didn't say film) that, to be projected (only 12 theaters have digital projectors), must be transferred to 35mm film at a cost ($300–$400 per minute) of $30,000–$50,000. Uh-oh! Your digital feature just got expensive.

2. *Shoot 16mm and blow up to 35mm:* There is 🔲 *only one way to make film look like film—shoot with film!* Buy film, rent a film camera, and shoot. Thus, your format options are either 16mm, super-16mm, or 35mm.

Many first-timers have a misconception that shooting in the 16mm format, instead of 35mm, saves large amounts of money. This is not true! Let's run the numbers. Shooting 16mm, instead of 35mm, saves you $6,000–$8,000 on purchasing film, $8,000–$10,000 in laboratory charges, and $3,000–$4,000 in equipment rentals, for a savings of $17,000–$22,000. But here's the rub: When finished, your 16mm film can't be projected in theaters unless it is blown up to 35mm.

The blow-up is not free. Labs charge $38,000–$45,000 ($400–$500 per minute) to blow up 90–120 minutes. And once you add the blow-up charges to the cost of shooting and editing your film, you'll discover that you haven't saved $17,000–$22,000, but actually spent an additional $21,000–$23,000. Bummer!

If your budget is over $80,000, but less than $150,000, and you want your final product to look like film, shoot 16mm and place your film in film festivals that have 16mm projectors, in hopes that a distributor will pick it up and pay the $38,000–$45,000 blow-up charges. It is a gamble, but the odds are still better than if you had a $20,000–$80,000 digital feature.

> **IMPORTANT POINT**   There are numerous magazine articles promoting the virtues of shooting with super-16mm film. This is 16mm film stock with sprocket holes on only one side of the filmstrip, making the frame rectangular and more conducive to a 35mm blow-up. The problem with super-16mm is, there are almost no super-16mm projectors in America. How are you going to screen it? You'll be stuck with a great super-16mm print that you can't show to anyone. That is, unless you spend that additional $38,000–$45,000 to blow it up to 35mm for one screening.

3. *Shoot 35mm:* If your budget is over $150,000—and for the purpose of the next 25 chapters, I assume you have $250,000–$500,000—then go

with 35mm film, with advantages to shooting 35mm, rather than 16mm, outweighing the slight cost disadvantage.

For instance, 35mm is easier to work with than 16mm. It is more precise. Also, 35mm film is easier to edit than 16mm film. The frames are larger. Finally, there is the massive motivational tool when shooting 35mm. When shooting 16mm, your cast and crew think of your film as "just a student film." But when you have a 35mm camera on the set, this alleged student film becomes a real movie. The cast and crew work harder and longer. The bottom line is: "Shoot 35mm if you can afford it."

HOW MUCH FILM DO YOU NEED?

Here's the formula: Film runs through the 35mm camera, and the projector, at a speed of 90 feet per minute (16mm film runs at a speed of 36 feet per minute). Therefore, your final 35mm movie, if its running time is 90 minutes, will be 8,100 feet long (90 feet/minute × 90 minutes).

To determine the amount of film you will purchase to commence your shoot, multiply the first number of the shooting ratio (the ratio between [a] how many feet of unexposed film you purchase to start your shoot and the number of [b] feet of film there is in your completed print) that you have budgeted for by the number of feet in your final print.

For example, if budgeting for a 3:1 shooting ratio (three takes of a single shot or three shots of one take each to make a scene) on a 90-minute film (8,100 feet), you'd probably purchase 24,300 feet of film (8,100 feet × 3).

For this book the assumption is that you will be shooting on a 6:1 shooting ratio. Therefore, your final 90-minute film (8,100 feet) will have you purchasing 48,600 feet (8,100 × 6) of unexposed 35mm film to start the shoot. For simplification, let's round off 48,600 feet to an even number and purchase 50,000 feet.

WHERE DO YOU BUY 50,000 FEET?

There are only two manufacturers of 35mm film that sell in the United States. They are:

1. Kodak
2. Fuji

You'll probably purchase Kodak film, not because it is better (when you see a movie, can you tell if Kodak or Fuji film was used? I doubt it), but because Kodak gives away free film to film schools and every graduating class of cinematographers learns to shoot with it. They're comfortable with how it develops and prints and become scared of Fuji. Keep your cinematographer happy and buy Kodak—if the price is right.

Now let's get a good price. Thirty-five-millimeter film comes in either, 1,000- or 400-foot rolls. The 1,000-footers are for dolly, tripod, and crane shots, and the 400-footers are for handheld shots. Cameras loaded with 1,000-foot rolls weigh 15 to 20 pounds more than those loaded with 400-foot rolls. Buy 400-foot rolls for handheld shots and 1,000-foot rolls for all other shots.

The next consideration is speed or ASA rating. Both Kodak and Fuji sell "high-speed" (400–500 ASA rating) and "regular-speed" (125–240 ASA rating) film. High speed means that the unexposed film captures the image quicker, when exposed to light, than low speed. Thus, a daylight shot doesn't require high-speed film. However, an exterior night shot with only a few lights requires high-speed film to capture the image.

Kodak and Fuji make comparable film in virtually every ASA speed and give them all weird stock numbers for the sole purpose of confusing you into believing there is something mystical about their film stock. You can mix high-speed and low-speed film from the same manufacturer, but don't mix manufacturers.

ASA	Kodak Stock #	Fuji Stock #
100	5248	8531
250	5246	8561
500	5279	8571

BOTTOM LINE Buy from only one manufacturer. Get regular-speed (125–240 ASA) film for your exterior day shots, high-speed (400–500 or 800 ASA) film for your interior and exterior night shots and daytime interior (indoor day locations are still dark) shots. Use 400-foot rolls for handheld shots and 1,000-foot rolls for all other shots. But don't pay retail!

WHAT DOES 35mm FILM COST?

There are four ways that 35mm film is sold:

1. New
2. Buybacks
3. Recans
4. Ends

New: Buy the film directly from the manufacturer. But this is expensive. A 1,000-foot roll is $600–$650 and a 400-foot roll is $240–$260. This translates to 60–65 cents per foot and costs $30,000–$32,500 for 50,000 feet.

■ *Nobody in Hollywood, except first-time filmmakers who just graduated from USC, UCLA, or NYU film schools, ever pays retail.* Thus, the best way to get a discount from Kodak is to say what they call "the F word"—Fuji! Play one company against the other. Let Kodak and Fuji bid on your film purchase and ask for "perks" on top of it. What else can they throw in? Maybe they'll discount your film to beat the competition and give you an additional 3,000 feet as a "courtesy." Also, never underestimate the impact of a few free T-shirts and caps on a crew that's working cheap.

If you are not a good negotiator, you merely say to the Kodak sales rep, "But I'm just a student filmmaker and I'm thinking about Fuji..." You will be amazed that you are instantly offered a 10–20 percent discount, saving you $3,000–$6,500.

Next, if you can't afford new film, then you purchase "buybacks," "recans," and "ends," or a combination of them, from a film/tape reseller (the "gray market") that gives 20–80 percent discounts.

Buybacks: Studio features purchase a minimum of 150,000 feet of film. When the movie is done the director might have only exposed 128,000 feet. Thus, there are 22,000 feet of brand-new unexposed film. The studio doesn't save this film. They sell the remaining 22,000 feet (maybe twenty 1,000-foot rolls and five 400-foot rolls) to a reseller at half price. The reseller then sells it to you at a price cheaper than if you bought it directly from Kodak or Fuji. These are buybacks (aka "factory sealed"). Buybacks typically can be bought for 40 to 45 cents per foot. That's $20,000 to $22,500 for 50,000 feet.

Recans: To start each day of the shoot, a cinematographer takes four new cans of film and has his assistant, the second assistant cameraman, load them into four magazines. If all four magazines aren't used, at the end of the day the film is taken out of the unused magazine, put back in the original cans, and resealed. This is a "recan." Though it has never been run through a camera, it has been handled, so it is less expensive than new film or buybacks. Recans sell for 20 to 30 cents a foot and cost only $10,000 to $15,000 for 50,000 feet.

Ends: Very often, an entire roll of film does not get used. When the cinematographer calls for a new film stock, and the magazines are changed, there is film left in the old magazine. This leftover, but unexposed, film is sold to the reseller as an "end." Anything less than 400 feet is a "short end" and anything over 700 feet is a "long end." You can buy long ends at 20 cents a foot and short ends for as little as 12 cents a foot, totaling $6,000–$10,000 for 50,000 feet.

Buying film is your first test in "film haggling" skills. And if you're not a good "film haggler" and can't negotiate savings on your film purchase, get out of the business!

The final place you can purchase your film is from "black market" sources that you may catch wind of through the grapevine. This is "liberated" film, i.e., stolen from someone else's film set. Bad karma. Don't do it. Why am I telling you about it, then? So you'll be aware that film is stolen from sets everywhere, every day. If you don't inventory your film daily and make it known that you're doing so, you're likely to find that some of your film gets "liberated" as well. Don't be an ogre, but do watch over your supply of film during the shoot.

LET'S SUMMARIZE

From your guesstimated budget you'll determine whether you are shooting with digital tape, or 16mm, super-16mm, or 35mm film. And since our budget is over $150,000, then you could and should shoot on 35mm. Further, with a budget of $250,000 to $500,000 you can and will allocate about **$20,000–$40,000** to purchase 35mm film.

Buy as many feet as possible, but don't pay retail. Purchase directly from either Kodak or Fuji, with a discount. And, toward the end of your shoot if you are running out of film (your cinematographer and director have allowed too many shots and too many takes), you will purchase more recans and ends.

Here are some of your choices, or combinations, thereof, for buying film that you will have with $20,000–$40,000:

65,000 feet at 60 cents/foot (new Kodak) = $39,000
65,000 feet at 50 cents/foot (new Fuji) = $32,500

50,000 feet at 50 cents/foot (Kodak discounted) = $25,000
50,000 feet at 40 cents/foot (Kodak buybacks) = $20,000
50,000 feet at 30 cents/foot (Fuji recans) = $15,000
50,000 feet at 12 cents/foot (Kodak short ends) = $6,000

TO DO:

1. Call film labs and find the cost to blow up 16mm to 35mm.
2. Get price lists from Kodak and Fuji.
3. Call film resellers and get recan, end, and buyback prices.

 FILM/TAPE SUPPLIERS

KODAK BRANCHES

Central States Office
61 W Eric St
Chicago, IL 60610
Ph: 630-910-4929

Southwest Office
11337 Indian Trail
Dallas, TX 75229
Ph: 972-481-1150

West Coast Office
6700 Santa Monica Blvd
Hollywood, CA 90038
Ph: 800-621-3456

East Coast Office
360 W 31st St
New York, NY 10001
Ph: 212-631-3418

Western Canada Office
4185 Still Creek Dr, Suite C150
Burnaby, BC V5C 6G9 Canada
Ph: 800-621-3456

Eastern Canada Office
3500 Eglinton Ave West
Toronto, ONT H3E 1J4 Canada
Ph: 416-761-4922

Europe Office
Kodak House
Hemel Hempstead, Herts HP1 1JU
    England
Ph: 44-1442-845-945

Latin America Office
8600 NW 17th St, Suite 200
Miami, FL 33126
Ph: 305-507-5656

FUJI BRANCHES

USA Office
Fuji Photo Film
1141 N Highland Ave
Hollywood, CA 90038
Ph: 323-957-8828
Fax: 323-962-0717

Canada Office
600 Suffolk Ct
Mississauga, ONT L5R 4G4 Canada
Ph: 905-890-6611
Fax: 905-890-7769

Latin America Office
Av Vereador Jose Diniz, 3.400
Campo Belo-CEP 04.604-901
Cx Postal 9.959 Sao Paulo, Brazil
Ph: 55-11-533-7493
Fax: 55-11-533-7383

Central America Office
Avenida Ejercito Nacional
#351 Col Granada
Delegacion Miguel Hidalgo
11520 Mexico DF, Mexico
Ph: 52-5-254-2000
Fax: 52-5-254-1508

England Office
Fuji Film House
125 Finchley Rd
London NW3 6JH England
Ph: 44-207-586-5900
Fax: 44-207-483-1419

France Office
45, Rue Pierre Charron
75008 Paris, France
Ph: 33-14-720-7690
Fax: 33-14-720-8428

Germany Office
Heesenstasse 31
40549 Dusseldorf, Germany
Ph: 49-211-5089134
Fax: 49-211-5089139

China Office
Beijing Fortune Building, Suite 817
5, Dong Sanhuan Bel-lu
Chaoyang District, Beijing
    100004 China
Ph: 86-10-6590-8370
Fax: 86-10-6590-8372

Japan Office
26-30, Nishiazabu 2-chome
Minato-ku, Tokyo 106-8620 Japan

Ph: 81-33-406-2458
Fax: 81-33-406-2713

Australia Office
114 Old Pittswater Rd
Brookvale, NSW 2100 Australia
Ph: 61-2-9466-2600
Fax: 61-2-9466-1975

WHOLESALE RESELLERS

Dr. Rawstock
6150 Santa Monica Blvd
Hollywood, CA 90038
Ph: 323-960-1781
Fax: 323-960-1780

Raw Stock
1133 Broadway, 5th Floor
New York, NY 10010
Ph: 212-255-0445
Fax: 212-463-9420

Edgewise Film & Tape
630 Ninth Ave, Suite 800
New York, NY 10036
Ph: 212-633-8172
Fax: 212-586-2420

SHORTenz
727 N La Brea Ave
Hollywood, CA 90038
Ph: 323-965-7465
Fax: 323-965-7455

The Tape Company
1014 N Highland Ave
Los Angeles, CA 90038
Ph: 323-993-3000
Fax: 323-461-8915
30 W 21st St
New York, NY 10010
Ph: 212-647-0900
Fax: 212-647-1534

Film Emporium
274 Madison Ave, Suite 204
New York, NY 10016
Ph: 212-683-2433
Fax: 212-683-2740

Super 8 Sound
2805 W Magnolia Blvd
Burbank, CA 91505
Ph: 818-848-5522
Fax: 818-848-5956

THE FILM LAB

"Negotiate the Deal"

Working with a film lab is simple. All you need to know is that you'll pay them three times: (1) during the shoot, (2) during the edit, and (3) to get your final answer print. This chapter is only concerned with what to pay a film lab during the shoot, to get the 50,000 feet of exposed 35mm film that you bought in the previous chapter developed and printed. The other two lab charges will be detailed in chapters 36 and 41.

Lab owners love independent filmmakers, and it isn't altruism. They make a lot of money from them. Even a low-budget feature, with 50,000 feet, will get the lab more money than five to eight big-budget commercials, with 5,000 feet each. That's why it is in the lab's interest to see that your dream becomes a reality. You're a very important client!

🔲 *Think of the lab owner as your silent partner—but a partner you pay.* He knows the local cinematographers and line producers, and can tell you which grips, gaffers, and soundmen have their own trucks and equipment. His facility, if you don't have an office, can be used as your sizzle to impress potential investors. The lab will always want to help you. Don't be shy. Ask for help.

WHAT A LAB CHARGES

Pick up your local production directory (see chapter 2). Find the closest film labs, get their rate cards, and look for the developing costs/foot and printing costs/foot, to obtain a "one-light," a technical phrase for dailies

PRODUCTION BUDGET

Title: "Your $1,000,000 Feature"   Executive Producer: _____

Producer: _____

Writer: ● _____   Director: _____

ACCOUNT NUMBER	DESCRIPTION	BUDGET
01-00	Producer	
02-00	Writer/Script	
03-00	Director	
04-00	Cast/Actors	
TOTAL ABOVE-THE-LINE (Pre-Production)		
BELOW-THE-LINE		
5-00	Film Stock	$20,000–$40,000
6-00	**FILM LAB (SHOOT)**	**$15,000–$30,000**
7-00	Camera	
8-00	Expendables	
9-00	Sound Equipment	
10-00	Sound Transfer	
11-00	Light/Grip	
12-00	Dolly	
13-00	Cinematographer	
14-00	PM & AD	
15-00	Production Designer	
16-00	Film Crew	
17-00	Art & Props	
18-00	Wardrobe & Makeup	
19-00	Permits	
20-00	Insurance	
21-00	Dailies	
22-00	FX/Stunts/Cars	
23-00	Locations	
24-00	Office & Paperwork	
25-00	Publicity	
26-00	Food	
TOTAL PRODUCTION BUDGET (In-the-Can)		
THE SHOOT (Total Above & Below)		
27-00	Film Edit	
28-00	Film Lab (Edit)	
29-00	Sound Edit	
30-00	ADR	
31-00	Foley	
32-00	Music/Score	
33-00	Mix (Re-record)	
34-00	Optical Transfer	
35-00	M&E	
THE EDIT (Post-Production)		
36-00	Titles	
37-00	Negative Cutting	
38-00	Film Lab (Answer Print)	
TOTAL PRODUCTION COSTS		

without sound. The rates will be 15–20 cents/foot to develop and 30–40 cents/foot to print, for a total of 45–60 cents/foot.

Don't pay that! Never pay retail! Thirty cents/foot will make a lab happy. Thus, get the 45 cents/foot lab to drop their price 30 percent to 30 cents/foot. Get the 60 cents/foot lab to drop their price 50 percent to, also, 30 cents/foot. Never pay more.

Also, it is often the case that dailies are transferred to videotape. This process is called telecine (tel-a-sinny). If you plan to edit your film on a digital desktop system, you will have to have your film telecined anyway. The lab charges you several times for this process. They charge by the foot (about 5 cents/foot) for "prep," then by the hour ($100–$200) for the telecine process. Estimate three hours of telecine time for each hour of film you shoot.

HOW DO YOU PAY THE LAB?

There are four ways to pay your film lab:

1. *The cash deal:* Money talks! A cash deal always gets you a negotiated 30–50 percent discount. Drop off a small check. Start shooting and the lab will process your film until your account runs out. They'll phone and ask you to put in more money, and they'll keep processing.

2. *Deferred billing:* This is a promise to pay at a later time. The benefit is that you save your cash for other costs. The disadvantages are, first, what if you can't pay? The lab forecloses on your negative. Also, a deferred billing will never get you a reduction on the rate card prices. You'll be billed at their highest rates and be charged for every little thing they do. Although deferred billing is possible and very tempting, try to make a cash deal.

3. *Partner deal:* This is similar to the deferred-billing arrangement. The lab will become your partner, so they will not charge for their services. In return, they expect a percentage of your sales, plus reimbursement for their services, at their highest book rates, prior to selling your film. Also, they'll probably demand the back-end print order once the distributor is secured.

4. *Credit cards:* This can get messy, but it's been done, and done successfully. Robert Townsend got a lot of press when he produced *The Hollywood Shuffle* this way, and a decade later Ed Burns produced *The Brothers Mc-Mullen* on weekends using credit cards. Using Visa and MasterCard (don't use Amex, they want all their money back every month), you can finance

your lab bill, but remember those big fat monthly bills at 22 percent interest. It's an option, but try very hard to avoid it.

Therefore, depending on how many feet of film you expose, you'll give the lab **$15,000–$30,000** (50,000 to 100,000 feet at 30 cents/foot) during production and another $10,000–$30,000 to finish your film. If you shoot on a lower shooting ratio, say 3:1 instead of 6:1, you'll obviously pay less. Be smart and economical. Every time you turn on that camera and expose film during the shoot, it costs you money. Don't cave in to actors' pleas for another five takes because they think they can do better.

> **BOTTOM LINE** Even though you see yourself as a small, low-budget feature filmmaker, to the lab, you're a big fish. Every lab wants your business. I beg you, don't pay retail. Haggle and get your developing and print costs down to at least 30 cents/foot.

TO DO:

1. Contact three film labs (two in-state and one out-of-state) and get their 35mm rates.

 FILM LABS

Foto-Kem Film Lab
2801 W Alameda Dr
Burbank, CA 91505
Ph: 818-846-3101
Fax: 818-941-2130

Consolidated Film Industries (CFI)
959 Seward St
Hollywood, CA 90038
Ph: 323-960-7444
Fax: 323-962-8746

Pacific Film Lab
823 Seward St
Hollywood, CA 90038
Ph: 323-461-9921
Fax: 323-464-6005

4 Media Corporation (4MC)
3611 N San Fernando Blvd
Burbank, CA 91505
Ph: 818-841-3812
Fax: 818-840-7802

Technicolor Film Lab
4050 Lankershim Blvd
Universal City, CA 91608
Ph: 818-769-8500
Fax: 818-761-4835
321 W 44th St
New York, NY 10036
Ph: 212-582-7310
Fax: 212-265-9089

DuArt Film and Video
245 W 55th St, 2nd Floor
New York, NY 10019
Ph: 212-757-4580
Fax: 212-757-5774

ColorLab NYC
27 W 20th Street, Suite 307
New York, NY 10011
Ph: 212-633-8172
Fax: 212-633-8241

Astro Color Lab
61 W Erie
Chicago, IL 60610
Ph: 312-280-5500
Fax: 312-280-5510

Continental Film Lab
1998 NE 150th St
Miami, FL 33181
Ph: 305-949-4252
Fax: 305-949-3242

Monaco Film Lab
234 9th St
San Francisco, CA 94103

Ph: 415-864-5350
Fax: 415-864-5682

Cinema Lab
2735 S Raritan St
Englewood, CO 80110
Ph: 303-783-1020
Fax: 303-806-0555

Alpha Cine Lab
1001 Lenora St
Seattle, WA 98121
Ph: 206-682-8230
Fax: 206-682-6649

CineFilm Transfer Lab
2156 Faulkner Rd NE
Atlanta, GA 30324
Ph: 404-633-1448
Fax: 404-633-3867

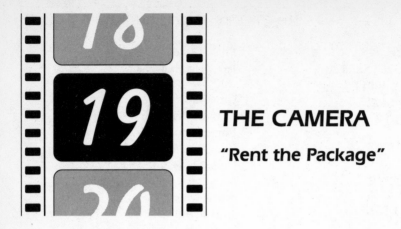

THE CAMERA
"Rent the Package"

An excellent 35mm camera package, to buy, costs upwards of $150,000. There is no cinematographer wealthy enough to purchase one. This is why you rent from camera rental facilities.

Renting a camera is not difficult. It is like renting a car, and you pay either a daily or a weekly fee. When you rent a car, you don't go to the manufacturer (Buick, Ford, Chrysler, etc.), you go to the rental facility (Hertz, Avis, Budget), which buys cars to rent. Likewise, when renting a 35mm camera, you go to a rental facility that buys cameras (Arriflex, Panavision, Aaton, and MovieCam) to rent.

A difference, however, is that when you rent a car, you get everything (seats, tires, radio, steering wheel, etc.) you need to drive away. This is not the case when renting a camera. Here the key words become "package" and "à la carte." You don't rent a camera, you rent a camera "package" that consists of 30–40 items. For a camera is just an engine in a body, and it won't work without "à la carte" accessories (batteries, lenses, magazines, tripods, handheld gear, matte boxes, etc.), which cost extra. Therefore, have your cinematographer make a detailed list of the accessories that he'll need to complement the camera you are about to rent.

Further, when renting a 35mm camera package don't obsess over every knob and gizmo. When you rent a car from Hertz or Avis do you obsess over distributor caps or hydraulic valves? No! You just assume the car works and want a good rental price. Cameras are the same. Just pick the one that you can afford, but make sure that it is sync-sound (meaning it's

PRODUCTION BUDGET

Title: "Your $1,000,000 Feature" Executive Producer: _____

Producer: _____

Writer: _____ Director: _____

ACCOUNT NUMBER	DESCRIPTION	BUDGET
01-00	Producer	
02-00	Writer/Script	
03-00	Director	
04-00	Cast/Actors	
TOTAL ABOVE-THE-LINE (Pre-Production)		
BELOW-THE-LINE		
5-00	Film Stock	$20,000–$40,000
6-00	Film Lab (Shoot)	$15,000–$30,000
7-00	**CAMERA**	**$12,000–$30,000**
8-00	Expendables	
9-00	Sound Equipment	
10-00	Sound Transfer	
11-00	Light/Grip	
12-00	Dolly	
13-00	Cinematographer	
14-00	PM & AD	
15-00	Production Designer	
16-00	Film Crew	
17-00	Art & Props	
18-00	Wardrobe & Makeup	
19-00	Permits	
20-00	Insurance	
21-00	Dailies	
22-00	FX/Stunts/Cars	
23-00	Locations	
24-00	Office & Paperwork	
25-00	Publicity	
26-00	Food	
TOTAL PRODUCTION BUDGET (In-the-Can)		
THE SHOOT (Total Above & Below)		
27-00	Film Edit	
28-00	Film Lab (Edit)	
29-00	Sound Edit	
30-00	ADR	
31-00	Foley	
32-00	Music/Score	
33-00	Mix (Re-record)	
34-00	Optical Transfer	
35-00	M&E	
THE EDIT (Post-Production)		
36-00	Titles	
37-00	Negative Cutting	
38-00	Film Lab (Answer Print)	
TOTAL PRODUCTION COSTS		

very quiet) and . . . 🎒 *for low-budget filmmakers there are actually only two rental choices—Arriflex or Panavision.*

Panavision, an American camera manufacturer, has six 35mm sync-sound models to choose from, which are the Millennium, the Platinum, the Gold, the Panaflex, the Panastar, and the X. Arriflex, a German camera manufacturer, has nine models to choose from, the 535B, the 535A, the 435, the BLIV (BL-4), the BLIII (BL-3), the BLII (BL-2), the IIC (2-C), and the brand-new ARRI LT and ARRI ST. All of these cameras, except the BL-2 (too heavy) and the 2-C (too noisy), are capable of doing everything you want.

> **AUTHOR'S NOTE** There are two other camera manufacturers—Aaton and MovieCam. Don't rent Aaton equipment. (It's made in France. I advise not using machinery made in France.) The couple of shoots for which I rented Aaton cameras had the magazines clog during the production. MovieCam equipment is excellent. However, it was just bought by Arriflex and is only available in three or four North American rental facilities.

If you want to use Panavision equipment (they don't sell their equipment to rental houses), you must rent directly from Panavision. Arriflex, however, sells its equipment to every camera rental facility. Thus, nine out of ten facilities have Arriflex cameras. Panavision (based in Woodland Hills, California) only has outlets in New York, Dallas, Chicago, Orlando, and Wilmington, N.C., and in Canada, Europe, Hong Kong, and Australia. My gut feeling is, if shooting away from a large metropolitan area (L.A., New York, Chicago, or Toronto), you'll probably use Arriflex equipment. If shooting near a large city, it is a toss-up between Arriflex and Panavision.

WHAT A CAMERA PACKAGE RENTS FOR

Like everything in the film business, camera rentals are negotiable. The rates vary from dealer to dealer and package to package. And when renting, you negotiate by using the phrase "days per week." For example, a rental house may give you a "four-day week." This means you pay for four days, but use the camera for seven days—a week. Call camera rental facilities and discover that their rate cards have two columns. The first itemizes cameras and accessories, and the second lists their rental fee per day.

A complete 35mm sync-sound camera package, with 30–40 "à la carte" attachments, may pencil out to $1,500–$2,500/day rental. Add on camera extras, for those special shots, and the package can rent for

$2,000–$3,000/day, or $14,000–$21,000/week, or $42,000–$63,000 for three weeks. This is not affordable.

Remember, never pay rate card. Camera rental facilities love to say they'll give you a "four-day week" (you get to use the equipment for seven days but pay for only four days). Thus, the $2,000–$3,000/day camera package can be rented for $8,000–$12,000/week ($2,000–$3,000 × 4), or $24,000–$36,000 for three weeks. This is not a good deal either.

Never, ever rent on a "four-day week"—that's what first-time suckers pay when they're fresh out of a four-year film school. Get a "three-day week." You'll get it, and, if it is off-season, you'll get a "two-day week" rate. Make it a point to know the name of a competing camera rental facility and say, "If you can beat or match their price [say a 'two-day week' amount] then I'll go with you." Rate cards are inflated B.S., and if you pay what they ask, you're stupid.

The bottom line is, if you accept a four-day week, the $2,000–$3,000/day 35mm camera package (Arriflex or Panavision) will cost $24,000–$36,000 for the entire shoot. If you haggle a "three-day week" for the shoot, the exact same package rents for $18,000–$27,000. And if you really know how to beg, cajole, and plead, you'll get a "two-day week" for the three-week shoot at $4,000–$6,000/week and pay only $12,000–$18,000.

For the purpose of our feature film budget I have allocated **$12,000–$30,000** to rent your camera package. This allows more than enough money to get your cinematographer almost all the new state-of-the-art 35mm camera gadgets and gizmos he desires to utilize for your three-week shoot.

TO DO:

1. Obtain rate cards from three camera rental facilities.
2. Ask for a two-day-week rate.

 BOOKS

from loading to shooting. Plus, digital shooting chapters.

ASC Manual, 8th edition
R. Hummel, 900 pp., $99.95
The must-have guide for cinematographers that covers all aspects of the job

The Camera Assistant's Manual
D. Elkins, 395 pp., $39.95
Discover the nuts and bolts of what everyone around a camera does and why.

Operating Cinematography
W. Hines, 255 pp., $24.95
An excellent book, which doesn't overwhelm with charts and details, on how to operate the camera.

Cinema Workshop
A. Wilson, 302 pp., $19.95
A wonderful guide for the technician who wants to be a professional cinematographer.

The Filmmaker's Pocket Reference
B. Brown, 249 pp., $36.95
Consolidates all the key data, with 150 easy-to-use tables, for the cinematographer and lighting director.

Motion Picture Camera Techniques
D. Samuelson, 191 pp., $32.95
Choice of film, shooting at night, shooting underwater . . . this book explains the DP's tasks during a shoot.

*Hands-On Manual for
  Cinematographers*
D. Samuelson, 401 pp., $54.95
The bible of details needed for the professional cinematographer to shoot effectively.

*The Bare Bones Camera Course for
  Film and Video*
T. Schroeppel, 90 pp., $10.95
Explains the craft of the cinematographer in extremely easy-to-understand terms. A marvel of clarity.

Cinematography
K. Malkiewicz, 213 pp., $23.00
From film stock, to filters, to lenses, to . . . this book outlines what a filmmaker needs to know about the camera.

The Five C's of Cinematography
J. Mascelli, 252 pp., $29.95
A classic. The most widely respected book on the craft of the camera.

Cinematography
P. Ettedgui, 189 pp., $41.95
An excellent gift book. Coffee table book, with over 500 photos, chronicling the cinematographer's craft.

 VIDEO

Visions of Light
VHS, 92 minutes, $39.95
Produced by the acclaimed American Society of Cinematographers, it visually explains the craft and history of cinematography.

 RENTAL HOUSES

PANAVISION EQUIPMENT

West Coast Facility
  6219 DeSoto Ave
  Woodland Hills, CA 91367
  Ph: 818-316-1000
  Fax: 818-316-1111

East Coast Facility
  540 W 36th St
  New York, NY 10018
  Ph: 212-606-0700
  Fax: 212-244-4457

South Facilities
1223 N 23rd St
Wilmington, NC 28405
Ph: 910-343-8796
Fax: 910-343-8275
2000 Universal Studio Plz,
 Suite 900
Orlando, FL 32819
Ph: 407-363-0990
Fax: 407-363-0180

Southwest Facility
8000 Jetstar
Irving, TX 75063
Ph: 972-929-8585
Fax: 972-929-8686

Canada Facilities
900A Don Mills Rd
Toronto, ONT N3C 1V6 Canada
Ph: 416-444-7000
Fax: 416-444-0192
5258 Lougheed Hwy
Burnaby, BC V5B 2Z6 Canada
Ph: 604-291-7262
Fax: 604-291-0422

Australia Facility
1 McLachlan Ave
Artarman, Sydney, NSW 2064
 Australia
Ph: 61-2-9436-1844
Fax: 61-2-9438-2585

Europe Facilities
Metropolitan Centre
Bristol Rd, Greenford
Middlesex UB6 86D England
Ph: 44-208-839-7333
Fax: 44-208-839-7300
35, Rue Pleyel
93200 Saint-Denis, Paris, France
Ph: 33-1-4813-2550

Fax: 33-1-4813-2551
Via delle Capannelle 95
00178 Rome, Italy
Ph: 3906-729-00235
Fax: 3906-729-00242
Schimmelmannstrabbe 1232-125
22043 Hamburg, Germany
Ph: 49-40-6549-6020
Fax: 49-40-6549-6028

Africa Facility
17 Eastern Service Rd
Eastgate #8, Sandton
Johannesburg, South Africa
Ph: 27-11-466-2380
Fax: 27-11-466-2387
Capetown, South Africa
Ph: 27-21-551-3265
Fax: 27-21-551-3292

Asia Facilities
5-5 Kojimachi, Chiyoda-ku
Tokyo, 102-0083 Japan
Ph: 81-3-5210-3322
Fax: 81-3-5210-2270
19 Bei San Huan West Rd
Beijing 100088 China
Ph: 86-10-6201-0134
Fax: 86-10-6204-0977

ARRIFLEX-MOVIECAM
EQUIPMENT

Hollywood Facilities
Clairmont Camera
4343 Lankershim
North Hollywood, CA 91602
Ph: 818-761-4440
Fax: 818-761-0861
Alan Gordon Enterprises
5625 Melrose Ave
Hollywood, CA 90036

Ph: 323-466-3561
Fax: 323-466-7806
Birns & Sawyer
1026 N Highland Ave
Hollywood, CA 90038
Ph: 323-466-8211
Fax: 323-466-7049

New York Facilities
Camera Service Center
619 W 54th St
New York, NY 10019
Ph: 212-757-0906
Fax: 212-620-8198
Du-All Camera
231 W 29th St, Suite 210
New York, NY 10001
Ph: 212-643-1042
Fax: 212-643-9335
Handheld Films
315 W 36th St, Suite 2E
New York, NY 10011
Ph: 212-502-0900
Fax: 212-502-0906
Technological Cinevideo Services
630 Ninth Ave, Suite 1004
New York, NY 10036
Ph: 212-247-6517
Fax: 212-489-4886

East Coast Office
617 Route 303
Blauvelt, NY 10913
Ph: 845-353-1400
Fax: 845-425-1250

West Coast Office
600 N Victory Blvd
Burbank, CA 91502
Ph: 818-841-7070
Fax: 818-848-4028

Canada Facility
415 Horner Ave, Unit 11
Etobicoke, ONT M8W 4W3 Canada
Ph: 416-255-3335
Fax: 416-255-3399

Europe Facilities
Arri GB Ltd
1-3 Airlinks, Spitfire Way
Heston, Middlesex
  TW5 9NR England
Ph: 44-208-848-8881
Fax: 44-208-561-1312
Arnold & Richter
Tuerkenstrasse 89
D-8000 Munich 40 Germany
Ph: 49-89-3809-1440
Fax: 49-89-3809-1798
Techni Cine Phot
64 bis, Blvd Jean-Jaures
Boite Postale 90
93402 St Ouen-Cedex, France
Ph: 33-40-10-55-55
Fax: 33-40-10-17-27

Asia Facilities
Jebsen & Co.
28/F, Caroline Centre
2-38 Yun Ping Rd
Causeway Bay, Hong Kong
Ph: 85-29-26-22-22
Fax: 85-28-82-17-87
NAC Incorporated
#2–7, Nishiazuabu
1-Chome, Minato-ku
Tokyo 106 Japan
Ph: 81-3-34-701-319
Fax: 81-3-34-798-842
S R Electronics
12/351 Nirlon Colony
Sidharth Naga, S V Road
Goregaon (West), Mumbai 400 062
  India

Ph: 91-22-875-9580
Fax: 91-22-876-2130

Australia Facility
  John Barry Group
  1 McLachlan Ave
  Artamon, Sydney, NSW Australia
  Ph: 61-2-9-439-6955
  Fax: 61-2-9-439-2375

Africa Facility
  ProGear Sales
  MCC, Parklands 2121
  PO Box 1185, Sandton
  Johannesburg, South Africa
  Ph: 27-11-804-3624
  Fax: 27-11-804-2440

EXPENDABLES

"Purchase the Supplies"

Expendables (sometimes called consumables) are items that you need (batteries, tape, gels, etc.), used once, and then disposed. They've been expended or consumed.

During your shoot you will discover that everybody in your crew needs something. Your gaffer will need a roll of gel, the grip will need extra clips, your assistant cameraman will need rolls of colored tape, and your soundman needs batteries. If you are missing any of these small items, it will hurt the film and may even shut down the production.

For instance, if you have a scary, evil-filled scene, you may want the room to have a red glow. It's Sunday at 6 P.M., the twilight outside the bedroom window is perfect, and it's time to get those last great shots of the day . . . but, oops! You don't have the red gels. Do you settle for a shot devoid of the mood that the red glow would provide? Do you stop production to send a production assistant to the store to purchase the gels? Expendables are important. Budget for them.

Expendables fall into three categories:

1. Gels and filters
2. Tape, tape, and tape
3. Miscellaneous

GELS AND FILTERS

Not all light is the same. Your cinematographer, gaffer, and grip use gels and filters to conform all forms of light, artificial or natural, to a constant color

PRODUCTION BUDGET

Title: "Your $1,000,000 Feature"   Executive Producer: _____

Producer: _____

Writer: _____   Director: _____

ACCOUNT NUMBER	DESCRIPTION	BUDGET
01-00	Producer	
02-00	Writer/Script	
03-00	Director	
04-00	Cast/Actors	
TOTAL ABOVE-THE-LINE (Pre-Production)		
BELOW-THE-LINE		
5-00	Film Stock	$20,000–$40,000
6-00	Film Lab (Shoot)	$15,000–$30,000
7-00	Camera	$12,000–$30,000
8-00	**EXPENDABLES**	**$2,000–$5,000**
9-00	Sound Equipment	
10-00	Sound Transfer	
11-00	Light/Grip	
12-00	Dolly	
13-00	Cinematographer	
14-00	PM & AD	
15-00	Production Designer	
16-00	Film Crew	
17-00	Art & Props	
18-00	Wardrobe & Makeup	
19-00	Permits	
20-00	Insurance	
21-00	Dailies	
22-00	FX/Stunts/Cars	
23-00	Locations	
24-00	Office & Paperwork	
25-00	Publicity	
26-00	Food	
TOTAL PRODUCTION BUDGET (In-the-Can)		
THE SHOOT (Total Above & Below)		
27-00	Film Edit	
28-00	Film Lab (Edit)	
29-00	Sound Edit	
30-00	ADR	
31-00	Foley	
32-00	Music/Score	
33-00	Mix (Re-record)	
34-00	Optical Transfer	
35-00	M&E	
THE EDIT (Post-Production)		
36-00	Titles	
37-00	Negative Cutting	
38-00	Film Lab (Answer Print)	
TOTAL PRODUCTION COSTS		

level. The gels and filters you need depend on the lighting conditions at locations, the hours shooting, the kinds of light rented, and the look you want.

Gels are variously colored sheets of transparent plastic that, when attached with clips, will alter or balance your lights. You will use a gel virtually every time you use lights. Gels are expensive.

Filters are transparent sheets of colored glass that are placed either in front of or just behind the lens of the camera to control light. Colored filters are used for moods. Polarized filters diminish sun glare. Diffusion filters create soft focus. Ultraviolet filters reduce haze. Some filters are actually used to make shooting in the day look like night. Now, stop worrying about all these filters. All you need to know is, budget for some, give that amount to your cinematographer and lighting director, and they'll get the best filters they can—but stay within your budget.

A cost-cutting trick when purchasing gels from your supplier is to get "remainder rolls" at discounts of 50–60 percent. However, the best cost-cutting method is to ask to use the cinematographer's, gaffer's, or grip's gels that they have accumulated from the other shoots they have been on.

🔲 *All DPs, gaffers, and grips maintain their own "kits" of expendables that they have "liberated" from past shoots.* So, when hiring, ask what they have, and purchase to supplement their supplies.

TAPE

It seems that someone on the set always needs tape. Red tape, white tape, two-sided sticky tape, duct tape, tape you can write on, etc. Tape is vitally important on a film set. You can't shoot without it, and you'll be surprised how much it costs. You'll need:

1. Grip tape
2. Camera tape
3. Paper tape
4. Double-sided tape

Grip tape is a two-inch gray fabric tape that looks like duct tape. It is very strong and is used to secure foamcore, duvetyne, art card, and the like.

Camera tape is a one-inch fabric tape that comes in a variety of colors. The camera team uses it to label camera magazines, mark the slate, and reseal film cans. Your camera team needs various colors to color-code unused, exposed, and damaged film.

Paper tape is one or two inches wide and has a matte finish, so it doesn't shine. It comes in black and white and is used by the prop department and production designer to alter the set.

Double-sided tape is ⅛-inch-wide tape that is sticky on both sides. It is used when something needs to be tacked down for a shot.

MISCELLANEOUS

There are 30–50 other incidental items that gaffers, camera crew, and set designers need to expedite the setups. They include:

1. Black wrap (black aluminum foil for heat shields)
2. Bobinett (mesh material for scrims)
3. "C-47s" (wooden clothespins used as clamps)
4. Dulling spray (to reduce shine on metal or glass surfaces)
5. Duvetyne (black canvas to cut or mask all window light)
6. Foamcore (white foam board to bounce light)
7. Art card (black/white cardboard to bounce light)
8. An assortment of nails, rope, sprays, glues, wires, staples batteries, etc.

It is these items that first-timers usually forget to budget into their production. Although termed "expendable," they are essential for your crew to do their jobs efficiently. If you don't plan (budget) for expendables, you will find yourself buying them on the first day of your shoot from money you allocated for post-production.

Plan, budget, and buy only what you need. Go to the expendables store with your cinematographer (allocate him $900), gaffer (allocate him $600), and key grip (allocate him $500) and make them squeeze their needs into those amounts. For **$5,000** your crew members will have everything they fantasize about, and for **$2,000** they will have their basic essentials.

TO DO:

1. Locate your local expendables supply store.
2. Itemize the expendables you need and price them.

SUPPLY STORES

Studio Depot
900 N La Brea Ave
Hollywood, CA 90038
Ph: 323-851-0111
Fax: 323-851-7854

FilmTools
3100 W Magnolia Blvd
Burbank, CA 91505
Ph: 818-845-8066
Fax: 818-845-8138

Castex
1044 N Cole Ave
Hollywood, CA 90038
Ph: 323-462-1468
Fax: 323-462-3719

Backstage Equipment
8052 Lankershim Blvd
North Hollywood, CA 91605
Ph: 818-504-6026
Fax: 818-504-6180

Barbizon
456 W 55th St
New York, NY 10019

Ph: 212-586-1620
Fax: 212-247-8818

B&H Photo & Video
420 Ninth Ave
New York, NY 10001
Ph: 212-239-7760
Fax: 212-239-7766

Set Shop
36 W 20th St
New York, NY 10011
Ph: 212-255-3500
Fax: 212-229-9600

Cine Rent West
2580 NW Upshur
Portland, OR 97210
Ph: 503-288-2048
Fax: 503-288-1789

Mark Clark Lighting & Expendables
4309 Briarbend
Houston, TX 77035
Ph: 713-723-1393
Fax: 713-723-3167

TexCam
3263 Branard
Houston, TX 7708
Ph: 800-735-2774
Fax: 713-524-2779

SOUND

"Get Your Sound Equipment"

Never underestimate the importance of sound.  *Sound will make the difference between a poor film and a good film and between a good film and a great film.* Obtaining excellent sound obviously starts with hiring the right person. To do this check the local production directory and get referrals from your film lab, film commissioner, and cinematographer. With respect to equipment, few, if any, cinematographers have their own, but 99 percent of soundmen own all the equipment needed for your shoot, which will include:

1. Sound recorder
2. Microphones
3. 6–12 channel mixer
4. Walkie-talkies

1. Sound recorder: Unlike videotape, motion picture film does not record sound. The sound is recorded independent of the film on tape (analog or DAT) and eventually placed onto your picture film. Sound recorders (aka tape recorders) especially if they are analog format, are many times referred to as Nagras (kinda like calling adhesive bandages Band-Aids or tissues Kleenex) because 80 percent of the recording machines used on movie sets are manufactured by Nagra.

2. Microphones, filters, cables: **Your sound will only be as good as your microphones.** Microphones, or lack of excellent ones, are the Achilles' heel of first-time filmmakers. For no matter how great the script is, and no matter how great the acting is, if you can't hear the performance it is all for

PRODUCTION BUDGET

Title: "Your $1,000,000 Feature"

Executive Producer: _____

Producer: _____

Writer: _____

Director: _____

ACCOUNT NUMBER	DESCRIPTION	BUDGET
01-00	Producer	
02-00	Writer/Script	
03-00	Director	
04-00	Cast/Actors	
TOTAL ABOVE-THE-LINE (Pre-Production)		
BELOW-THE-LINE		
5-00	Film Stock	$20,000–$40,000
6-00	Film Lab (Shoot)	$15,000–$30,000
7-00	Camera	$12,000–$30,000
8-00	Expendables	$2,000–$5,000
9-00	**SOUND EQUIPMENT**	**$6,000–$11,000**
10-00	**SOUND TRANSFER**	**$3,000–$5,000**
11-00	Light/Grip	
12-00	Dolly	
13-00	Cinematographer	
14-00	PM & AD	
15-00	Production Designer	
16-00	Film Crew	
17-00	Art & Props	
18-00	Wardrobe & Makeup	
19-00	Permits	
20-00	Insurance	
21-00	Dailies	
22-00	FX/Stunts/Cars	
23-00	Locations	
24-00	Office & Paperwork	
25-00	Publicity	
26-00	Food	
TOTAL PRODUCTION BUDGET (In-the-Can)		
THE SHOOT (Total Above & Below)		
27-00	Film Edit	
28-00	Film Lab (Edit)	
29-00	Sound Edit	
30-00	ADR	
31-00	Foley	
32-00	Music/Score	
33-00	Mix (Re-record)	
34-00	Optical Transfer	
35-00	M&E	
THE EDIT (Post-Production)		
36-00	Titles	
37-00	Negative Cutting	
38-00	Film Lab (Answer Print)	
TOTAL PRODUCTION COSTS		

naught. Be absolutely sure your soundman has an excellent package of microphones.

These packages must include (a) a directional (or cardioid) microphone for recording sound from one or two actors; (b) an omnidirectional microphone to capture sound from a group or crowd; (c) a shotgun microphone to record from a distance; and (d) small wireless lavalier microphones that can be hidden on an actor's clothing. Your equipment should also include a windscreen (to eliminate "crackle" when shooting outdoors) and a healthy supply of cables and coils to connect the Nagra and microphones.

3. *Mixing board:* You can use either the Nagra or a lower-end board with 6 to 12 channels. The board allows the sound mixer to record multiple microphones, on separate tracks, and adjust sound levels individually. For instance, if the first actor is in the foreground and the other is 10 feet behind him, the soundman can raise or lower either voice levels.

4. *Walkie-talkies:* It is not essential that you have them, but they definitely make production easier. A series of four-channel walkie-talkies will enhance efficiency. One channel will be used by the camera and light crew (orchestrating lights and camera placement); another channel by the production manager, assistant director, makeup, and hair (got to get those damn actors out of makeup and on the set); a third channel by the director (for personal chats with his production designer, trainer, and nutritionist); and a fourth channel for the producer (to eavesdrop on everyone else).

WHAT TO PAY FOR CREW AND EQUIPMENT

At the high end, you'll pay union (see chapter 2) wages with the soundman at $40/hour and your boom operator $30/hour. Your shoot will have a 70–90 hour workweek. If you signed with IATSE (the crew's union), you'll pay overtime and your sound crew will cost $15,000–$20,000 for three weeks. Renting equipment (a Nagra, a cart to put it on, microphones, a mixer, and walkie-talkies with extra batteries) costs an additional $1,000–$1,500/week or $3,000–$4,500 for three weeks. Therefore, the sound equipment and sound crew for your shoot, without negotiating, will be $18,000–$24,500.

Don't pay this. Here's why. Supply and demand! There are a lot of soundmen and not many feature films. Thus, budgeting $2,000–$3,500/week is more than enough to hire an excellent soundman, with his own equipment, who pays for his assistant (boom operator at $500–$700/week) from his own salary. For three weeks, this will be **$6,000–$11,000.**

WHAT TO PAY FOR TRANSFER

Your next cost will be for sound transfers. Once your sound is recorded on magnetic or DAT tape, it must be transferred to film so that it can be projected and edited with the picture. The sound transfer is done usually at a film lab and the charge is approximately $60/hour. You should allocate two hours of transfer time for each hour of sound recorded.

If you recorded sound for 50,000 feet of film, that's roughly nine hours. Your transfer time will cost $1,080 (18 hours × $60). But there's more. You also have to pay for the stock onto which your sound is transferred. The rate card lists that stock at five cents/foot. If you're buying 50,000 feet of stock you will pay $2,500.

Remember, never pay retail! It will be easy to haggle transfer time to $40/hour, lowering the transfer expense from $1,080 to just $720. And negotiating just a one-cent reduction on the transfer stock brings your stock cost from $2,500 down to $2,000. Depending on how many feet of film (50,000 to 80,000 feet) you use, your sound transfer and sound film stock cost will be **$3,000–$5,000.**

> **IMPORTANT POINT**   Sound is super important! No matter how beautiful your film looks, no matter how great your acting is, no matter how gripping your story is, your film will flop if you have lousy sound. Make sure your sound is excellent.

The bottom line is that good sound does not cost a lot, but it does demand attention to detail. A good sound crew and equipment cost only $6,000–$11,000 and sound transfers will cost an additional $3,000–$5,000.

———

TO DO:

1. Get the names of three soundmen with their own equipment.
2. Call three sound facilities or film labs and get transfer rates.

BOOKS

Sound for Film and Television
T. Homlinson, 254 pp., $44.95
Covers all the sound fundamentals
associated with filmmaking, from
recording to editing to mixing. Audio
CD included. A must!

Practical Art of Motion Picture Sound
D. Yewdall, 266 pp., $49.95
A Hollywood sound pro with over 150
feature film credits details what to do
with sound from pre-production to
production to post-production.

Audio Post-Production for Digital Video
J. Rose, 256 pp., $44.95
The bible for digital post-audio techniques. Includes streaming audio and
video for the Internet.

Sound Design
D. Sonnenschein, 245 pp., $19.95
Details the importance of sound design,
from music to voice to effects, and how
to use them to improve your film.

Sound Assistance
M. Talbot-Smith, 245 pp., $36.95
Thorough sound explanation, in easy-
to-understand terms, of what occurs
in television and radio studios.

VIDEO

Sound Success
VHS, 30 minutes, $22.95
An A–Z of basic sound from
microphones to post-production.

RENTAL FACILITIES AND SUPPLIERS

Coffey Sound Services
3353 Cahuenga Blvd
Hollywood, CA 90068
Ph: 818-759-0240
Fax: 323-876-4775

Wilcox Sound & Communications
4545 Shermak St
Burbank, CA 95105
Ph: 818-557-3377
Fax: 818-557-3367

Adolph Gasser, Inc.
181 Second St, 2nd Floor
San Francisco, CA 94105
Ph: 415-495-3852
Fax: 415-543-2615

Dreamhire Pro Audio Rentals
137-139 W 25th St, 8th Floor
New York, NY 10001
Ph: 212-691-5544
Fax: 212-627-4763

Soho Audio
376 Broome St, 4th Floor
New York, NY 10013
Ph: 212-226-2429
Fax: 212-966-7650

Charter Broadcast
870 W Division, Unit E
Chicago, IL 60622
Ph: 312-944-2770
Fax: 312-944-1587

Fletcher Chicago
1000 N Branch St
Chicago, IL 60622
Ph: 312-226-2223
Fax: 312-421-6654

CEAVCO Audio
6240 W 54th Ave
Arvada, CO 80002
Ph: 303-539-3400
Fax: 303-539-3401

Gemini Sound
10218 Miller Rd
Dallas, TX 75238

Ph: 214-341-6922
Fax: 214-341-9363

Szabo Sound
2400 Central Pkwy, Suite C
Houston, TX 77092
Ph: 713-956-7451
Fax: 713-956-2244

LIGHTING AND GRIP

"Rent Light and Grip Equipment"

So why use lights? You *can* shoot without any and still capture an image—but you don't want to, because what looks great to your eye won't look great on film. The reason is twofold—depth and darkness.

The lens of the camera is merely a cheap replication of a human eye. Humans have two lenses (left eye and right eye) on their head. Eyes adapt and focus quickly, pick up color and shadow details, and create depth perception. The greatest camera and lens in the world will never capture what the human eye sees. A camera has only one lens (one eye) and thus the captured image will be flat.

Next, for whatever reason, developed film always appears darker than what the naked eye sees. Thus you want lights to brighten the captured image. Now you understand that a scene that is not lit will appear flat and dark. If you want your picture to show details, be bright, and have a feeling of depth perception, then you need lights. You literally 📁 *light a scene to make it unnatural and to call it natural.*

HOW TO LIGHT

The basic lighting setup used for every shot is called the "three-point setup." This means placing three lights (the key light, the back light, and the fill light) and pointing them from varying angles, onto the actor(s) or object(s) that is the scene's center of attention. Lighting is not rocket science.

1. *Key light:* This light, the first light placed, points directly at the subject and eliminates all unseemly shadows from the actors' faces and

PRODUCTION BUDGET

Title: "Your $1,000,000 Feature"   **Executive Producer:** _____
Producer: _____
Writer: _____   **Director:** _____

ACCOUNT NUMBER	DESCRIPTION	BUDGET
01-00	Producer	
02-00	Writer/Script	
03-00	Director	
04-00	Cast/Actors	
TOTAL ABOVE-THE-LINE (Pre-Production)		
BELOW-THE-LINE		
5-00	Film Stock	$20,000–$40,000
6-00	Film Lab (Shoot)	$15,000–$30,000
7-00	Camera	$12,000–$30,000
8-00	Expendables	$2,000–$5,000
9-00	Sound Equipment	$6,000–$11,000
10-00	Sound Transfer	$3,000–$5,000
11-00	**LIGHT/GRIP**	**$6,000–$24,000**
12-00	Dolly	
13-00	Cinematographer	
14-00	PM & AD	
15-00	Production Designer	
16-00	Film Crew	
17-00	Art & Props	
18-00	Wardrobe & Makeup	
19-00	Permits	
20-00	Insurance	
21-00	Dailies	
22-00	FX/Stunts/Cars	
23-00	Locations	
24-00	Office & Paperwork	
25-00	Publicity	
26-00	Food	
TOTAL PRODUCTION BUDGET (In-the-Can)		
THE SHOOT (Total Above & Below)		
27-00	Film Edit	
28-00	Film Lab (Edit)	
29-00	Sound Edit	
30-00	ADR	
31-00	Foley	
32-00	Music/Score	
33-00	Mix (Re-record)	
34-00	Optical Transfer	
35-00	M&E	
THE EDIT (Post-Production)		
36-00	Titles	
37-00	Negative Cutting	
38-00	Film Lab (Answer Print)	
TOTAL PRODUCTION COSTS		

especially his/her eye sockets. Although this light makes your actors' complexions smooth and more attractive, it also creates a flat look, which is why a key light is not used alone.

2. *Back lights:* After the key light is placed, the lighting director then thinks back lighting. These are the lights that are used to create a feeling of depth. Ever notice how the main actor in a scene always seems to have a halo around his head? This halo or glow comes from two lights being placed above and behind him, shining on the back of his head, that visually kick the actor forward from the background. Back lighting is also referred to as a "kicker," "rim lighting," or a "hair light."

3. *Fill lights:* Now, after the key and back lights are set, the fill lights are placed to the sides and above and below the actors, but in front of them, to bring added dimension to their faces (which are flattened by the key light). Fill lights, besides being used to create additional depth, also are blocked, bounced, filtered, and gelled to create drama, mood, and the subtle "look" of a scene.

At a minimum every scene should have a key light (to make the actor pretty), one or two back lights (to create depth), and fill lights (to get a mood). There is a fourth light commonly used called an "eye light." This is a small light that places a little twinkle in each of the actor's eyes. The eye light is only used when the cinematographer notices that the key light has not put a twinkle in the actor's eyes. It's this twinkle that makes the actor and his/her performance come alive.

Now, with this understanding of lighting, you should rent just enough light and grip equipment (what holds, or grips, the lights) to perform a three-point lighting setup. Strike a deal similar to the camera rental one: Rent the light and grip equipment for seven days, but pay for three or two.

Normally, you rent a light and grip package, after your cinematographer and gaffer (lighting director) have scouted the film's locations and put together their wish list, at a cost of about $4,000/day. And, if you accept a "four-day week" from the rental facility, this will be $48,000 ($4,000 × 4 days × 3 weeks). Even a two-day week will be $24,000.

You don't have $24,000–$48,000 in your budget for lights and grip equipment. Therefore, the secret to getting a good deal lies in finding a gaffer or grip who owns his own truck. Every city in America has three to six of these fully equipped trucks (aka independent trucks) that are easily rented at a rate of $2,000–$3,000/week (that's enough), for a total of $6,000–$9,000.

You'll find independent lighting-grip trucks by either calling your film commissioner, looking in the local production directory, or asking your cinematographer. These trucks are always owned by either a former cinematographer, now working as a gaffer, or a key grip, who thought that by buying equipment he'd get more jobs. But what actually happened is that he stumbled into the equipment rental business.

For the $2,000–$3,000/week you'll obtain (a) the truck owner to be your gaffer or grip, (b) get the use of all his equipment, (c) including the truck (which you'd have to rent). And, if you're really a good bargainer, you'll get him to throw in (d) an assistant (best boy electrician or dolly grip) as part of the package.

If all else fails, go to your local light and grip rental source and cry "student film." Ask if you can rent the equipment for a paperwork processing and equipment packing fee. One filmmaker was able to rent very costly, lightweight Kino Flo lights for $40/weekend by appealing to a salesman's sympathies. Then her gaffer, paid with cases of beer, borrowed a lighting truck from a lighting rental house and they let him take all the stands he needed. It's all who you know. If you don't "know" someone, find someone who does (usually your cinematographer) and ask for favors.

The bottom line is that **$6,000** can get you an independent lighting truck, containing all the equipment needed to light your film, with the truck owner becoming your gaffer or key grip. And, if you have upwards of **$24,000** you'll be able to rent everything that your gaffer and DP fantasize about on a four-day week from a rental facility.

TO DO:

1. Scout locations, with your DP and gaffer, and assess lighting needs.
2. Get the names of grips or gaffers with their own trucks.

BOOKS

Painting with Light
J. Alton, 191 pp., $27.50
A lighting classic! Written in 1949, when lighting was extremely important, it is still relevant today.

Masters of Light
D. Schaefer and L. Salvato, 356 pp., $24.95
The theory of lighting is explained, with discussions with 15 lighting pros ranging from Zsigmond to Wexler to Storaro.

A–Z of Lighting Terms
B. Fitt, 240 pp., $36.95
Want to light? Then you must know the lighting terminology and understand all the charts.

Film Lighting
K. Malkiewicz, 195 pp., $22.00
Twenty cinematographers and gaffers detail, with hundreds of drawings, how they light scenes.

Lighting for Film and Television
G. Millerson, 466 pp., $59.95
If you're getting just one book on lighting, this is the book.

Lighting for Digital Video and TV
J. Jackman, 416 pp., $44.95
Lighting digital video is different. This book reveals the secrets Hollywood pros use.

Gaffer's Set Lighting Handbook
H. Box, 432 pp., $44.95
Need to know the equipment? This book, which is loaded with photos and line drawings, is the one.

Uva's Basic Grip Book
M. Uva, 258 pp., $27.95
The first book to get when learning the craft. A must-have.

Uva's Rigging Guide
M. Uva, 263 pp., $49.95
Shooting in a tree, under a car, or on a plane's wing? This book details how to rig for the shot.

 VIDEOS

Light It Right
VHS, 30 minutes, $22.95
The A–Z of lighting properly for film or video.

Basic Lighting for DV
VHS, 72 minutes, $29.95
How to shoot stunning digital video using lighting techniques of the pros.

 RENTAL SOURCES

Mole-Richardson
937 N Sycamore Ave
Hollywood, CA 90038
Ph: 323-851-0111
Fax: 323-851-5593

Acey Decy
200 Parkside Dr
San Fernando, CA 91340
Ph: 818-408-4444
Fax: 818-408-2777

The Rosenthal Group
10625 Cohasset St
Sun Valley, CA 91352
Ph: 818-252-1010
Fax: 818-252-1070

Culver Studio Light & Grip
9336 W Washington Blvd
Culver City, CA 90232
Ph: 310-202-3363
Fax: 310-202-3516

Angstrom Stage Lighting
837 N Cahuenga Blvd
Hollywood, CA 90038
Ph: 323-462-5923
Fax: 323-462-0623

Paskal Lighting
6820 Romaine St
Hollywood, CA 90038
Ph: 323-466-5233
Fax: 323-466-1071

ABC&G Lighting/GDR
236 W 61st St
New York, NY 10023
Ph: 212-956-6447
Fax: 212-397-9579

CECO International
440 W 15th St
New York, NY 10011
Ph: 212-206-8280
Fax: 212-727-2144

East Coast Lighting
353 W 39th St, Suite 202
New York, NY 10018
Ph: 212-643-9727
Fax: 212-643-9740

See Factor Industry
37-11 30th St
Long Island City, NY 11101

Ph: 718-784-4200
Fax: 718-784-0617

CSC Lighting Center
619 W 54th St
New York, NY 10019
Ph: 212-757-0906
Fax: 212-713-0075

DTC Grip & Electrical
809 Anthony St
Berkeley, CA 94710
Ph: 510-665-1100
Fax: 510-665-1109

Common Productions
Spencer Commons
311 El Carmelo Ave
Palo Alto, CA 94306
Ph: 650-493-1720
Fax: 650-493-1461

Cinema Trucks of Texas
2003 Briargreen
Houston, TX 77077
Ph: 713-522-7265
Fax: 281-497-7125

MC Lighting & Production Services
4309 Briarbend
Houston, TX 77035
Ph: 713-723-1393
Fax: 713-723-3167

Pacific Grip & Lighting
10401 Martin Luther King Way South
Seattle, WA 98178
Ph: 206-622-8540
Fax: 206-292-2919

Jonas Jensen Studios
2141 W Valley Hwy North
Auburn, WA 98001
Ph: 253-833-0800
Fax: 253-833-4099

Bexel Corp
3314 Fourth Ave South
Seattle, WA 98134
Ph: 206-628-7000
Fax: 206-628-7003

Lighting Services
241 S Cherokee St
Denver, CO 80223
Ph: 303-722-4747
Fax: 303-722-4537

Gripworks & Electrical
41 Skyline Dr
Denver, CO 80215
Ph: 303-525-4747
Fax: 303-239-1210

Chicago Studio City
5660 W Taylor
Chicago, IL 60644
Ph: 773-261-3400
Fax: 773-261-6290

Essanay Studio and Lighting
1346 N North Branch
Chicago, IL 60622
Ph: 312-664-4400
Fax: 312-664-4430

Lite-It Grip Trucks
450 S Andrews Ct
West Chicago, IL 60185
Ph: 630-231-1671
Fax: 630-231-1672

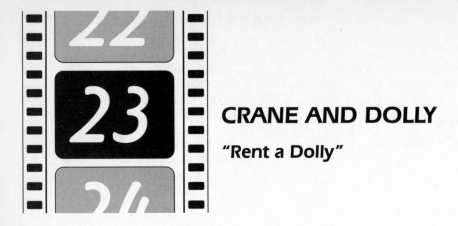

CRANE AND DOLLY
"Rent a Dolly"

Move the camera on your shots, but be sure that you keep it steady. Bouncing the camera around like they do on TV shows like *ER* and *NYPD Blue* gives shots that look cool—on TV. However, the same bouncing camera shot affects a movie audience differently and makes them seasick and nauseous. This is not good! For camera movement shots that will be viewed in a movie theater it is imperative to use a dolly, steered by a human pushing a handlebar. The dolly can move back and forth and side to side. The dolly is weighted and balanced to provide stable mobility, so your picture is smooth and not jumpy like handheld movement. The best dolly shots are the ones the audience doesn't even notice.

On micro-budget films, DPs have been known to rig a pseudo-dolly using a wheelchair or shopping cart. Hopefully, you won't need to do this—your camera might be ruined. For transporting equipment, your dolly choices are the doorway dolly, the western dolly, and the tube dolly. For mounting and moving your camera, you can choose among dollies manufactured by Fisher (Fisher-11, Fisher-10, Fisher-9) and Chapman (Hybrid, Hustler, PeeWee). There are other dolly manufacturers, but Fisher and Chapman are the manufacturers that most rental facilities stock.

Dollies are inexpensive, easy to use, and provide a slight (three- to four-foot) hydraulic elevation capability, giving a small crane movement for those expensive-looking shots. The biggest cranes (oversized dollies) give your camera an elevation of about 40 feet. The smallest cranes have a maximum lift of about 11 feet. If your production is on a limited budget and, therefore, a limited time schedule, you'll forgo using a crane (setting

PRODUCTION BUDGET

Title: "Your $1,000,000 Feature" Executive Producer: _____

Writer: _____ Producer: _____

Director: _____

ACCOUNT NUMBER	DESCRIPTION	BUDGET
01-00	Producer	
02-00	Writer/Script	
03-00	Director	
04-00	Cast/Actors	
TOTAL ABOVE-THE-LINE (Pre-Production)		
BELOW-THE-LINE		
5-00	Film Stock	$20,000–$40,000
6-00	Film Lab (Shoot)	$15,000–$30,000
7-00	Camera	$12,000–$30,000
8-00	Expendables	$2,000–$5,000
9-00	Sound Equipment	$6,000–$11,000
10-00	Sound Transfer	$3,000–$5,000
11-00	Light/Grip	$6,000–$24,000
12-00	**DOLLY**	**$2,000–$3,000**
13-00	Cinematographer	
14-00	PM & AD	
15-00	Production Designer	
16-00	Film Crew	
17-00	Art & Props	
18-00	Wardrobe & Makeup	
19-00	Permits	
20-00	Insurance	
21-00	Dailies	
22-00	FX/Stunts/Cars	
23-00	Locations	
24-00	Office & Paperwork	
25-00	Publicity	
26-00	Food	
TOTAL PRODUCTION BUDGET (In-the-Can)		
THE SHOOT (Total Above & Below)		
27-00	Film Edit	
28-00	Film Lab (Edit)	
29-00	Sound Edit	
30-00	ADR	
31-00	Foley	
32-00	Music/Score	
33-00	Mix (Re-record)	
34-00	Optical Transfer	
35-00	M&E	
THE EDIT (Post-Production)		
36-00	Titles	
37-00	Negative Cutting	
38-00	Film Lab (Answer Print)	
TOTAL PRODUCTION COSTS		

up, practicing, and blocking a crane shot can take three or four hours), and rely on a dolly.

WHAT IT COSTS

When you rent a dolly—just like when you rent a camera—the rate card price is only for the body. You need to select accessories, including risers, tracks (straight and curved), seats, adapters, tracking bars, jib arms, platforms, track wheels, etc.—all of which carry additional charges. However, the total cost for a dolly, with all accessories, won't be more than $1,000/week. For a three-week shoot, you will pay $2,000 to $3,000.

> **IMPORTANT POINT**   Your objective is to have dolly shots (aka camera movement) rather than static tripod and zoom shots as often as possible. **Dolly shots are one of the keys to giving your film "production value."** But here's the problem. Although inexpensive to rent, dollies are heavy and cumbersome. They slow you down when maintaining a 25–35 shot/day schedule. Therefore, rent a dolly but never allow it to slow you down.

Dolly shots are difficult to execute. The camera moves, the focal point changes, the lens adjusts, and the composition changes. This is expert territory, so be absolutely sure, upon viewing dailies, that every shot is sharp and in frame. If any dolly shot is out of focus (the DP will never admit to this—he'll call it "soft focus"), immediately fire the first assistant cameraman (aka the focus puller), hire a new one, and work just as fast the next day. And, if—in the worst-case scenario—the dolly puts you more than one day behind schedule, go back to using just the tripod, zoom, and handheld shots until back on schedule.

Using a dolly and, at times, a crane to get 25–35 shots/day greatly adds to your production value. The cost will be only **$2,000–$3,000,** but make sure that this equipment doesn't slow you down and put you behind schedule. Rent a dolly. Get a good deal. But be careful.

TO DO:

1. Ask your camera rental facility what dollies they rent.
2. Get rates for a Chapman (Hybrid or PeeWee) or Fisher (#9 or #10) dolly, with accessories.

 BOOKS

Uva's Guide to Cranes, Jibs and Dollies
M. Uva and S. Uva, 268 pp., $37.99
The definitive book on how to operate
this important filmmaking equipment.

The Grip Book
M. Uva, 378 pp., $32.95
This is the classic. This book details
what cranes and dollies to use and
why. Loaded with illustrations.

Uva's Rigging Guide
M. Uva and S. Uva, 263 pp., $49.95
Shooting in a tree, under a car, or on a
plane's wing? This book details how to
rig for the shot.

 **RENTAL
FACILITIES**

Chapman Leonard
12950 Raymer St
North Hollywood, CA 91605
Ph: 818-764-6726
Fax: 818-764-2728
1901 E 501st St, Suite 38
Austin, TX 78723
Ph: 512-473-0084
Fax: 512-473-0042

5045 Still Creek Ave
Burnaby, Vancouver, BC V5C 5V1
   Canada
Ph: 604-299-0913
Fax: 604-299-0913

J L Fisher, Inc.
1000 W Isabel St
Burbank, CA 91506
Ph: 818-846-8366
Fax: 818-846-8699

Camera Service Center
619 W 54th St
New York, NY 10019
Ph: 212-757-0906
Fax: 212-713-0075

Panavision New York
540 W 36th St
New York, NY 10018
Ph: 212-606-0700
Fax: 212-244-4457

The Shotmaker Company
10909 Vanowen St
North Hollywood, CA 91605
Ph: 818-623-1700
Fax: 818-623-1710

Camera Cars Unlimited
5331 Derry Ave, Suite A
Agoura Hills, CA 91301
Ph: 818-889-9903
Fax: 818-889-4970

Action Car Cameras
508 Nepperhan Ave
Yonkers, NY 10701
Ph: 914-964-5816
Fax: 914-964-5836

Tracking Shot
203 Meserole Ave
Brooklyn, NY 11222
Ph: 718-956-7995
Fax: 718-349-9148

ABOVE-THE-LINE

"What Talent Costs"

Everyone has read about astronomical amounts paid to established writers, directors, and actors. Most of the stories and amounts paid are close to correct. And you have nowhere near that type of money to hire celebrities. You'll hire talented people who, like you, are starting careers and are looking for opportunities to secure a credit and experience on a feature film.

You will literally pay these people with opening title credits supplemented with just enough salary to pay their rent during the weeks they're working for you.

PRODUCER: WHAT TO PAY YOURSELF

The politically correct answer: $25,000–$40,000
Your answer: $10,000–$20,000

Producers pay other people. Producers rarely get paid unless the film makes profits. Film schools and filmmaking books tell you that the standard producer's fee is 10 percent of the total production budget. This is simply not true on your first feature, especially if funding comes from friends and relatives.

The goal of your first film is not to get a paycheck but rather a calling card to launch your career. Put the extra production money you might gain on the screen, not in your pocket, and only keep enough to subsist (rent, food, insurance, gas, etc.) during the months that you are working to obtain your first opening title credit.

PRODUCTION BUDGET

Title: "Your $1,000,000 Feature" Executive Producer: _____

Producer: _____

Writer: _____ Director: _____

ACCOUNT NUMBER	DESCRIPTION	BUDGET
01-00	**PRODUCER**	**$10,000–$20,000**
02-00	**WRITER/SCRIPT**	**$5,000–$10,000**
03-00	**DIRECTOR**	**$10,000–$15,000**
04-00	**CAST/ACTORS**	**$6,000–$9,000 (+$25,000)**
TOTAL ABOVE-THE-LINE (Pre-Production)		**$31,000–$54,000 (+$25,000)**
BELOW-THE-LINE		
5-00	Film Stock	$20,000–$40,000
6-00	Film Lab (Shoot)	$15,000–$30,000
7-00	Camera	$12,000–$30,000
8-00	Expendables	$2,000–$5,000
9-00	Sound Equipment	$6,000–$11,000
10-00	Sound Transfer	$3,000–$5,000
11-00	Light/Grip	$6,000–$24,000
12-00	Dolly	$2,000–$3,000
13-00	Cinematographer	
14-00	PM & AD	
15-00	Production Designer	
16-00	Film Crew	
17-00	Art & Props	
18-00	Wardrobe & Makeup	
19-00	Permits	
20-00	Insurance	
21-00	Dailies	
22-00	FX/Stunts/Cars	
23-00	Locations	
24-00	Office & Paperwork	
25-00	Publicity	
26-00	Food	
TOTAL PRODUCTION BUDGET (In-the-Can)		
THE SHOOT (Total Above & Below)		
27-00	Film Edit	
28-00	Film Lab (Edit)	
29-00	Sound Edit	
30-00	ADR	
31-00	Foley	
32-00	Music/Score	
33-00	Mix (Re-record)	
34-00	Optical Transfer	
35-00	M&E	
THE EDIT (Post-Production)		
36-00	Titles	
37-00	Negative Cutting	
38-00	Film Lab (Answer Print)	
TOTAL PRODUCTION COSTS		

Everyone has a different lifestyle. Some people can live on $500 a month; others need $10,000 a month for basic bills.

IMPORTANT POINT Even though your film is only a three-week shoot, you will eat up 12 hours a day every day for five months while producing your first feature.

Thus, guesstimate an amount (e.g., $2,000 to $4,000) you will need to live each month and multiply by five months to establish a producer's fee of **$10,000–$20,000.**

WRITER/SCRIPT: WHAT TO PAY A TYPIST

The politically correct answer: $70,000–$80,000
Your answer: $5,000–$10,000

What you can afford, once you've discovered your unknown writing talent, is $2,500–$5,000 ($500–$1,000/week for five weeks) for a first draft. Next, get coverage from two professional script readers for $100–$250 each. Then pay the writer $1,500–$3,000 ($500–$1,000/week for three weeks) for the second draft. Keep a final $1,000–$2,000 aside for a second writer to do a polish, and you've gotten a very good shot at getting an excellent script for **$5,000–$10,000.**

DIRECTOR: WHAT TO PAY A WANNABE

The politically correct answer: $70,000–$120,000
Your answer: $10,000–$15,000

You are about to make someone famous. The director always gets famous. You are about to give someone $250,000–$500,000 (plus a great script) to launch a career. Isn't that enough? I believe that a first-time feature film director should pay *you,* yes, that's correct, they should pay you $25,000–$50,000, if you're giving him/her $250,000–$500,000 for the opportunity to demonstrate his talent.

The Directors Guild used to call low-budget anything under $500,000 but recently raised it to under $1.2 million. At that level, the Guild allows its members to negotiate their own salaries. However, the Guild still mandates that even on a three-week shoot, you're obligated to pay the director, along with the assistant director and production manager (both who are in the Directors Guild), for a minimum eight-week period. And don't forget that no matter what rate your director accepts, you still have to pay dues of 5.5 percent pension and 4.5 percent health, and owe the director an additional 125 percent of scale when the film reaches break-even during distribution. This could easily amount to $70,000–$120,000. This is not in your budget. You can only afford $10,000–$15,000, which is more than enough to pay someone to become famous.

The best way to allocate this money is to (1) pay your director $3,000–$4,000 ($750–$1,000/week for four-weeks) during pre-production, (2) then pay $4,500–$6,000 ($1,500–$2,000/week for three weeks) during the shoot, and (3) remit the final $2,500–$5,000 (intervals of $100–$200/day) during post-production.

If you are producing and also directing the film, you will pay yourself the producer's fee while making the film and defer (to be paid at a later time) your director's salary (usually at Directors Guild minimums) until after the film is made, distributed, and the investors have recouped their investment.

For non-celebrity first-time directors, **$10,000–$15,000** is more than enough. Pay any more and you're a fool.

ACTORS: WHAT TO PAY WAITERS

The politically correct answer: $40,000–$60,000
Your answer: $6,000–$9,000

A three-week shoot with 15–18 actors should not require more than 50–60 acting days. Whether or not you sign with SAG on a low-budget (limited exhibition [LEA] or experimental filmmaker) agreement, $100/day is fair. What do you think? The **$6,000–$9,000** will get you 15–20 actors for your film. The numbers break down (for a three-week shoot with 20 actors at $100/day or $500/week) like this:

Part	# of Days	Salary
Star (3 weeks)	15–18	$1,500+
Co-star (2 weeks)	10–12	$1,000+
Actors #3–5 (1 week)	15–18	$1,500+
Actors #6–8 (3 days)	9	$900+
Actors #9–20 (1 day)	12	$1,200+
20 Actors	61–69 Days	$6,100–$9,000

What about a celebrity? You want to get a recognizable "name" for a more marketable film. Put in $25,000 to hire him/her. Budget a one-day hire at $25,000 instead of $100. *$25,000 is a lot of money, especially if it's only for one day of work!* Name actors will take **$25,000** to come to your set, instead of sitting at home, for one, two, or three days to play a judge in your courtroom scene.

Once you have the great script and $250,000–$500,000 in the bank, you will be amazed how easy it will be to hire talent, even names. They actually need you *more* than you need them. There is no need to pay superstar rates.

ABOVE-THE-LINE COSTS

Your total above-the-line (producer, writer, director, actors) costs total **$31,000–$54,000, plus $25,000** set aside to hire a name actor midway into the shoot.

TO DO:

1. Figure out your living expenses for five months. That's your producer's fee.

 BOOKS

Agents and Managers
HCD staff, 302 pp., $59.95
Updated every six months. Contact information for 1,500 agencies and 5,500 individuals to include agents, talent managers, and casting directors.

Producers 411
Variety staff, 400 pp., $49.00
An entertainment directory for serious professionals that lists producers and production companies with financing.

Producers
HCD staff, 402 pp., $59.95
Contains contact information for 1,750 companies and 9,900 individuals who are either studio and network execs or producers with pre-approved film funding deals.

Film Actors
HCD staff, 400+ pp., $85.00
Six thousand listings of film actors and over 15,000 film titles. Includes agent contact information.

Film Writers
HCD staff, 400+ pp., $85.00

Eight thousand screenwriter listings with over 35,000 film and television titles. Includes agent contact information.

Film Directors
HCD staff, 400+ pp., $75.00
Five thousand five hundred individual listings with over 43,000 film titles. Includes agent contact information.

DGA Directory of Members
DGA staff, 771 pp., $39.95
A list of all members of the DGA, with their credits and contact information.

 GUILDS AND UNIONS

USA

Writers Guild of America
WGA/East
555 W 57th St, 12th Floor
New York, NY 10019
Ph: 212-767-7800
Fax: 212-582-1909
Web: www.WGAEast.org
WGA/West
7000 W 3rd St
Los Angeles, CA 90048
Ph: 323-951-4000
Fax: 323-782-4800

Directors Guild of America (DGA)
110 W 57th St
New York, NY 10019
Ph: 212-581-0370
Fax: 212-581-1441
Web: www.DGA.org
7920 Sunset Blvd
Los Angeles, CA 90046
Ph: 310-289-5333
Fax: 310-289-2029

International Alliance of Theatrical Stage Employees (IATSE)
1515 Broadway, Suite 601
New York, NY 10036
Ph: 212-730-1770
Fax: 212-730-7809
Web: www.IATSE.lm.com
10045 Riverside Dr, 2nd Floor
Toluca Lake, CA 91602
Ph: 818-980-3499
Fax: 818-980-3496

Screen Actors Guild (SAG)
360 Madison Ave
New York, NY 10017
Ph: 212-944-1030
Fax: 212-944-6774
Web: www.SAG.org
5757 Wilshire Blvd
Los Angeles, CA 90036
Ph: 323-954-1600
Fax: 323-549-6603

SAG BRANCHES

Arizona
Ph: 602-264-7571
Fax: 602-264-7571

Boston
Ph: 617-742-2688
Fax: 617-742-4904

Chicago
Ph: 312-573-8081
Fax: 312-573-0318

Cleveland
Ph: 216-579-9305
Fax: 216-781-2257

Dallas
Ph: 214-363-8300
Fax: 214-363-5386

Denver
Ph: 303-757-6226
Fax: 303-757-1769

Detroit
Ph: 248-355-3105
Fax: 248-355-2879

Miami
Ph: 305-670-7677
Fax: 305-670-1813

Orlando
Ph: 407-649-3100
Fax: 407-649-7222

Atlanta
Ph: 404-239-0131
Fax: 404-239-0137

Honolulu
Ph: 808-596-0388
Fax: 808-593-2636

Houston
Ph: 713-972-1806
Fax: 713-780-0261

Minneapolis
Ph: 612-371-9120
Fax: 612-371-9119

Nashville
Ph: 615-327-2944
Fax: 615-329-2803

Las Vegas
Ph: 702-737-8818
Fax: 702-737-8851

Wilmington
Ph: 910-762-1889
Fax: 910-762-0881

Portland
Ph: 503-279-9600
Fax: 503-279-9603

Philadelphia
Ph: 215-545-3150
Fax: 215-732-0086

Puerto Rico
Ph: 737-289-7832
Fax: 737-289-8732

San Francisco
Ph: 415-391-7510
Fax: 415-391-1108

Seattle
Ph: 206-270-0493
Fax: 206-282-7073

St. Louis
Ph: 314-231-8410
Fax: 314-231-8412

Washington, DC
Ph: 301-657-2560
Fax: 301-656-3615

CANADA

Writers Guild/Canada
1225-123 Edward St
Toronto, ONT M5G 1E2 Canada
Ph: 416-979-7907
Fax: 416-979-9273

Directors Guild/Canada
One Eglinton Ave E, Suite 604
Toronto, ONT M4P 3A1 Canada
Ph: 416-482-6640
Fax: 416-482-6639
Web: www.DGA.ca
430-1152 Mainland St
Vancouver, BC V6B 4X2 Canada
Ph: 604-688-2976
Fax: 604-688-2610

ACTRA Performers Guild
2239 Yonge St
Toronto, ONT M4S 2B5 Canada

Ph: 416-489-1311
Fax: 416-489-8076
Web: www.actra.com
400-856 Homer St
Vancouver, BC V6B 2W5 Canada
Ph: 604-689-0727
Fax: 604-689-1145

ENGLAND

Directors Guild of Great Britain
Acorn House
314-320 Grays Inn Rd
London WC1X 8DP England
Ph: 44-207-278-4343
Fax: 44-207-278-4742
Web: www.dggb.co.uk

British Actors' Equity Association
Guild House
Upper St Martins Ln
London WC2H 9EG England
Ph: 44-207-379-6000
Fax: 44-207-379-7001
Web: www.equity.org.uk

Writers' Guild of Great Britain
430 Edgware Rd
London W2 1EH England
Ph: 44-207-723-8074
Fax: 44-207-706-2413
Web: www.writersguild.org.uk

Broadcasting, Entertainment,
    Cinematograph and Theatre Union
    (BECTU)
111 Wardour St
London W1F 0AY England
Ph: 44-207-437-8506
Fax: 44-207-437-8268
Web: www.bectu.org.uk

Producers Alliance for Cinema &
    Television (PACT)
45 Mortimer St
London W1W 7TD England
Ph: 44-207-331-6000
Fax: 44-207-331-6700
Web: www.pact.co.uk

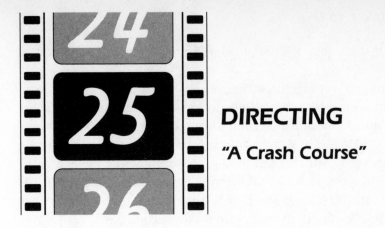

DIRECTING

"A Crash Course"

Listening to Spielberg, Scorsese, Coppola, Tarantino, or Soderbergh tell you how they'll approach directing their next feature does you little good. What you want to know is how they directed their first feature—how they directed when they didn't know what they were doing, when they had little to no money, when they were running out of film, when they had energetic (i.e., incompetent) but inexperienced crew, etc.

DIRECT YOUR FIRST FEATURE

Let me give you a straight, no-nonsense, simple-to-understand approach to how to direct. Then, armed with this you will either direct or hire someone to direct *but not be intimidated by the craft*. Here goes.

I have discovered that directing breaks down to four things.

1. Direct the actor (Pick actors who act, not talk)
2. Direct the edit (Get the shots to save the film)
3. Direct the schedule and budget (Get the master, then say no)
4. Direct the camera (Get coverage and don't flop the I-line)

1. DIRECT THE ACTOR

After script and money, the most important ingredient to a successful film is the cast. If you select the right actors, it is almost impossible to screw up a great script. Therefore, handling the casting session is an extremely important part of directing. 💼 *Stop thinking of the casting session as a fashion parade!*

When word gets out (agents, acting studios, breakdown services, etc.) that you are shooting a feature, you'll be inundated with actors' headshots and résumés. Spend a nominal amount of money ($500–$1,000) to hire a casting director, who'll save you an amazing amount of time. The casting director will set up a casting room (400 square feet, with a table, a video camera and monitor, and a Polaroid) for two days and screen the 100 to 200 actors who submitted résumés and narrow them down to three to five per role who receive a "callback" to read again on the second day.

On the callback day, you will sit behind the table with the casting director, and possibly an assistant and the producer. Then, one by one, the actors enter the room for their 10-minute audition. Once again, this is not a fashion parade.

You want actors to be creative. They can always add depth to their character with body movements, unique facial gestures, distinct vocal intonations, etc. Creative actors make a great script greater. So when the actor asks, "What are you looking for?" tell him, "We'll be here long enough for you to read it three times. The first time, try it your way." Giving the actor this freedom increases the likelihood that he will come up with something creative (a lisp, a twitch, a vocal nuance, etc.) that will enhance the character.

After the actor reads the two-minute scene his way, tell him, "That was wonderful," if it was. If it wasn't wonderful, tell him that anyway (only say positive things to actors). In either case give him some direction by stating, "Try it this way, please." This direction becomes the test to see if the actor is really an actor or just a "talker," and if he is willing and capable of taking direction. 💼 *If you want to direct, all it takes is five words, which are, "Try it this way, please."* You are giving direction. This simple phrase, combined with a reassuring nod every now and then, will start your directing career.

Your concern is that you may hire an actor who looked right and was great in the first read-through. Then, on the third day of the shoot, you discover, upon giving him direction, that he can't or won't follow it. Now, after the fact, you realize that in the casting session, the actor wasn't acting, he was just talking. Talking loud or talking slowly, but just talking—and you're stuck with him. This happens time and time again, especially when a first-time director falls in love with someone's physical looks.

Most first-time directors are intimidated by actors and treat that casting session as if it's a modeling runway. Don't let this happen! Pick actors who are right for the part, but make sure you pick actors *who can act and who are willing to take direction from you.* Once your cast is chosen, you will have two days, at the most, of "table readings" (reading the script line-by-line around a table) to help them get into character. During these table readings and rehearsal, at the actual set if possible, be sure that you are in charge. You are the director. Don't be shy.

2. DIRECT THE EDIT

You will quickly discover that during post-production, the film editor always feels that he/she "saved the film." They always do, or so they think. The truth is, the film editor couldn't save the film if you hadn't gotten him/her the shots to save the film. Thus, the film editor really didn't save the film—he/she was just doing their job. Therefore, it is the director's job to get the shots that the film editor, two months later, will need to save the film. These shots are called cutaways, reaction, or cat-in-the-window shots. Here is why you get them.

With a high budget, you have the luxury of renting three cameras, with corresponding crews, to get a master shot (camera #1), a medium over-the-shoulder (OTS) shot (camera #2), and a reverse medium over-the-shoulder shot (camera #3) simultaneously. This is referred to as getting the "master and two pops." For when shooting with three cameras running simultaneously, the editor has three shots from different angles, with exactly the same acting performance, that all match and cut together easily.

With a low budget you only have enough money to rent one 35mm camera (chapter 19). Thus, you'll shoot the scene three times, approximately 30 minutes apart, one after the other. First you will set up, light, and shoot a master shot. Then you'll move the camera, set up, light, and shoot the OTS shot. Then you'll move the camera again, set up, light, and shoot the reverse OTS shot. The actors repeat the same scene three times. Although this style is slightly beneficial for lighting, the big problem is that the actors never give identical performances. An eyebrow gesture, a word, a hand movement—something will be slightly different each time.

Thus, two months later, when the editor is editing, he will see that the shots don't exactly match. And when the editor cuts a medium shot into the master, there will be a second or two when it will not be smooth. The audience will notice. To cover up this edit blemish, the editor will look for a one- to two-second cutaway, reaction, or cat-in-the-window shots.

Cutaways could be a hand tapping, a foot stomping, a faucet dripping, etc. Reaction shots, usually close-ups, are facial expressions of actors reacting to the drama. Cat-in-the-window shots are just that. Literally put a putty cat in the window and get a five-second shot of it meowing. Audiences love shots of animals. Cut to the cat, or a dog, or a frog—it always produces a laugh or a warm feeling, but make sure that the audience knows that in the master shot there's a window with a cat in it.

Get these shots! Down the road in post-production, when the editor is trying to cover up actors' gaffes, poor performances, or rough transitions and save the film, you'll be ecstatic that you have these shots. Make sure to get three to four cutaway, reaction, or cat-in-the-window shots for each scene.

3. DIRECT THE SCHEDULE AND BUDGET

Understand that being on schedule and being on budget are two entirely different concepts. Your schedule is simply the page count—how many pages are covered each day. You have enough money to direct or shoot 90 pages during three weeks (18 days), which becomes a five-page/day schedule. At the end of shooting day #1, ask the script supervisor whether you got five pages shot. If so, you're on schedule. If not, you're behind schedule. The next day, you must compensate and shoot extra pages to get back on your schedule.

Getting more specific: There are usually 10 hours of shooting each day. On a three-week, five page/day shoot you'll have approximately two hours to get one script page in the can. And, while shooting that page, if you want production value, you'll get five shots (master shot, medium shot[s], close-up[s], reaction shot[s], etc.)—with camera movement (dolly shots) and lighting (key, back, and fill)—during those two hours. Thus, your schedule becomes one shot every 20–25 minutes, which becomes five to six shots every two hours, to accomplish one page of script. Maintain this for 10 hours and you have five pages in the can with 25–35 shots.

IMPORTANT POINT   Everything is not fine even if you're on schedule. For, *being on schedule is useless if you aren't simultaneously on budget.*

What if, while shooting five pages a day, you wrote some extra checks? You gave the cinematographer some more money, the production designer rented some more props, and eight more actors were needed for the crowd scene. You are on schedule, but over budget. Where's this extra money going to come from? The answer is post-production! But if you take the money that was budgeted for post-production to pay for little extras during the shoot, you will run out of money during post and not finish your film. Bummer!

So how do you stay on budget? Simple! Once you start your shoot, never write an extra check. Don't listen to crew members who tell you producers always come up with money when needed. Don't worry about everyone liking you. Matter of fact, expect that during the production the crew will actually hate you. You have stopped writing checks. Remember, a good producer and director sticks to the budget and get the film done.

> **IMPORTANT POINT**   You must understand that a budget is not measured in just money, it is also film stock (chapter 17). The biggest check you write will be to purchase film stock. Film is much more expensive than tape. In the video or electronic world, when a producer-director runs out of tape stock, he pulls out a $100 bill and buys 10–15 hours. In the film world, another 10–15 hours translates to another $20,000–$40,000.

Your budget permits you to buy approximately 50,000 feet of 35mm film. Treat the 50,000 feet as if it were gold. Budget and allocate it wisely. You cannot expose more than 550 feet (50,000 feet divided by 90 pages) of film stock per script page. When you run out of film stock, your movie is done. Allocate it wisely.

The rule of thumb is, if you're 10 percent over shooting ratio for more than two days in a row, the shoot is a fiasco. Assume you're planning for a 6:1 shoot and shooting (actors want more takes, cinematographer wants more angles, etc.) a 7:1. This is more than 10 percent over your planned shooting ratio, and on the afternoon of the 14th day of your 18-day shoot you will run out of film, with 15–17 pages still to be shot. You now have a massive problem and will probably use money budgeted for post-production to buy more film, and, although the film will get shot, it will never get finished. Bummer!

4. DIRECT THE CAMERA

Unquestionably, the biggest fear first-time directors face is what the heck to do with the camera—which lenses to use, where to place it, where to position the actors, which shot to get first. Stop worrying. Here's the golden rule: 🛄 *First get the master shot, then go in for coverage.*

For the master shot, you put a small-number lens (20mm, 25mm, 30mm, etc.) on the camera and pull it back far enough so that everything that is written on the script page (set, actors, props, etc.) is viewed in the camera's eyepiece. The master shot captures the entire set with all the actors in that scene.

For the next shot(s), move the camera in, change the lens (35mm, 50mm, etc.), and get the two OTS (over-the-shoulder) medium shots (actors are framed from above their heads to just below their waists), in which you see only part of the set. You may choose not to run the entire scene with this setup. Perhaps you will pick the action up after the cast is seated. Then you'll get the close-ups, focusing on the dialogue. Then you'll get your extreme close-ups and cutaways.

All shots, other than the master shot, comprise coverage. Coverage shots consist of:

Medium shot (MS)
Over-the-shoulder shot (OTS)
Close-up (CU)
Extreme close-up (ECU)
Establishing shot (ES)
Reaction shot
Point-of-view shot (POV)

You want these extra shots. But first *get the master and then get coverage.* Why? The master shot is the easiest shot to get. There is so much latitude that it is impossible for the actors to move in and out of the frame. Close-ups, contrary to belief, are the difficult shots to get, for they leave actors very little space to move. During close-ups, the actor may move his head slightly and be out of frame. But it is almost impossible to get a bad master shot unless a prop falls down or an actor flubs his lines.

If you're having a problem visualizing what I'm explaining, go rent *Stranger Than Paradise,* the film that launched Jim Jarmusch's career. It was commercially successful, and in my opinion, it was a piece of crap. I'm not saying that I am a better director than Jim Jarmusch. But you will see that *Stranger Than Paradise* is nothing but 40–50 master shots. Not a single medium shot, close-up, or reaction shot in the entire movie. He just put the camera on a tripod, hit the on button, and told the actors to talk for two to three minutes. He didn't even pan or tilt. Also rent *Clerks,* the film that launched Kevin Smith's career. You'll discover only one scene in the entire film with an over-the-shoulder medium shot or two. Every other scene was done with only a master.

DIRECTING OVERVIEW

Let's assume you're about to direct a one-page scene and your budget permits a three-week shoot with 50,000 feet of film. Earlier in this chapter, I explained how this allows you 20–25 minutes per shot. In these minutes, you rehearse and shoot the scene with a master shot, exposing 90 feet of film stock. You're on schedule and on budget, and if you are Jarmusch or Smith, you are done. Now let's think art (aka coverage) and get production value.

You've scheduled 120 minutes and budgeted 550 feet of film and have only used 20–25 minutes and 90 feet. You now have 460 feet and almost 95–100 minutes left to create art with a selection of medium shots, close-ups, cutaways, over-the-shoulder shots, etc. If directing on a 6:1 shooting ratio, you could get the master shot six times (six takes). Or you could get the master shot with one take and use the remaining budgeted film to get five different shots (master and coverage) with one take each.

THE I-LINE RULE

The final rule to follow when directing the camera is known as the imaginary-line, the I-line, the 180-degree, or the center-of-action rule. This states that through the middle of every scene, there is an imaginary line. On one side of that line there are 180 degrees. On the other side of the line are the other 180 degrees of a 360-degree circle.

For the first shot, the master shot, of every scene, place the camera on one side or the other of the imaginary line (center of action). Once you have shot the master, you have shown the direction in which all the actors are facing or the cars are driving. You must make sure that in all the other shots for that scene's coverage, you never place the camera on the other side of the line (called "flopping the I-line") to get a medium shot or a close-up.

DIRECTOR'S CRASH COURSE RECAP

1. Cast: Pick the right actors. Make absolutely sure that they aren't just talkers and that they are willing and capable of taking direction from you.

2. Edit: Approach each scene knowing that the editor will eventually need shots to edit smoothly. Get close-ups and/or cutaways for each scene.

3. Schedule and budget: To stay on schedule, start each scene with a master shot. Then, don't write any extra checks, and be extremely anal about exposing your precious film stock with too many takes or angles.

4. Shot selection: First get your master shot, then go in for the smaller (medium) and smaller (close-up) and smaller (extreme close-up) shots. And while doing this never flop the I-line.

If you do this, you will have excellent actors, a happy crew, an efficient shoot, and, most important, a film that gets done on schedule and on budget.

TO DO:

1. Notify agents, acting studios, and breakdown services that you're casting.
2. Figure out your shooting schedule.
3. Rent *Stranger Than Paradise* and *Clerks*.

 BOOKS

Film Directing Shot by Shot
S. Katz, 365 pp., $27.95
If you're getting just one book on directing, then this is the one. A must!

Film Directing: Cinematic Motion
S. Katz, 291 pp., $26.95
An excellent companion book to *Shot by Shot*. Details staging scenes.

Beginning Guide to Directing
R. Harmon, 196 pp., $16.95
A basic book for the first-time film director.

Film Directing Fundamentals
N. Proferes, 242 pp., $29.95
An excellent beginner's book. Shows how to break down a script, get a schedule, and shoot.

Directing: Film Techniques
M. Rabiger, 542 pp., $49.95
Dispenses the A–Z of directing in more depth than a beginner's directing book.

Film Directing
R. Harmon, 219 pp., $22.95
An excellent beginner's book. Geared for a film school grad who needs more info.

Directing 101
E. Pintoff, 223 pp., $16.95
A beginner's book that provides a
solid intro.

The Film Director
R. Bare, 273 pp., $18.95
An industry classic that has been
recently updated.

Directing Your Directing Career
K. Callan, 348 pp., $18.95
Directing is a business. This is the only
book that teaches the business of how
to launch your career.

Fight Directing for Theatre
J. Suddeth, 343 pp., $39.95
Whether stage or film, this book
teaches how to choreograph those
amazing fight scenes.

Directing for Film and Television
C. Lukas, 235 pp., $19.95
The basics for the first-time film
director.

Making Movies
S. Lumet, 220 pp., $14.00
A directing genius describes how he
created a process that works.

Setting Up Your Shots
J. Vineyard, 135 pp., $19.95
An excellent visual book that shows in
line-drawing detail how to get great
camera moves.

On Directing
H. Clurman, 308 pp., $16.95
A classic. Elia Kazan calls it the most
influential book on how to obtain performances. A must!

Directing Actors
J. Weston, 315 pp., $26.95

Focuses solely on working with actors
and getting them to deliver
memorable performances.

The Director's Journey
M. Travis, 301 pp., $26.95
Details how to work, as a director,
with writers and actors during the
pre-production and rehearsal periods.

The Film Director's Team
A. Silver and E. Ward, 248 pp., $19.95
Paperwork is imperative. This book
details how to do all the paperwork
expected of a director. A must!

Actors Turned Directors
J. Stevens, 381 pp., $19.95
If you're an actor who wants to direct,
this book is a must.

Directing Feature Films
M. Travis, 395 pp., $26.95
Takes you through the entire creative
process, with emphasis on collabo-
ration.

The Directors: Take One
R. Emery, 413 pp., $19.95
Interviews with 15 contemporary di-
rectors like Cameron, Carpenter,
Howard, and Lee.

The Directors: Take Two
R. Emery, 389 pp., $19.95
The follow-up to *Take One,* with an
additional 15 interviews with
Avildsen, Reiner, Zemeckis, etc.

The Directors: Take Three
R. Emery, 400 pp., $21.95
Twenty more directors, including
Steven Spielberg, Robert Altman,
Tim Burton, Barry Levinson . . .

Basic Studio Directing
R. Fairwether, 192 pp., $31.95
A technical book on the process of
directing in studio for broadcasting.

Directing
M. Goodridge, 176 pp., $41.95
An excellent gift. Coffee table book,
with 500 photos, for a wannabe
director.

Film Directors
HCD staff, 400+ pp., $75.00
Contains 5,500 individual listings with
over 43,000 film titles. Includes information on how to contact them.

 VIDEOS

Directing Workshop: Action/Cut
Six VHS tapes, 12 hours, Guy Magar,
$329.95
A step-by-step and shot-by-shot
explanation of the directing process,
with an intensive interactive
workbook. An excellent directing
course on tape.

First Works, Volume 1
VHS, 122 minutes, $34.95
Compare yourself to the first films
directed by Roger Corman, Spike Lee,
Oliver Stone, Bob Zemeckis, and more.

First Works, Volume 2
VHS, 120 minutes, $34.95
More first films directed by Martin
Scorsese, Ron Howard, John Milius,
John Carpenter, and others.

 BANKABLE STUDIO DIRECTORS

Steven Spielberg
DreamWorks SKG
100 Universal Plz, Bungalow 477
Universal City, CA 91608
Ph: 818-695-5000

James Cameron
Lightstorm Entertainment
919 Santa Monica Blvd
Santa Monica, CA 90401
Ph: 310-587-2500

George Lucas
Lucasfilm Ltd.
PO Box 10228
San Rafael, CA 94912
Ph: 415-662-1800

Ron Howard
Imagine Entertainment
9465 Wilshire Blvd, 7th Floor
Beverly Hills, CA 90212
Ph: 310-858-2000
Fax: 310-858-2020

Tim Burton
Tim Burton Productions
1990 S Bundy Dr, Suite 200
Los Angeles, CA 90025
Ph: 310-571-4000

Martin Scorsese
Cappa Productions
445 Park Ave, 7th Floor
New York, NY 10022
Ph: 212-906-8800

John Woo
Garth Productions
2450 Broadway, Suite E590
Santa Monica, CA 90404

Ph: 310-449-3205
Fax: 310-276-8310

Ridley Scott
Scott Free
634 N La Peer Dr
West Hollywood, CA 90069
Ph: 310-360-2250
Fax: 310-288-4545

Robert Zemeckis
Gelfand, Rennert & Feldman
1880 Century Park East, Suite 900
Los Angeles, CA 90067
Ph: 310-556-6652

Michael Bay
Bay Films
631 Colorado Ave
Santa Monica, CA 90401
Ph: 310-829-7799

Clint Eastwood
Malpaso Productions
Contact: Leonard Hirshan
William Morris Agency
151 El Camino Dr
Beverly Hills, CA 90212
Ph: 310-859-4224

Mel Gibson
Contact: Bruce Davey
c/o Icon Productions
808 Wilshire Blvd, 4th Floor
Santa Monica, CA 90401
Ph: 310-434-7400

Robert Redford
Contact: David O'Connor
c/o Creative Artists Agency (CAA)
9830 Wilshire Blvd
Beverly Hills, CA 90212
Ph: 310-288-4545

Francis Ford Coppola
American Zoetrope
916 Kearny St
San Francisco, CA 94133
Ph: 415-788-7500

Michael Mann
Contact: Richard Lovett
c/o Creative Artists Agency (CAA)
9830 Wilshire Blvd
Beverly Hills, CA 90212
Ph: 310-451-4150

Oliver Stone
Contact: Rick Nicita
c/o Creative Artists Agency (CAA)
9830 Wilshire Blvd
Beverly Hills, CA 90212
Ph: 310-451-4150

 BANKABLE INDEPENDENT DIRECTORS

Joel and Ethan Coen
Contact: Jim Berkus
c/o United Talent Agency
9560 Wilshire Blvd, Suite 500
Beverly Hills, CA 90212
Ph: 310-273-6700

Andy and Larry Wachowski
Contact: Dave Wirtschafter
c/o William Morris Agency
151 El Camino Dr
Beverly Hills, CA 90212
Ph: 310-274-7451

Bobby and Peter Farrelly
Contact: Bradley Thomas
325 Wilshire Blvd, Suite 201
Santa Monica, CA 90401

Ph: 310-319-2800
Fax: 310-319-2802

Quentin Tarantino
Contact: Mike Simpson
William Morris Agency
151 El Camino Dr
Beverly Hills, CA 90212
Ph: 310-859-4000

Lasse Hallstrom
Contact: De Blois Mejia & Co.
9171 Wilshire Blvd, Suite 541
Beverly Hills, CA 90210
Ph: 310-273-7769
Fax: 310-273-8965

Brian De Palma
Contact: Bart L. Fooden
c/o Reminick Aaron & Co., LLP
1430 Broadway, 17th Floor
New York, NY 10017-4037
Ph: 212-697-6900

Neil Jordan
c/o International Creative
    Management (ICM)
8942 Wilshire Blvd
Beverly Hills, CA 90211
Ph: 310-550-4000
Fax: 310-550-4100

Paul Thomas Anderson
Contact: John Lesher
c/o United Talent Agency
9560 Wilshire Blvd, Suite 500
Beverly Hills, CA 90212
Ph: 310-273-6700

Ang Lee
Contact: Tory Metzger
c/o Creative Artists Agency (CAA)
9380 Wilshire Blvd
Beverly Hills, CA 90212

Ph: 310-288-4545
Fax: 310-288-4800

Spike Jonze
Contact: Tory Metzger
c/o Creative Artists Agency (CAA)
9830 Wilshire Blvd
Beverly Hills, CA 90212
Ph: 310-288-4545
Fax: 310-288-4800

Spike Lee
c/o 40 Acres & a Mule Filmworks
75 S Elliot Pl, 3rd Floor
Brooklyn, NY 11217
Ph: 718-624-2974

James Ivory
c/o Merchant Ivory Productions
250 W 57th St, Suite 1825
New York, NY 10107
Ph: 212-582-8049

Kevin Smith
Contact: Gail Stanley
c/o View Askew Productions
3 Harding Rd
Red Bank, NJ 07701
Ph: 732-842-6933

Atom Egoyan
Contact: Robert Newman
c/o International Creative
    Management (ICM)
80 Niagara St
Toronto, ONT M5V 1C5 Canada
Ph: 310-550-4000
    416-703-2137

Richard Linklatter
Contact: Beth Swofford
c/o Creative Artists Agency (CAA)
9830 Wilshire Blvd
Beverly Hills, CA 90212
Ph: 310-288-4545

DEPARTMENT HEADS

"Hire Key People"

Procuring an excellent crew is not difficult. 🧳 ***To hire a superb crew all you need to do is hire four department heads.*** They, in turn, hire the remaining 20–30 crew members. Concern yourself only with hiring the four key people. They have Rolodexes loaded with crew who owe them favors. Once you've hired a department head, just tell him/her what you budgeted for each supporting crew person and have the key hire them.

The department heads are:

1. Director of Photography
2. Production Manager
3. Assistant Director
4. Production Designer

1. DIRECTOR OF PHOTOGRAPHY

This is the first person you hire. The director of photography (aka DP, DOP, or cinematographer) knows how to make a film. You don't. Hiring your DP is almost as important as acquiring a great script. Choose wisely.

The DP will get you a crew. Plus, he understands the mechanics of shooting film, including grades of film stock, the camera, lenses, camera movement, focal points, creative angles, and light and shadows, and will become the person you depend on to take you step-by-step through the post-production process.

Of course the DP should be a visual artist, but he is also the captain of your crew. He should be a leader with an amazing work ethic. You need a

PRODUCTION BUDGET

Title: "Your $1,000,000 Feature"   Executive Producer: _____

Producer: _____

Writer: _____   Director: _____

ACCOUNT NUMBER	DESCRIPTION	BUDGET
01-00	Producer	$10,000–$20,000
02-00	Writer/Script	$5,000–$10,000
03-00	Director	$10,000–$15,000
04-00	Cast/Actors	$6,000–$9,000 (+$25,000)
TOTAL ABOVE-THE-LINE (Pre-Production)		**$31,000–$54,000 (+$25,000)**
BELOW-THE-LINE		
5-00	Film Stock	$20,000–$40,000
6-00	Film Lab (Shoot)	$15,000–$30,000
7-00	Camera	$12,000–$30,000
8-00	Expendables	$2,000–$5,000
9-00	Sound Equipment	$6,000–$11,000
10-00	Sound Transfer	$3,000–$5,000
11-00	Light/Grip	$6,000–$24,000
12-00	Dolly	$2,000–$3,000
13-00	**Cinematographer**	**$10,000–$15,000**
14-00	**PM & AD**	**$14,500–$21,000**
15-00	**Production Designer**	**$6,000–$8,500**
16-00	Film Crew	
17-00	Art & Props	
18-00	Wardrobe & Makeup	
19-00	Permits	
20-00	Insurance	
21-00	Dailies	
22-00	FX/Stunts/Cars	
23-00	Locations	
24-00	Office & Paperwork	
25-00	Publicity	
26-00	Food	
TOTAL PRODUCTION BUDGET (In-the-Can)		
THE SHOOT (Total Above & Below)		
27-00	Film Edit	
28-00	Film Lab (Edit)	
29-00	Sound Edit	
30-00	ADR	
31-00	Foley	
32-00	Music/Score	
33-00	Mix (Re-record)	
34-00	Optical Transfer	
35-00	M&E	
THE EDIT (Post-Production)		
36-00	Titles	
37-00	Negative Cutting	
38-00	Film Lab (Answer Print)	
TOTAL PRODUCTION COSTS		

DP with a substantial body of work, great connections, and understands budget and time restrictions. If he doesn't, he can easily waste film, or take too long with setups and cost you time. You can't afford either.

It is imperative that your DP be excellent. And I beg you not to make the common first-timer's mistake of hiring a DP who is really only an AC (assistant cameraman). Here's what I mean. The camera crew consists of four people:

1. Director of Photography
2. Camera Operator
3. First Assistant Cameraman (first AC or focus puller)
4. Second Assistant Cameraman (second AC or clapper/loader)

A kid graduates from film school with a degree in cinematography and comes to Hollywood with a 16mm short. He quickly discovers that no one will hire him to shoot a 35mm feature. So, to pay rent, the first job he gets is at a camera rental facility as a gofer/driver or a maintenance assistant.

At the camera rental facility, as working DPs pick up camera packages for their shoots, the college grad introduces himself and asks for a job—as a second AC (aka second assistant cameraman or clapper/loader). This person's responsibility is to load magazines, work the slate (the clapper), and keep the camera reports.

The kid eventually hooks up with a DP, leaves the rental facility, becomes a second AC, and works on 20–30 shoots over two years, and—if he doesn't screw up—he eventually becomes a first AC (aka first assistant cameraman or focus puller). This person is in charge of focus and keeps the camera, magazines, and film gate clean and clear. He does this for two years, works on another 20–30 projects, and "pulls focus" on 1,000–10,000 shots. If all these shots are sharp and clear, he moves up the ladder to become a camera operator. This is the person who frames the shot, with or without the actor, for maximum dramatic effect.

After five or six years operating the camera, he is qualified to be a feature film DP. During this time he has worked on almost 100 projects and actively participated in 10,000–50,000 shots. This is the person you should hire.

Who to hire
Optimal: Hire a seasoned feature film DP who understands your budget restraints.

Next best: Hire a DP who has been working for five to seven years on rock videos, commercials, and industrials.

Not bad: Hire the camera operator who has been working for the feature film DP who refused your project because of budget restraints.

Who not to hire

A recent college graduate who has only shot 16mm shorts.

A seasoned DP who is used to big-budget shoots and who thinks your budget is too low.

Anyone who has shot only video, never film.

How to find a DP

Call the local film lab and ask for referrals.

Call the local camera rental facility and ask for referrals.

Call the local film commissioner and ask for referrals.

Once you've hired your DP, he will hire a crew of assistants (operator, first AC, and second AC) within 24 hours.

What to Pay

You'll need the DP for two or three weeks ($1,000/week) during pre-production and for three weeks ($2,000–$3,000/week) during production. Finally, you'll rely on him during the two or three months of post-production ($1,000/month), as your guide through each phase of editing and lab work. This totals:

$2,000–$3,000 (pre-production)
$6,000–$9,000 (production)
$2,000–$3,000 (post-production)
$10,000–$15,000

2. PRODUCTION MANAGER

With your script, shooting schedule, and DP in place, it's time to have a professional to double-check your work. This person is the production manager (PM or line producer). He will find the little details you missed by going through checklists, refining your budget, and evaluating your schedule.

The PM also is valuable for his Rolodex, to assemble a great crew at a modest cost. His knowledge of where to rent camera, light, and sound equipment; where to buy short ends film stock; and who to contact for inexpensive expendables can also save you thousands. And, should there be a problem on the set (equipment needed, location secured, etc.), the PM will make sure everyone is happy.

How to Find a PM

You can call film labs, camera rental facilities, and film commissioners for referrals. But, your DP, who will have worked with 10–15 PMs in the past, will be very specific about who he would like to work with.

What to Pay

You'll need the PM for one month of pre-production ($750–$1,000/week) to assemble a crew, find suppliers, secure locations, and oversee paperwork. During the three-week production ($1,500–$2,000/week), the PM makes sure everyone gets to the set on time, the scenes are shot, the overnight work of developing, printing, transfers, and dailies is accomplished, and the next day's schedule is prepared. During post-production the PM has little to do, except inventory and return all rented equipment ($1,000–$1,500 for one or two weeks) and transfer control to the post-production supervisor or the film editor.

$3,000–$4,000 (pre-production)
$4,500–$6,000 (production)
$2,000–$3,000 (post-production)
$9,500–$13,000

3. ASSISTANT DIRECTOR

Where the PM thinks about later today and tomorrow, the AD (assistant director) thinks about the next shot. The job of the assistant director is to assist the director. For example, when the director confers with the cast after each shot, the AD utilizes a stand-in and readies the next setup (camera, lights, dolly) for the director when he returns with the cast. Further, the AD handles call times to actors, maintains paperwork and time cards, supervises extras, and knows when to announce, "Quiet on the set" as he keeps the shoot on schedule.

How to Find an AD

Do the same thing you did to find your PM. Ask your DP for referrals. Plus, ask your PM if he knows of ADs he likes to work with.

> **IMPORTANT POINT**   You don't want your director to come with his own AD. This will make it harder for you to control the director (it's now two against one) if he goes over schedule. However, if you hire the AD, then, the AD being your employee, you have more control over the director— if you need to use it.

What to Pay

ADs get paid slightly less than PMs. You'll need an AD for only two weeks ($750–$1,000/week) of pre-production, three weeks of production ($1,000–$1,500/week), and for a few days during the wrap ($250/day) while everything is inventoried and returned.

$1,500–$2,000 (pre-production)
$3,000–$4,500 (production)
$500–$1,500 (wrap)
$5,000–$8,000

So your total for the PM ($9,500–$13,000) and the AD ($5,000–$8,000) is **$14,500–$21,000.**

4. PRODUCTION DESIGNER

The production designer (aka PD) manufactures the look of your film. He is part artist, part architect, and part carpenter. From mega-budget multi-location shoots to small one-location films, the production designer is responsible for every facet of the set from construction to design. The production designer is an artist who is resourceful in scouting materials, props, and locations that fit your budget. He should own a van or truck (for schlepping) and be ready to pick up a hammer and drill.

The production designer will have a three- to four-person staff that includes an art director, a set decorator, a prop master, and a gofer, all willing to rent, borrow, or steal whatever is needed to build and design the sets needed within your budget.

How to Find a Production Designer

First, get referrals from DPs and PMs. Also, try your local theater set designers. They will be ecstatic to have an operating title credit on a feature film as a production designer. Finally, department store window dressers know how to build visual environments on small budgets and will be even cheaper to hire.

What to Pay

The production designer is usually the first department head you hire who works full-time (70–90 hours/week). He must have his job done (sets designed and built) before the movie can be shot. Thus, the production designer is needed for at least four weeks of pre-production ($750–$1,000/week) and the three weeks ($1,000–$1,500/week) of the production. There is no need for a production designer during post-production.

$3,000–$4,000 (pre-production)
$3,000–$4,500 (production)
$6,000–$8,500

As you can see, $30,500 to $44,500 will hire a professional director of photography (**$10,000–$15,000**), production manager (**$9,500–$13,000**), assistant director (**$5,000–$8,000**), and production designer (**$6,000–$8,500**) for your movie.

The game plan is to first hire the DP, who will point you to a PM, who knows an AD, who all know PDs. Once the department heads are hired, the remaining crew members magically appear.

TO DO:

1. Get three recommendations (labs, film commissioner) for your DP.
2. Get three recommendations from your DP for your department heads.

BOOKS

Below-the-Line Talent
HCD staff, 400 pp., $75.00
Contains 6,000 crew and department head contacts with over 15,000 film listings throughout North America.

Job Descriptions
W. Hines, 342 pp., $27.95
Defines each crew and technician position with very specific job details.

Production Management
B. Cleve, 210 pp., $29.95
Explains the job of the production manager.

Surviving Production
D. Patz, 262 pp., $26.95
Also explains the job of the production manager.

The Film Director's Team
A. Silver and E. Ward, 248 pp., $19.95
Explains the job of the assistant director.

Cinematography
J. Mascelli, 251 pp., $29.95
Explains the job of the cinematographer.

Continuity Supervisor
A. Rowlands, 194 pp., $34.95
Explains the job of the script supervisor.

The Technique of the Professional Make-up Artist
V. Kehoe, 289 pp., $57.95
Explains the job of the makeup artist.

Art Direction for Film and Video
R. Olson, 143 pp., $31.95
Explains the job of the production designer.

What an Art Director Does
W. Preston, 190 pp., $21.95
Explains the job of the art director/production designer.

Production Design and Art Direction
P. Ettedgui, 209 pp., $41.95
A gift book. Explains the craft of the production designer with interviews loaded with 100s of photos.

The Filmmaker's Guide to Production Design
V. LoBrutto, 240 pp., $19.95
Explains how to turn a simple screenplay into a visual masterpiece.

Editing and Post-Production
D. McGrath, 186 pp., $39.95
A gift book. Explains the craft of the editor with 500 photos and numerous interviews.

 KEY PERSONNEL SOURCES

Production Managers (Union)
Contact: Directors Guild of America
Ask for: Directory of Members
110 W 57th St
New York, NY 10019
Ph: 212-581-0370
Fax: 212-581-1441
Web: www.DGA.org
7920 Sunset Blvd
Hollywood, CA 90038
Ph: 310-289-2000
Fax: 310-289-2029

Assistant Directors (Union)
Contact: Directors Guild of America
Ask for: Directory of Members
110 W 57th St
New York, NY 10019
Ph: 212-581-0370
Fax: 212-581-1441
Web: www.DGA.org
7920 Sunset Blvd
Los Angeles, CA 90046
Ph: 310-289-2000
Fax: 310-289-2029

Cinematographers (Union)
Contact: IATSE, Local 600
International Cinematographers
7715 Sunset Blvd, Suite 300
Los Angeles, CA 90046
Ph: 323-876-0160
Fax: 323-876-6383
80 Eighth Ave, 14th Floor
New York, NY 10011
Ph: 212-647-7300
Fax: 212-730-7809

Cinematographers (Union)
Contact: ASC
American Society of
   Cinematographers
1782 N Orange Dr
Los Angeles, CA 90046
Ph: 323-969-4333
Fax: 323-882-6391

Production Designers (Union)
Contact: IATSE, Local 876
Art Directors Guild
11969 Ventura Blvd, Suite 200
Studio City, CA 91604
Ph: 818-762-9995
Fax: 818-769-9997

Key Personnel (Non-union)
Contact: Independent Feature Project
Ask for: Resource Directory
IFP/West
8750 Wilshire Blvd, 2nd Floor
Beverly Hills, CA 90211
Ph: 310-475-4379
Fax: 310-432-1203
IFP/New York
104 W 29th St, 12th Floor
New York, NY 10001
Ph: 212-465-8200
Fax: 212-465-8525
IFP/North
401 N 3rd St, Suite 450
Minneapolis, MN 55401
Ph: 612-338-0871
Fax: 612-338-4747
IFP/South
210 2nd St
Miami Beach, FL 33139
Ph: 305-538-8242
IFP/Midwest
33 E Congress Pkwy, Room 505
Chicago, IL 60605
Ph: 312-435-1825
Fax: 312-435-1828

Non-union Key Personnel
Contact: AFC and respective area's film
   commissioner
Ask for: Referrals
Association of Film Commissioners
835 N Stanley Ave
Los Angeles, CA 90046
Ph: 323-852-4747
Fax: 323-852-4904
Web: www.aifc.org
(See chapter 31 for individual
commissions.)

PRODUCTION CREW

"Hire Crew"

Your staff will consist of four groups: (1) the above-the-line talent, (2) the department heads, (3) the film crew, and (4) the post-production personnel. In the previous chapters you learned how to secure the above-the-line talent and the department heads who in turn hire 25 individuals to comprise your fully staffed crew. Let's take a closer look at who hires the 25 crew members and what to pay them:

Crew Hired by the DP
1. Camera Operator
2. First Assistant Cameraman
3. Second Assistant Cameraman

Crew Hired by the PM
4. Sound Mixer
5. Boom Operator
6. Production Coordinator
7. Script Supervisor
8. Gaffer
9. Best Boy Electrician
10. Key Grip
11. Dolly Grip
12. Grip(s)
13. Key Makeup–Hairstylist
14. Assistant Makeup–Hairstylist

PRODUCTION BUDGET

Title: "Your $1,000,000 Feature"   Executive Producer: _____
                                     Producer: _____
Writer: _____   Director: _____

ACCOUNT NUMBER	DESCRIPTION	BUDGET
01-00	Producer	$10,000–$20,000
02-00	Writer/Script	$5,000–$10,000
03-00	Director	$10,000–$15,000
04-00	Cast/Actors	$6,000–$9,000 (+$25,000)
TOTAL ABOVE-THE-LINE (Pre-Production)		**$31,000–$54,000 (+$25,000)**
BELOW-THE-LINE		
5-00	Film Stock	$20,000–$40,000
6-00	Film Lab (Shoot)	$15,000–$30,000
7-00	Camera	$12,000–$30,000
8-00	Expendables	$2,000–$5,000
9-00	Sound Equipment	$6,000–$11,000
10-00	Sound Transfer	$3,000–$5,000
11-00	Light/Grip	$6,000–$24,000
12-00	Dolly	$2,000–$3,000
13-00	Cinematographer	$10,000–$15,000
14-00	PM & AD	$14,500–$21,000
15-00	Production Designer	$6,000–$8,500
16-00	**FILM CREW**	**$23,000–$35,500**
17-00	Art & Props	
18-00	Wardrobe & Makeup	
19-00	Permits	
20-00	Insurance	
21-00	Dailies	
22-00	FX/Stunts/Cars	
23-00	Locations	
24-00	Office & Paperwork	
25-00	Publicity	
26-00	Food	
TOTAL PRODUCTION BUDGET (In-the-Can)		
THE SHOOT (Total Above & Below)		
27-00	Film Edit	
28-00	Film Lab (Edit)	
29-00	Sound Edit	
30-00	ADR	
31-00	Foley	
32-00	Music/Score	
33-00	Mix (Re-record)	
34-00	Optical Transfer	
35-00	M&E	
THE EDIT (Post-Production)		
36-00	Titles	
37-00	Negative Cutting	
38-00	Film Lab (Answer Print)	
TOTAL PRODUCTION COSTS		

15. Wardrobe
16. Craft Service

Crew Hired by the Production Designer
17. Art Director
18. Set Decorator
19. Set Dresser
20. Prop Master

Crew Hired by the First AD
21. Second Assistant Director
22. Second Second Assistant Director
23–25. Production Assistants

1. Camera Operator ($2,000–$3,000): To save money, most low-budget shoots use a three-man camera crew, with the DP operating the camera. However, if your budget permits (and yours does), have a four-man camera crew (DP, operator, first AC, and second AC) and free the DP to focus on art (lighting, filters, etc.) rather than on operating the camera. Pay the camera operator $150/day to prep the camera (check out the gear), then $700–$900/week during the shoot, and $150/day to return the camera equipment.

2. First Assistant Cameraman ($1,500–$2,000): The first AC (aka focus puller) is needed for two or three days of camera prep at $100/day, then $500–$700/week during the shoot, with no wrap or post-production time required.

3. Second Assistant Cameraman ($1,000–$1,500): The second AC (aka clapper/loader) loads the magazine, slates each shot, and keeps the camera reports. Pay him $400–$500/week during the shoot. You will not need him during prep or post-production.

4. Sound Mixer ($0): Pay the sound mixer (already budgeted, chapter 21) $1,500–$2,000/week, which includes use of his sound gear. You'll need the sound mixer for three to four pre-production days and the three-week shoot.

5. Boom Operator ($0): The boom operator (already budgeted, chapter 21) is hired and paid by your sound mixer out of his fee ($1,500–$2,000/week) at a rate of $400–$500/week.

6. Production Coordinator ($2,000–$3,000): This is your guy or girl Friday (aka your office manager). You'll need the production coordinator for two to three weeks of pre-production at $300/week, then during the shoot at $400/week, with one week of wrap and one week of post-production at $300/week.

7. *Script Supervisor ($1,500–$2,000):* Another unsung hero on the film set, the script supervisor keeps the script notes (needed to expedite editing); is in charge of continuity (makes sure that everything from props to makeup match from shot to shot); and covers the director's ass (makes sure camera setups don't flop the I-line). You'll need the script supervisor for one pre-production week at $100/week, then at $500/week during the shoot, with two or three days of post-production at $100/day.

8. *Gaffer ($0):* His salary is included in the flat rate ($2,000–$3,000/week) you negotiate for the light-grip truck (chapter 22). The gaffer is needed for one pre-production week and for the shoot.

9. *Best Boy Electrician ($0):* The best boy is the gaffer's assistant, and is paid by the gaffer out of the flat rate for the use of his truck (chapter 22). Gaffers, on low-budget shoots, usually pay their best boy(s) $500–$700/week.

10. *Key Grip ($2,500–$3,500):* The key grip is in charge of the equipment (rigging, scaffolding, etc.) that holds or grips the lights. The key grip will be needed during pre-production, depending on the amount of rigging, for one to three weeks at $600/week, then for the shoot at $800/week.

11. *Dolly Grip ($1,500–$2,000):* He is the key grip's assistant. Rigging and scaffolding are heavy, and because you want camera movement, someone has to operate the heavy dolly. He is needed for the entire shoot at $500–$700/week.

12. *Grip(s) ($1,000–$2,000):* You need one or two extra grips, who are labor-intensive production assistants, to haul and rig lights for the production at $300/week.

13. *Key Makeup–Hairstylist ($2,000–$3,000):* You need this person for a pre-production week at $100–$150/day, assuming actors have been selected, and during the shoot at $600/week. You might pay an additional $50–$150/week for the use and resupply of his makeup "kit."

14. *Assistant Makeup–Hairstylist ($500–$1,000):* The assistant is needed for the shoot at $200–$300/week. Although he/she will be willing to do it for just a film credit and experience, I advise you to pay him. Paying someone, even if a token salary, is the best way to make sure that they show up on time every day. You can find extra assistants at the local makeup or beauty school.

15. *Wardrobe ($2,000–$3,000):* You need the wardrobe head (aka costume designer) during pre-production, once actors have been cast. This

person designs each character's wardrobe, then rents, purchases, or makes the costumes and ensures that they fit. He will be paid $300–$400/week during pre-production and $500–$700/week during the shoot.

16. *Craft Service ($500–$1,000):* This is the first person on the set each morning. He makes coffee (remember, no one works until they see coffee perked), prepares a continental breakfast (juice, muffins, fruit, yogurt, etc.), and resupplies the snack table at $250–$300/week. It's wise to give him one day to shop at $100, and then one day at $100 during wrap to return rented or borrowed items such as tables, mini-fridges, coffee urns, chairs, etc.

17. *Art Director ($2,500–$3,000):* The production designer's first assistant is called the art director. He's hired by the production designer and is needed for four pre-production weeks and the shoot at $400–$500/week.

18–19. *Set Decorator and Dresser:* See production assistants.

20. *Prop Master ($1,500–$2,500):* Once the assistant director breaks down the script during early pre-production, you will obtain a list of props. The prop master, hired by the production designer, will get these items and have a van to store them in. You need him for two weeks of pre-production at $300–$400/week and $400–$600/week during the shoot.

21. *Second Assistant Director ($500–$1,000):* This will probably be an extremely efficient production assistant who, thanks to his dependability and organizational skills, you've bumped up to the better position and title. He will be in charge of call sheets, paperwork, and crowd control during scenes with extras. Pay him $250–$300/week during the shoot.

22. *Second Second Assistant Director:* See production assistants.

23–25. *Production Assistants ($500–$2,000):* The production assistants (PAs or Gofers) are your only recent-college-grad employees. Each is assigned to a department head and sometimes given a nicer title like set decorator, set dresser, second second assistant director, etc. However, be sure to hire only those who ask, "How high?" when you say, "Jump." You do not want PAs who think they can make films better than you can. You'll need two to four PAs during the shoot at $150/week each. Plus, save $2,000–$3,000 by hiring only PAs who have a pickup or van. Why rent them when the PAs bring them for free?

This is your 25-person crew. Only the PAs, an assistant makeup person, the second AD, and a third grip will possibly be first-timers. All others will be professionals with numerous shoots under their belts. Your total payroll will be **$23,000–$35,500.**

HOW DO YOU PAY A CREW?

There are three ways to pay:

1. Salary
2. Cash (independent contracting)
3. Salary and deferrals

Salary

Negotiate a weekly fee, set up a payroll system (withholding tax, etc.) and pay accordingly.

Independent Contracting

This will save bookkeeping costs and additional payroll taxes. You and the crew member agree upon a weekly, monthly, or project rate. Pay accordingly, without making deductions for state and federal taxes, Social Security, or Medicare. The independent contractor pays his/her own withholding taxes and the contractor—you or your company—files a 1099 IRS form. It is important to consult with an attorney and/or an accountant about who is and who isn't considered an "independent contractor."

Salary and Deferrals

The procedure of combining salary and deferrals, although not recommended, is commonly used by first-timers. Beginning producers always feel that to attract competent talent, they must pay large salaries. They accomplish this illusion by offering a deferral agreement, in which a predetermined amount is paid at a later date.

A first-time filmmaker, hearing that a director should get $10,000 a week, a DP $6,000 a week, an actor $5,000 a week, etc., feels compelled to match that salary. However, knowing that these amounts are unavailable to him, the inexperienced producer tells the director that he'll get $10,000/week: $3,000 in cash, and $7,000/week deferred. The DP is told he'll be paid $6,000/week: $1,000 cash and $5,000 deferred. The cycle continues until hundreds of thousands of dollars are built up in deferrals.

The upside of deferrals is that cast and crew feel more appreciated. The downside is that if you're not extremely careful, you will encumber the sale of your finished project to a distributor because the outstanding deferrals, which are actually debts, could be ridiculously high.

> IMPORTANT POINT   If you use deferrals with crew, be sure to state that deferrals will be paid out of profits. This sounds fair. However, when you write the employment contract, use the phrase "net producer's profits" in the place of the more generic "profits." The reason is that there probably won't be profits, there likely won't be net profits, and there very likely won't be net producer profits. In effect, you'll owe them nothing, even though the film got made, distributed, and earned revenues.
>
> Finally, a word to the wise: Based on years of hiring non-union, low-budget crews, I recommend not using deferrals. It merely complicates matters. I discovered that I can hire the same person whether I say, "I'll pay you $2,000 a week; $600 in cash, with $1,400 deferred," or simply say, "I know what you're worth. If you're not doing anything for the next one to three weeks please help me. . . . But I only have $600 a week." I have always gotten the employee I wanted, if he/she was available, without the bullshit and the complications created by using deferrals.
>
> However, I realize that most first-timers are insecure about negotiating with crew and talent. Therefore, if necessary, use deferrals, but be sure to define "deferred" as being until the film makes "net producer profits."

Below-the-line crew are everywhere. They are in every city and state. They are looking for opportunities. Just call the local film commissioner. Get the respective production directory. Budget what you can pay, and don't be embarrassed if it is a low number. For **$23,000–$35,500** you will be able to obtain a 25-person professional crew for your production. Don't pay more!

TO DO:

1. Get an independent contractor's form and IRS regulations for 1099 employees.
2. Get the union (IATSE) rate card and use the recommended low-budget wages as a reference point.

BOOKS

Gaffers, Grips, and Best Boys
E. Taub, 276 pp., $15.95
Outlines each crew position and
explains their specific daily functions.

Job Descriptions
W. Hines, 342 pp., $27.95
Defines each crew and technician po-
sition with very specific job details.

Below-the-Line Talent
HCD staff, 400+ pp., $80.00
Lists 6,000 crew and department head
contacts with over 15,000 film listings.

 **HIRING
SOURCES**

Camera Operator (Union and
   non-union)
Assistant Cameramen (Union and
   non-union)
Contact: SOC
Society of Operating Cameramen
PO Box 2006
Toluca Lake, CA 91610
Ph: 818-382-7070

Sound Technician (Union)
Boom Operator (Union)
Contact: IATSE, Local 695
5439 Cahuenga Blvd
North Hollywood, CA 91601
Ph: 818-985-9204
Fax: 818-985-9204

Script Supervisor (Union)
Production Coordinator (Union)

Contact: IATSE, Local 871
11519 Chandler Blvd
North Hollywood, CA 91601
Ph: 818-509-7871
Fax: 818-506-1555

Grips (Union)
Contact: IATSE, Local 80
2520 W Olive Ave
Burbank, CA 91505
Ph: 818-526-0700
Fax: 800-994-1080

Gaffers (Union)
Lighting Technicians (Union)
Contact: IATSE, Local 728
14629 Nordhoff St
Panorama City, CA 91402
Ph: 818-891-0728
Fax: 818-891-5288

Makeup and Hairstylist (Union)
Contact: IATSE, Local 706
828 Hollywood Way
Burbank, CA 91505
Ph: 818-295-3933
Fax: 818-295-3930

Wardrobe and Costumers (Union)
Contact: IATSE, Local 705
1427 N La Brea Ave
Hollywood, CA 90028
Ph: 323-851-0220
Fax: 323-851-9062

Editors (Union)
Contact: IATSE, Local 700
7715 Sunset Blvd, Suite 200
Los Angeles, CA 90046
Ph: 323-876-4770
Fax: 323-876-0861

Stuntmen (Union and non-union)
Contact: Stuntmen's Association of
   Motion Pictures

10660 Riverside Dr, 2nd Floor, Suite E
Toluca Lake, CA 91602
Ph: 818-766-4334
Fax: 818-766-5943

Stuntwomen (Union and non-union)
Contact: Stuntwomen's Association of
   Motion Pictures
12457 Ventura Blvd, Suite 506
Studio City, CA 91604
Ph: 818-762-0907
Fax: 818-762-9534

Non-union Crew
Contact: Any IFP office
Ask for: Crew Referral Database
(See chapter 26.)

Non-union Crew
Contact: Respective area's film
   commissioner
Ask for: Referrals
Association of Film Commissioners

835 N Stanley Ave
Los Angeles, CA 90046
Ph: 323-852-4747
Fax: 323-852-4904
(See chapter 31 for individual
   commissions.)

Canadian Crew (Union)
Contact: ACFC
Association of Canadian Film
   Craftspeople
3993 Henning Dr, Suite 108
Burnaby, BC V5C 6P7 Canada
Ph: 604-299-2232
Fax: 604-299-2243

English Crew (Union)
Contact: BECTU
Broadcasting, Entertainment,
   Cinematograph and Theatre Union
111 Wardour St
London W1F 0AY England
Ph: 44-207-437-8506
Fax: 44-207-437-8268

WHAT TO EXPECT

"Get Ready for the Shoot"

PRE–PRODUCTION (WHAT TO EXPECT)

Get ready for eighteen ball-busting, mind-numbing 18-hour days. Here's why. You can't manufacture daylight. Therefore, if you want your first shot when it's light at 7 A.M., you wake everyone at 5 A.M. to be at the set and working by 6 A.M. You shoot until 7 P.M. when it's dark. Then you have two to three hours of preparation for tomorrow and an hour or two of dailies. This is an 18-hour day during production. Now do this every day for three weeks. Whew!

During pre-production your work schedule will be 8–10 hour days until the last week of pre-production, when the 10–12 hour days commence until the shoot, when exhaustive 18-hour days take over. I hope you're ready for this! In pre-production you're consumed with checking and double-checking everything, including:

- Locations secured and prepared, and property releases signed
- Production board and shooting schedule prepared
- Camera package rented and picked up
- Light-grip truck/equipment rented and picked up
- Sound equipment rented and picked up, and tape stock purchased
- Expendables purchased and inventoried
- Film stock purchased and refrigerated
- Film lab contracted with prices in writing
- Sound transfers contracted with prices in writing
- Permits and insurance finalized

- Insurance certificates faxed to suppliers and locations
- Actors committed, rehearsed, and signed to deal memos
- Wardrobe, props, and makeup selected and obtained
- Crew hired, committed, and signed to deal memos
- Location(s) scouted by department heads
- Storyboard and shot list finalized
- Cast and crew list prepared and distributed
- Sets designed and dressings and props secured
- Caterer chosen, menus reviewed, and contract signed
- Production notebooks handed out

WEEKEND PRIOR TO THE SHOOT

Friday morning, have the "cast meeting" along with the department heads, hair, makeup, and wardrobe personnel. Have the actors read the script from beginning to end. Hearing the lines spoken creates a visual image for the department heads. Each and every scene will be dissected to make sure everyone has every last thing they need. Your production coordinator will take notes and makes a final to-do list.

Friday afternoon, have a "crew meeting" with everyone from department heads to the last production assistant. Each department head brings his/her production notebook, and the script will be reviewed in the scheduled shooting order. Each department head states his special needs and discusses assistance needed from other departments. Once again the production coordinator takes notes and prepares another final to-do list.

Friday evening, have a complete "cast and crew meeting," where everyone meets. This meeting should have a buffet; this is really a "getting acquainted" party. Everyone schmoozes, checks out each other's bods and wedding bands, and shares a couple of laughs as the production coordinator distributes a photocopied cast and crew (C&C) list that includes everyone's pager and phone number(s), a list of vendors and suppliers, and maps to each shooting location with driving directions from north, east, west, and south.

The next day you meet with the production coordinator to check and double-check again. The locations are secured and dressed. The equipment has been picked up. The crew knows where to go. Everything is ready—or so it appears. Then on the next day, the quiet before the storm, there is nothing left to do but relax, go to sleep, and dream about tomorrow—the first day of your shoot.

FIRST DAY OF THE SHOOT (WHAT TO DO)

Craft service arrives first and prepares coffee and breakfast, then hair and makeup arrive, then actors get their cup of java and go for makeup. Then camera crew. Then light crew. Then sound crew. One by one they arrive. The key to getting your film made is to take things one step at a time. Don't think your film to death. You have done your pre-planning, you're organized, the sets are built, the actors rehearsed, the crew is ready—so shoot the film! Get the first shot but always make sure that 🧳 *the first shot every day is a simple master shot, possibly with a simple dolly movement.*

Have the actors walk through their lines once.
Place the camera in position on a tripod or dolly.
Block for the master shot.
Do a technical run-through.
The director nods ready.
The AD calls, "Last looks."
The script supervisor announces scene and take numbers.
The sound mixer repeats scene and take numbers.
The director nods to the AD that he's ready.
The AD yells, "Quiet on the set!"
When all is quiet, the AD asks, "Sound ready?"
Sound replies, "Sound is ready."
The AD then yells, "Roll sound!"
The sound mixer yells, "Speed!"
The AD then yells, "Roll camera!"
The second AC holds the slate in front of the camera.
The camera operator or first AC turns on the camera and says, "Camera rolling."
The AD says, "Mark it!" and the second AC "claps" the slate.
The director calls, "Action!"
The actors perform their lines.
The dolly moves.
The director observes and calls, "Cut!"

EVERY OTHER DAY (WHAT TO ACCOMPLISH)

First call will be at sunrise, usually 6:00 A.M., which means everyone wakes up at 5:00 to shower and drive to the set (at least for the first few days; after that, showers seem to be given less priority). You power through, achieve 25–35 shots by moving the equipment every 20–25 minutes.

"Cut!" is announced at the end of each shot. The three people who can say "Cut" during filming are the director, the camera operator, and/or the soundman. The director will always call "Cut" when the shot is finished to his satisfaction. Then again, the director may call "Cut" if the take isn't to his liking—due to performance, framing, camera movement, etc. The camera operator and soundman also have the authority to call "Cut" should the camera jam, or if there is a "rollout" (the film in the magazine has run out), or if the boom is not properly placed, or a disruptive sound is detected—but not because they don't like the performance. That is the sole privilege of the director.

"Print" is announced at the end of each shot if the director feels it is good enough to have the lab print it. The second AC pencils a circle around the shot number on the camera report. This is called a "circle take," and you can save money at the film lab by only processing the "circle takes" (the good performances) rather than printing everything.

"Wrap" is called after you've gotten your last shot. What dictates the last shot is inevitably the sun. Daylight is the only thing that can't be manufactured. Thus, max out your daylight hours and keep shooting until sunset. Then, assuming no night shots are scheduled, you call "Wrap." But just because you've called "Wrap" doesn't mean that the day is over. You still make sure that:

- (Security) Department heads secure and lock up all valuable equipment.
- (Scheduling) The director and script supervisor are on schedule (pages covered) and the production coordinator distributes "call sheets" (call times, locations, scenes scheduled, and special needs) for the next day's shoot.
- (Film stock) All the film stock is accounted for.
- (Film processing) All of the day's exposed film stock is sent to the lab, with camera reports (with circle takes), and yesterday's processed film is ready for viewing.
- (Paperwork) All forms (call sheets, camera report, sound report, script notes, releases, contracts, etc.) have been completed, distributed, and/or filed.

- (Syncing) The day's sound is taken to the sound transfer facility and yesterday's transfers are picked up and brought to the editing room for syncing.
- (Organizing) The production manager/line producer has double-checked to make sure that the next day's location(s) is available.
- (Financial coordinating) All petty cash spent is accounted for.
- (Production planning) All department heads, after receiving their call sheets, check the script breakdowns for the next day's needs.
- (Actors availabilities) All actors are available and have their call times.

FIRST, SECOND, AND THIRD WEEKS

Despite the long hours, expect the first week of your shoot to be filled with excitement. I call the first week the "Fun Week." By the second week, the "Zombie Week," after six 18-hour days, everyone is exhausted. The crew has become the walking dead, so expect to use all of your motivational skills to keep up a 25–35 shots/day schedule. As burnt out as you feel, you must be the most together person on the set.

The final week, the third week, everyone is beyond burnout. Nerves are frazzled. Every crew person hates you. Nobody sits at your table during lunch. Filmmaking is no longer glamorous. The excitement and enthusiasm is long gone. By this time everyone has had some sort of argument, conflict, or gripe that has gone unanswered or unfulfilled. Yet they don't quit, because they are going to make a film either "to spite you" or "in spite of you." I call this the "Hell Week."

Twenty-five to thirty-five shots a day is an extremely difficult job for even the most experienced crew, let alone the low-budget crew you've assembled. Fall behind schedule, and your film will be unfinished and useless. So keep the camera moving, keep the crew jumping, keep the takes to a minimum while getting a master and the best coverage you can, and understand that to do this, you will become something of a tyrant.

TO DO:

1. Take vitamins. Get into shape. You'll need energy and stamina.
2. Check the amount of film exposed each day—don't run out.
3. Make an end-of-the-day checklist, and stick to it.

BOOKS

Rebel Without a Crew
R. Rodriguez, 285 pp., $14.00
How a 23-year-old produced *El Mari-achi* for $7,000 and became a
Hollywood player. A fun read.

*The Beginning Filmmaker's Guide to a
   Successful First Film*
R. Harmon, 183 pp., $15.95
Takes you through the process of pro-
ducing and/or directing your first film.

Low-Budget Films That Sell
R. Harmon, 153 pp., $12.95
An introduction to the ins and outs of
successful low-budget production.

Feature Filmmaking at Used-Car Prices
R. Schmidt, 409 pp., $16.95
An excellent book! How to write, produce, direct, shoot, edit, and promote
a feature film for under $15,000.

*Hollywood on $5,000, $10,000 or
   $25,000 a Day*
P. Gaines and D. Rhodes, 147 pp.,
$11.95
The survival guide for low-budget
filmmakers.

The Guerilla Film Maker's Handbook
C. Jones and G. Jolliffe, 640 pp., $34.95
A must! The ultimate guide to
independent filmmaking. Comes with
free filmmaking software, forms, and
contracts.

The Filmmaker's Handbook
S. Ascher and E. Pincus, 614 pp., $20.00

Technically details each mechanical
step of making your film.

 VIDEOS

Basic Shooting
VHS, 30 minutes, $22.95
The A–Z of video shooting.

Advanced Shooting
VHS, 30 minutes, $22.95
Shot sheets, lenses/filters,
exposure/shutter, camera moves,
composition, etc.

 **TOP FEMALE
DIRECTORS**

Barbra Streisand
Contact: Jeff Berg
c/o International Creative
   Management (ICM)
8942 Wilshire Blvd
Beverly Hills, CA 90211
Ph: 310-550-4000

Penny Marshall
Contact: Jim Wiatt
c/o William Morris Agency (WMA)
151 El Camino Dr
Beverly Hills, CA 90212
Ph: 310-274-7451

Jodi Foster
Contact: Meg Lefauve
c/o Egg Pictures
5555 Melrose Ave
Jerry Lewis Building Annex
Los Angeles, CA 90038
Ph: 323-956-8400

Nora Ephron
Contact: Sam Cohn
c/o International Creative
    Management (ICM)
40 W 57th St
New York, NY 10019
Ph: 212-556-5600

Kathryn Bigelow
Contact: Ken Stovitz
c/o Creative Artists Agency (CAA)
9830 Wilshire Blvd
Beverly Hills, CA 90212
Ph: 310-288-4545

Mimi Leder
Contact: Byrdie Lifson Pompan
c/o Creative Artists Agency (CAA)
9830 Wilshire Blvd
Beverly Hills, CA 90212
Ph: 310-288-4545

Jane Campion
Contact: Vicky Harper
c/o HLA Management
PO Box 1536
Strawberry Hills, NSW, 2012 Australia
Ph: 61-2-29310-4948

Diane Keaton
Contact: John Burnham
c/o William Morris Agency (WMA)
151 El Camino Dr
Beverly Hills, CA 90212
Ph: 310-274-7451

Amy Heckerling
Contact: Ken Stovitz
c/o Creative Artists Agency (CAA)
9830 Wilshire Blvd
Beverly Hills, CA 90212
Ph: 310-288-4545

Betty Thomas
Contact: Brian Lourd
c/o Creative Artists Agency (CAA)
9830 Wilshire Blvd
Beverly Hills, CA 90212
Ph: 310-288-4545

Sue Seidelman
Contact: Gail Pearl
c/o William Morris Agency (WMA)
1325 Ave of the Americas
New York, NY 10019
Ph: 212-586-5100

Allison Anders
Contact: Shana Eddy
c/o United Talent Agency (UTA)
9560 Wilshire Blvd, Suite 500
Beverly Hills, CA 90212
Ph: 310-273-6700

Randa Haines
Contact: David Wirtschafter
c/o William Morris Agency (WMA)
151 El Camino Dr
Beverly Hills, CA 90212
Ph: 310-274-7451

Martha Coolidge
Contact: Robert Stein
c/o William Morris Agency (WMA)
151 El Camino Dr
Beverly Hills, CA 90212
Ph: 310-274-7451

Mira Nair
Contact: Bart Walker
c/o International Creative
    Management (ICM)
40 W 57th St
New York, NY 10019
Ph: 212-556-5600

Penelope Spheeris
Contact: David Gersh
c/o The Gersh Agency
232 N Canon Dr
Beverly Hills, CA 90210
Ph: 310-274-6611

Gillian Armstrong
Contact: Beth Swofford
c/o Creative Artists Agency (CAA)
9830 Wilshire Blvd
Beverly Hills, CA 90212
Ph: 310-288-4545

Sally Potter
Contact: Alexandra Cann
    Representation
c/o Principle Agency
12 Abingdon Rd
London, England
Ph: 44-207-938-4002

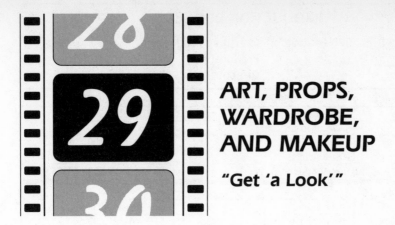

ART, PROPS, WARDROBE, AND MAKEUP

"Get 'a Look'"

Pretty sets make pretty pictures and realistic sets create realistic drama. 🔲 *Well-dressed sets and actors have as much to do with the "look" of a film as do cameras and lights.* You desire your film to be visually distinctive. This "look" comes from the design of the sets and actors.

The production designer is responsible for "the look," or the overall visual design, of your film. He chooses colors, moods, and themes for the physical sets to enhance the story. The production designer researches the time period, the location, the economic status, the professions, etc. of the script's characters. He scouts locations and determines whether to rent a small soundstage and build one-, two-, and three-wall movable sets. He brings the cinematographer and gaffer to each of the live locations he might use to discuss lighting. The production designer draws up his budget, gets approval from the director (artistically) and the producer (financially), and proceeds to build the sets.

WHAT "THE LOOK" WILL COST—SETS AND PROPS

What your art and prop budget includes is:

1. Nominal travel (car, gas, etc.)
2. Drawings/sketches (paper, pencil, and time)
3. Set construction (building materials, one-wall, two-wall flats, etc.)
4. Prop rentals (cell phones, lighters, guns, etc.)
5. Set dressings (furniture, draperies, paintings, plants, etc.)

PRODUCTION BUDGET

Title: "Your $1,000,000 Feature"   Executive Producer: _____

Producer: _____

Writer: _____   Director: _____

ACCOUNT NUMBER	DESCRIPTION	BUDGET
01-00	Producer	$10,000–$20,000
02-00	Writer/Script	$5,000–$10,000
03-00	Director	$10,000–$15,000
04-00	Cast/Actors	$6,000–$9,000 (+$25,000)
TOTAL ABOVE-THE-LINE (Pre-Production)		$31,000–$54,000 (+$25,000)
BELOW-THE-LINE		
5-00	Film Stock	$20,000–$40,000
6-00	Film Lab (Shoot)	$15,000–$30,000
7-00	Camera	$12,000–$30,000
8-00	Expendables	$2,000–$5,000
9-00	Sound Equipment	$6,000–$11,000
10-00	Sound Transfer	$3,000–$5,000
11-00	Light/Grip	$6,000–$24,000
12-00	Dolly	$2,000–$3,000
13-00	Cinematographer	$10,000–$15,000
14-00	PM & AD	$14,500–$21,000
15-00	Production Designer	$6,000–$8,500
16-00	Film Crew	$23,000–$35,500
17-00	**ART & PROPS**	**$5,000–$9,000**
18-00	**WARDROBE & MAKEUP**	**$3,000–$5,000**
19-00	Permits	
20-00	Insurance	
21-00	Dailies	
22-00	FX/Stunts/Cars	
23-00	Locations	
24-00	Office & Paperwork	
25-00	Publicity	
26-00	Food	
TOTAL PRODUCTION BUDGET (In-the-Can)		
THE SHOOT (Total Above & Below)		
27-00	Film Edit	
28-00	Film Lab (Edit)	
29-00	Sound Edit	
30-00	ADR	
31-00	Foley	
32-00	Music/Score	
33-00	Mix (Re-record)	
34-00	Optical Transfer	
35-00	M&E	
THE EDIT (Post-Production)		
36-00	Titles	
37-00	Negative Cutting	
38-00	Film Lab (Answer Print)	
TOTAL PRODUCTION COSTS		

6. Picture vehicles (any car driven by a character on camera)
7. Signage (printing, posters, photos, etc.)

The wrong way to approach a production designer is to ask, "What do you need?" You're naive. You're asking for it and you'll get a laundry list of everything under the sun that you can't afford. This ain't *Gone With the Wind.* Simply pick an affordable dollar amount and tell the production designer, "That's your budget. What can you do for that?" Stand back and watch how creative he becomes.

Let's say your film takes place at three locations: a suburban house, a bowling alley, and a restaurant. When these locations are found, you'll probably want to replace the furnishings. You'll change the living room or redesign the bedroom. You might decide the bathroom is too small to accommodate a camera and crew, so you'll rent a 1,000-foot soundstage and build a two-wall bathroom set. This involves paying for carpenters, as well as materials. You may find a bowling alley you like, but it will look contemporary, and your film takes place in the 1950s. That's gonna cost some bucks. The restaurant might look perfect, but you'll have to make up a few menus and rent neon signs for the windows. More bucks.

With a $250,000–$500,000 budget you can't permit the production designer to have carte blanche. Pick an amount of money you can afford, which does not include his/her salary, and allocate it wisely. Be sure to get a production designer who is able to beg, borrow, and steal creatively. Budget **$5,000–$9,000** for sets and props.

PRODUCTION DESIGN TIPS

Product placement: Companies called product placement agencies specialize in getting consumer products into movies. It is no accident that the hero in that mega-budget movie wears Ray•Bans, uses a Motorola cell phone, drinks Coke, and drives a BMW. Corporations think of product placement as advertising and pay producers up to $150,000 for a five-second logo spot. A typical Schwarzenegger or Stallone movie has 15–20 products strategically placed to be seen for several seconds. These 15–20 logo IDs of Coke cans, or Sony TV sets, or Snickers candy bars can bring $2–$3 million in added revenue.

Be wary, though. It's not as easy as it sounds. Questions a product placement agency will want answered are, "What's your budget?" and "Who's your distributor?" and "How many prints are they making?" You're an independent. You don't have a distributor. And, even if you did have one, your film won't be a major release (1,500–6,000 prints), like Sly and Arnie's films. You will be lucky to get a distributor to release your films with 20–50 prints.

If your film isn't a major studio release then a product placement agency won't pay $150,000 to show a can of Coke for a five-second logo ID. What you will be able to get from Coca-Cola is ten to twenty cases of free soda for your crew. Product placement agencies can also get you props for free that you otherwise would have to buy or rent.

You can find Product placement agencies listed in *The Blu-Book,* an annual directory published by the *Hollywood Reporter.* A lot of companies handle product placement requests in-house, as well. Call corporate headquarters and ask for the marketing department.

Studio rentals: Every movie lot (Warner Bros., Paramount, etc.) and TV studio (ABC, NBC, etc.) has a prop department where it stores the props and set dressings used for previous movies and TV shows. You'll be surprised how inexpensively you can rent them.

Student films: Try the old, "But I'm just a student filmmaker" on anyone you're trying to buy or rent props from. This usually gets you a reduced rate from prop rental facilities and costume houses.

Film commissioners: Your local film commissioner will be very helpful when scouting locations. They always have notebooks full of photos of homes, restaurants, and buildings that the locals want filmmakers to rent. The film commissioner can also help secure a park or municipal building from the city, county, or state.

WARDROBE

Once you have hired the production designer, he will know, based on the salaries you've provided, whom to hire as the wardrobe and makeup heads. Both will probably need an assistant.

The wardrobe head (or costume designer) will read the script and itemize how many costumes each character needs, and make a wardrobe checklist. After the actors are cast, he will get their sizes or measurements, and either rent costumes, buy them, or make them.

Also be aware that during the shoot there are dry cleaning charges—invariably you will pay rush charges. Remember, if you are doing any scene with water or effects, you need two identical wardrobes if you shoot two takes. Shoot three takes, three identical costumes will be needed.

Renting, buying, sewing, and dry cleaning are not free. Budget **$2,000–$3,000** for wardrobe.

MAKEUP

Makeup is not free either. Every makeup person has his own makeup kit. The issue, however, is who pays for the actual supplies—the creams, the lotions, the pads, etc. What I've discovered is that if you tell the makeup person you will give him $700/week to include use of his supplies, he skimps on applying makeup. However, if you pay him $600/week and give him a $100/week allowance for makeup (still totaling $700/week) he won't skimp, and will feel much freer in designing and applying makeup.

A hidden makeup and wardrobe cost is Polaroids—the instant camera. Although the camera is cheap, the film is expensive (about $1 per shot). Each time actors are made up and/or dressed in costume, they have their photos taken by both wardrobe and makeup. You will have to match that actor's makeup and wardrobe for scenes that are shot days later. Allocate **$1,000–$2,000** for makeup and Polaroid film.

The total cost for art, props, wardrobe, and makeup will be **$8,000–$14,000.** The production designer will budget and oversee the disbursement of this money to the individual departments.

Art and Props	$5,000–$9,000
Wardrobe	$2,000–$3,000
Makeup and Film	$1,000–$2,000
	$8,000–$14,000

TO DO:

1. Call your local TV station. Ask about using their sets and props.
2. Check your film commissioner's location books.

BOOKS

Hair, Makeup & Styling Career Guide
C. Wright, 380 pp., $39.95
Besides describing how to launch a
career, it details the craft of the
hair–makeup person.

*The Technique of the Professional
Make-up Artist*
V. Kehoe, 289 pp., $57.95
Excellent how-to book on the nuts
and bolts of professional makeup.

TV Scenic Design
G. Millerson, 265 pp., $49.95
Details the art and craft of designing
and building film and stage sets.

Costume Design 101
R. La Motte, 178 pp., $19.95
Explains the art and business of
costume design for film and television.

*Designer Drafting for the Entertainment
World*
P. Woodbridge, 365 pp., $54.95
The definitive textbook for design
and drafting of sets for film, stage,
and television.

*The Filmmaker's Guide to Production
Design*
V. LoBrutto, 240 pp., $19.95
An indispensable resource that
explains the nuts and bolts of design-
ing sets cost-effectively.

What an Art Director Does
W. Preston, 191 pp., $21.95
An excellent introduction to motion
picture production design.

Art Direction for Film and Video
R. Olson, 144 pp., $24.95
Dispenses a very good introduction
into the craft of the production
designer.

 **PROP RENTALS
AND PRODUCT
PLACEMENT**

STUDIO PROP RENTALS

Sony Pictures Studios
Attn: Prop Department
5300 Alla Rd
Los Angeles, CA 90066
Ph: 310-244-5999
Fax: 310-244-0999

Universal Studios
Attn: Prop Department
100 Universal City Plz
Universal City, CA 91608
Ph: 818-777-2784
Fax: 818-866-0293

Walt Disney Studios
Attn: Prop Department
500 S Buena Vista St
Burbank, CA 91521
Ph: 818-560-1191
Fax: 818-566-7451

Warner Bros. Studios
Attn: Prop Department
4000 Warner Blvd
Burbank, CA 91522
Ph: 818-954-2181
Fax: 818-954-4965

PRODUCT PLACEMENT
COMPANIES

Handler Public Relations
801 N Brand Ave, Suite 620
Glendale, CA 91203
Ph: 818-552-7300
Fax: 818-545-9116

Initiative Media-Promotion House
8544 Sunset Blvd
West Hollywood, CA 90069
Ph: 310-854-4887
Fax: 310-967-2450

Motion Picture Magic
17337 Ventura Blvd, Suite 120
Encino, CA 91316
Ph: 818-905-9814
Fax: 818-905-8560

Vista Group
805 S San Fernando Blvd
Burbank, CA 91502
Ph: 818-840-6789
Fax: 818-840-6880

AIM Productions
37-1135th Ave, Suite 3B
Astoria, NY 11101
Ph: 718-729-9288
Fax: 718-786-0137

George Fenmore, Inc.
250 W 54th St, Suite 712
New York, NY 10019
Ph: 212-977-4140
Fax: 212-977-4404

Impact Product Placement
62-54 97th Pl, Suite 14C
Rego Park, NY 11374
Ph: 718-271-5271
Fax: 718-699-4963

RENTAL STAGES

Century Studio Corporation
8660 Hayden Pl, Suite 100
Culver City, CA 90232
Attn: Gary Klimmer
Ph: 310-287-3600
Fax: 310-287-3608

GMT Studios
5751 Buckingham Pkwy
Culver City, CA 90230
Attn: Jennifer Harley
Ph: 310-649-3733
Fax: 310-216-0056

Hollywood Center Studios
1040 N Las Palmas
Los Angeles, CA 90038
Attn: Richard Schnyder
Ph: 323-860-0000
Fax: 323-860-8105

Raleigh Studios
5300 Melrose Ave
Hollywood, CA 90038
Attn: Mary Fry
Ph: 323-466-3111
Fax: 323-871-5600

Ren-Mar Studios
846 N Cahuenga Blvd
Hollywood, CA 90038
Attn: Carol Cassella
Ph: 323-463-0808
Fax: 323-465-8173

Silvercup Studios
42-22 22nd St
Long Island City, NY 11101
Attn: Lisa Sanchez
Ph: 718-906-2000
Fax: 718-906-2585

Broadway Stages
39-25 21st St
Long Island City, NY 11101
Attn: Jeanette Argento
Ph: 718-786-5428
Fax: 718-706-2433

City Stage
435 W 19th St
New York, NY 10011

Attn: Brian Coles
Ph: 212-627-3400
Fax: 212-633-1228

Shadow Studios
531 W 19th St
New York, NY 10011
Attn: Joe O'Brien
Ph: 212-691-1167
Fax: 212-691-1791

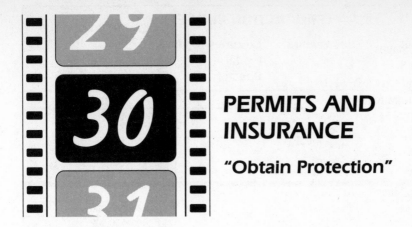

PERMITS AND INSURANCE

"Obtain Protection"

This chapter, on film permits and film insurance, will not be exciting or exotic, but that's the insurance business. Now don't get lazy and skip to an exciting chapter like film festivals or dealmaking. Read this chapter!

PERMITS

A film permit is basically a license to conduct a temporary business, a film production, in the city where you're about to shoot. Once you know the exact locations for your shoot, contact the local film commissioner to obtain one or information about how to obtain one. Even if you are shooting at your own house (your house is either in the city or the county), you are still obligated to obtain a film permit from the city or county.

What Permits Cost

Film permits vary from $25 to $4,000 per day, generally depending on the size of the community. Beware when a film commissioner says it's free to shoot in their state. 📁 *When film commissioners say the word "free," it's a lie.* Well, not a lie. Just misleading. Most film commissioners, to entice you to shoot in their region, claim there are no permit fees. What they mean is no daily fees. However, you still must pay for insurance (read on) and usually a police officer ($45–$85/hour) or two. Then this allegedly free permit gets expensive.

Also, in many cities you're required to notify in writing everyone within

PRODUCTION BUDGET

Title: "Your $1,000,000 Feature"   Executive Producer: _____

Producer: _____

Writer: _____   Director: _____

ACCOUNT NUMBER	DESCRIPTION	BUDGET
01-00	Producer	$10,000–$20,000
02-00	Writer/Script	$5,000–$10,000
03-00	Director	$10,000–$15,000
04-00	Cast/Actors	$6,000–$9,000 (+$25,000)
TOTAL ABOVE-THE-LINE (Pre-Production)		**$31,000–$54,000 (+$25,000)**
BELOW-THE-LINE		
5-00	Film Stock	$20,000–$40,000
6-00	Film Lab (Shoot)	$15,000–$30,000
7-00	Camera	$12,000–$30,000
8-00	Expendables	$2,000–$5,000
9-00	Sound Equipment	$6,000–$11,000
10-00	Sound Transfer	$3,000–$5,000
11-00	Light/Grip	$6,000–$24,000
12-00	Dolly	$2,000–$3,000
13-00	Cinematographer	$10,000–$15,000
14-00	PM & AD	$14,500–$21,000
15-00	Production Designer	$6,000–$8,500
16-00	Film Crew	$23,000–$35,500
17-00	Art & Props	$5,000–$9,000
18-00	Wardrobe & Makeup	$3,000–$5,000
19-00	**PERMITS**	**$2,000–$6,000**
20-00	**INSURANCE**	**$3,000–$10,000**
21-00	Dailies	
22-00	FX/Stunts/Cars	
23-00	Locations	
24-00	Office & Paperwork	
25-00	Publicity	
26-00	Food	
TOTAL PRODUCTION BUDGET (In-the-Can)		
THE SHOOT (Total Above & Below)		
27-00	Film Edit	
28-00	Film Lab (Edit)	
29-00	Sound Edit	
30-00	ADR	
31-00	Foley	
32-00	Music/Score	
33-00	Mix (Re-record)	
34-00	Optical Transfer	
35-00	M&E	
THE EDIT (Post-Production)		
36-00	Titles	
37-00	Negative Cutting	
38-00	Film Lab (Answer Print)	
TOTAL PRODUCTION COSTS		

a five-block radius of your location that you're making a film. Duh! What do you think happens? The people you just notified always object, and you'll be forced to pay them for their inconvenience. Your free permit just got even more expensive.

Therefore, when budgeting for film permits always include (a) the daily or weekly fee, (b) the cost of police or firemen, (c) the possibility of inconvenience payoffs to local residents, and (d) the cost of insurance.

The cost for a permit to include a cop's salary but exclude insurance (see below), for a 12–18 day shoot, will be **$2,000–$6,000.**

What if you don't get a film permit? Then you're called a guerrilla film-maker.

Guerrilla Filmmaking

No-budget filmmakers do this for one reason: Money! Or lack of it. They would rather allocate the small amount of money they have to purchase more film or hire more crew than give it to a government agency, a cop, and an insurance salesman. Ever see a small crew shooting? Ninety-nine times out of a hundred, if you don't see a police officer on the set, that shoot doesn't have a film permit. And every cop driving by knows they don't have a permit, but they rarely stop and shut down the shoot. Why?

Cops have higher priorities (robberies, rapes, murders) than bugging filmmakers who may not have permits. Besides, policemen like filmmakers. Not because we're cute or interesting, but because we aid their retirement. A retired cop supplements his pension fund by putting on his old uniform, sitting on a movie set, and collecting $45–$85/hour while he hits on starlets.

Do not be concerned with police officers. Although their job is to control what's going on in their community, they're not scouting for low-budget filmmakers to harass. Do, however, be concerned about any other uniformed employees (security guards, park rangers, etc.). I hate life-guards. Try to shoot at any beach and those damn Baywatch Bimbettes will shut you down in a minute. A $6/hour security guard, an $8/hour campus cop, or a $12/hour lifeguard will shut you down. A $45–$85/hour cop will look the other way.

The worst that can happen if you shoot a film guerrilla-style is that you get "busted" by a cop who forces you, for three to four hours, to stop shooting while you go to the film commissioner and pay for the permit.

IMPORTANT POINT Cops only stop you when you're impeding on their turf. What's their turf? The street. If you're stopping traffic to get a shot, you're asking to be busted. If, however, your vans and trucks are parked and you're shooting on someone's property, with permission, away from the street, or in a building, the cops invariably look the other way.

In your budget, you have more than enough money to get a permit, pay for a cop, and buy insurance. Now let's take a look at what insurance you should get.

INSURANCE

Insurance means different things to different people. To camera rental houses, it means they are reimbursed if someone breaks or steals their equipment. To investors, film commissioners, and cities, it means they're not liable should an accident take place on your set. To distributors, it safeguards against misuse of names, addresses, phone numbers, and similarities between film characters and real people. To the federal government, it means your employees are protected if injured on your shoot.

Production insurance can cover 100 different contingencies: faulty film stock, damage to locations, stolen or damaged equipment, injured personnel holding up a shoot, etc. Insurance companies offer many options, and getting insurance can be mind-boggling and expensive. Get insured for everything, if you can afford it. If not, concern yourself only with the following five:

1. Equipment Insurance: Mechanical equipment, theft/damage insurance
2. Liability Insurance: General comprehensive and liability insurance
3. Workers' Comp: Workers' compensation insurance
4. E&O: Errors and omissions insurance
5. The bond: Completion bond

1. EQUIPMENT INSURANCE

No rental house will rent their equipment to you without it. The reason is simple: They know that at your budget you can't afford security personnel. They're letting you have equipment worth $150,000–$250,000. There is a good chance of damage and a likelihood that something will be stolen.

What It Costs

Don't overpay. Your equipment insurance will range from **$1,500–$4,500,** depending upon the value of the rented equipment and the length of the shoot. Occasionally, a camera rental facility offers its own insurance policy, and it may be less expensive. Ask prices, shop, compare, and you'll save 10–30 percent.

2. LIABILITY INSURANCE

This insurance is required in order to get a film permit. Also, managers or owners of the buildings and property where you're filming might require you to get this insurance, in case an accident happens.

What It Costs

Depending on the amount the film commissioner tells you to get ($1 million is normal), the policy will cost **$1,000–$3,500.**

> COST-SAVING TIP   If the film commissioner asks to read your script, be careful. He's looking for scenes that entail fire, explosions, or car chases. If so, the likelihood of accidents and litigation is high, and he'll demand you get $10 million rather than $1 million. A two-page car chase can cost an extra $5,000.
>
> If you have a 90-page script with a two-page car chase in it, and the film commissioner asks to read it, you *could* send an 88-page script. I guarantee the commissioner won't call you back wanting to talk about a two-page plot point scene that appears to be missing.

3. WORKERS' COMPENSATION

Workers' comp is federally mandated. It provides medical and disability benefits to an employee injured in the course of production. There's a saying on film sets: "It's not a film unless somebody gets a broken bone or requires stitches." There are always accidents on film sets, so make sure you have workers' comp.

What It Costs

When you contact your insurance agent, he/she will ask, "What do you think your weekly payroll will be?" Workers' compensation rates are based on your payroll. Since you have a small payroll, your total package should not cost more than **$500–$2,000.**

4. ERRORS AND OMISSIONS

The errors and omissions policy (aka E&O) insures the distributor or broadcaster that all rights, releases, and legal clearances have been obtained from actors, writers, property owners, musical composers, and others whose actual or intellectual property you are using. To make sure your film is eligible for E&O, you must have proof that you have permission to use certain locations. You also must make sure that if you mention an address or phone number in your film, it doesn't belong to anyone. You don't have to pay for this insurance, the distributor will. Just make sure you have the paperwork (contracts, agreements, releases, etc.) needed to get it.

> **INTERESTING POINT**   Have you noticed that when someone in a movie mentions a phone number, it always starts with 555? Why does Hollywood use 555? Everyone knows it's weird. Here's why. Pick up your phone and dial 555 and four digits. You'll discover that no such phone number exists. Now imagine that you put a real phone number into your movie and a million people hear it. For whatever reason, 1 out of 200 people, lonely souls with nothing to do, go home, dial the number, and hang up. Your film has just instigated 5,000 phone calls. If this was your phone number, I guarantee that you'd be pissed and sue the film's distributor.

If you have made an error in your film or omitted someone's rights, then that person probably will sue. And, if there is a lawsuit, the insurance company that provided the E&O insurance will pay for the litigation and damages.

E&O insurance is very important. You must make sure that you deliver, along with your finished film, all the forms and releases that prove you have the rights to everything. Then, when the distributor picks up your film, with these forms and releases, he'll pay for the E&O insurance, which he'll eventually inflate and recoup, with creative bookkeeping, from your profits, at a cost of **$8,000–$20,000.**

5. COMPLETION BOND

A completion bond is an insurance policy that guarantees that if—for whatever reason—you don't finish your film on schedule or your production goes over budget, the insurance company will provide the finishing funds.

Sounds great, huh? An insurance policy that guarantees finishing your film! Here's reality: You ain't getting a completion bond. Insurance companies don't bond low-budget, first-time filmmakers who barely know how to buy film. They're not stupid. They know you don't know what you're doing. They know you're really under budget. You're too high a risk.

> **KEEP THIS IN MIND**   Completion bond executives are important. Kiss ass. If this film is successful, your second and third film will have a high enough budget to require a completion bond. If you don't get the bond, you don't get the production money. Develop a relationship with the bonding companies so that when you need a bond, they'll know and trust you.

What It Costs

Budget completion bonds are approximately 6 percent of the budget. On a $3 million film, $180,000 would be required. However, due to competition within the bond industry, you can be refunded 50 percent of that initial policy if you finish your shoot without needing finishing funds. But remember there will be no completion bond on your first low- to no-budget film.

BOTTOM LINE:

Here's your insurance cost. You will plan for E&O insurance, forget about a completion bond, and pay for (a) equipment insurance, (b) liability insurance, and (c) workers' compensation, at a cost of **$3,000–$10,000.**

1. Equipment Insurance	$1,500–$4,500
2. Liability Insurance	$1,000–$3,500
3. Workers' Comp	$500–$2,000
4. E&O	$0 (but plan for it)
5. Completion Bond	$0 (forget it)
	$3,000–$10,000

The final tally for insurance and permits combined, if you're not guerrilla filmmaking, is $2,000–$6,000 for permits (fees, cops, and liability coverage) and $3,000–$10,000 for insurance (equipment, liability, and workers' compensation) totaling **$5,000–$16,000** for a three-week shoot.

TO DO:

1. Ask your film commissioner for fees, insurance, and police/fire requirements.
2. Phone three insurance agents and compare the equipment, liability, and workers' comp rates.

 INSURANCE AGENTS

INSURANCE COMPANIES

American International
  Entertainment
Contact: Aggi Phard
80 Pine St, 3rd Floor
New York, NY 10005
Ph: 212-770-7000
Fax: 212-809-1533

Chubb Group
Contact: David Seaman
801 S Figueroa St, Suite 2400
Los Angeles, CA 90017
Ph: 213-612-0880
Fax: 213-612-5721

Fireman's Fund Insurance
Contact: Robert Bailey
10940 Wilshire Blvd, Suite 1900
Los Angeles, CA 90024
Ph: 213-861-7300
Fax: 310-208-8094

INSURANCE BROKERS

Albert G. Ruben Services
Contact: Brian Kingman
10880 Wilshire Blvd, Suite 700
Los Angeles, CA 90024
Ph: 310-234-6800
Fax: 310-446-7839

Entertainment Brokers International
Contact: Martin Ridgers
10940 Wilshire Blvd, 17th Floor
Los Angeles, CA 90024
Ph: 310-824-0111 ext 214
Fax: 310-824-5733

Marsh Arts Inc.
Contact: LeCont Moore
1166 Ave of the Americas
New York, NY 10036
Ph: 212-345-6000
Fax: 212-345-5811

Near North Entertainment Insurance
Contact: Sheldon Bachrach
1840 Century Park East, Suite 1100
Los Angeles, CA 90067
Ph: 310-556-1900
Fax: 310-556-4702

D.R. Reiff & Associates
Contact: Dennis Reiff
320 W 57th St, 2nd Floor
New York, NY 10019
Ph: 212-603-0231
Fax: 212-247-0739

Speare & Co.
Contact: Tom Alper
15303 Ventura Blvd, 7th Floor
Sherman Oaks, CA 91403
Ph: 818-464-9300
Fax: 818-464-9398

Encore Entertainment Insurance
Contact: Guy De Marco
10969 Ventura Blvd, Suite 300
Studio City, CA 91604
Ph: 818-358-0500
Fax: 818-358-0501

Taylor & Taylor
Contact: Darren Rosenbaum
12100 Wilshire Blvd
Los Angeles, CA 90025
Ph: 310-826-7200
Fax: 310-826-9300

Truman Van Dyke Co.
Contact: Kent Hamilton
6255 Sunset Blvd, Suite 1401
Hollywood, CA 90028
Ph: 323-462-3300
Fax: 323-462-4857

USI Entertainment Insurance
Contact: Bobbi Curry
14140 Ventura Blvd, 3rd Floor
Sherman Oaks, CA 91423
Ph: 818-704-1000
Fax: 818-704-4699

COMPLETION BOND COMPANIES

Aberdeen Film Completions
Contact: Les Eckert

300 E Magnolia Blvd
Burbank, CA 91502
Ph: 818-841-9880
Fax: 818-841-9840

Cinefinance
Contact: Fred Milstein
1925 Century Park East, Suite 1010
Los Angeles, CA 90067
Ph: 310-226-6800
Fax: 310-226-6810

Film Finances
Contact: Stuart Ransohoff
9000 Sunset Blvd, Suite 1400
Los Angeles, CA 90069
Ph: 310-275-7323
Fax: 310-275-1706

International Film Guarantors
Contact: Steve Mangel
10940 Wilshire Blvd, Suite 2010
Los Angeles, CA 90024
Ph: 310-208-4500
Fax: 310-443-8998

Motion Picture Bond Company
Contact: Leonard Ephraim
1801 Ave of the Stars, Suite 2000
Los Angeles, CA 90067
Ph: 310-551-0371
Fax: 310-551-0518

Worldwide Film Completion Inc.
Contact: Steve Cardone
2901 28th St, Suite 290
Santa Monica, CA 90405
Ph: 310-450-1600
Fax: 310-450-3399

ENTERTAINMENT INSURANCE WEB SITES

AON/Albert Ruben
www.albertruben.aon.com

C&S International
www.csins.com

Chubb Group
www.chubb.com/businesses/industry
  groups

Cinema Completion International
www.cnacci.com

Encore Insurance
www.encoreinsurance.com

Film Finances
www.ffi.com

Fireman's Fund
www.the-fund.com

Global Entertainment Insurance
www.globalentins.com

International Film Guarantors
www.nnng.com/ifg.htm

Marshall Entertainment Insurance
www.marshallentertainment.com

D.R. Reiff & Associates
www.reiffinsurance.com

Taylor & Taylor
www.taylorinsurance.com

LOCATIONS

"Secure the Locations"

A location is not Germany, or downtown Philadelphia, or a suburb of Toledo, or a small Hobbit hamlet. For your purpose, think of a location as a fuse box. It takes time to connect and disconnect from a power source. The fewer the moves, the fewer the connects and disconnects. The fewer connects and disconnects, the greater the efficiency. Keep it simple. For your first feature you should never attempt more than six locations (six fuse boxes) as Steven Soderbergh did with his first film, *sex, lies and video-tape,* within a short radius.

SOUNDSTAGES VS. ACTUAL LOCATIONS

Big-budget films use a combination of soundstages for interiors and actual locations for exteriors. The lower your budget, the more actual locations you will use. If you're guerrilla filmmaking, you will quite likely use only actual locations. However, with our budget, there is enough money to rent three or four actual locations for a couple of days each, assuming you get them cheaply, and a soundstage, where you'll build a couple of sets (two- and three-wall) to double for interior locations that are too constrictive to shoot in.

A soundstage is nothing more than a huge, high-ceilinged barn or warehouse that is isolated from street noise. Soundstage advantages include convenience, flexibility, quick setups, soundproofing, ample parking, protection from inclement weather, smooth floor surfaces for easy dolly movement, and high ceilings to expedite lighting. Plus, there is the

PRODUCTION BUDGET

Title: "Your $1,000,000 Feature" **Executive Producer:** _____
                                        Producer: _____
Writer: _____   **Director:** _____

ACCOUNT NUMBER	DESCRIPTION	BUDGET
01-00	Producer	$10,000–$20,000
02-00	Writer/Script	$5,000–$10,000
03-00	Director	$10,000–$15,000
04-00	Cast/Actors	$6,000–$9,000 (+$25,000)
TOTAL ABOVE-THE-LINE (Pre-Production)		**$31,000–$54,000 (+$25,000)**
BELOW-THE-LINE		
5-00	Film Stock	$20,000–$40,000
6-00	Film Lab (Shoot)	$15,000–$30,000
7-00	Camera	$12,000–$30,000
8-00	Expendables	$2,000–$5,000
9-00	Sound Equipment	$6,000–$11,000
10-00	Sound Transfer	$3,000–$5,000
11-00	Light/Grip	$6,000–$24,000
12-00	Dolly	$2,000–$3,000
13-00	Cinematographer	$10,000–$15,000
14-00	PM & AD	$14,500–$21,000
15-00	Production Designer	$6,000–$8,500
16-00	Film Crew	$23,000–$35,500
17-00	Art & Props	$5,000–$9,000
18-00	Wardrobe & Makeup	$3,000–$5,000
19-00	Permits	$2,000–$6,000
20-00	Insurance	$3,000–$10,000
21-00	Dailies	
22-00	FX/Stunts/Cars	
23-00	**LOCATIONS**	**$2,000–$10,000**
24-00	Office & Paperwork	
25-00	Publicity	
26-00	Food	
TOTAL PRODUCTION BUDGET (In-the-Can)		
THE SHOOT (Total Above & Below)		
27-00	Film Edit	
28-00	Film Lab (Edit)	
29-00	Sound Edit	
30-00	ADR	
31-00	Foley	
32-00	Music/Score	
33-00	Mix (Re-record)	
34-00	Optical Transfer	
35-00	M&E	
THE EDIT (Post-Production)		
36-00	Titles	
37-00	Negative Cutting	
38-00	Film Lab (Answer Print)	
TOTAL PRODUCTION COSTS		

added bonus of making your crew feel like it has a base of operations. The cons are cost, availability, set construction, union issues, restricted working hours, and power.

Actual locations such as bowling alleys, schools, churches, convenience stores, homes, hotels, etc. are already constructed and have interiors, exteriors, and set dressings. No matter how hard your crew works at constructing a genius set, nothing beats the look and feel of a real location. The cons of actual locations are low ceilings, difficult lighting, small rooms, stationary walls, uneven floors, and the inability to control noise. Before deciding on whether to use actual locations over soundstages or a combination of both, you will first educate yourself by scouting.

LOCATION SCOUTING

When scouting your priorities are:

A. Location (Does it look good?)
B. Cost (Is it affordable?)
C. Power (Where is the electrical panel box?)
D. Parking (Where are 30–40 cars going to park?)
E. Photocopy (Where is the closest Kinko's?)
F. Permits (What are city costs/fees?)

The first thing you do when location scouting is to contact the film commission, tell them what you're looking for and what you can afford. The film commissioner will refer you to a location coordinator who knows every house, barn, park, and restaurant in the city, and charges $700–$1,000/week. If you don't want to pay for a location coordinator, then you will spend hours in the film office, poring over thousands of photos of available locations that they've accumulated.

Once you've discovered the perfect locations(s) for your shoot, you must get permission to shoot on the property. If the location is private property, then get a property release from the owner. The E&O insurance agent (chapter 30) will ask for it. Once signed, this release grants you permission to be on the property for a specified time and to use the visual image of the property in your film.

Always remember, 🔲 *only go to a location once—the owner will never let you back.* Why? Film crews destroy property. Things get damaged. Lawns get ruined. Holes appear in walls, carpets get stained, and windows get broken. I'm warning you, if you use your friend's house as a set he won't be your friend anymore. Make sure you get every single shot you want before you leave a location.

> **PRODUCER TIP**   Always have a roll of $100 bills (bribe money) when shooting. After two days at any location, the neighbors always bitch about how much of a nuisance you are. Argue and they'll call the cops. So when a neighbor walks up and asks to have a word with you, dig into your pocket, palm a $100 bill, and give it to him while telling him how wonderful he is. Don't let him talk; if you do he will tell you to get the hell off his street.
>
> I've tried $20s—they didn't work. I've tried $50s—they didn't work. Only $100s will work. During the shoot, many problems will be solved by palming $100.

WHAT TO PAY

Locations cost anywhere from nothing (your own home, a friend's restaurant, an open field) to thousands of dollars a day. Shop for what you can afford. Property owners have delusions that filmmaking means big money, and it often is impossible to convince them that you don't have $5,000 a day for their location. Find the best location that you can afford, but make sure to get a property release (needed for E&O) from the owner.

At the least, budget $100 a day for 18 shooting days, for a maximum of six locations, and you'll spend **$2,000.** However, let's say two locations (restaurant and bowling alley) want $500 a day for three days. One location (church) wants $1,000 a day. Another location (exclusive mansion) wants $5,000 a day. One location (your friend's house) is free for five days, and the last location (your house) will cost you $1,000 to pay your four neighbors $50 a day each for the inconvenience caused by the 30 crew cars parked in front of their houses for five days.

Restaurant	3 days @ $500/day	$1,500
Bowling Alley	3 days @ $500/day	$1,500
Mansion	1 day @ $5,000/day	$5,000
Church	1 day @ $1,000/day	$1,000
Friends' House	5 days @ $0	$0
Your House	5 days @ $200/day	$1,000
	18 days	**$10,000**

When you know how to scout and shop properly, for a three-week shoot (18 shooting days), renting your locations will cost **$2,000–$10,000.**

TO DO:

1. Contact the film commissioner and view location photos.
2. Visit locations, checking for power and parking.
3. Obtain property release forms.

 FILM COMMISSIONERS

USA

Alabama
Alabama Film Office
401 Adams Ave
Montgomery, AL 36104
Contact: Michael Boyer
Ph: 334-242-3990
Fax: 334-242-2077
Web: www.telefilm-south.com/
    alabama/alablam.html

City of Mobile Film Office
150 S Royal St
PO Box 1827
Mobile, AL 36693
Contact: Eva Golson
Ph: 334-208-7305
Fax: 334-208-7659

Alaska
Alaska Film Office
3601 C St, Suite 700
Anchorage, AK 99503
Contact: Mary Pignalberi
Ph: 907-269-8137
Fax: 907-269-8136
Web: www.alaskafilmoffice.com

Arizona
Arizona Film Commission
3800 N Central Ave, Bldg D
Phoenix, AZ 85012
Contact: Linda Peterson Warren
Ph: 602-280-1380
    800-523-6695
Fax: 602-280-1384
Web: www.state.az.us/commerce

Arkansas
Arkansas Film Office
1 Capitol Mall, Room 4B-505
Little Rock, AR 72201
Contact: Joe Glass
Ph: 501-682-7676
Fax: 501-682-Film

California
California Film Commission
7080 Hollywood Blvd, Suite 900
Hollywood, CA 90028
Contact: Pamela Powell
Ph: 323-860-2960
    800-858-4749
Fax: 323-860-2972
Web: www.film.ca.gov

Entertainment Industry Development
    Corporation
7083 Hollywood Blvd, 5th Floor
Hollywood, CA 90028

Contact: Lindslay Parsons Jr.
Ph: 323-957-1000
Fax: 323-463-0613
Web: www.eidc.com

San Diego Film Commission
1010 Second Ave, Suite 1600
San Diego, CA 92101-4912
Contact: Cathy Anderson
Ph: 619-234-3456
Fax: 619-234-4631
Web: www.sdfilm.com

San Francisco Film & Video Arts
    Commission
1 Dr. Carlton B. Goodlett Pl, Suite 473
San Francisco, CA 94102
Contact: Patrick Johnston
Ph: 415-554-6244
Fax: 415-554-6503
Web: www.ci.sf.ca.us/film

Colorado
Mayor's Office of Art, Culture & Film
303 W Colfax Ave, Suite 615
Denver, CO 80204
Contact: Ronald F. Pinkard
Ph: 303-640-2686
Fax: 303-640-2737

Boulder County Film Commission
PO Box 73
Boulder, CO 80306
Contact: Shelly Helmerick
Ph: 303-442-1044
    800-442-0447
Fax: 303-938-8837

Connecticut
Connecticut Film, Video &
    Media Office
505 Hudson St
Hartford, CT 06106
Contact: Katherine Ray
Ph: 860-270-8084

Fax: 860-270-8077
Web: www.state.ct.us/tourism

Delaware
Delaware Film Office
99 Kings Hwy
Dover, DE 19901
Contact: Jennifer Hastings
Ph: 302-739-4271 ext. 140
    800-441-8846
Fax: 302-739-5749
Web: www.state.de.us

District of Columbia
Mayor's Office of Motion Picture & TV
717 14th St, NW, 12th Floor
Washington, DC 20005
Contact: Crystal Palmer
Ph: 202-727-6607
Fax: 202-727-3787

Florida
Broward Alliance Film and Television
    Commission
350 SE 2nd St, Suite 400
Fort Lauderdale, FL 33301
Contact: Elizabeth Wentworth
Ph: 954-524-3113
    800-741-1420
Fax: 954-524-3167
Web: www.browardalliance.org

Jacksonville Film Commission
220 E Bay St, Suite 404
Jacksonville, FL 32202
Contact: Todd Roobin
Ph: 904-630-2522
Fax: 904-630-1485
Web: www.ci.jax.fl.us/pub/film/
    film.htm

Miami/Dade Office of Film &
    Entertainment
111 NW 1st St, Suite 2510
Miami, FL 33128

Contact: Jeff Peel
Ph: 305-375-3288
Fax: 305-375-3266

Tampa/Hillsborough County Film
  Commission
400 N Tampa St, Suite 1010
Tampa, FL 33602
Contact: Edie Emerald
Ph: 813-223-1111 ext. 58
Fax: 813-229-6616
Web: www.thcva.com

Georgia
Georgia Film & Videotape Office
285 Peachtree Center Ave, Suite 1000
Atlanta, GA 30303
Contact: Greg Torre
Ph: 404-656-3591
Fax: 404-651-9063
Web: www.film.georgia.org

Hawaii
Hawaii Film Office
PO Box 2359
Honolulu, HI 96804
Contact: Georgette Deemer
Ph: 808-586-2570
Fax: 808-586-2572

Idaho
Idaho Film Bureau
700 W State St, Box 83720
Boise, ID 83720
Contact: Peg Owens
Ph: 208-334-2470
    800-942-8338
Fax: 208-334-2631

Illinois
Illinois Film Office
100 W Randolph, Suite 3-400
Chicago, IL 60601
Contact: Ron Ver Kuilen
Ph: 312-814-3600

Fax: 312-814-8874
Web: www.commerce.state.il.us

Chicago Film Office
1 N LaSalle, Suite 2165
Chicago, IL 60602
Contact: Richard Moskal
Ph: 312-744-6415
Fax: 312-744-1378
Web: www.ci.chi.il.us

Indiana
Indiana Film Commission
1 N Capitol, Suite 700
Indianapolis, IN 46204-2288
Contact: Jane Rulon
Ph: 317-232-8829
Fax: 317-233-6887
Web: www.al.com/derringer/
    filmcomm.html

Iowa
Iowa Film Office
200 E Grand Ave
Des Moines, IA 50309
Contact: Wendol M. Jarvis
Ph: 515-242-4726
Fax: 515-242-4859
Web: www.state.ia.us/film

Kansas
Kansas Film Commission
700 SW Harrison St, Suite 1300
Topeka, KS 66603
Contact: Vicky Henley
Ph: 785-296-4927
Fax: 785-296-6988
Web: www.kansascommerce.com

Kentucky
Kentucky Film Commission
500 Mero St
2200 Capitol Plaza Tower
Frankfort, KY 40601
Contact: Jim Toole

Ph: 225-564-3456
Fax: 502-564-7588

Louisiana
Louisiana Film Commission
343 3rd St, Suite 400
Baton Rouge, LA 70804-4320
Contact: Peter Loop II
Ph: 225-342-8150
Fax: 225-342-7988
Web: www.lafilm.org

New Orleans Film and Video
   Commission
1515 Poydras St, Suite 1200
New Orleans, LA 70112
Contact: Kimberly Carbo
Ph: 504-565-8104
Fax: 504-565-8108

Maine
Maine Film Office
State House Station 59
Augusta, ME 04333-0059
Contact: D. Lea Girardin
Ph: 207-287-5703
Fax: 207-287-8070
Web: www.state.me.us/decd/film

Maryland
Maryland Film Office
217 E Redwood St, 9th Floor
Baltimore, MD 21202
Contact: Michael B. Styer
Ph: 410-767-6340
   800-333-6632
Fax: 410-333-0044
Web: www.mdfilm.state.md.us

Baltimore Film Commission
34 Market Plz, Suite 200
Baltimore, MD 21202
Contact: Rose Greene
Ph: 410-396-4550
Fax: 410-272-5850

Massachusetts
Massachusetts Film Office
10 Park Plz, Suite 2310
Boston, MA 02116
Contact: Robin Dawson
Ph: 617-973-8800
Fax: 617-973-8810
Web: www.state.ma.us/film

Michigan
Michigan Film Office
201 N Washington Sq
Lansing, MI 48913
Contact: Janet Lockwood
Ph: 517-973-8800
   800-477-3456
Fax: 517-373-0059
Web: www.michigan.org

Minnesota
Minnesota Film Board
401 N 3rd St, Suite 460
Minneapolis, MN 55401
Contact: Randy Adamsick
Ph: 612-332-6493
Fax: 612-332-3735
Web: www.mnfilm.org

Minneapolis Office of Film/Video/
   Recording
323M City Hall
350 S 5th St
Minneapolis, MN 55415
Contact: Janet Zahn
Ph: 612-673-2947
Fax: 612-673-2011

Mississippi
Mississippi Film Office
PO Box 849
Jackson, MS 39205
Contact: Ward Emling
Ph: 601-359-3297
Fax: 601-359-5048
Web: www.mississippi.org

Missouri
Missouri Film Commission
301 W High St, Room 720
PO Box 118
Jefferson City, MO 65102
Contact: Richard Smreker
Ph: 573-751-9050
Fax: 573-751-7384
Web: www.ecodev.state.mo.us/film/

Kansas City, Missouri Film Office
10 Petticoat Ln, Suite 250
Kansas City, MO 64106
Contact: Patti Watkins
Ph: 816-221-0636
    800-889-0636
Fax: 816-221-0189
Web: www.kcfilm.com

Saint Louis Film Office
1 Metropolitan Sq, Suite 1100
Saint Louis, MO 63102
Contact: James Leonis
Ph: 314-992-0609
Fax: 314-421-0394
Web: www.stlfilm.com

Montana
Montana Film Office
1424 Ninth Ave
Helena, MT 59620
Contact: Lonie Stimac
Ph: 406-444-3762
    800-553-4563
Fax: 406-444-4191
Web: www.montanafilm.com

Nebraska
Nebraska Film Office
PO Box 98907
Lincoln, NE 68509-8907
Contact: Laurie J. Richards
Ph: 402-471-3680
    800-228-4307

Fax: 402-471-3026
Web: www.film.nebraska.org

Nevada
Nevada Film Office
555 E Washington, Suite 5400
Las Vegas, NV 89101
Contact: Charles Geocaris
Ph: 702-486-2711
    877-638-3456
Fax: 702-486-2712
Web: www.nevadafilm.com

New Hampshire
New Hampshire Film & TV Bureau
172 Pembroke Rd
PO Box 1856
Concord, NH 03302
Contact: Laura Simoes
Ph: 603-271-2665
Fax: 603-271-6784
Web: www.visitnh.gov

New Jersey
New Jersey Motion Picture/TV
    Commission
153 Halsey St
PO Box 47023
Newark, NJ 07101
Contact: Joseph Friedman
Ph: 973-648-6279
Fax: 973-648-7350
Web: www.nj.com/njfilm

New Mexico
New Mexico Film Office
1100 S St. Francis Dr
PO Box 20003
Santa Fe, NM 87505-5003
Contact: Nancy Everist
Ph: 800-545-9871
    505-827-9810
Fax: 505-827-9799
Web: www.newmexico
    development.com

Santa Fe Film Office
201 W Marcy St
Santa Fe, NM 87501
Contact: Kathy Madden
Ph: 505-984-6760
    800-984-9984
Fax: 505-984-6679
Web: www.santafe.org

New York
New York State Governor's Office
    for Motion Picture and TV
    Development
633 Third Ave, 33rd Floor
New York, NY 10017
Contact: Pat Kaufman
Ph: 212-803-2330
Fax: 212-803-2339
Web: www.nyfilm.com

NYC Mayor's Office of Film, Theatre
    & Broadcasting
1697 Broadway, Suite 602
New York, NY 10019
Contact: Patricia Reed Scott
Ph: 212-489-6710
Fax: 212-307-6237
Web: www.ci.nyc.ny.us/html/
    filmcom.html

North Carolina
North Carolina Film Office
301 N Wilmington St
Raleigh, NC 27626
Contact: William Arnold
Ph: 919-733-9900
    800-232-9227
Fax: 919-715-0151
Web: www.telefilm-
    south.com/nc/olnc.html

Charlotte Region Film Office
112 S Tryon St, Suite 900
Charlotte, NC 28284

Contact: Marcie Oberndorf-Kelso
Ph: 800-554-4373
    704-347-8942
Fax: 704-347-8981
Web: www.charlotteregion.com

North Dakota
North Dakota Film Commission
604 East Blvd, 2nd Floor
Bismark, ND 58505
Contact: Pat Hertz
Ph: 800-328-2871
    701-328-2525
Fax: 701-328-4878

Ohio
Ohio Film Commission
77 S High St, 29th Floor
PO Box 1001
Columbus, OH 43216
Contact: Steve Cover
Ph: 614-466-2284
    800-230-3523
Fax: 614-466-6744
Web: www.ohiofilm.com

Greater Cincinnati Film
    Commission
602 Main St, Suite 712
Cincinnati, OH 45202
Contact: Lori Holladay
Ph: 513-784-1744
Fax: 513-768-8963
Web: www.film-cincinnati.org

Greater Cleveland Media
    Development Corporation
(Greater Cleveland Film Commission)
825 Terminal Tower
Cleveland, OH 44113
Contact: Christopher Carmody
Ph: 216-623-3910
    888-746-Film

Fax: 216-736-7792
Web: www.clevelandfilm.com

Oklahoma
Oklahoma Film Commission
15 N Robinson, Suite 801
Oklahoma City, OK 73102
Contact: Charles (Bud) Elder
Ph: 800-766-3456
    405-521-2407
Fax: 405-521-3992

Oregon
Oregon Film & Video Office
121 SW Salmon St, Suite 300A
Portland, OR 97204
Contact: David Woolson
Ph: 503-229-5832
Fax: 503-229-6869

Pennsylvania
Pennsylvania Film Office
Forum Building, Room 210
Harrisburg, PA 17120
Contact: Brian Kreider
Ph: 717-783-3456
Fax: 717-787-0687
Web: www.dced.state.pa.us

Greater Philadelphia Film Office
100 S Broad St, Suite 600
Philadelphia, PA 19110
Contact: Sharon Pinkenson
Ph: 215-686-2668
Fax: 215-686-3659
Web: www.film.org

Pittsburgh Film Office
223 Fourth Ave, Suite 1300
Pittsburgh, PA 15222
Contact: Dawn Keezer
Ph: 412-261-2744
    888-744-3456
Fax: 412-471-7317

Rhode Island
Rhode Island Film & TV Office
1 W Exchange St
Providence, RI 02903
Contact: Rick Smith
Ph: 401-222-2601
Fax: 401-273-8270
Web: www.rifilm.com

South Carolina
South Carolina Film Office
1205 Pendleton St, Suite 110
PO Box 7367
Columbia, SC 29202
Contact: Isabel Hill/Jeff Monks
Ph: 803-737-0490
Fax: 803-737-3104
Web: www.scfilmoffice.com

South Dakota
South Dakota Film Commission
711 E Wells Ave
Pierre, SD 57501-3369
Contact: Chris Hull
Ph: 605-773-3301
    800-952-3625
Fax: 605-773-3256
Web: www.state.sd.us

Tennessee
Tennessee Film/Entertainment/Music
   Commission
320 Sixth Ave North, 7th Floor
Nashville, TN 37243-0790
Contact: Anne Pope
Ph: 615-741-3456
    877-818-3456
Fax: 615-741-5554
Web: www.film.state.tn.us

Memphis & Shelby County Film,
   Tape & Music Commission
Beale Street Landing

245 Wagner Pl, Suite 4
Memphis, TN 38103-3815
Contact: Linn Sitler
Ph: 901-527-8300
Fax: 901-527-8326

Nashville Mayor's Office of Film
117 Union St
Nashville, TN 37201-1301
Contact: Kym Gerlock Jackson
Ph: 615-862-4700
Fax: 615-862-6025
Web: www.nashville.net/~cinevent

Texas
Texas Film Commission
PO Box 13246
Austin, TX 78711
Contact: Tom Copeland
Ph: 512-463-9200
Fax: 512-463-4114
Web: www.governor.state.tx.us/film

Austin Film Office
201 E 2nd St
Austin, TX 78701
Contact: Gary Bond
Ph: 512-404-4562
    800-926-2282
Fax: 512-404-4564

Dallas/Fort Worth Regional Film
  Commission
504 Business Pkwy
Richardson, TX 75081
Contact: Roger E. Burke
Ph: 972-234-5697
    800-234-5699
Web: www.dfwfilm.org

Houston Film Commission
901 Bagby, Suite 100
Houston, TX 77002

Contact: Rick Ferguson
Ph: 713-227-3100
    800-365-7575

Utah
Utah Film Commission
324 S State, Suite 500
Salt Lake City, UT 84111
Contact: Leigh Von Der Esch
Ph: 801-538-8740
    800-453-8824
Fax: 801-538-8886
Web: www.film.state.ut.us

Vermont
Vermont Film Commission
10 Baldwin St
PO Box 129
Montpelier, VT 05601
Contact: Loranne Turgeon
Ph: 802-828-3618
Fax: 802-828-2221

Virginia
Virginia Film Office
901 E Byrd St
Richmond, VA 23219-4048
Contact: Rita McClenny
Ph: 800-854-6233
    804-371-8204
Fax: 804-371-8177
Web: www.film.virginia.org

Washington
Washington State Film Office
2001 Sixth Ave, Suite 2600
Seattle, WA 98121
Contact: Suzy Kellett
Ph: 206-956-3200
Fax: 206-956-3205
Web: www.wafilm.wa.gov

City of Seattle—Mayor's
  Film Office
600 Fourth Ave, 2nd Floor
Seattle, WA 98104-1826
Contact: Donna James
Ph: 206-684-5030
Fax: 206-684-0379

West Virginia
West Virginia Film Office
State Capital, Bldg 6, Room 525
Charleston, WV 25305-0311
Contact: Mark McNabb
Ph: 304-558-2234
Fax: 800-982-3386

Wisconsin
201 W Washington Ave, 2nd Floor
Madison, WI 53702-0001
Contact: Stan Solheim
Ph: 608-267-3456
    800-345-6947
Fax: 608-266-3403

Greater Milwaukee Convention &
  Visitors Bureau
510 W Kilbourn Ave
Milwaukee, WI 53203
Contact: Patti Gorsky
Ph: 414-273-2879
    888-571-2879
Fax: 414-273-5596

Wyoming
Wyoming Business Council—
  Film & Arts
214 W 15th Street
Cheyenne, WY 82002
Contact: Michell Phelan
Ph: 307-777-3400
    800-458-6657
Fax: 307-777-2838
Web: www.wyomingfilm.org

INTERNATIONAL

Australia
New South Wales Film & Television
  Office
1 Francis St, Level 6
Sydney, NSW 2010 Australia
Contact: Trisha Rothkrans
Ph: 61-2-9380-5599
Fax: 61-2-9360-1090

Pacific Film & Television Commission
111 George St, Level 15
PO Box 94
Brisbane Albert St
Queensland 4002 Australia
Contact: Robin James/Barbara Edols
Ph: 61-7-3224-4114
Fax: 61-7-3224-6717
Web: www.pftc.com.au

Melbourne Film Office
3 Treasury Pl
GPO Box 4361
East Melbourne, Victoria 3002 Australia
Contact: Louisa Coppel
Ph: 61-3-9651-0610
Fax: 61-3-9651-0665
Web: www.cinemedia.net

Canada
Alberta Film Commission
639 Fifth Ave SW, Suite 660
Standard Life Tower
PO Box 2100, Station M (#6)
Calgary, AB T2P 2M5 Canada

British Columbia Film Commission
375 Water St, Suite 350
Vancouver, BC V6B 5C6 Canada
Contact: Peter Mitchell
Ph: 604-660-2732
Fax: 604-660-2732
Web: www.bcfilmcommission.com

Ontario Film Development
  Corporation
175 Bloor St East, Suite 300
  North Tower
Toronto, ONT M4W 3R8 Canada
Contact: Gail Thomson
Ph: 416-314-6858
Fax: 416-314-6876
Web: www.to-ontfilm.com

Toronto Film and Television Office
West Tower, 2nd Floor, New City Hall
Toronto, ONT M5H 2N2 Canada
Contact: Rhonda Silverstone
Ph: 416-392-7570
Fax: 416-392-0675
Web: www.to-ontfilm.com

Montreal Film & Television
  Commission
275 Notre Dame East, Suite R-100
Montreal, QUE H2Y 1C6 Canada
Contact: Andre Lafond
Ph: 514-872-2883
Fax: 514-872-3409

France
Commission Nationale du Film France
30 Ave de Messine
Paris 75008 France
Contact: Benoit Caron
Ph: 33-1-53-83-9898
Fax: 33-1-53-83-9899
Web: www.filmfrance.com

Germany
Berlin-Brandenburg Film Commission
August Bebel Str 26-53
Potsdam-Babelsberg, D-14482
  Germany
Contact: Roland Schmidt
Ph: 49-331-743-87-30
Fax: 49-331-743-87-99
Web: www.filmboard.de/koordi.htm

FFF FilmFernsehfonds Bayern GmbH
Schwanthaleistrasse 69
Munich 80336 Germany
Contact: Dr. Herbert Huber/
  Anja Metzger
Ph: 49-89-544-60-216
Fax: 49-89-544-60-223
Web: www.fff-bayern.de

Hong Kong
Television and Entertainment Licens-
  ing Authority
39/F, Revenue Tower
Wan Chai, Kowloon, Hong Kong
Contact: Eddy Chan Yuk-Tak
Ph: 852-2594-5888
Fax: 852-2507-2219

Italy
Italian Film Commission
1804 Ave of the Stars, Suite 700
Los Angeles, CA 90067
Contact: Pasquale Bova
Ph: 310-879-0950
Fax: 310-203-8335

Mexico
National Film Commission—Mexico
Av. Division Del Norte # 2462 5to. PISO
Col. Portales, C.P. 03300 Mexico DF
Contact: Jorge Santoyo
Ph: 52-5-688-0970
Fax: 52-5-688-7027
Web: www.imcine.gob.mx/
  conafili.html

New Zealand
Film New Zealand
The Production Village
26 Wright St
PO Box 24142
Wellington, New Zealand

Contact: Jane Gilbert
Ph: 64-4-802-4577
Fax: 64-4-385-8755
Web: www.filmnz.org.nz

Norway
Norwegian Film Commission
Bergen Media By
Geogernes Verft 3
N-5011 Bergen, Norway
Contact: Torill Svege
Ph: 47-55-56-0510
Fax: 47-55-66-0355

Portugal
Portugal Film Commission
Rua de S. Pedro de Alcantara, 45-Io
Lisboa, 1269-138 Portugal
Contact: Margarida Costa
Ph: 3511-323-0800
Fax: 3511-347-8643

Puerto Rico
Puerto Rico Film Commission
355 F.D. Roosevelt Ave
Fomento Building, Suite 106
San Juan, PR 00918 USA
Contact: Manuel A. Biascoechea
Ph: 787-758-4747
Fax: 787-756-5706

Scotland
Scottish Screen
74 Victoria Crescent Rd
Glasgow G12 9JN Scotland,
    United Kingdom
Contact: Kevin Cowle
Ph: 44-141-302-1724
Fax: 44-141-302-1711
Web: www.scottishscreen.demon.co.uk

Spain
Barcelona Plato Film Office—
    Barcelona City Council
Palau Nou, La Rambla 88-94, 3a pl.
Barcelona, Catalonia 08002 Spain
Contact: Julia Goytisolo
Ph: 34-93-301-7775
Fax: 34-93-302-6233
Web: www.bcn.es/icub/filmoffice

United Kingdom
British Film Commission
70 Baker St
London W1M 1DJ England,
    United Kingdom
Contact: Steve Norris
Ph: 44-171-224-5000
Fax: 44-171-224-1013
Web: www.britfilmcom.co.uk

DAILIES, FX/STUNTS/CARS

"Keep It Simple"

Once you are shooting you'll expose an average of 3,000 feet per day, on a schedule of five pages a day. After a couple of shooting days you will want to see what your film looks like (view dailies).

Dailies (aka rushes, one-lights, work prints) are the developed shots that you get back from the lab. When you negotiate with the lab, you call the film a "one-light." When you screen it, you'll call the film "dailies" or "rushes." When you edit it, you'll call this same film a "work print." 🧳 *Dailies, rushes, one-lights, and work prints are the same piece of celluloid* but are given different names at different stages to confuse you into thinking that you need to hire expensive pros.

Most first-timers don't understand the purpose of dailies. They believe that they allow the director and actors to review dramatic performances. Wrong! 🧳 *Never, ever let actors see dailies.* Know what actors see when they see dailies? They see how fat they are. They see that their makeup is not right. They see that they are losing hair. Vanity takes over and the next day you'll never get them out of makeup and you'll have a dilettante on your set.

Why would you want to see dailies, anyway? You saw the performance on the set when you announced, "Print. That's a take." The performance doesn't change when you look at the film. So why have dailies? The answer is simple. To see if the shots are in focus, if they are framed properly, if there are scratches on the print, if there are any focal soft spots, and if the dolly shots are steady, etc.! And if you notice any of these problems then you instantly correct them by firing an employee or replacing equipment before you shoot another day.

PRODUCTION BUDGET

Title: "Your $1,000,000 Feature"   Executive Producer: _____

Producer: _____

Writer: _____   Director: _____

ACCOUNT NUMBER	DESCRIPTION	BUDGET
01-00	Producer	$10,000–$20,000
02-00	Writer/Script	$5,000–$10,000
03-00	Director	$10,000–$15,000
04-00	Cast/Actors	$6,000–$9,000 (+$25,000)
TOTAL ABOVE-THE-LINE (Pre-Production)		**$31,000–$54,000 (+$25,000)**
BELOW-THE-LINE		
5-00	Film Stock	$20,000–$40,000
6-00	Film Lab (Shoot)	$15,000–$30,000
7-00	Camera	$12,000–$30,000
8-00	Expendables	$2,000–$5,000
9-00	Sound Equipment	$6,000–$11,000
10-00	Sound Transfer	$3,000–$5,000
11-00	Light/Grip	$6,000–$24,000
12-00	Dolly	$2,000–$3,000
13-00	Cinematographer	$10,000–$15,000
14-00	PM & AD	$14,500–$21,000
15-00	Production Designer	$6,000–$8,500
16-00	Film Crew	$23,000–$35,500
17-00	Art & Props	$5,000–$9,000
18-00	Wardrobe & Makeup	$3,000–$5,000
19-00	Permits	$2,000–$6,000
20-00	Insurance	$3,000–$10,000
21-00	**DAILIES**	**$4,000–$6,000**
22-00	**FX/STUNTS/CARS**	**$0**
23-00	Locations	$2,000–$10,000
24-00	Office & Paperwork	
25-00	Publicity	
26-00	Food	
TOTAL PRODUCTION BUDGET (In-the-Can)		
THE SHOOT (Total Above & Below)		
27-00	Film Edit	
28-00	Film Lab (Edit)	
29-00	Sound Edit	
30-00	ADR	
31-00	Foley	
32-00	Music/Score	
33-00	Mix (Re-record)	
34-00	Optical Transfer	
35-00	M&E	
THE EDIT (Post-Production)		
36-00	Titles	
37-00	Negative Cutting	
38-00	Film Lab (Answer Print)	
TOTAL PRODUCTION COSTS		

Whether you view dailies with or without sound will be determined by how soon, after you drop the exposed film at the lab, you want to see them. You can always get dailies without sound within two days. Dailies with sound are put through a couple of steps to marry the sound film with the picture film, which takes the extra time. Obviously, if you are on location or in a remote area, it will take longer. Also, you can always place a rush order on an important scene (DP wants to see how the lighting came out) and screen it the next morning, for an additional charge.

What Does It Cost?

To screen your film you eventually write three small checks. The first ($2,000–$3,000) is to hire an assistant editor to synchronize the sound transfers to the one-light print. Next, you'll need to rent editing equipment to synchronize, for a cost of $1,000.

The third check ($1,000–$2,000) will be to print a series of numbers on the film (every 20 frames on 16 mm and every 16 frames on 35 mm). These numbers, called edge code or key numbers, will be indispensable during editing. The total cost for these three checks will amount to **$4,000–$6,000.**

SPECIAL EFFECTS/STUNTS/CAR CHASES

I'm going to make this very, very, very simple. What do special effects (abbreviated SFX or FX), stunts, and car chases cost? They cost NOTHING! Here's why. You ain't gonna have any! It is tough enough to make a film—don't try to make a complicated one. Save the special effects and stunts for your second film.

———————

 BOOKS

Art of Visual Effects
P. Rogers, 357 pp., $41.95
Interviews with the contemporary geniuses on the tools of the trade.

Visual Effects Cinematography
Z. Perisic, 275 pp., $49.95
A how-to book explaining the techniques used to create those visual effects that dazzle audiences.

Video and Film Effects for Television
M. Mitchell, 224 pp., $24.99

Step-by-step coverage for special effects in TV, from moving the camera through to post-production.

 STUNT EFFECTS AND STUNT EXPERTS

STUNT PROFESSIONALS

Stuntmen's Association
10660 Riverside Dr, 2nd Floor, Suite E
Toluca Lake, CA 91602
President: Carl Ciarfalio
Ph: 818-766-4334

Stunts Unlimited
4421 Riverside Dr, Suite 210
Toluca Lake, CA 91505
President: Ron Stein
Ph: 323-874-0050

International Stunt Association
11331 Ventura Blvd, Suite 205
Studio City, CA 91604
President: Michael Haynes
Ph: 818-760-2072
Fax: 818-760-2217

Stuntwoman's Association United
PO Box 1483
Studio City, CA 91614
President: Leigh Hennessey
Ph: 818-508-4651

Stuntwomen's Association of Motion
   Pictures
12457 Ventura Blvd, Suite 208
Studio City, CA 91604
President: Jane Austin
Ph: 818-762-0907

SPECIAL EFFECTS EXPERTS

Scott Anderson
Contact: Paul Hook
c/o International Creative
   Management (ICM)
8942 Wilshire Blvd
Beverly Hills, CA 90211
Films: *Die Hard, Starship Troopers*
Ph: 310-550-4474
Fax: 310-550-4100

Eric Brevig
c/o Industrial Light & Magic (ILM)
PO Box 2459
San Rafael, CA 94912
Films: *Wild Wild West, Men in Black*
Ph: 415-258-2000

Mat Beck
c/o Light Matters
15332 Antioch, Suite 150
Pacific Palisades, CA 90272
Films: *X-Files, Star Trek*
Ph: 310-454-5104

John Dykstra
c/o Sony Pictures Imageworks
9050 W Washington Blvd
Culver City, CA 90232
Films: *Batman, Star Wars*
Ph: 310-840-8000
Fax: 310-840-8100

Richard Edlund
c/o Boss Film Studios
13335 Maxella Ave
Marina Del Rey, CA 90292
Films: *Ghostbusters, Air Force One*
Ph: 310-823-0433
Fax: 310-305-8576

Volker Engel
Contact: Bob Coleman
c/o Digital Artists Agency
2131 Century Park Ln, Suite 313
Los Angeles, CA 90067
Films: *Godzilla, Universal Soldier*
Ph: 310-788-3918

Anna Foerster
c/o Sightline Productions
PO Box 722142
San Diego, CA 92172
Films: *Independence Day,*
   Pitch Black
Ph: 858-538-9616
Fax: 858-538-8853

John Knoll
c/o Industrial Light & Magic (ILM)
PO Box 2459
San Rafael, CA 94912
Films: *Mission Impossible, Hook*
Ph: 415-258-2000

Ken Ralston
c/o Sony Pictures Imageworks
9050 W Washington Blvd
Culver City, CA 90232
Films: *Cocoon, Who Framed*
   Roger Rabbit
Ph: 310-840-8000
Fax: 310-840-8100

Mark Stetson
c/o Digital Domain
300 Rose Ave
Venice, CA 90291
Films: *Right Stuff, Blade Runner*
Ph: 310-314-2800
Fax: 310-314-2888

Doug Trumbull
c/o Entertainment Design Workshop
PO Box 1250
1375 Boardman St
Sheffield, MA 01257
Films: *2001, Silent Running*
Ph: 413-229-3101
Fax: 413-229-9930

PAPERWORK

"Organization Is Imperative"

Organization revolves around paperwork. Procrastinate, don't do your paperwork, and your film will suffer. Here are the 20–30 forms, releases, checklists, and contracts that, at a minimum, you will deal with. They are all important!

Forms
    Production Board
    Shooting Schedule
    Storyboards
    Continuity Breakdown
    Script Supervisor Notes
    Cast and Crew List
    Locations List
    Equipment and Suppliers List
    Camera Reports
    Sound Reports
    Call Sheets
    Production Reports

Releases
    Actor's Release
    Property Release
    Music Release
    Group Release
    Script Release

PRODUCTION BUDGET

Title: "Your $1,000,000 Feature" 　　**Executive Producer:** _____
　　　　　　　　　　　　　　　　　　　Producer: _____
Writer: _____ 　　　　　　　**Director:** _____

ACCOUNT NUMBER	DESCRIPTION	BUDGET
01-00	Producer	$10,000–$20,000
02-00	Writer/Script	$5,000–$10,000
03-00	Director	$10,000–$15,000
04-00	Cast/Actors	$6,000–$9,000 (+$25,000)
TOTAL ABOVE-THE-LINE (Pre-Production)		**$31,000–$54,000 (+$25,000)**
BELOW-THE-LINE		
5-00	Film Stock	$20,000–$40,000
6-00	Film Lab (Shoot)	$15,000–$30,000
7-00	Camera	$12,000–$30,000
8-00	Expendables	$2,000–$5,000
9-00	Sound Equipment	$6,000–$11,000
10-00	Sound Transfer	$3,000–$5,000
11-00	Light/Grip	$6,000–$24,000
12-00	Dolly	$2,000–$3,000
13-00	Cinematographer	$10,000–$15,000
14-00	PM & AD	$14,500–$21,000
15-00	Production Designer	$6,000–$8,500
16-00	Film Crew	$23,000–$35,500
17-00	Art & Props	$5,000–$9,000
18-00	Wardrobe & Makeup	$3,000–$5,000
19-00	Permits	$2,000–$6,000
20-00	Insurance	$3,000–$10,000
21-00	Dailies	$4,000–$6,000
22-00	FX/Stunts/Cars	$0
23-00	Locations	$2,000–$10,000
24-00	**OFFICE & PAPERWORK**	**$2,000–$7,000**
25-00	**PUBLICITY**	**$2,000–$10,000**
26-00	Food	
TOTAL PRODUCTION BUDGET (In-the-Can)		
THE SHOOT (Total Above & Below)		
27-00	Film Edit	
28-00	Film Lab (Edit)	
29-00	Sound Edit	
30-00	ADR	
31-00	Foley	
32-00	Music/Score	
33-00	Mix (Re-record)	
34-00	Optical Transfer	
35-00	M&E	
THE EDIT (Post-Production)		
36-00	Titles	
37-00	Negative Cutting	
38-00	Film Lab (Answer Print)	
TOTAL PRODUCTION COSTS		

Checklists
    Production Manager's Checklist
    Assistant Director's Shot List
    Gaffer and DP Checklist
    Property and Wardrobe Checklist

Contracts
    Story Rights
    Script Ownership
    Actor/talent Agreements
    Music/score Rights
    Independent Contractor Agreements
    Deferral Agreements

Production Board (aka breakdown, strip board, or board): This is prepared during pre-production by the PM or AD to establish an efficient order for shooting scenes.

Shooting Schedule: It states the order in which the scenes are to be shot and what (cast, props, locations, etc.) logistics are needed for each scene.

Storyboards: These sketches, which resemble a comic book, allow the director to conceptualize his thoughts and work efficiently. Even if you only draw stick figures, you must storyboard, for 🧳 ***if you can't direct a pencil, you can't direct a camera.***

Continuity Breakdown: After the board and schedule are prepared, the script supervisor, first AD, and PM make a detailed accounting (breakdown sheets) of all props, wardrobe, actors, equipment information, etc. that are needed. These sheets are photocopied, placed in loose-leaf notebooks, and distributed to key crew members.

Cast and Crew List: The production coordinator compiles the C&C list. It contains the names, addresses, phone numbers (home, cellular, and pager) of all cast and crew, so they can get in touch with one another, if and when a location or schedule change is planned.

Locations List: This is an itemization that gives addresses, descriptions (with photos, if available), directions, parking instructions, and phone numbers for each location. Always prepare driving instructions from every possible direction (north, east, west, and south).

Equipment and Suppliers List: The production coordinator compiles this list of suppliers, vendors, and miscellaneous support companies (addresses, phone numbers, calling hours, and persons to contact) and distributes it to the crew.

Camera Reports: Prepared by the second AC during the shoot, these reports itemize the details (footage, filters, film speed, etc.) for each shot, along with printing instructions, and is sent to the film lab with the exposed film.

Sound Reports: Prepared by the sound mixer, these daily reports are sent to the transfer facility. Normally the audio tapes and sound reports will accompany the film and camera reports to expedite synchronizing the sound with picture for dailies.

Call Sheets: The first AD and PM prepare these reports daily and distribute them to the crew at each day's wrap. This enables everyone to know what scenes and locations are scheduled for tomorrow, what cast members are needed, what equipment is required, and what time everyone must arrive.

Production Reports: At the end of each day, the PM and first AD fill in a report detailing everything that occurred that day, including time of first shot, lunchtime, time of final shot, number of scenes and pages shot, and amount of film footage used. This allows the studio executives to see what was accomplished and if everything is on schedule.

Checklists: Literally every department—camera, sound, wardrobe, makeup, props, set design, production, etc.—maintains a laundry list (checklist) of things to be ordered, things to do, and things to have ready for each day.

Contracts and Agreements: Do not make any handshake, oral, or loosely arranged agreements—get it in writing! After the film is completed, you must be able to show that you own all rights (talent, script, music) and have obtained all clearances (property, names, songs, etc.) to obtain an errors and omissions (E&O) insurance policy.

What Does Paperwork Cost?

The actual paper and software is not expensive. However, the professionals who prepare the paperwork can become expensive.

Film labs will give you free forms for camera and sound reports. Production forms come on pads of 25–50 sheets that you can purchase for $4–$7 each, for a cost of $100–$150. The production board (10–12 panels), with colored strips and a header panel, will cost about $150. You might also want to purchase a software program or two for screenwriting, budgeting, or scheduling, for $250–$700, for a total cost of **$500–$1,000.**

OFFICE

You're a low-budget filmmaker with limited money, so spend it wisely. Low-budget means low-rent. Seven hundred square feet is adequate for a production office. Don't look in a part of your city that has a Starbucks within five blocks and a Kinko's within ten blocks. Find a neighborhood with a bail bondsman on every other block, and there will be low-rent buildings offering short-term rentals.

Buy a couch (or even rent one), get two telephones, a fax, file cabinets, a computer (Internet DSL connected), a URL address and an e-mail account, two desks, folding director's chairs for meetings, a coffee table, and a good answering service. You'll also need a coffee pot and a small refrigerator for those 18-hour workdays. Dress the place up by getting a big bulletin board and adorning it with the headshots of potential cast members and framed movie posters. Now this is a production office.

Your temporary lease should cover five months. Month 1, during pre-production, you will use it for meetings, casting, and rehearsals. Month 2, during production, the office will be empty during the day while everyone is at the location shooting. Months 3–5, during post-production, it will become your editing suite.

Pay no more than $1/square foot or $700/month. For five months, that's $3,500. Also, you'll have phone fees and furniture costs. Depending on how much furniture you own and how much you borrow or buy, you'll spend $500–$3,000. The total cost to rent and set up a production office for five months will be $4,000–$6,000. At the very lowest (working out of your home), you will have a $1,500 phone bill ($300 × 5 months). Thus, your cost for having an office for five months will be **$1,500–$6,000,** and when combined with paperwork costs ($500–$1,000) will total **$2,000–$7,000.**

PUBLICITY

Every distributor is looking for you. Why are you hiding? Chapter 43, "Publicity," will outline what to do, what it costs, and why you do it. However, for the sake of this chapter and filling in the budget just allocate **$2,000–$10,000** for publicity.

TO DO:

1. Call Realtors and look for office space.
2. Order the forms you need!

 BOOKS

Film and TV Contracts
P. Alberstadt, 476 pp., $54.95
Contracts! An excellent book that details the contracts and agreements needed by an independent producer, with a CD-ROM template to use and adapt.

Contracts for the Film and Television Industry
M. Litwak, 455 pp., $35.00
Legal forms! Sixty-two useful contracts for producers that cover all areas of film and television production.

Film Scheduling
R. Singleton, 246 pp., $22.95
Scheduling! If you don't prepare your own shooting schedule you'll never understand what's being accomplished. This book explains how.

The Film Director's Team
A. Silver and E. Ward, 248 pp., $19.95
Paperwork! There are over 15 forms and checklists filled in daily during a shoot. This book explains them to a first-timer.

The Complete Film Production Handbook
E. Honthaner, 514 pp., $54.95
Forms! Forms! Forms! This book, with a CD-ROM, will allow you to print forms, adapt them, and organize your shoot.

Film Scheduling and Film Budgeting Workbook
R. Singleton, 298 pp., $19.95
Budgeting and scheduling! This book will give you the paperwork and needed information on how to fill it in for an efficient shoot.

 PRODUCTION MANAGERS AND ASSISTANT DIRECTORS

Contact the local film commissioner. (See chapter 31.)
Then contact local production manager(s) or assistant director(s).

FOOD AND CRAFT SERVICE

"Fuel Your Crew"

I didn't understand why a producer is supposed to feed his crew. That is, until 1982, when I stupidly attempted to not feed one. I wasn't trying to starve my employees. My thought was that by having everyone brownbag it I'd save money to buy more film stock, rent better equipment, have more takes, and make a better film. I thought everybody would agree to that. Boy, was I wrong.

Here was my logic: Producers are employers. Film crews are employees. Employees bring their lunch to work or they go out during a lunch break. The only employees that I know who get fed daily, by their boss, work in either the restaurant industry . . . or the Army.

So on that shoot, when I hired my crew, I told them that they'd be responsible for bringing their own lunches. I'd supply snacks and fast food (burgers, fries, and sodas) every now and then. Then, on the third day, after two grueling 18-hour shooting days, my six-foot-four-inch, 250-pound key grip approached me, wrapped his hands around my neck, and explained filmmaking to me. His grasp got tighter and tighter. My face got bluer and bluer. This was one pissed-off dude.

He gathered his composure (he didn't want a dead line producer on his hands) and said, 🧳 **"It isn't food. It's fuel. Skimp on food, don't feed your crew, and the film will suffer."**

As soon as he said the word "fuel" I got it. Your crew is waking at 5:00 A.M. and getting home at 10:00 P.M. They don't have the time or energy to buy groceries and prepare meals. McDonald's isn't open late or at 5:30 A.M., Starbucks isn't even open. Thus, all the energy and nourishment needed for those labor-intensive, anxiety-ridden 18-hour days will come from the fuel you provide.

PRODUCTION BUDGET

Title: "Your $1,000,000 Feature" Executive Producer: _____

Producer: _____

Writer: _____ Director: _____

ACCOUNT NUMBER	DESCRIPTION	BUDGET
01-00	Producer	$10,000–$20,000
02-00	Writer/Script	$5,000–$10,000
03-00	Director	$10,000–$15,000
04-00	Cast/Actors	$6,000–$9,000 (+$25,000)
TOTAL ABOVE-THE-LINE (Pre-Production)		**$31,000–$54,000 (+$25,000)**
BELOW-THE-LINE		
5-00	Film Stock	$20,000–$40,000
6-00	Film Lab (Shoot)	$15,000–$30,000
7-00	Camera	$12,000–$30,000
8-00	Expendables	$2,000–$5,000
9-00	Sound Equipment	$6,000–$11,000
10-00	Sound Transfer	$3,000–$5,000
11-00	Light/Grip	$6,000–$24,000
12-00	Dolly	$2,000–$3,000
13-00	Cinematographer	$10,000–$15,000
14-00	PM & AD	$14,500–$21,000
15-00	Production Designer	$6,000–$8,500
16-00	Film Crew	$23,000–$35,500
17-00	Art & Props	$5,000–$9,000
18-00	Wardrobe & Makeup	$3,000–$5,000
19-00	Permits	$2,000–$6,000
20-00	Insurance	$3,000–$10,000
21-00	Dailies	$4,000–$6,000
22-00	FX/Stunts/Cars	$0
23-00	Locations	$2,000–$10,000
24-00	Office & Paperwork	$2,000–$7,000
25-00	Publicity	$2,000–$10,000
26-00	**FOOD**	**$6,000–$9,000**
TOTAL PRODUCTION BUDGET (In-the-Can)		
THE SHOOT (Total Above & Below)		
27-00	Film Edit	
28-00	Film Lab (Edit)	
29-00	Sound Edit	
30-00	ADR	
31-00	Foley	
32-00	Music/Score	
33-00	Mix (Re-record)	
34-00	Optical Transfer	
35-00	M&E	
THE EDIT (Post-Production)		
36-00	Titles	
37-00	Negative Cutting	
38-00	Film Lab (Answer Print)	
TOTAL PRODUCTION COSTS		

I'm a quick study, and became a popular PM because of the way I fueled (fed) my crew from that day forward. Food prepared properly is not expensive. However, food prepared improperly will destroy the morale on your set and quite possibly induce your crew to quit.

Here's how to fuel your crew. In pre-production, hire a craft service person and a caterer. The craft service person is the first to arrive each day at the set, instantly prepares coffee and a continental breakfast. Then, six to seven hours later, your crew needs lunch. If you let them leave, and hope they'll come back and instantly resume shooting, you're naive. You want your crew to stay on the set. Hire a caterer and contract for a different meal each day at a price of $8-$13 per person. Have a hot meal, with vegetables and dessert, prepared daily and presented with china and silverware (not paper and plastic).

HELPFUL HINT   When hiring cast and crew, always ask their dietary habits (vegetarian, low-salt, Zen macrobiotic, etc.) and have the caterer prepare special meals for them daily. This is easy to do and the crew will think you're wonderful.

Next, make sure there is a snack table, loaded with munchies, maintained by the craft service person, for cast and crew to nibble on throughout the day. Doughnuts, freshly brewed coffee, sodas, candy, cookies, juices, and gum are common staples.

HELPFUL HINT   Contrary to what you've heard or believe, absolutely no drugs or alcohol are permitted on a set. However, when you enter the second week, the Zombie Week, of your shoot, and everyone is exhausted, have the snack table loaded with drinks (caffeine- and sugar-loaded) like Jolt, Burst, or Red Bull for that spurt in energy.

Finally, on days when working 15 hours or more, you will supply a second meal approximately six hours after the caterered lunch meal. Your craft service person will get 10 pizzas, or 40 burgers, or 8 buckets of chicken for a 30-minute break early in the evening.

Cost for your entire food budget will amount to **$6,000–$9,000.**

Breakfast	$1,000–$1,500
Lunch	$4,000–$5,000
Snacks	$500–$1,000
Second meal	$500–$1,500
	$6,000–$9,000

Feed your crew well. Aside from being assured that their weekly pay-checks don't bounce, good food is the only thing that they expect. I have heard some film people flippantly state that your film will only be as good as the food you feed your crew. You don't have to serve lobster thermidor, but feed them well.

TO DO:

1. When hiring, make a list of special food needs.
2. Get bids ($8–$13/person) from caterers.

 **FILM CATERERS**

Contact any caterer.
(See local Yellow Pages.)

THE FILM IS SHOT

"The Post-production Process"

Your feature film is shot and you've spent **$179,500–$354,000** of the $250,000–$500,000 budget. Now, with the remaining **$70,500–$146,000**, let's move into post-production and finish your film.

After 18 grueling days you got the Martini Shot (final shot of shoot), broke out the flat champagne, proposed a toast, and passed out. You come to (notice I didn't say "wake up") three days later and go to your office where your dailies (about to be called the "work print") are neatly stacked in 1,000-foot cans. Everyone is gone. Your crew has departed for other projects. What do you do?

The answer is obvious: You start post-production. The question, however, becomes: But how?

"Help" goes the cry, as you phone your DP. Remember, I told you to budget 10 percent of your DP's total salary for post-production. This allows you to write a $100 check 15–20 times, as if it were a consulting fee, each and every time that you phone or meet with your DP. You sit with him, schtup him $100, analyze the $70,500–$146,000 that is left, and figure how to allocate it to best finish your film and whom to hire as the editor.

IMPORTANT POINT   Post-production is simple. Don't be overwhelmed. *Post-production is easy because it happens in a very logical step-by-step order.* The shoot is overwhelming because everything happens at once every day. But post is simply one step at a time.

First, hire an editor (chapter 36). Walk away and let the editor edit. Then hire a sound editor (chapter 37). Walk away and let the sound editor

PRODUCTION BUDGET

Title: "Your $1,000,000 Feature"   Executive Producer: _____
                                    Producer: _____
Writer: _____   Director: _____

ACCOUNT NUMBER	DESCRIPTION	BUDGET
01-00	Producer	$10,000–$20,000
02-00	Writer/Script	$5,000–$10,000
03-00	Director	$10,000–$15,000
04-00	Cast/Actors	$6,000–$9,000 (+$25,000)
TOTAL ABOVE-THE-LINE (Pre-Production)		**$31,000–$54,000 (+$25,000)**
BELOW-THE-LINE		
5-00	Film Stock	$20,000–$40,000
6-00	Film Lab (Shoot)	$15,000–$30,000
7-00	Camera	$12,000–$30,000
8-00	Expendables	$2,000–$5,000
9-00	Sound Equipment	$6,000–$11,000
10-00	Sound Transfer	$3,000–$5,000
11-00	Light/Grip	$6,000–$24,000
12-00	Dolly	$2,000–$3,000
13-00	Cinematographer	$10,000–$15,000
14-00	PM & AD	$14,500–$21,000
15-00	Production Designer	$6,000–$8,500
16-00	Film Crew	$23,000–$35,500
17-00	Art & Props	$5,000–$9,000
18-00	Wardrobe & Makeup	$3,000–$5,000
19-00	Permits	$2,000–$6,000
20-00	Insurance	$3,000–$10,000
21-00	Dailies	$4,000–$6,000
22-00	FX/Stunts/Cars	$0
23-00	Locations	$2,000–$10,000
24-00	Office & Paperwork	$2,000–$7,000
25-00	Publicity	$2,000–$10,000
26-00	Food	$6,000–$9,000
TOTAL PRODUCTION BUDGET (IN-THE-CAN)		**$148,500–$300,000**
THE SHOOT (TOTAL ABOVE & BELOW)		**$179,500–$354,000**
27-00	Film Edit	
28-00	Film Lab (Edit)	
29-00	Sound Edit	
30-00	ADR	
31-00	Foley	
32-00	Music/Score	
33-00	Mix (Re-record)	
34-00	Optical Transfer	
35-00	M&E	
THE EDIT (Post-Production)		
36-00	Titles	
37-00	Negative Cutting	
38-00	Film Lab (Answer Print)	
TOTAL PRODUCTION COSTS		

edit. Then hire a musician/arranger for your score (chapter 38). Then do ADR (automatic dialogue replacement; chapter 39). Then do Foley (chapter 39). Then get your titles (chapter 40). Then order your final print at the lab (chapter 41) with the DP, film editor, and sound editor overseeing each step. All you do is observe, recommend, and approve. This you can handle.

There will be 12 steps (yep, another Hollywood 12-step program) during three stages—(a) splicing the film, (b) creating sound, (c) striking an answer print—of post-production when you are forced to write bank checks. They are:

1. The film edit
2. The sound edit
3. The ADR session
4. The Foley session
5. The music score
6. The re-recording session
7. The M&E track
8. The titles
9. The optical transfers
10. The negative cutting
11. The color correcting
12. And, striking a print

FILM EDIT VS. ELECTRONIC EDIT

There are two ways of editing—the old way, which is to physically cut film (the work print); or the newer method, which is to electronically (non-linear) edit using a computer. The new way, although the most common, is not necessarily the best way for you. Here's why.

When you edit on film (the old way) you literally splice the print that you get from the lab each day. This print, called your dailies when you screened it, is now called your work print when editing. This method worked for *Casablanca, Gone With the Wind, Miracle on 34th Street,* and all the classics. If the old edit system was good enough for them, shouldn't it be good enough for you?

To edit the new way (electronic editing, digital editing, desktop editing, or non-linear editing), your film is shot the same as the old way, but the film lab only develops the negative. They don't make a print. Instead they take your developed negative and either transfer it to tape (telecine) or digitize it onto a hard drive. Then, rather than physically splicing film, you edit with a computer.

The old way, you cut film. The new way, you slide digitized clips around with the mouse. The new way is faster. The new way is the way that most first-timers edit today. 🔳 *However, the new way is not automatically the way you want to go.* Don't assume it's the best way; stop, think for a moment, and contemplate the four problems with the newer electronic method.

1. Cost
2. Edit style
3. Dead sync
4. 3/2 pulldown

COST

To edit on film, you get a print at the lab and rent a film editing machine (for about $1,000 a month) that is manufactured by Moviola, KEM, or Steenbeck. It will take about 10 weeks to finish your edit. Let's do the math. There are about 700 hours in a month. Divide the 700 hours into $1,000 and you get a rental fee of $1.43/hour. Do you know any electronic editing facility or computer editing equipment that you can rent for that hourly rate? No way, Jose! Don't even try to say the word Avid (manufacturer of computer editing systems) to me. Can you get an hourly rate of $1.43 for an Avid? No! How about $3/hour for an Avid? No! $10/hour for an Avid? No! $20–$75/hour is the going rate to rent an Avid. Computers loaded with Final Cut Pro (Mac) or Adobe Premiere (Windows) editing software aren't even that cheap.

To edit electronically, you rent an electronic editing machine ($20–$75 per hour), usually manufactured by Avid. Editing this way, you'll finish your edit in only seven weeks. So the new way is definitely faster. Now, let's compare cost.

The old way, although a little slower, will cost, at $1,000 a month for a Moviola rental, about $2,500 for 10 weeks. The new way, at $20–$75 an hour for an Avid, will cost $5,600–$21,000 for seven weeks. The new way is faster, but more expensive, and aren't you trying to save money?

When salesmen who are selling editing time or machines tell you, "Everyone's doing it the new way," they are lying. Spielberg, Scorsese, and Stone—who can edit any way they want—still prefer the old way. Get a print, call KEM, Steenbeck, or Moviola (film editing machine manufacturers), rent a flatbed or upright (types of film editing machines), and splice.

> **AUTHOR'S NOTE**   Please don't misinterpret me. I'm not saying to not edit electronically, or rent an Avid, or use your Mac G4 loaded with the latest version of Final Cut Pro. What I'm saying is that there are two ways of going. And I want you to think twice before you just jump on the everyone's-doing-it-electronic bandwagon.

EDIT STYLE

Another problem with electronic post-production is in the visual edit rhythm. What I mean is, your editor is used to editing for broadcast, cable, or video. When you edit electronically, you put in more splices per minute and get what's nicknamed the "Pepsi Cut" or the "MTV Cut." This edit, with its fast cut pace, is visually entertaining when seen on television but overbearing when seen on the big screen. Too many fast, choppy slices give theatrical audiences eyestrain and one hell of a headache.

DEAD SYNC

Be careful, you may face a problem syncing your picture with audio. When you edit electronically, you sit six to eight feet from the monitor. Light and sound move at different speeds. When you are six to eight feet away from the monitor while editing, and then six to eight feet away from a TV set when viewing at home, the difference in the two speeds is not noticeable and everything appears synchronized.

However, when you watch the film in a movie theater from a distance of 150–300 feet (called the "throw"), the difference between the speed of sound and the speed of light becomes noticeable. The result is that your picture which was edited to be in sync on TV, is not in sync in a theater. Bummer! This is a big problem. Electronic editing facilities know synchronization problems exist. They even have a phrase for it; they call it "dead sync." Put in the back of your mind that dead sync is an issue that you will deal with if your film is to be viewed in a movie theater.

3/2 PULLDOWN

The electronic edit system and the film edit system run at different speeds. Film runs at 24 frames per second (fps), and video runs at 30 frames per second. Thus, the edit list you made from your electronic edit system is based on a 30 fps system, and the negative cutter cuts at 24 frames per second. Get it? The numbers won't match. If you give the 30 fps edit decision list (EDL) to a negative cutter, the final print will look like Fellini dropped acid. Yikes! Your job is to be sure that the editing facility performs a proper 3/2 pulldown (conforms the 30 fps EDL to a 24 fps EDL) so that you can properly cut the film negative to strike your final print.

WHAT'S THE POINT?

Here's the point regarding choosing an edit method: The old way, although it seems archaic, works and is still used by Coppola, Spielberg, and Scorsese, when they're not making a film that's loaded with digital effects. The new method, although faster, is more expensive and has other shortcomings. I'm quite sure that most of you will choose the newer electronic edit method on a desktop computer. *But,* please know that (a) it will probably be more expensive; (b) you must make sure your splice rhythm is suited for a movie theater, not a TV; (c) your film must be synchronized for a 150–300 foot theatrical throw; and (d) you must be very anal when obtaining your EDL.

Whether you edit the old way or the new way, you will still go through the 12 steps of post-production, step-by-step-by-step-by-step-by-step . . . until you get to your answer print. Let's look at those 12 steps.

————————

TO DO:

1. Reverse-budget your post.

BOOKS

First Cut
G. Oldham, 421 pp., $21.95
Conversations with 20 great film editors who explain the craft and process.

Guide to Post-production for TV and Film
B. Clark and S. Spohr, 256 pp., $41.95
An excellent book that takes you step-by-step through the process of finishing your film.

Film Technology in Post-Production
D. Case, 221 pp., $30.00
This updated second edition takes you through the mechanical process of finishing your film.

Film Editing Room Handbook
N. Hollyn, 582 pp., $24.95
A must-have that will outline the step-by-step process of finishing your film after the shoot.

The Guerilla Film Maker's Handbook
C. Jones and G. Jolliffe, 640 pp., $35.00
Superior chapters, with photos and line drawings, that detail the steps as you go from your shoot to your final answer print.

Editing and Post-Production
D. McGrath, 186 pp., $39.95
Although a gift book, it explains the editor's craft with 500 photos and numerous interviews.

 **POST-PRODUCTION SUPERVISORS**

Contact the film lab.
(See chapter 18.)

Contact the local film commissioner.
(See chapter 31.)

THE PICTURE EDIT

"Pick an Editor"

There are two post-production methods: the old way (the film way), which still works and entails getting a print of the developed negative from the lab to splice on film editing equipment (an upright or a flatbed); or the new way (electronic post), which is to transfer the developed negative to tape or digitize it, and edit electronically with a computer-based system.

Avid is the largest manufacturer of these computer-based systems, but with the prices of computers dropping so fast, most of today's first-time filmmakers make their own inexpensive computer editing system with either the latest version of Adobe Premiere (PC-based) or Final Cut Pro (Macintosh-based) software.

Whether you decide to edit using the old method or the newer method, the steps of post-production are pretty much the same. Pick a picture editor—cut the picture. Pick a sound editor—cut the sound. Adjust the dialogue tracks. Add sound effects. Do ADR. Do Foley. Pick a composer, etc.

But the first step is always "pick an editor."

WHEN TO HIRE THE EDITOR

Do you hire an editor before you shoot or wait until after the shoot? No one really knows. Ask an editor and of course he'll say, "When shooting your film." Naturally he/she wants to work during the shoot—it means a longer-paying job. But does the extra money you pay him outweigh what he saves you?

In the low-budget world, I don't believe so. If there's extra money in

PRODUCTION BUDGET

Title: "Your $1,000,000 Feature" Executive Producer: _____

Producer: _____

Writer: _____ Director: _____

ACCOUNT NUMBER	DESCRIPTION	BUDGET
01-00	Producer	$10,000–$20,000
02-00	Writer/Script	$5,000–$10,000
03-00	Director	$10,000–$15,000
04-00	Cast/Actors	$6,000–$9,000 (+$25,000)
TOTAL ABOVE-THE-LINE (Pre-Production)		**$31,000–$54,000 (+$25,000)**
BELOW-THE-LINE		
5-00	Film Stock	$20,000–$40,000
6-00	Film Lab (Shoot)	$15,000–$30,000
7-00	Camera	$12,000–$30,000
8-00	Expendables	$2,000–$5,000
9-00	Sound Equipment	$6,000–$11,000
10-00	Sound Transfer	$3,000–$5,000
11-00	Light/Grip	$6,000–$24,000
12-00	Dolly	$2,000–$3,000
13-00	Cinematographer	$10,000–$15,000
14-00	PM & AD	$14,500–$21,000
15-00	Production Designer	$6,000–$8,500
16-00	Film Crew	$23,000–$35,500
17-00	Art & Props	$5,000–$9,000
18-00	Wardrobe & Makeup	$3,000–$5,000
19-00	Permits	$2,000–$6,000
20-00	Insurance	$3,000–$10,000
21-00	Dailies	$4,000–$6,000
22-00	FX/Stunts/Cars	$0
23-00	Locations	$2,000–$10,000
24-00	Office & Paperwork	$2,000–$7,000
25-00	Publicity	$2,000–$10,000
26-00	Food	$6,000–$9,000
TOTAL PRODUCTION BUDGET (In-the-Can)		**$148,500–$300,000**
THE SHOOT (Total Above & Below)		**$179,500–$354,000**
27-00	**Film Edit**	**$12,000–$18,500**
28-00	**Film Lab (Edit)**	**$2,000–$3,000**
29-00	Sound Edit	
30-00	ADR	
31-00	Foley	
32-00	Music/Score	
33-00	Mix (Re-record)	
34-00	Optical Transfer	
35-00	M&E	
THE EDIT (Post-Production)		
36-00	Titles	
37-00	Negative Cutting	
38-00	Film Lab (Answer Print)	
TOTAL PRODUCTION COSTS		

the budget I'd rather it be used on buying more film stock, allowing the actors more takes and the director more angles, rather than having an editor hang around the set with a cup of coffee hitting on starlets.

The only way an editor saves you money during the shoot is if he edits fast enough to discover that a vital shot in a scene is missing before you leave the location. On low-budget films, however, it is common practice to shoot the film, take a one-week break, and only then concern yourself with selecting a film editor.

WHERE TO FIND AN EDITOR

First, ask your DP (remember, give him a $100 for each phone call or meeting). Then query the film lab and the film commissioner, while simultaneously perusing the local production directory. This will garner three to five names. Phone them and ask if they want to edit a feature. Tell them how many feet of film (or hours of tape) you shot and your pay scale.

If interested, each editor will come to the interview, where you'll be with your DP (yep, another $100 check), with a demo tape. Obviously, it will look good or he wouldn't let you see it. You view each of their tapes and talk film theory. How do you know which to hire? I truly wish I knew. There is no sure method, and unless there's a strong referral you will probably go with just a gut feeling.

> **IMPORTANT POINT**   Editor A shows you a half-hour drama that looks good, and, in a nice way, lets you know that he saved the film. Editor B shows you a half-hour drama that also looks good, and, in a nice way, lets you know that he saved the film. **Every film editor believes he saved the film.** What you won't know is that Editor A had a great script, great film footage, and great acting, and edited something that is good. Editor B had a rotten script, rotten footage, and rotten acting, and edited something that is good. So Editor A is only an average editor, and Editor B is an excellent editor.

WHAT FILM EDITING COSTS

You will write four checks—(1) editor's salary, (2) assistant editor's salary, (3) equipment rental, and (4) editing supplies—to achieve six edits (cuts of your film) over an 8–10 week period. The first edit is either called the rough cut, the assemble edit, or the first cut. The second edit is called the second cut; the third edit, the third cut, etc.

The first cut is nothing but the master shots, in the order they appear in the script. Remember in the directing chapter I said to get the master shot and then get coverage. If you did this, you will have a master shot for every scene. However, you didn't shoot page 1 first, then page 2 second, then page 3 third—you shot out of reading order to accommodate efficiency. Now, the first edit simply places the master shots (shot out of order) back into their proper script reading order.

HOW TO EDIT If editing on a flatbed, you will have 50 cans (1,000-foot reels) of film. Let's assume that scene 1 is exactly one page long (one page of script equals one minute of running time equals 90 feet of 35mm film). The editor, with the script notes, finds that the 90-foot master shot of scene 1 is on reel 19, footage 220–310. The editor spools reel 19 to 220 feet, marks it, and makes a cut. He then spools forward 90 feet to footage 310, cuts again, removes the 90 feet, and cements back together the remaining 910 feet (0′–220′ and 310′–1,000′) and puts it back into its original can.

The 90-foot (60 seconds of running time) master shot is now the first minute of your movie.

Now, assume that scene 2 (script pages 2 and 3) is a two-minute scene. Two minutes is 180 feet of film. The editor checks the script notes and determines that scene 2's master shot (180 feet) is on reel 12, footage 640–820. He takes reel 12, cuts out the 180 feet, and splices it onto the end of scene 1's 90 feet for a total of three minutes (60 seconds of scene 1 and 120 seconds of scene 2), or 270 feet.

Now, assume that scene 3 is only 15 seconds long. It comprises the top fourth of script page 4. The editor looks for the 20 feet (15 seconds) of the master shot of scene 3. It's on reel 21, footage 370–390. The editor cuts the 20 feet from reel 21 and splices it onto the end of scene 2's two-minute (180 feet) master shot, which is just after scene 1's one-minute (90 feet) master shot.

You now have 3 minutes and 15 seconds of the film edited with three master shots. The rest of the film, master shot after master shot after master shot, is assembled the same way. This is not difficult. And if you were Jim Jarmusch or Kevin Smith editing their first films (*Stranger Than Paradise* and *Clerks*), you'd be almost done.

Anyone, if they can read script notes and splice, can do a rough cut. It is not an artistic endeavor. It ain't rocket science. It is just mechanical. The rough cut takes approximately one week and has the 50,000 feet spliced down to 12,000–13,000 feet. The second edit (another week) trims this to 10,000–12,000 feet with medium shots in it. The third edit (another week) trims this to 8,500–11,000 feet with close-ups, over-the-shoulder, and re-action shots in it. Finally, the fourth, fifth, and sixth edits rearrange scenes, fine-tune the film, and get it down to 8,100–10,800 feet.

The bottom line is to budget enough money to hire an editor, with an assistant, to give you six cuts in an 8–10 week period. The film editor will cost $800–$1,000/week ($6,400–$10,000). He will need an assistant editor at $400–$500/week ($3,200–$5,000). The film editing equipment (splicers, stools, sound heads, rewinds, flatbeds, etc.) will rent for about $1,000/month ($2,000–$2,500). You should also count on spending another $400–$1,000 on supplies for the editor (grease pencils, bulbs, gloves, tape, cement, film cores, etc.), for a total cost of **$12,000–$18,500.**

Editor	$6,400–$10,000
Assistant Editor	$3,200–$5,000
Equipment Rental	$2,000–$2,500
Editing Supplies	$400–$1,000
	$12,000–$18,500

IMPORTANT POINT If you decide to edit electronically (you probably will), realize that the edit will go faster, maybe 6–8 weeks instead of 8–12. Also, be very careful when you transfer your electronic image to the film image for theatrical distribution, for there are always glitches. It never goes as smoothly as those salesmen say. Ask them about guaranteeing "dead sync" (synchronizing picture to sound for a theatrical throw, not a broadcasting throw) and the "3/2 pulldown" (converting the 30 frames/second electronic edit list to a 24 frames/second film edit list).

Also, during the edit you will incur lab charges called reprints. The film editor might want to creatively cut in a flashback. He will call the lab and reprint the scene from the original developed negative. Maybe some footage is too light, too dark, too red, or too green. The editor might want it reprinted. Possibly, during the splicing, the work print got ripped or mutilated. Then reprint it. All you need to know is that there will be reprints (or retransfers, if electronic editing) during this stage. The lab will charge about 20 cents/foot, with the total cost being **$2,000–$3,000.**

Two or three months later, your 50,000 feet is spliced to 8,100–10,800 feet that portrays the visual story. You project it. It fills the screen. The color is good. The scenes are in order. However, something looks flat about your film. You're not sure what it is. You ask your DP (another $100 check), "What's wrong?" and he tells you that your movie doesn't come alive until you add 20–40 tracks of sound.

_____

TO DO:

1. View videos and count the splices in several scenes.

 BOOKS

Film Editing Room Handbook
N. Hollyn, 582 pp., $24.95
A must-have that will outline the step-by-step process of finishing your film after the shoot.

The Technique of Film and Video Editing
K. Dancyger, 381 pp., $32.95
The book is described as the best training for directors-to-be. Examples from recent films shot by Spike Lee, Atom Egoyan, and Quentin Tarantino.

Video Editing
S. Browne, 312 pp., $34.99
A complete how-to of contemporary video editing techniques for the new digital technologies.

Nonlinear Editing Basics
S. Browne, 221 pp., $36.95

A user-friendly, heavily illustrated guide for anyone editing with a non-linear system.

Editing Digital Film
J. Fowler, 187 pp., $29.95
Gives a basic intro to Final Cut Pro, Avid, and Media 100.

The Avid Digital Editing Room Handbook
T. Solomons, 233 pp., $26.95
This book is a must for first-timers using an Avid editing system.

Avid Editing
S. Kauffmann, 294 pp., $52.95
If you are using either Media Composer or Avid Express, this book, with its demonstration-loaded CD-ROM, will give you the nuts and bolts.

Digital Desktop Nonlinear Editing
S. Schenk, 401 pp., $49.95
This book demystifies the art of digital editing. Its CD-ROM is loaded

with demos, tutorials, and numerous visual clips.

 VIDEOS

Video Editing
VHS, 30 minutes, $22.95
Basic editing techniques and more.

Desktop Video
VHS, 30 minutes, $22.95
Computer video tips and techniques.

 FILM EDITORS

Motion Picture Editors Guild/West
(IATSE, Local 700)
7715 Sunset Blvd, Suite 200
Los Angeles, CA 90046

Ph: 323-876-4770
Fax: 323-876-0861
Web: www.editorsguild.com

Motion Picture Editors Guild/East
(IATSE, Local 771)
165 W 46th St, Suite 900
New York, NY 10036
Ph: 212-302-0700
Fax: 212-302-1091

Contact the local film commissioner.
(See chapter 31.)

THE SOUND EDIT

"Pick a Sound Editor"

When a film is successful, the writer gets credit, the director gets credit, and the actors get credit. Even the cinematographer, composer, production designer, and film editor get accolades. One of the tragedies of filmmaking is that the sound editor goes unnoticed. Don't believe me? Then name one sound editor. Without a sound editor your film's visual look and the actors' performances appear flat and uninteresting. Without a sound editor the Denzels, Dustins, Coppolas, and Spielbergs will get no Oscars. Now, once again, name me a sound editor.

WHAT A SOUND EDITOR DOES

The sound is always taken for granted. Sound is never noticed when it's good, but when it's bad everyone notices. Poor or mediocre sound will destroy even the best film. **The sound recorded at the shoot, the real sound recorded with the best equipment, isn't good. Matter of fact, it sucks.**

Here's why. The human ear receives hundreds, maybe thousands, of tracks of sound from every direction simultaneously. Yet when we capture sound with a microphone, those thousands of tracks are condensed down into one track. Consequently, the sound recorded during your shoot is flat. It is almost mono. During post-production, it becomes the sound editor's job to take this flat sound, take it apart, enhance it, create more tracks, then layer these tracks on top of each other and make this artificial sound appear as if it is the "true" dimensional sound.

The first step in sound editing is a "spotting session" where the sound editor views the dailies with the director to discern what he has in mind for

PRODUCTION BUDGET

Title: "Your $1,000,000 Feature" Executive Producer: _____
                                  Producer: _____
Writer: _____   Director: _____

ACCOUNT NUMBER	DESCRIPTION	BUDGET
01-00	Producer	$10,000–$20,000
02-00	Writer/Script	$5,000–$10,000
03-00	Director	$10,000–$15,000
04-00	Cast/Actors	$6,000–$9,000 (+$25,000)
TOTAL ABOVE-THE-LINE (Pre-Production)		**$31,000–$54,000 (+$25,000)**
BELOW-THE-LINE		
5-00	Film Stock	$20,000–$40,000
6-00	Film Lab (Shoot)	$15,000–$30,000
7-00	Camera	$12,000–$30,000
8-00	Expendables	$2,000–$5,000
9-00	Sound Equipment	$6,000–$11,000
10-00	Sound Transfer	$3,000–$5,000
11-00	Light/Grip	$6,000–$24,000
12-00	Dolly	$2,000–$3,000
13-00	Cinematographer	$10,000–$15,000
14-00	PM & AD	$14,500–$21,000
15-00	Production Designer	$6,000–$8,500
16-00	Film Crew	$23,000–$35,500
17-00	Art & Props	$5,000–$9,000
18-00	Wardrobe & Makeup	$3,000–$5,000
19-00	Permits	$2,000–$6,000
20-00	Insurance	$3,000–$10,000
21-00	Dailies	$4,000–$6,000
22-00	FX/Stunts/Cars	$0
23-00	Locations	$2,000–$10,000
24-00	Office & Paperwork	$2,000–$7,000
25-00	Publicity	$2,000–$10,000
26-00	Food	$6,000–$9,000
TOTAL PRODUCTION BUDGET (In-the-Can)		**$148,500–$300,000**
THE SHOOT (Total Above & Below)		**$179,500–$354,000**
27-00	Film Edit	$12,000–$18,500
28-00	Film Lab (Edit)	$2,000–$3,000
27-00	**SOUND EDIT**	**$7,500–$12,000**
29-00	ADR	
30-00	Foley	
31-00	Music/Score	
32-00	Mix (Re-record)	
33-00	Optical Transfer	
34-00	M&E	
THE EDIT (Post-Production)		
36-00	Titles	
37-00	Negative Cutting	
38-00	Film Lab (Answer Print)	
TOTAL PRODUCTION COSTS		

each scene. The sound editor then becomes a kind of composer as he creates, re-creates, and gathers the sounds to enhance the mood of each scene.

For example, take a simple scene in an inexpensive motel room. A woman enters, turns on the light, drops her keys and purse on the dresser, removes her blouse and tosses it on the coffee table, revealing a blood-soaked bra, then flops onto the bed with a moan. The sound effects the sound editor will gather will probably include:

- City traffic
- Cars honking
- A siren blaring
- Key in lock
- Doorknob turning
- Door squeaking
- Door slamming shut
- Lock bolted shut
- Footsteps on carpet
- Keys hitting dresser
- Purse hitting dresser
- Blouse rustling
- Blouse hitting coffee table
- Bed squeaking
- Moan

Each sound is created, cut, and placed to match the action on the screen. The sounds add depth to the visual image.

Next, the sound editor separates the recorded dialogue (cuts the dialogue tracks) onto different tracks. For example, when several people are talking to each other, he separates each person's dialogue onto its own audio track so that during the mix (re-recording session) the mixer will be able to raise or lower an actor's voice without affecting the voice(s) of the other actor(s) in the scene.

Further, the sound editor is responsible for preparing the "cue sheets." These are charts that indicate the precise spots where a sound effect either fades in or fades out. Having these cues ready will save hours of time, and therefore money, at the very expensive mixing session.

If this appears complicated, it is. But don't worry about it and all the technical details, for the bottom line is that all you're going to do is hire someone to do it for you. Your job is to hire the right sound editor at the right price.

HOW TO FIND A SOUND EDITOR

The best way is to get referrals from your film editor. Believe me, if a sound editor ever ruined a film editor's cut with poor sound, that film editor will make sure never to work with him again. By the same token, if a film editor's cut was improved with excellent sound, he will praise and work with that sound editor again and again. Also get recommendations from the manager of the sound facility where you're planning to book ADR (chapter 39), Foley (chapter 39), and mixing (chapter 39) time. Finally, your cinematographer ($100 check) will have the name of a sound editor or two.

Between these three sources you will get several names. Interview them with your DP ($100 check) and film editor present and, as with hiring your film editor, go with a gut feeling.

WHAT TO PAY

You will need the sound editor for five to seven weeks at $700–$900/week ($3,500–$6,300). He, in turn, will need an assistant at $400–$500/week ($2,000–$3,500). Finally, the editing equipment and supplies will cost approximately $2,000. This totals **$7,500–$12,000.**

TO DO:

1. Call sound facilities and get referrals.

 BOOKS

Practical Art of Motion Picture Sound
D. Yewdall, 266 pp., $49.95
An excellent book. Provides a thorough A–Z of creating great sound from the shoot, to the edit, to the final print.

Producing Great Sound for Digital Video
J. Rose, 428 pp., $44.95
If you are shooting your movie with digital video, this book is a must.

Audio Post-production in Video and Film
T. Amyes, 243 pp., $42.95
A good introduction for a filmmaking beginner, and loaded with enough technical depth to suit the professional.

Sound-On-Film
V. LoBrutto, 301 pp., $19.95
Learn from the best. Interviews with
27 creators of sound for movies like
Star Wars, Apocalypse Now, and
Raging Bull.

SOUND EDITORS

Contact the local film commissioner.
(See chapter 31.)

Contact your film editor.
(See chapter 36.)

Coffey Sound & Communications
(West Coast sound rental facility with
   bulletin board)
3353 W Cahuenga Blvd
Hollywood, CA 90068
Ph: 323-876-7525
Fax: 323-876-4775

Lentini Communications
(East Coast sound rental facility with
   bulletin board)
54 W 21st St, Suite 301
New York, NY 10010
Ph: 212-206-1452
Fax: 212-206-1453

Fletcher Chicago
1000 N Northbranch
Chicago, IL 60607

Ph: 312-932-2700
Fax: 312-932-2799

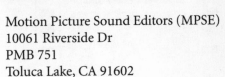

SOUND ASSOCIATIONS

Motion Picture Sound Editors (MPSE)
10061 Riverside Dr
PMB 751
Toluca Lake, CA 91602
Ph: 818-506-7731

Association of Motion Picture Sound
   (AMPS)
28 Knox St
London W1H 1FS England
Ph: 44-207-723-6727
Web: www.amps.net

Cinema Audio Society (CAS)
12414 Huston St
Valley Village, CA 91607
Fax: 818-752-8624
E-mail: CinAudSo@aol.com

American Cinema Editors (ACE)
100 Universal City Plz, Bldg 2282,
   Room 234
Universal City, CA 91608
Ph: 818-777-2900
Fax: 818-733-5023

MUSIC/SCORE

"Hire a Composer"

Music sets the dramatic tone. What is a kiss without violins? A cavalry charge without a bugle? Music establishes moods, intensifies emotions, and maintains the story by connecting scenes and shots. It is especially important on low-budget productions because it disguises imperfections in the dialogue and effects tracks. Be careful! Be very careful! Most first-timers make big mistakes when approaching music for their film. Permit me to explain how to obtain your music/score inexpensively by first explaining what not to do.

WHAT NOT TO DO

First, *don't* use "prerecorded" songs. I know you think it's a great idea. A Moody Blues album, a couple of Grateful Dead songs, a Metallica cut, a '50s Frankie Avalon beach song. Studio features use them. Why not you? Simple: They're outrageously expensive. Popular tunes that pop up during films cost $25,000–$200,000 each—and that's for only 10–15 seconds. Using any Beatles song for 5–10 seconds will cost at least $200,000. The cheapest licensing fee I ever heard of for a popular song was $6,000.

Now, consider 12–15 songs for 10–15 second segments at $6,000–$50,000 each, and your music budget skyrockets to $60,000–$750,000. You can't afford that. *Almost Famous,* the Cameron Crowe film about his escapades as a 15-year-old reporter for *Rolling Stone* magazine had a music budget of almost $3.5 million for prerecorded songs of the '60s.

PRODUCTION BUDGET

Title: "Your $1,000,000 Feature"   Executive Producer: _____
                                     Producer: _____
Writer: _____   Director: _____

ACCOUNT NUMBER	DESCRIPTION	BUDGET
01-00	Producer	$10,000–$20,000
02-00	Writer/Script	$5,000–$10,000
03-00	Director	$10,000–$15,000
04-00	Cast/Actors	$6,000–$9,000 (+$25,000)
TOTAL ABOVE-THE-LINE (Pre-Production)		**$31,000–$54,000 (+$25,000)**
BELOW-THE-LINE		
5-00	Film Stock	$20,000–$40,000
6-00	Film Lab (Shoot)	$15,000–$30,000
7-00	Camera	$12,000–$30,000
8-00	Expendables	$2,000–$5,000
9-00	Sound Equipment	$6,000–$11,000
10-00	Sound Transfer	$3,000–$5,000
11-00	Light/Grip	$6,000–$24,000
12-00	Dolly	$2,000–$3,000
13-00	Cinematographer	$10,000–$15,000
14-00	PM & AD	$14,500–$21,000
15-00	Production Designer	$6,000–$8,500
16-00	Film Crew	$23,000–$35,500
17-00	Art & Props	$5,000–$9,000
18-00	Wardrobe & Makeup	$3,000–$5,000
19-00	Permits	$2,000–$6,000
20-00	Insurance	$3,000–$10,000
21-00	Dailies	$4,000–$6,000
22-00	FX/Stunts/Cars	$0
23-00	Locations	$2,000–$10,000
24-00	Office & Paperwork	$2,000–$7,000
25-00	Publicity	$2,000–$10,000
26-00	Food	$6,000–$9,000
TOTAL PRODUCTION BUDGET (In-the-Can)		**$148,500–$300,000**
THE SHOOT (Total Above & Below)		**$179,500–$354,000**
27-00	Film Edit	$12,000–$18,500
28-00	Film Lab (Edit)	$2,000–$3,000
29-00	Sound Edit	$7,500–$12,000
30-00	ADR	
31-00	Foley	
27-00	**MUSIC/SCORE**	**$5,000–$7,000**
32-00	Mix (Re-record)	
33-00	Optical Transfer	
34-00	M&E	
THE EDIT (Post-Production)		
36-00	Titles	
37-00	Negative Cutting	
38-00	Film Lab (Answer Print)	
TOTAL PRODUCTION COSTS		

WARNING   If you don't license these songs properly (technically called "music clearance"), you won't get an E&O insurance policy. And, remember, without E&O insurance you won't get a distributor.

Second, *don't* use "pre-cleared" (canned or stock) music from those CDs advertised for $99 in the back of filmmaker magazines. They're actually okay, but do you really want something that's just "okay" for your film's score?

Next, *don't* use "public domain" (free) music. Public domain is basically anything that was recorded or written over 75 years ago. Do you know of any music written in the early '20s or before that you want for your score?

Now, *don't* get smart and say "classical." Although Beethoven's Fifth Symphony is public domain, what you *can't* use is a 1986 recording of Leonard Bernstein conducting the New York Philharmonic in a rendition of Beethoven's Fifth. This recording will not be public domain for 60 years. You can purchase ($3) the sheet music of Beethoven's Fifth, rent a music hall ($10,000+), hire an orchestra ($20,000–$100,000/day) and a conductor ($10,000–$30,000), project the work print ($2,000+), and have the conductor, with the $3 sheet music, conduct the orchestra. It just got expensive, didn't it?

WHAT TO DO

Now that you know what you aren't going to do, what you *are* going to do is hire a composer. **Every city has hundreds, if not thousands, of unemployed musicians, and every one of them would love an opening title credit** on a feature film that says "Composed By," "Music By," or "Orchestrated By." Hire a composer/musician/arranger, just like you hired a writer. It is a composer-for-hire. It's that simple, and you own everything.

HELPFUL HINTS

- Beware of musicians who quote inflated rates when they've never scored a film. Don't be intimidated—they're employees.
- With studio features, the producer or studio owns all rights. Treat your low-budget composer just like a studio would treat him. Pay

a salary and keep all "licensing and publishing rights." You pay. You own.

- Most music publishers allow you to use their songs inexpensively, sometimes for free, if you intend to showcase at a festival. They do this hoping that if a distributor buys the film, they'll want the music also. Then it gets expensive.
- Although it's not legal, many first-time filmmakers just put (aka steal) popular music, without proper licensing, in their film for festival screenings. If a distributor buys the film, they dump the illegal music and license songs (possibly the same ones) after the fact.

FINDING COMPOSERS

Of course, first check your local film directory. Next, all post-production facilities have bulletin boards loaded with composers' and musicians' business cards. Also, there are talent agencies and associations that specialize in music composers. You can browse through record stores for local bands (contact numbers are always on those CDs), and check out acts in your local lounges, clubs, and rock venues. Make your calls and you will have dozens of composers/musicians competing to create music for you.

WHAT COMPOSERS DO

Your composer views the final cut and conducts "spotting sessions" with the director, where each scene's mood and theme are discussed, and makes a list of "music cues." From these cues, he compiles a music "timing sheet" listing the footage and time (frames and seconds) where the music is placed. The composer then creates the score, working with the director, fitting music into the footage and time allotted within each cue. Finally, the composer records the score at his studio with his synthesizer and several additional musicians, and delivers the final product, with the cue sheets, for approval.

WHAT TO PAY

A $500,000–$1 million feature film can easily allocate $25,000–$50,000 for music. This allows for 8–15 studio musicians, two or three recording sessions, a day or two of mixing time, the contracted fees for composing and orchestrating, stock costs, licensing fees (music clearance for two or three songs), and studio and equipment rental fees.

With your budget, this is not affordable. Thus, looking for a composer who needs his first feature credit, but who has his own recording studio (a second bedroom or garage) is your best choice. Negotiate a flat fee of **$5,000–$7,000** to include the composer's fee, recording studio time, additional musicians, tape stock, and transfer costs. Don't pay more.

TO DO:

> **1.** Get composer referrals and ask for demo tapes.

 BOOKS

The Score
M. Schelle, 429 pp., $19.95
Interviews with film composers that reveal the craft and secrets behind the marriage of music and image.

Creating the Best Score for Your Film
D. Bell, 112 pp., $12.95
An excellent how-to book for the first-time filmmaker. A must-have!

The Reel World: Scoring for Pictures
J. Rona, 272 pp., $24.95
A very practical guide to the art, technology, and business of composing for film and TV.

Film and Television Composer's
  Resource Guide
M. Northam and L. Miller, 220 pp., $36.95

For the working composer. A superb guide to organizing and building his/her music business. Loaded with forms, checklists, and agreements.

Music for the Movies
T. Thomas, 326 pp., $19.95
An excellent read. A total history of film music from the '30s to the '90s.

 SOFTWARE

Automated Contracts for the Music
  Industry
J. Earp, Windows or Macintosh, $199.95
A $450/hour entertainment attorney in a disc. Over 65 "fill in the blanks" contracts for musicians.

LICENSING SITES

www.EnableYourMusic.com
Founder: Steve Love
Founded: March 2001

www.SongCatalog.com
Founder: Steven McClintock
Founded: November 2000

www.Taxi.com
Founder: Michael Laskow
Founded: January 1992

www.MusicMatch.com
Founder: Dennis Mudd
Founded: April 1997

www.MusicNet.com
Founder: Rob Glaser
Founded: December 2001

 PERFORMING RIGHTS SOCIETIES

American Society of Composers,
   Authors and Publishers (ASCAP)
Los Angeles: 7920 Sunset Blvd, Suite 300
Los Angeles, CA 90046
323-883-1000
Fax: 323-883-1049
New York: 1 Lincoln Plz
New York, NY 10023
212-621-6000

Broadcast Music Incorporated (BMI)
Los Angeles: 8730 Sunset Blvd,
   3rd Floor West
Los Angeles, CA 90069

Ph: 310-659-9109
New York: 320 W 57th St
New York, NY 10019
Ph: 212-586-2000

Society of Composers and Lyricists
   (SCL)
400 S Beverly Dr, Suite 214
Beverly Hills, CA 90212
310-281-2812

 MUSIC CLEARANCE COMPANIES

BZ/Rights and Permissions
121 W 27th St, Suite 901
New York, NY 10001
Ph: 212-924-3000

Clearing House Ltd.
6605 Hollywood Blvd, 2nd Floor
Los Angeles, CA 90028
213-469-3186

Copyright Music & Vocals
67 Portland St, 1st Floor
Toronto, ONT M5V 2M9 Canada
416-979-3333

Diamond Time Ltd.
73 Spring St, Suite 504
New York, NY 10012
212-274-1006

Clearance Quest
116 Harding Pl, Suite A4
Nashville, TN 37205

Harry Fox Agency
711 Third Ave
New York, NY 10017
212-370-5330

Media Music Consultants
1551 Ocean Ave, Suite 260
Santa Monica, CA 90401
310-576-1387

Media Rights Inc.
6100 Wilshire Blvd, Suite 1500
Los Angeles, CA 90048
213-954-0181

Screenmusic International
18034 Ventura Blvd, Suite 450
Encino, CA 91316
818-789-2954

Suzy Vaughn Associates
6848 Firmament Ave
Van Nuys, CA 91406
818-988-5599

 COMPOSER AGENTS

Blue Focus Management
152333 Ventura Blvd, Suite 200
Sherman Oaks, CA 91403
Ph: 818-380-1919
Web: www.bluefocusmgmt.com

Derek Power Co.
818 N Doheny Blvd, Suite 1003
Los Angeles, CA 90069
Ph: 310-550-0770
Web: www.Music4Film.com

Gorfaine/Schwartz Agency
13245 Riverside Dr, Suite 450
Sherman Oaks, CA 91423

Ph: 818-461-9600
Web: www.gsamusic.com

Greenspan Artists Management
6777 Hollywood Blvd, Suite 514
Los Angeles, CA 90028
Ph: 323-468-1540
Web: www.GreenArtMan.com

Seth Kaplan Entertainment
8440 Santa Monica Blvd
West Hollywood, CA 90069
Ph: 323-848-3700

The Kordek Agency
211 W Alameda Ave, Suite 101
Burbank, CA 91502
Ph: 818-559-4248
Web: www.KordekAgency.com

Kraft-Benjamin Agency
8491 Sunset Blvd, Suite 492
West Hollywood, CA 90048
Ph: 310-652-6065

Robert Light Agency
6404 Wilshire Blvd, Suite 900
Los Angeles, CA 90048
Ph: 323-651-1777
E-mail: rlatalent@aol.com

Working Artists Agency
13525 Ventura Blvd, Suite 102
Sherman Oaks, CA 91423
Ph: 818-907-1122
Web: www.WorkingArtistsAgency.com

POST-SOUND

"ADR, Foley, Mix, M&E, and Opticals"

The picture edit is done. The sound edit is done. The music score is done. Now don't get lazy. Ninety-eight percent of first-timers relax at this point, feeling they're almost finished, and get sloppy with the final post-production steps. Big mistake! Get lethargic now and your film becomes bland and flat. The finish line is in sight and . . . 📦 *excellent sound isn't recorded. It's manufactured.* Achieving excellent sound entails making one deal to write five checks one month into post-production. Here's how to make the best deal, keep the five checks small, and get the best sound for only $13,000–$19,000.

THE POST-PRODUCTION SOUND FACILITY

First find a post-production sound facility (aka mixing studio), which is a "one-stop shop" that includes an ADR-Foley room, a sound effects library, and a recording studio. These facilities are typically run by a veteran musician who started the studio to record his own music, and, as his equipment grew, he helped out on a short film, then an industrial, then a commercial, etc. And, within a few years, this former musician, now an expert on film sound, makes his living by renting his facility and personnel to filmmakers.

FINDING THE FACILITY

First, as always, check your local film directory. Next, ask your DP ($100 check), your film lab, your film editor, and your sound editor for referrals.

PRODUCTION BUDGET

Title: "Your $1,000,000 Feature"   Executive Producer: _____
                                     Producer: _____
Writer: _____   Director: _____

ACCOUNT NUMBER	DESCRIPTION	BUDGET
01-00	Producer	$10,000–$20,000
02-00	Writer/Script	$5,000–$10,000
03-00	Director	$10,000–$15,000
04-00	Cast/Actors	$6,000–$9,000 (+$25,000)
TOTAL ABOVE-THE-LINE (Pre-Production)		**$31,000–$54,000 (+$25,000)**
BELOW-THE-LINE		
5-00	Film Stock	$20,000–$40,000
6-00	Film Lab (Shoot)	$15,000–$30,000
7-00	Camera	$12,000–$30,000
8-00	Expendables	$2,000–$5,000
9-00	Sound Equipment	$6,000–$11,000
10-00	Sound Transfer	$3,000–$5,000
11-00	Light/Grip	$6,000–$24,000
12-00	Dolly	$2,000–$3,000
13-00	Cinematographer	$10,000–$15,000
14-00	PM & AD	$14,500–$21,000
15-00	Production Designer	$6,000–$8,500
16-00	Film Crew	$23,000–$35,500
17-00	Art & Props	$5,000–$9,000
18-00	Wardrobe & Makeup	$3,000–$5,000
19-00	Permits	$2,000–$6,000
20-00	Insurance	$3,000–$10,000
21-00	Dailies	$4,000–$6,000
22-00	FX/Stunts/Cars	$0
23-00	Locations	$2,000–$10,000
24-00	Office & Paperwork	$2,000–$7,000
25-00	Publicity	$2,000–$10,000
26-00	Food	$6,000–$9,000
TOTAL PRODUCTION BUDGET (In-the-Can)		**$148,500–$300,000**
THE SHOOT (Total Above & Below)		**$179,500–$354,000**
27-00	Film Edit	$12,000–$18,500
28-00	Film Lab (Edit)	$2,000–$3,000
29-00	Sound Edit	$7,500–$12,000
27-00	**ADR**	**$2,000–$3,000**
28-00	**FOLEY**	**$2,000–$3,000**
27-00	Music/Score	$5,000–$7,000
29-00	**MIX (RE-RECORD)**	**$5,000–$7,000**
30-00	**OPTICAL TRANSFER**	**$2,000–$3,000**
31-00	**M&E**	**$2,000–$3,000**
THE EDIT (POST-PRODUCTION)		**$39,500–$59,500**
36-00	Titles	
37-00	Negative Cutting	
38-00	Film Lab (Answer Print)	
TOTAL PRODUCTION COSTS		

When choosing a facility, after price and equipment, your next priority is, "Who is the chief mixer?" who many times is the owner of the facility. Make sure you're comfortable with his capabilities and commitment to quality.

THE FIVE BANK CHECKS

Once you've identified your facility, you'll negotiate a flat deal or five small deals (five bank checks) for the following post-sound steps:

ADR and Foley

Bank check #1 is for two or three days of ADR (automatic dialogue replacement) time. Your edited work print (chapter 36) is projected in a small theater (ADR room) and the actor(s) return to match lines (i.e., lip-sync) to their mouth movements. This enables you to capture clearer individual tracks of dialogue without background noise. In some cases, voice actors (aka loopers) create background dialogue and chatter that is used ("looping") to fill up a scene with the sounds of a crowd.

Check #2 is for two or three days of Foley time. A Foley stage is stocked with hand props, different kinds of doors, and "Foley pits." These pits, which ain't actually pits, are three-foot-by-three-foot surfaces (cement, gravel, carpet, tile, linoleum, wood, dirt, grass, water, etc.) upon which Foley artists (aka walkers) enhance the sound of every actor's footsteps. Priority is first to re-create the footsteps, then to secure clothes-rustling sounds, then paper-crinkling noises, then miscellaneous sounds like keys jiggling, doors opening, etc.

Re-recording

Check #3 pays for three to five days of studio time when the chief sound mixer and your sound editor mix the 30–40 tracks (3–4 dialogue tracks, 10–15 effects tracks, 5–6 ADR tracks, 5–6 Foley tracks, and 3–5 music tracks) down to three tracks, known as M, E, and V. The M track is for music, the E track is for sound effects, and the V track is for voices. This is the re-recording session, and the film on which the three tracks are placed is called "3-stripe" (aka "full coat").

M&E and Opticals

Check #4 is for obtaining a separate M&E (35mm film with no picture but only audio music and sound effects) track on 3-stripe where the V stripe (voices or dialogue) or track is left blank. The M&E track will be needed when you are selling your film around the world. In nations that don't speak English, they will dub their own language in the track that you've left blank. Without an M&E track foreign buyers are forced to use subtitles. With an M&E track they can dub in their respective nation's language. Dubbed films make more money than subtitled films. Thus, get an M&E track.

Check #5 is for converting your 3-stripe sound into an optical sound track. Eventually, you'll marry the sound film onto the picture film. But you can't simply put the 3-stripe on the picture frame, for it'll blot out the image. A step is needed to get sound in the shape of a thin squiggly line (optical sound) that is placed on the picture film, but between the picture frames and the sprocket holes, so that it doesn't block the visual image. This type of sound is called optical sound.

WHAT IT COSTS

Sound facilities rent by the hour and give discounts if you book a full day. A full day is 10 hours. Strive for two to three days of ADR time (20–30 hours), two to three days of Foley time (20–30 hours), and five to seven days (50–70 hours) of mix time. Phone local sound facilities and have them forward their rate cards for ADR ($150–$250/hour), Foley ($150–$250/hour), and mix ($250–$450/hour) time.

To get a great deal it is best to negotiate a flat rate. Let the facility manager know that you and your sound editor are ready to come in at any time. Tell him you'll need 30 hours (10 hours/day) of ADR time, 30 hours of Foley time, and 70 hours of mix time—and all you have is $9,000. Pause. Stay silent. The facility manager will probably give you 20 hours (two days) of ADR, 20 hours (two days) of Foley, and 50 hours (five days) of mix for the $9,000.

This is an excellent deal. You rented the $150–$450/hour studio for approximately $100/hour. However, play it safe and budget **$2,000–$3,000** for ADR, **$2,000–$3,000** for Foley, **$5,000–$7,000** for re-recording, **$2,000–$3,000** for an M&E track, and **$2,000–$3,000** for an optical track, for a total of $13,000–$19,000.

Your total editing stage, which takes three months, is done at a cost of only **$39,500–$59,500.**

TO DO:

1. Select a facility with ADR and Foley capability.
2. Be sure that your cue sheets are prepared.

 BOOKS

 SOUND RENTAL FACILITIES

Guide to Post-Production
B. Clark and S. Spohr, 223 pp., $41.95
The best book on walking you through the steps of post-production sound. A must-have!

The Guerilla Film Maker's Handbook
C. Jones and G. Jolliffe, 640 pp., $35.00
Contains superb visual chapters on the nuts and bolts of post-production sound, ADR, Foley, and music.

Sound for Film and Television
T. Holman, 249 pp., $44.95
Contains detailed chapters on mixing, audio editing, Foley, and ADR up to obtaining your perfect final print.

The Filmmaker's Handbook
S. Ascher and E. Pincus, 614 pp., $20.00
Contains over 100 pages dedicated to audio, music, and post-production sound. A superb post primer!

LOS ANGELES BASED

Universal Studios
100 Universal City Plz
Universal City, CA 91608
Ph: 818-777-2211
Web: www.UniversalStudios.com/
    Studio

The Bakery
10709 Burbank Blvd
North Hollywood, CA 91601
Ph: 818-508-7800
Fax: 818-508-7122
Web: www.bakerydigitalpost.com

The Village
1616 Butler Ave
West Los Angeles, CA 90025
Ph: 310-478-8227
Fax: 310-479-1142
Web: www.VillageStudio.com

Intersound
962 N La Cienega Blvd
Los Angeles, CA 90069
Ph: 310-652-3741
Fax: 310-652-5973
Web: www.intersound.com

Laser Pacific Digital Studios
823 N Seward
Hollywood, CA 90038
Ph: 323-960-2125
Fax: 323-466-5047

NEW YORK BASED

Back Pocket Studio
37 W 20th St
New York, NY 10011
Ph: 212-255-5313
Fax: 212-633-8697
Web: www.baronandbaron.com

GLC Productions
302A W 12th St
New York, NY 10014
Ph: 212-691-1038
Fax: 212-242-4911
Web: www.glc.com

Gun For Hire Post
110 Leroy St, 8th Floor
New York, NY 10014
Ph: 212-609-9000
Fax: 212-691-9148
Web: www.gunforhire.com

Kas Music Sound
34-12 36th St
Long Island City, NY 11106
Ph: 718-786-3400
Fax: 718-729-3007
Web: www.mastersound.com

Now Hear This
250 W 49th St, Suite 704
New York, NY 10019
Ph: 212-265-1188
Fax: 212-265-6363

Planet V, Inc.
31 Bond St, 3rd Floor
New York, NY 10012
Ph: 212-253-1788
Fax: 212-353-1744
Web: www.PlanetVinc.com

Sony Music Studios
460 W 54th St
New York, NY 10019
Ph: 212-833-7373
Fax: 212-833-8412
Web: www.SonyMusic.com

ALL OTHER AREAS

Contact the local film commissioner.
(See chapter 31.)

TITLES

"Give Credit"

Remember that happy-but-neurotic family (your crew) who loved you during pre-production and hated you during production? Well, they'll love you again during post-production when it's "Title and Credit time." You'll get phone calls. "How ya doing?" asks a grip who now wants a dolly grip credit. "Anything I can do to help?" offers a three-day-hire actor you hated, who's vying for an opening rather than closing credit.

The phone rings. A cast member who was a one-day hire—and a royal pain in the ass during his only day on the set—asks if his credit, instead of "Thug #4" in the rear crawl, could actually be a name. This will set him apart from Thugs 1, 2, and 3. Then, instead of a production assistant credit, a crew member asks for a second assistant director credit. A principal actor, who worked the entire shoot, but is not famous, will ask that his opening title credit be ahead of the celebrity actor who only worked three days.

When approaching credits, a rule of thumb is to keep each opening title on the screen just long enough to be read aloud twice. If the titles are too fast, the audience is frustrated. If the titles are too slow, the audience gets bored. Experiment with pacing and rhythm and don't ever forget or misspell anyone's name. Your production crew credits mut be scrutinized, and add post-production personnel and facilities to incude film editors, sound engineers/mixers, sound assistants, Foley artists, mixers, negative cutter, the post-sound house, the mixing facility, the lab, the sound transfer facility, the optical facility, etc. Once again, make absolutely sure that every name is spelled correctly.

Titles can be as simple as white letters on a black background or as

PRODUCTION BUDGET

Title: "Your $1,000,000 Feature" Executive Producer: _____
                                   Producer: _____
Writer: _____   Director: _____

ACCOUNT NUMBER	DESCRIPTION	BUDGET
01-00	Producer	$10,000–$20,000
02-00	Writer/Script	$5,000–$10,000
03-00	Director	$10,000–$15,000
04-00	Cast/Actors	$6,000–$9,000 (+$25,000)
TOTAL ABOVE-THE-LINE (Pre-Production)		**$31,000–$54,000 (+$25,000)**
BELOW-THE-LINE		
5-00	Film Stock	$20,000–$40,000
6-00	Film Lab (Shoot)	$15,000–$30,000
7-00	Camera	$12,000–$30,000
8-00	Expendables	$2,000–$5,000
9-00	Sound Equipment	$6,000–$11,000
10-00	Sound Transfer	$3,000–$5,000
11-00	Light/Grip	$6,000–$24,000
12-00	Dolly	$2,000–$3,000
13-00	Cinematographer	$10,000–$15,000
14-00	PM & AD	$14,500–$21,000
15-00	Production Designer	$6,000–$8,500
16-00	Film Crew	$23,000–$35,500
17-00	Art & Props	$5,000–$9,000
18-00	Wardrobe & Makeup	$3,000–$5,000
19-00	Permits	$2,000–$6,000
20-00	Insurance	$3,000–$10,000
21-00	Dailies	$4,000–$6,000
22-00	FX/Stunts/Cars	$0
23-00	Locations	$2,000–$10,000
24-00	Office & Paperwork	$2,000–$7,000
25-00	Publicity	$2,000–$10,000
26-00	Food	$6,000–$9,000
TOTAL PRODUCTION BUDGET (In-the-Can)		**$148,500–$300,000**
THE SHOOT (Total Above & Below)		**$179,500–$354,000**
27-00	Film Edit	$12,000–$18,500
28-00	Film Lab (Edit)	$2,000–$3,000
29-00	Sound Edit	$7,500–$12,000
30-00	ADR	$2,000–$3,000
31-00	Foley	$2,000–$3,000
27-00	Music/Score	$5,000–$7,000
32-00	Mix (Re-record)	$5,000–$7,000
33-00	Optical Transfer	$2,000–$3,000
34-00	M&E	$2,000–$3,000
THE EDIT (Post-Production)		**$39,500–$59,500**
36-00	**TITLES**	**$1,500–$3,000**
37-00	Negative Cutting	
38-00	Film Lab (Answer Print)	
TOTAL PRODUCTION COSTS		

elaborate as animation superimposed over live action, utilizing stop-action. First determine your budget. The simplest method is to type the titles into your computer, using the fonts you prefer, and print the titles with a laser printer. Then make photolith negatives of each sheet and shoot them with a pin-registered camera, with fadeouts, using high-contrast black-and-white negative stock, and deliver this to the lab on clear leader strips. The lab will make an interpositive and superimpose it over the original moving picture. You'll have your credits and they won't cost more than $1,000. If this sounds too technical then call your DP ($100 check) and he/she will tell you what to do.

If you're lucky, you'll have a lab that does credits. See if you can negotiate eight to ten opening title cards and the closing crawl to be included in your lab deal. In this case, you provide the lab with clean computer print-outs of the titles, and they shoot them and take care of the rest. If you're not shooting the titles yourself, and your lab is not playing hero, then you will get bids from title houses that specialize in film credits, or optical houses that have title departments. Then outline the titles you need and negotiate a flat deal.

> **IMPORTANT POINT**   When creating your titles, remember that they jiggle. If you're superimposing them over action, create a drop shadow to rim the letters and separate them from the backdrop. If superimposing, be sure the backdrop action does not have excessive movement. Also, keep your opening title cards within the TV safe area (4:3 aspect ratio) so that when your movie shows on TV, the titles will be seen in their entirety. Otherwise, a title card created for a wide movie screen will be cut off when shown on the narrower TV screen.

If you have signed with any guilds or unions, their rules and regulations will dictate the sequence of the titles. If you haven't, the general rule for opening title card order is: actor (if anyone has negotiated for an above-the-title credit), movie title, actors, production designer, composer, editor, director of photography, executive producer(s), producer(s), writer(s), and director last. If you have an associate producer, line producer, or co-producer, their credits go between the director of photography and the executive producer(s). The pecking order for the rear title crawl is usually: actors, production manager, assistant director, cinematographer, camera crew, lighting crew, sound crew, art crew, editors, post-production personnel, facilities, music credits, special thanks, and your copyright notice. Your final decision is whether to give yourself the ego-oriented possessory credit of "A Film By" in the opening titles.

Although titles you create will cost no more than $1,000, for an additional $500 you can hire a storyboard artist or cartoonist to draw 10–15 panels at $30–$50 each. You'll place these illustrations under the opening titles (one drawing per title), with some slight camera movement toward the lettering. Finally, you can hire a company with a graphic designer that specializes in titles, or an optical effects house. But never pay more than $3,000. Your titles will be done for **$1,500–$3,000.**

TO DO:

1. Get the names of three title houses from your lab or film directory. Get their rate cards and compare prices.
2. Price typesetting, shooting, and developing 10–15 title cards.

 OPTICAL HOUSES

LOS ANGELES BASED

Artifact, Inc.
505 N Sycamore St
Santa Ana, CA 92701
Ph: 714-564-1090
Fax: 714-569-9292

Consolidated Film Industries
959 Seward St
Hollywood, CA 90038
Ph: 323-960-7444
Fax: 323-962-8746

Hollywood Title
201 N Hollywood Way, Suite 212
Burbank, CA 91505
Ph: 818-845-1159
Fax: 818-845-1199

Howard Anderson Company
5161 Lankershim Blvd, Suite 120
North Hollywood, CA 91601
Ph: 818-623-1111
Fax: 818-623-7761

Klaspy Csupo Inc.
6353 Sunset Blvd
Los Angeles, CA 90028
Ph: 323-463-0145
Fax: 323-468-3020

Pacific Title and Art Design
6350 Santa Monica Blvd
Hollywood, CA 90038
Ph: 323-464-0121
Fax: 323-463-7549

Walt Disney Studios
500 S Buena Vista St
Burbank, CA 91521
Ph: 818-560-5284
Fax: 818-563-4375

NEW YORK BASED

ChromaVision
49 W 27th St, 8th Floor
New York, NY 10001
Ph: 212-686-7366
Fax: 212-686-7310
Web: www.ChromaVision.com

DuArt Film & Video
245 W 55th St
New York, NY 10019
Ph: 212-757-4580
Fax: 212-262-3381
Web: www.DuArt.com

HeavyLight
115 W 27th St, 12th Floor
New York, NY 10001
Ph: 212-645-8216

Fax: 212-367-8861
Web: www.heavylightdigital.com

Interface Arts
241 16th St
Brooklyn, NY 11215
Ph: 718-788-0335
Fax: 212-779-2207
Web: www.Interface_arts.com

Rhinoceros Visual Effects and Design
50 E 42nd St
New York, NY 10017
Ph: 212-986-1577
Fax: 212-986-2113

ALL OTHER AREAS

Contact the local film commissioner.
(See chapter 31.)

FINISH THE MOVIE

"Strike a Final Print"

Almost done! Just two checks away from finishing. It was only four months ago that you purchased 50,000 feet of film, spent three unglamorous weeks shooting, and a couple of months watching editors, a musician, and post-production technicians mold your baby into 8,100–10,800 feet. You feel you have the perfect film. Slow down. You still have two more checks to write. The first is to cut the negative, and the second, and last (phew!), is to color-correct and obtain your final print.

The film you now have is only an edited work print. This is not your final product. Its color is adequate but not great. It has been spliced, cemented, and scratched. The final step is to get a print without splices or scratches with superb color and a superior audio track. To do this you hire a negative cutter (aka conformer), who literally cuts the original negative, which has been stored (three months) at the lab since the shoot, to exactly match (conform) to the 300–500 splices that are in your edited work print. Negative cutting is a precise profession; one tiny mistake and your negative is ruined forever.

No one on your crew will know a negative cutter. Check your local directory. Then ask your DP ($100 check), film editor, and sound facilities manager for referrals. Don't bother schmoozing a negative cutter with an offer of a film credit. He doesn't care. It's just a job. He'll want to know how many feet of film you exposed. The more feet, the more work. Hearing only 50,000 feet, he'll figure it's an easy job. He'll also want to know what type of film it is, and the last thing he wants to hear is "action-adventure," which translates to splice, splice, splice—a lot of work.

PRODUCTION BUDGET

Title: "Your $1,000,000 Feature" Executive Producer: _____

Producer: _____

Writer: _____ Director: _____

ACCOUNT NUMBER	DESCRIPTION	BUDGET
01-00	Producer	$10,000–$20,000
02-00	Writer/Script	$5,000–$10,000
03-00	Director	$10,000–$15,000
04-00	Cast/Actors	$6,000–$9,000 (+$25,000)
TOTAL ABOVE-THE-LINE (Pre-Production)		**$31,000–$54,000 (+$25,000)**
BELOW-THE-LINE		
5-00	Film Stock	$20,000–$40,000
6-00	Film Lab (Shoot)	$15,000–$30,000
7-00	Camera	$12,000–$30,000
8-00	Expendables	$2,000–$5,000
9-00	Sound Equipment	$6,000–$11,000
10-00	Sound Transfer	$3,000–$5,000
11-00	Light/Grip	$6,000–$24,000
12-00	Dolly	$2,000–$3,000
13-00	Cinematographer	$10,000–$15,000
14-00	PM & AD	$14,500–$21,000
15-00	Production Designer	$6,000–$8,500
16-00	Film Crew	$23,000–$35,500
17-00	Art & Props	$5,000–$9,000
18-00	Wardrobe & Makeup	$3,000–$5,000
19-00	Permits	$2,000–$6,000
20-00	Insurance	$3,000–$10,000
21-00	Dailies	$4,000–$6,000
22-00	FX/Stunts/Cars	$0
23-00	Locations	$2,000–$10,000
24-00	Office & Paperwork	$2,000–$7,000
25-00	Publicity	$2,000–$10,000
26-00	Food	$6,000–$9,000
TOTAL PRODUCTION BUDGET (In-the-Can)		**$148,500–$300,000**
THE SHOOT (Total Above & Below)		**$179,500–$354,000**
27-00	Film Edit	$12,000–$18,500
28-00	Film Lab (Edit)	$2,000–$3,000
29-00	Sound Edit	$7,500–$12,000
30-00	ADR	$2,000–$3,000
31-00	Foley	$2,000–$3,000
27-00	Music/Score	$5,000–$7,000
32-00	Mix (Re-record)	$5,000–$7,000
33-00	Optical Transfer	$2,000–$3,000
34-00	M&E	$2,000–$3,000
THE EDIT (Post-Production)		**$39,500–$59,500**
36-00	Titles	$1,500–$3,000
37-00	**NEGATIVE CUTTING**	**$5,000–$6,500**
38-00	**FILM LAB (ANSWER PRINT)**	**$8,000–$15,000**
TOTAL PRODUCTION COSTS		**$233,500–$438,000**

The cutter, thinking not a lot of cuts, will offer a flat fee of $600–$800 per 1,000-foot reel, rather than a per-splice fee. Write the check and get the negative cut to conform exactly to the work print's edit list. Your film is 8,100 feet (eight reels), so your cost will be **$5,000–$6,500.**

THE FINAL BANK CHECK

The very last check you write will be to the film lab, to secure your final color-corrected print from the cut negative. The lab has an employee called a timer. The name is a holdover from the days when colorizing a film was determined by how long (time) the actual negative sat in a developer. 🔖 *The timer, or color corrector, is the only person at the film lab who is an artist.* Whenever I make a deal at a lab, I always want to meet the timer who will be assigned to my project and say hello with a bottle of wine. This will be the best $25 you spend on your film.

The timer takes the cut negative and corrects color (adjusts printing lights) until he gets the right look for each scene. Normally, he starts with skin tones and adjusts accordingly. He can add orange to the sky. He can make the pastures greener. There is a lot he can do. However, he is limited once an actor is in the frame. If he puts orange in the sky the actor's skin could turn bright red.

The lab then makes a print from the timer's adjusted printing lights. This is almost your final print. When you view it you'll gush with pride. It's as if your first child was born. There's your film filling the screen with actors, color, fades, dissolves, music, and titles. But hold back on your emotions when screening your first attempt at an answer print. Make color correction notes, with your DP (another $100), during the screening, and have the lab strike a second print. Wait a couple of days and screen your film again at the lab.

The lab charges $1.00–$1.50 per foot to print your film, with two color-correcting attempts. If you have 8,100 feet and negotiate a price of $1.00/foot, the cost is about $8,000. If you have 10,800 feet and only negotiate a price of $1.50/foot (sucker's deal), then it will cost about $15,000. So securing (aka striking) your final answer print will cost **$8,000–$15,000.**

Voilà! It's done! You've made a feature film.

Now let's add up all the checks. Above-the-line costs for talent (producer, writer, director, and actors) cost $31,000 to $54,000. Then, to shoot your film (vendors, crew, locations, permits, etc.) cost an additional $148,500 to $300,000, for a grand total of $179,500 to $354,000 to get your film in the can over three weeks. Next, the three-month post-production period (edit, sound, music, etc.) cost an additional $39,500 to $59,500, and when added to the final lab (titles, cutting, coloring) charges of $14,500 to $24,500, you have spent $233,500–$438,000 to produce a feature film that looks like a million dollars.

TO DO:

1. Get referrals for negative cutters; negotiate a flat fee.
2. Meet your timer; make sure you get two attempts at color correcting.

 BOOKS

 SCREENING ROOMS

Guide to Post-Production
B. Clark and S. Spohr, 223 pp., $41.95
The best book on walking you through post-production and obtaining your final print. A must-have!

The Guerilla Film Maker's Handbook
C. Jones and G. Jolliffe, 640 pp., $35.00
Contains superb visual chapters on the nuts and bolts of post-production and your final lab work.

The Filmmaker's Handbook
S. Ascher and E. Pincus, 614 pp., $20.00
Contains over 100 pages dedicated to post-production and obtaining your final print.

LOS ANGELES BASED

American Film Institute
2021 N Western Ave
Los Angeles, CA 90027
Ph: 323-856-7600
Fax: 323-467-4578

Charles Aidikoff Screening Room
150 S Rodeo Dr, Suite 140
Beverly Hills, CA 90212
Ph: 310-274-0866
Fax: 310-550-1794

Culver Studios Screening Rooms
9336 W Washington Blvd
Culver City, CA 90232
Ph: 310-202-3253
Fax: 310-202-3536

Directors Guild of America
  Screening Rooms
7920 Sunset Blvd
Los Angeles, CA 90046
Ph: 310-289-2021
Fax: 310-289-5398

Raleigh Studios
5300 Melrose Ave
Hollywood, CA 90038
Ph: 323-466-3111
Fax: 323-871-5600

Sunset Screening Rooms
8730 Sunset Blvd
West Hollywood, CA 90069
Ph: 310-652-1933
Fax: 310-652-3828

Warner Bros. Studio Projection
  Rooms
4000 Warner Blvd
Burbank, CA 91522
Ph: 818-954-2220
Fax: 818-954-4138

NEW YORK BASED

Goldcrest Post Production
799 Washington St
New York, NY 10014
Ph: 212-243-4700
Fax: 212-243-4453
Web: www.goldcrest.org

Magno Sound & Video
729 Seventh Ave
New York, NY 10019
Ph: 212-302-2505
Fax: 212-764-1679
Web: www.magnosoundand
  video.com

Mark Forman Productions
300 W 23rd St, Suite 14A/B
New York, NY 10011
Ph: 212-633-9960
Fax: 212-807-0121
Web: www.screeningroom.com

Quad Cinemas
34 W 13th St
New York, NY 10011
Ph: 212-255-2243
Fax: 212-255-2247
Web: www.quadcinemas.com

Technicolor East Coast
321 W 44th St, Suite 138
New York, NY 10036
Ph: 212-582-7310
Fax: 212-265-9089
Web: www.technicolor.com

Tribeca Film Center
375 Greenwich St
New York, NY 10013
Ph: 212-941-4000
Fax: 212-265-9089
Web: www.tribecafilm.com

Walt Disney Screening Room
500 Park Ave
New York, NY 10022
Ph: 914-260-1067
Web: www.nyscreening.disney.com

ALL OTHER AREAS

Contact the local film commissioner.
(see chapter 31.)

Contact the local film lab.
(See chapter 18.)

FILMMAKING A–Z

"The $5,000 to $10,000,000 Feature"

You just screened your film at the lab. The final print is gorgeous . . . absolutely frickin' gorgeous. You are proud. Your heart bubbles with excitement. But before you practice your Oscar thank-yous, let's take a quick A–Z recap at what you accomplished.

A. Idea: You got an idea that was great.

B. Low-budget: You adapted it to a limited-location story.

C. Treatment: You fleshed it out into a four-page treatment.

D. Register: You took $20 to the WGA and registered it.

E. Screenplay: You expanded it into 40–60 scenes and a first draft.

F. Rewrite: You rewrote it, focusing on dialogue and character development.

G. Copyright and CYA: You registered and copyrighted it again.

H. Form a company: You got your business license and filed your DBA statement.

I. Studio dealmaking: You tried getting an agent and selling to studios, but without pay-or-play money you opted to go independent.

J. Independent financing: You got a DP and his demo reel, offered investors 50 percent of profits, and raised $250,000–$500,000.

K. Reverse budget: You squeezed the 38 budget line items into $250,000–$500,000 and set out to make a film that looks like a million bucks.

L. Shooting schedule: You scheduled a three-week shoot, with five pages and 25–30 shots/day.

M. Director: You hired a director (probably yourself) who understands low-budget filmmaking.

N. Guilds and unions: You weren't intimidated, and decided to only sign with SAG on a LEA agreement.

O. Key personnel: You hired your cinematographer, production manager, assistant director, production designer, and production coordinator.

P. Crew: You told each of them what you could afford and they hired everyone else.

Q. Equipment: You rented camera(s), on a two-day week rate, and made separate deals for lights, sound, and a dolly.

R. Film and lab: You bought 50,000 feet of film, at a discount, and made a deal with a film lab.

S. The shoot: You spent three grueling weeks (18 shooting days) and got your 90 pages in the can.

T. Film editor: You hired a film editor and sat back.

U. Sound editor: You hired a sound editor and sat back.

V. Music: You hired a composer and sat back.

W. Sound facility: You recorded ADR, then Foley, then mixed the 30–40 tracks down to three tracks and ordered your M&E.

X. Titles: Almost done, you spelled everyone's name correctly and contracted for your titles.

Y. Answer print: You cut the negative, color-corrected it, and got your final print.

Z. 60–80 percent discount: Depending on how good you are at negotiating, *You made a $1 million feature at a 60–80 percent savings for $233,500–$438,000.*

Let's get real! How many of you readers actually have access to $233,500–$438,000? Very few! So let's go down in budget to dollar amounts that you, the first-time independent filmmaker, can truly afford.

Let's get even more frugal, go down in budget, and learn how to produce a feature for as little as $5,000. Then let's go up in budget and discover how to produce (your second and third features) for as much as $10 million, the result being that you will truly know how to produce any feature film from as little as $5,000 to as high as $10 million.

GOING DOWN IN BUDGET

"$150,000" Budget (aka "The Low-Budget Feature")

If you have access to $150,000, you can still produce a 35mm, three-week shoot, but must cut $83,500 from the prior $233,500 budget (million-dollar feature) that you produced in chapters 17–41. 🗂 *The first draft of every budget is always prepared in pencil.* Now, take out your eraser and let's go line item by line item as you trim $69,000.

> Line item 1—*producer:* Instead of a $10,000 fee, take only $7,000. *You'll save $3,000!*
>
> Line item 2—*writer/script:* Instead of $5,000, you only have $4,000. Take $100/week off the writer's salary, possibly offset with offering the writer 5 percent of the film's profits. *You'll save $1,000!*
>
> Line item 3—*director:* Instead of $10,000, pay him $2,000 for pre-production, $1,000/week during the shoot, and $1,000 during post, for a total of $6,000. *You'll save $4,000!*
>
> Line item 4—*cast/actors:* Instead of paying $6,000 ($100/day), you can only afford $3,000 at $50/day. *You'll save $3,000!*
>
> Line item 5—*film stock:* Instead of 50,000 feet at 40 cents/foot for $20,000, you get 40,000 feet (buybacks and recans) at 30 cents/foot for $12,000. *You'll save $8,000!*
>
> Line item 6—*film lab:* Instead of paying $15,000 to develop 50,000 feet at 30 cents/foot, you develop 40,000 feet at 25 cents/foot for $10,000. *You'll save $5,000!*
>
> Line item 7—*camera:* Instead of paying $12,000 to rent a camera package, you spend only $6,000, forgoing many of the expensive add-ons. *You'll save $6,000!*

We have gone through only 7 of 38 line items and already deducted $30,000. Go through the remaining items, cutting $1,000 here and $2,000 there, and you'll get down to $150,000. Let's not fool anyone. The film you make for $150,000 will not be as good as the film you make for $233,500. But, the bottom line is, if all you have is $150,000 and you want to produce a 35mm feature film on a three-week shoot, it is doable.

"$120,000" Budget (aka "The Blow-up Feature")

With only a $120,000 you can't produce a 35mm feature film on a three-week shoot, but you will have two choices. Choice #1 is to shoot 35mm on a three-week schedule, but only have enough money to get a rough cut that you submit to festivals as a work-in-progress. Or, choice #2 is to forget 35mm, and shoot 16mm for three weeks. This way, you can finish your film and also enter film festivals, where you hope that a distributor will pay the $45,000–$55,000 for the 35mm blow-up.

"$80,000" Budget (aka "The Ultra-Low-Budget Feature")

With only $80,000, you only have enough money for a two-week (13 shooting days) shoot with 35,000 feet of film. Hire a crew for two weeks instead of three. Rent equipment for two weeks instead of three. Do everything for two weeks instead of three. Instead of a five pages/day schedule, you will have a seven pages/day schedule. And as long as you don't have many location moves, you have enough time to get the master shot, with less coverage, and still make a 35mm film with a rough cut, or a 16mm film that is finished.

"$50,000" Budget (aka "The No-Budget Feature")

With only $50,000, all you can afford is a one-week (nine shooting days over two weekends) shoot, getting 10 pages/day. If you shoot 35mm (20,000 feet), you will get a rough cut, and that's it. If you choose 16mm, you will finish your film, but will inevitably have a lab debt of about $25,000. The lab will give you one print to enter festivals, but will hold on to the negative, and if you don't pay the debt, it will foreclose. Other than a digital shoot, a 16mm one-week shoot is the most common type of film made by neophyte directors. Maybe you should think strongly about this.

"$20,000" Budget (aka "The Guerrilla or Digital Feature")

With approximately $20,000 you can't afford a film format (35mm or 16mm), and must shoot with tape. You'll probably use (chapter 50) mini–DV camera(s), $200 worth of tape, a seven-person crew, two vans, three lights, a good sound setup, have a one- to two-week shoot, and a two-month edit on your home computer.

"$5,000" Budget (aka "The Real-Time Feature")

Here's how to shoot a 35mm movie (yes, that's correct—I said 35mm film, not that inexpensive mini–digital video) for less than $5,000.

First, attend local live theater until you discover that great one-room play that totally captivates an audience for 90 minutes. You have just discovered liquid gold. After the play find the writer. Introduce yourself as a producer, and partner with him to make it into a movie. He ain't gonna say no. You put up the money ($5,000), the writer puts up the script, and together you co-produce and co-direct.

On Monday, cast the actors, offering deferral deals (paying out of profits). Rehearse on Tuesday, Wednesday, Thursday, and Friday. On Saturday, go to the actual location (possibly a bowling alley, church, courtroom, etc.) and rehearse again. Meanwhile, on Thursday write two $300 checks to hire a DP and PM for a weekend shoot. The DP will rent a 35mm camera package (an Arri BLIV, rigged for handheld, with a 10:1 zoom lens, and two 1,000-foot magazines) to be picked up Friday and returned Monday, for $800. The PM will buy 10,000 feet (remember a 90-minute movie is 8,100 feet) of recans (20 cents/foot) for $2,000.

On Saturday, at the location, get everyone together and give a great Knute Rockne rah-rah speech. On Sunday, have a soundman ($300) and a gaffer ($300) come with their equipment for a half-day. The actors will rehearse in the morning. In the afternoon, there will be only eight shots. They're called "fluid master shots"—love that Hollywoodese. Load a 1,000-foot magazine and shoot an 11-minute (1,000 feet) master shot scene. After 11 minutes the magazine will run out of film. Tell the actors to hold their marks and stay in character. Your DP reloads and shoots another 11-minute segment.

Reload and do it again, again, and again, until in a little over two hours (changing magazines takes time) you've exposed eight reels (8,000 feet) and have shot a 90-minute 35mm movie in "real time," for just under $5,000.

■ *You can produce a 35mm feature for only $5,000.* If you don't believe this, rent Alfred Hitchcock's *Rope* to see how he did it. While you're at it, check out Hitchcock's classic *Rear Window*, starring Grace Kelly and James Stewart—a two-room location shot. Then check out Hitchcock's *Lifeboat*, a movie set in a small rowboat with eight people. Now you'll understand why Hitchcock's a genius. He knew how to do it cheap. And now, so do you!

GOING UP IN BUDGET

Now let's assume you have $500,000–$700,000. How will you spend the extra $200,000 to make the $250,000–$500,000 (chapters 17–41) movie a better movie? What if you had $700,000–$1 million? How will you spend the extra $200,000–$300,000 to make the $500,000–700,000 movie a better movie? Etcetera. Obviously, as you go up in budget you spend more money on extra weeks, better crew, more takes, name actors, and other items, but watch, as the budget goes up, how certain aspects kick in at each budget increase.

"$250,000–$500,000" Budget (aka "The Million-Dollar Feature")

This is what you just learned to make (chapters 17–41): a 35mm, three-week shoot, working with one guild (SAG on a limited exhibition agreement), purchasing 50,000 feet of film, with experienced key people, a three- to four-month post period, and an original score. 🧳 *As the budget increases, above-the-line amounts increase 100–10,000 percent and below-the-line items increase only 2–4 percent each.* Watch.

"$500,000–$700,000" Budget (aka "The $1–$2 Million Feature")

With this extra $200,000, you can now do a 35mm, four-week shoot (not three), buy 80,000 feet of film (not 50,000), sign with two guilds (not one), cast a name actor for two or three days, double the production design budget, pay your crew much better, license one popular song to use under the titles and hire a composer for the rest of the score. The result is that a movie that people think costs $1 to $2 million was produced for only $500,000–$700,000.

"$700,000–$1,200,000" Budget (aka "The $2–$3 Million Feature")

With another $200,000, you can shoot for five weeks (not four), sign with all three guilds (WGA, DGA, and SAG), and have enough film (120,000 feet) and time (30 days) to allow the actors three takes of each shot. It is usually on the third take (the "golden take") that the actor gives the best performance. And the editor will probably opt for the third takes. With the previous budgets the editor didn't have choices, he had only one take to edit. Thus, this film will appear as a much better acted film.

"$1–$2 Million" Budget (aka "The $3–$5 Million Feature")

This is the budget range assigned to the Movie-of-the-Week (aka MOW), which is usually a three-week, 35mm shoot, with three guilds, in which one actor, almost always a woman, is paid $200,000–$300,000 to be the star and a second actor is paid $100,000–$150,000 to be the co-star. 🖾 *Ninety-nine percent of all MOWs star a woman.*

Twenty-five years ago *Monday Night Football* appeared. Guys tuned in to football and the competing networks counter-programmed for women. While men like action and sports, women like stories. Stories about women—a woman in a crisis, a woman and her family, her house, her career, and her relationships—which always are based on a true story.

Thus, the easiest way to break into the industry, which is still not easy, is to option an event or a true story (JonBenet Ramsey, Amy Fisher, Monica Lewinsky, Chandra Levy) and then partner with an established episodic TV actress (*ER, Law & Order, Friends*), who has a development deal with the TV network to make a MOW starring herself.

The TV networks finance MOWs for $1.2 million–$2 million. If the network funds almost $2 million, then you shoot the movie in the actual city where the true story took place. If the network lowballs and funds closer to $1.2 million, then your film becomes a runaway production. You go to Canada to shoot, because Toronto and Vancouver look like any American city, you get a 35 percent discount on the dollar, and the Canadian government agencies (city, province, and national) give refunds totaling almost 25 percent on all monies spent in Canada.

Anyway, back to the budget. With $1.2 million–$2 million you can produce a MOW, starring a famous TV actress ($200,000–$300,000) and the co-star ($100,000–$150,000), with an excellent crew, running three cameras simultaneously, over a three-week shoot, which you will eventually call a "just under" $3–$5 million feature.

"$2–$3 Million" Budget (aka "The $5–$7 or $7–$10 Million Feature")

With the extra $1 million you can hire a "movie actor," rather than a "TV actor," and your three-week shoot will become a five- to seven-week shoot. You will sign with three guilds, obtain a completion bond, and have a lot of blood, violence, sex, and swearing in the movie. What I have just described is not a MOW for television, but an HBO special or Show-time Original Picture for pay cable.

When you subscribe to HBO or Showtime you want movies. They're movie channels. What's a movie? Movies are those newspaper ads. However, the movie studios (Paramount, Warner Bros., Fox, Sony, etc.) don't make enough movies for HBO or Showtime to program 24 hours a day. Thus, HBO, Showtime, and even Encore/Starz had to vertically integrate and manufacture their own product. But these cable movies have to feel and look like a movie-movie that you might pay $10 to see at a theater. This is accomplished by always putting one "movie actor" ($1 million-plus salary), instead of a "TV actor" ($200,000–$300,000 salary), in a film with a cash budget of $2–$3 million and calling it a $5–$7 million feature or a "just under" $7–$10 million feature.

TV ACTOR VS. MOVIE ACTOR

Let's play the name game. 🗄 *There is a big difference between a TV actor and a movie actor, and it has nothing to do with their abilities.* It is about their name marketability. Ninety-nine percent of all actors who achieve fame and fortune do it via primetime (8 P.M.–11 P.M.) episodic TV. The double-edged sword, however, is that after the actor is on TV every Tuesday night (paid $100,000–$750,000 per episode) for five years, the viewers think of that actor as free and they balk at paying $10 to see this "free" actor in a movie.

It is very hard for a TV actor to become a famous movie actor. All TV actors try it, but four out of five fail and come back to TV three years later. Michael J. Fox came back. Ted Danson came back. Kirstie Alley came back. Tom Selleck came back. And let's not even talk about David Caruso. But one out of five succeed, like Denzel Washington (*St. Elsewhere*), Helen Hunt (*Mad About You*), Bruce Willis (*Moonlighting*), George Clooney (*ER*), and Danny De Vito (*Taxi*), and launch successful movie careers. I know you're thinking of names of this actor and that actor—but the bottom line is, once an actor becomes famous by starring in a weekly prime-time TV series, it is extremely hard to get a movie audience to pay to see him/her. Why pay when you can see them every night for free?

Now, on to movie actors. These are the actors who became famous by only being in movies. If you want to see Tom Cruise, Dustin Hoffman, Harrison Ford, Edward Norton, Brad Pitt, Julia Roberts, or Angelina Jolie at a movie theater you must shell out $10.

Every year one or two actors/actresses become famous without ever being in a TV series. They're nicknamed the "flavor of the month" and are considered to be movie actors. Recent examples are Mira Sorvino, Salma Hayek, Catherine Zeta-Jones-Douglas, Jennifer Lopez, Charlize Theron, etc. If you want to look at them you pay $10, and their salaries start at $1 million.

Thus, with a $2–$3 million cash budget you can afford a movie actor ($1 million+), instead of a TV actor ($200,000+), and probably be producing an HBO special or a Showtime Original starring Ray Liotta, Chaz Palmentieri, or Holly Hunter, with a budget allegedly "just under" $7–$10 million.

> **IMPORTANT POINT**   You should know, however, that it is easy to get episodic TV actors in your movie for less money than they're paid for a half-hour TV episode. The TV actor sees your film as an opportunity to prove to the movie studios that he/she can pull an audience. You are really paying that actor not in cash, but with the opportunity to become a movie star.

We have now gone from $5,000 to $10 million to produce your first feature. Where do you think you'll start—at the top, or at the bottom of the budget ladder? The answer, of course, is at the bottom. And your first feature film will either be a $250,000–$500,000 (35mm, three-week shoot) production that you'll call a "million-dollar feature," a $50,000–$150,000 (16mm, one-week) shoot that you'll call a "guerrilla feature," or an ultra-low-budget $5,000–$50,000 (digital) feature.

Now the real issue becomes how to sell it. It doesn't matter if your budget is $5,000 or $500,000 or $5 million—the bottom line to always remember is that you have spent your money, you are broke, and you want to sell your film. So let's start publicity, attend a festival or two, attract a distributor, and make a deal.

———

TO DO:

1. For $500,000–$700,000, write down which guilds you'll sign with, what you'll pay a star, and how long your shoot will be.
2. Do the same for $700,000–$900,000.

3. Do the same for $900,000–$1 million.
4. Do the same for $2.5 million+.

 BOOKS

Micro-Budget Hollywood
P. Gaines and D. Rhodes, 219 pp.,
$17.95
Details budgeting feature films that
are produced for $50,000 to $500,000.

Film Budgeting
R. Singleton, 465 pp., $22.95
An in-depth explanation of how to
prepare budgets for feature films in
the $1 million to $50 million range.

Film and Video Budgets
D. Simon and M. Wiese, 461 pp.,
$26.95
From no-budget to high-budget, from
digital to film, this book explains the
budgeting process in depth.

 **HOLLYWOOD
GOSSIP SITES**

www.Aint-It-Cool.com
www.MrShowBiz.com

www.Eonline.com
www.FilmShark.com
www.RoughCut.com
www.IfilmPro.com
www.Variety.com
www.HollywoodReporter.com
www.MovieMaker.com

 **HOLLYWOOD
DATABASE SITES**

www.Imdb.com
www.Baseline.Hollywood.com
www.FilmBiz.com
www.InHollywood.com
www.HCDonline.com
www.IndieNetwork.com
www.IndustryCentral.net
www.Producers-source.com
www.CreativePlanet.com

PUBLICITY

"Promote, Market . . . Sell"

Your film is finished and it's time to make money. But to do this you'll need a distributor and the hunt is on. However, looking for a distributor isn't that difficult when you realize that they're looking for you harder than you're looking for them. Here's why.

Distributors love independent filmmakers. They truly love you. You're creative (unique scripts and stories). You're guaranteed (they don't gamble on scripts, they see final films). You don't cost them a penny (investors funded the film not them). And, best of all, when you're done you're begging (broke).

This is an important point so I'll repeat it. Don't be naive. Distributors love independent filmmakers because (1) you're cheap, you have no overhead; (2) you're free, investors pay for everything; (3) you're guaranteed, you've finished the film; (4) you're broke and begging. If I were a distributor I'd love you too.

Now, watch how that articulate and allegedly altruistic distribution executive, who was just on the *Charlie Rose* show proclaiming how filmmaking is an indigenous American art form, becomes a shark when you, the broke filmmaker, want to sell your art. Distributors know that they can "pick up" (aka purchase or license) a wonderful film for next to nothing and a promise of net profits.

Thus, why find a distributor when they're looking for you? Your job, which is what your publicity budget is for, while making your film, is to stop hiding and allow the distributors to know that you exist. This is why you do publicity. But do the proper publicity. Getting an article written about your film in local newspapers is useless. Film distributors, the buyers, don't read local newspapers. You must target your entire publicity budget ($2,000–$10,000 [chapter 33]) on ways to make it easy for distributors to discover you.

KNOW THE BUYERS

There are 40–60 North American distributors, who make 250–450 movies a year, and who are also looking for inexpensive independent films. These distributors fall into four classifications:

1. The major studios: These are the six or seven distributors (Universal, Fox, Paramount, Sony, etc.) that each make 20–30 movies a year at $10–$70 million budgets.
2. The mini-majors: The six or seven distributors (Miramax, New Line, MGM/UA, Artisan, etc.) that each make 5–20 movies a year at $5–$20 million budgets.
3. The independents: The 10–15 distributors (Fox Searchlight, Orion Classics, Samuel Goldwyn, Sony Classics, etc.) that each make three to five movies a year at $1–$5 million budgets.
4. Exploitation: The 20–30 companies (Concorde, Crown, Troma, Curb, Trident, etc.) that each make 3–15 movies a year, with words like "Blood," "Zombie," "Slime," "Nightmare," or "Massacre" in the titles, at budgets under (well under) a million, and generate mostly foreign and video revenues.

Additionally, each year, there are always at least 200 filmmakers (people like you) who make a movie ($10,000–$3 million budgets) hoping it will be the next *Easy Rider; sex, lies and videotape; The Blair Witch Project; My Big Fat Greek Wedding;* or *Barbershop.*

DISTRIBUTOR CATEGORY	HOW MANY	FILMS/ YEAR	BUDGETS
Major Studios	6–7	20–30	$10–$70 million
Mini-Majors	6–7	5–20	$5–$20 million
Independents	10–15	3–5	$1–$5 million
Exploitation	20–30	3–15	$1 million
Distributors	*40–60*	*250–450*	*$17–$100 million*
Filmmakers	*200*	*1*	*$0.1–$3 million*

The above 40–60 distributors, besides making films, also acquire independently made films. To find them, each distributor has an employee, called the acquisition executive (AE), who combs the woods, film labs, and film festivals to find you. They are looking for you! 🗄 *You never call a distributor. They will call you. Just stop hiding.* AEs make the deals and write the checks and the 40–60 of them are the total target of your $2,000–$10,000 publicity budget.

HIRE A PUBLICIST

🗄 *Toot your own horn and you're an egomaniac. Have someone else toot your horn and you're undiscovered talent.* Get a publicist. They're listed in your local film directory. You can also get a directory of members from the Publicists Guild of America (323-876-0160). They charge $1,500–$5,000 a month (four to six months), plus expenses, for a total of $6,000–$30,000 plus $6,000–$40,000 in expenses. This is not in your budget. You will be forced to do the publicity yourself, with some consulting guidance by a publicist—and here is what you do.

THE PRODUCTION CHARTS

First, during pre-production, a month prior to your shoot, be sure to get your film listed in the trades' "Production Charts." These charts appear in *Daily Variety* (Friday's issue) and the *Hollywood Reporter* (Tuesday's issue).

To get listed, phone *Daily Variety* (323-857-6600) and the *Hollywood Reporter* (323-525-2126) and speak to the editor in charge of the chart. You'll probably get a recording instructing you to leave your name and fax number and a submission form will be faxed to you. The form always requests:

- A. The title of your film
- B. Production company address, phone, and fax
- C. Actors/cast (stars only)
- D. Department heads
- E. Date your shoot begins
- F. How long the shoot will last
- G. Distributor (if any)

Fill it in, fax it back instantly, and your film will almost automatically appear in the "Films in Pre-Production" or "Future Feature Films in Production" column of the two "Production Charts" each Tuesday and Friday. And when your film begins shooting (the date you provided), your listing is moved to the "Films in Production" section. Thus, you'll be listed for six to eight weeks in both newspapers for no cost.

IMPORTANT POINT   The first week you're listed in *Daily Variety*, a gray tint highlights your information to indicate that it is a new listing. The *Hollywood Reporter*, trying to be different, puts a box around first-week listings.

Why the tinting? Why the box? These boring charts are read by out-of-work actors, out-of-work crew, people trying to sell you T-shirts, and AEs. The tinting and the box are like flashing neon signs to the AEs, telling them that a new sucker (you) somewhere in America is spending his own money. And they will instantly call you. Miramax will call you. New Line will call you.

When your film is listed you will get phone calls from distributors. It is guaranteed. Who is phoning will be the acquisition executive, who will titillate you with their desire to screen your film. Don't get excited. You are in pre-production and have nothing to show. The best thing to do is to stay cool and to politely hang up on each distributor—I guarantee they'll remember you. This is publicity.

FILM FINDERS

Simultaneous to your production chart listing, phone Film Finders (323-308-3489, filmfinders@filmfinders.com) and get listed in their production directory. This company publishes a quarterly compendium of literally every film and TV program that is being made in the world. The listing is free; Film Finders makes their money by selling annual subscriptions for $5,000 to AEs, broadcast and cable program directors, and video/DVD buyers.

PRODUCTION STILLS

Next, during the shoot be sure to get your photos. Another mistake first-time filmmakers make is not taking quality still photos during the shoot. You will need them for your press kits, film festivals, and eventually for newspaper ads and the video/DVD box design. You can't get these photos after the shoot. Hire a still photographer ($150–$250/day) to come to the set on the days that your film looks like it's big-budget and get plenty of black-and-white and color shots, for a cost of **$500–$1,000.**

> **IMPORTANT POINT**   Be sure to take action photos of yourself. When the photographer comes, take off your damn baseball cap, lose the shades, and get photos of you pointing. Always point, point, point—it makes it look like you're in charge.

PRESS KIT

Next, armed with your photos, prepare a press kit. If you really had a $1 million budget, you'd make 1,000 electronic press kits (EPKs—VHS tapes with interviews and isolated scene footage) and 2,000 print press kits for journalists. You don't have that kind of money. But let's make the AEs think you do to incite more excitement. So make only 100 print press kits and, instead of sending them to the media, mail them to the AEs that you hung up on when they called three months prior (they'll remember you), and hold the remaining ones for festival submissions.

Your press kit should contain:

1. A glossy two-pocket folder.
2. 7–10 photos from the shoot (inside right pocket)
3. 3–4 actors' headshots (inside right pocket)
4. 1–2 action photos of you (inside right pocket)
5. 1–2 page synopsis of the film (inside left pocket)
6. 1–2 page biography of you (inside left pocket)
7. 1–2 page story about making the film (inside left pocket)
8. Cute tchotchke, gizmo, or toy (key ring, pen, etc.)

Each press kit will cost $6–$7, plus $3 to mail, so you'll spend about $10 per press kit. It will cost about **$1,000** for 100 kits.

When the AEs get your press kits, they will phone you again and ask, "When can I see your film?" If they ask if you have your film on tape say, "No, it's a film." (Even if it's digital say no.) If you say yes they'll want you to send the tape. Letting them view a tape in their office is the least effective way to induce them to buy. Never send a tape!

Instead, offer to screen your movie for them in front of a paying audience. The AEs will love this; it enables them to better gauge your film's commerciality. In reality, what you're really telling the AE is the date and time of your upcoming film festival screening, where an audience pays to see your film. The bottom line of your publicity budget is to titillate the AEs enough to get them to leave their offices (usually in L.A. or New York), get on a plane, rent a car, book a hotel, and attend the film festival where your film is screening. This will not be easy.

Film festivals are extremely important to independent filmmakers and they will comprise a major part of your publicity budget. 🧳 *Film festivals are not free.* Therefore, let's take a more in-depth look at what they are, why you go to them, what you accomplish at them, and what they cost.

TO DO:

1. Get a list of publicists from the Publicists Guild.
2. Compile an acquisition executive list to target.

 BOOKS

Selling Your Film
E. Sherman, 167 pp., $19.95
A guide for independent filmmakers that takes you through the steps of financing, selling, and marketing a feature film.

Publicity Advice and How-to Handbook
R. Gompertz, 154 pp., $22.95
Your film is finished but no one in Hollywood knows about it. This book will explain what to do.

Publicity Writing for TV and Film
R. Gompertz, 222 pp., $26.95
Writing an effective press release and

creating a press kit is imperative for promoting your film.

Marketing and Selling Your Film Around the World
J. Durie and N. Watson, 167 pp., $19.95
The best on what to do with your film once it is finished.

Movie Marketing
T. Lukk, 274 pp., $19.95
This book demystifies the complex marketing issues and techniques used by distributors.

Selling the Sizzle
B. Avrich, 178 pp., $24.95
The Toronto Film Festival's director explains the nuts and bolts of marketing a film into a box-office winner.

PUBLICITY ORGANIZATIONS

Publicists Guild of America
7715 Sunset Blvd, Suite 300
Los Angeles, CA 90046
Ph: 323-876-0160
Fax: 323-876-6383

Public Relations Society of America
   (PRSA)
33 Irving Pl
New York, NY 10003
Ph: 212-995-2230
E-mail: hq@prsa.org

Entertainment Publicists Professional
   Society (EPPS)
PO Box 5841
Beverly Hills, CA 90209
Ph: 888-399-EPPS
Fax: 310-452-9005
E-mail: epps@p3corp.com

PUBLICITY FIRMS

Henri Bollinger Public Relations
Ph: 818-784-0534
Fax: 818-789-8862

Burson-Marsteller
Ph: 310-226-3000
Fax: 310-226-3030

Warren Cowan & Associates
Ph: 310-275-0777
Fax: 310-247-0810

Dennis Davidson Associates Inc.
Ph: 323-525-1030
Fax: 323-525-1034

Indie P.R.
Ph: 323-964-0700
Fax: 323-964-0704

Julian Myers Public Relations
Ph: 310-827-9089
Fax: 310-827-9838

Rogers & Cowan
Ph: 310-201-8800
Fax: 310-788-6600

PMK Public Relations
Ph: 212-582-1111
Fax: 212-582-6666

Premiere PR
Ph: 310-285-7070
Fax: 310-285-7055

FILM FESTIVALS

"Enter, Attend . . . Win"

The success of an independent film is almost totally dependent on how it plays at a film festival. At this cultural event films, from first-timers, get discovered, attract distributors, and get sold. **[TOP SECRET]** *Film festivals are every-where and easy to enter.* There are at least 300–2,000 festivals held yearly, which translates to 6–40 festivals per week. And you must attend—but which ones and why?

WHAT EXACTLY IS A FILM FESTIVAL?

A film festival is a cultural event. Every city likes to think it has culture—you know, the opera, the symphony, the ballet, etc. And a city without a film festival is obviously a city without culture.

> **IMPORTANT POINT**   Cultural events don't make profits. Otherwise they'd be called business ventures. Thus, if your city or town doesn't have one, don't think about creating one unless you have plenty of free time and can afford to lose money.

To create a film festival, a theater is rented for a week or a weekend. All theaters are for rent if you pay the owner above his "house nut" (i.e., cost to operate the theater per week). This guarantees the theater owner a profit, plus the bonus of the candy counter sales as each screening attracts 200–400 popcorn eaters. Theater owners love having a festival at their theater.

Festivals screen one film every two hours, or about seven films per day. For a weeklong festival this translates to 50 films (seven films a day at

12:00, 2:00, 4:00, etc. times seven days), and for a weekend festival it's 20 films (seven films a day times three days). Festivals like Toronto, which have four theaters, with multiple screens projecting films silmultaneously for 10 days, book over 150 films. Sundance books 60–70 films.

The format of every festival with 50 films over a week (25 films if each film is screened twice, once during the day and once at night) always consists of (a) an opening and closing film, (b) three sidebars (i.e., Early Film Noir, New Women Directors, Best of Latin America, etc.) comprised of 15–20 films, (c) four or five seminars, (d) a couple of breakfast-with-directors lectures, (e) an over-the-hill actor's retrospective, and (f) 25–30 films from independent filmmakers, like you.

Festivals are looking for you, more than you are looking for them. Only about 20 of the 300–2,000 festivals annually are highly selective. Thus, over 95–99 percent of the film festivals each year are easy to get into, as long as you have 90 minutes that is in focus. But they are not free.

WHAT FESTIVALS COST

Your first cost is a submission fee. It won't be much, maybe $50. However, you must send your film in a tape format to be judged. This costs another $100 to create and dupe (duplicate). If you're accepted, you pay an additional $200–$500 acceptance fee. Then you realize you only have one print, so you pay the lab $1,500 to strike a second print. Next is the cost of attending. You pay your own way—airplane ticket, hotel costs, car rentals, etc. And, if you can afford a publicist, you pay to have him attend—another plane ticket, hotel room, etc. Basically, it costs **$2,000–$6000** to attend a film festival, which doesn't include posters and festival catalogue ads, making it the largest portion of your **$2,000–$10,000** publicity budget.

HOW TO FIND FESTIVALS

You can get a list of festivals from any number of Web sites. Just type "film festival" into your search engine (Google, AltaVista, Excite, etc.) and print. Besides the film festival guidebooks, browsing through film magazines (*Release Print, The Independent, MovieMaker, Filmmaker,* etc.) with their "call for entries" notices in the classified sections will get you numerous names, dates, and addresses.

WHICH FESTIVALS ARE BEST

Remember, when you finish making your film, you've spent your money. You're close to broke and feeling pressure to pay back investors. You won't want to wait long to attend a festival or two. 🧳 *Only attend festivals that the distributors send their AEs to.* And the ones most commonly attended by AEs are:

1. Sundance (January, 801-328-3456)
2. Slamdance (January, 323-466-1786)
3. Palm Springs (January, 760-322-2930)
4. Berlin (February, 49-30-254-890)
5. Rotterdam (February, 31-10-411-8080)
6. Santa Barbara (March, 805-963-0023)
7. South by Southwest (March, 512-467-7979)
8. L.A. Independent Film Fest (April, 323-937-9155)
9. Seattle (May, 206-324-9996)
10. TriBeCa (May, 212-941-2400)
11. Cannes (May, 33-1-4561-6600)
12. Hong Kong (June, 852-2584-4333)
13. Karlovy Vary (July, 420-224-235412)
14. Edinburgh (August, 44-131-228-4051)
15. Hollywood Film Festival (August, 310-288-1882)
16. Montreal (August, 514-848-3883)
17. Telluride (September, 303-643-1255)
18. Toronto (September, 416-967-7371)
19. Venice (September, 39-41-521-8711)
20. Hamptons (October, 516-324-4600)
21. New York (October, 212-875-5638)
22. Raindance (October, 44-207-287-3833)
23. Tokyo (November, 81-3-3563-6305)
24. Pusan, Korea (November, 82-51-747-3010)

ENTERING FILM FESTIVALS

Entering is simple. Call, fax, or e-mail the festival and request an application. Most entry forms are one page, with a page or two of rules and guidelines, peppered with a little PR about the festival and its history. Fill out (neatly) and return the entry form, and include:

A. The completed application form
B. The submission fee
C. A VHS viewing copy of your film
D. Your press kit
E. A self-addressed, stamped envelope (if you'd like your materials returned)
F. A cover letter (kiss-ass) explaining why it's an honor to be included

WHY GO TO FESTIVALS?

Film festivals are vital for three reasons. The first, of course, is to win awards. The second is to start the buzz and hype. The third, and by far the most important, which is phrased three different ways, is to either (a) be discovered, (b) get a distributor, or (c) sell your film.

> **IMPORTANT POINT** Only attend festivals that AEs attend. You'll be well received at Philadelphia or Virginia festivals. You'll be the big fish in a little pond. But no AEs attend, so you won't sell your film. And more than likely, you'll never get it into Sundance, Toronto, or Telluride, because you've given away the "World Premiere," "North American Premiere," and "USA Premiere" of your film to Philadelphia or Virginia. Dummy! You gave away all your premieres to festivals that have no AEs in attendance.

1. "Award-Winning Filmmaker"

Have you ever noticed the phrase "an award-winning filmmaker" after someone's name and wondered what award he won? If the award had the prestige, for instance, of an Oscar, an Emmy, the Sundance Grand Jury Prize, or the Palme d'Or, the person would identify himself as "an Oscar winner" or "an Emmy winner."

If someone has won an award that truly has merit they'd be glad to announce it. But if they've only received an award that has little to no merit, then they'll call himself the generic "award-winning filmmaker." When someone announces they're an "award-winning filmmaker," you can assume they've received a certificate that no one has ever heard of and has little to no merit.

I apologize for ruthless honesty. I myself am a multiple "non-meritorious" award-winning filmmaker. The first award I won was in a science fiction, live-action, 35mm category. The festival gave out five awards in this category. I came in second (there were only two films entered!). I'm an award-winning filmmaker. Two weeks later, I entered the Seattle Film Festival. They gave everyone who entered a certificate of accomplishment. It's an award? I am now a multiple-award-winning filmmaker. 📁 *Everyone who enters a festival becomes an award-winning filmmaker. So what?* The key, of course, is to win an award at an elite festival.

2. Buzz and Hype

The second reason to attend festivals is to have your film reviewed and you interviewed. Festival directors try to make a profit. Thus, a week before your screening, the festival director gets the local media to screen and review your film. It is actually in your favor that you are cheap. Reviewers love to say they discovered some "little jewel."

And, with good reviews, your film will sell out. If it sells out, the reviewers then want to interview you. People hear about you. People tell their friends. People love to say that they saw a great film before its release. The buzz and hype starts, and you now have clippings to include in your press kit, to further entice distributors.

3. Selling Your Film

The third, and by far the most important, reason to enter a festival is that it allows you the opportunity to either (a) sell your film, (b) be discovered, or (c) get a distributor. Here's how it happens.

When an acquisition executive goes to a festival and sees that your screening has sold out, he literally doesn't have to see it. *The film makes money!* People are paying to see it. Next, he scans the sold-out audience in hopes of finding a clearly defined demographic in attendance. Finally, the AE buys a ticket and screens your film, not really to see if he/she likes it, but more to see if the audience likes it. Does the audience laugh when they are supposed to laugh? Cry when they are supposed to cry?

Then, when the rear title crawl appears, if the audience applauds, not with politeness but with enthusiasm, and exits the theater with "the buzz" (that "positive word of mouth" that can't be bought), the AEs approach you (you're the overly dressed neurotic one) in the lobby during your "15 minutes of Warhol," as you're nibbling your fingernails down to the cuticles.

🗄️ *Independent deals aren't made in Hollywood offices, but at candy counters.* (That's why the trades call it a "popcorn deal.") In the theater lobby, each AE will want to whisk you away in a limousine (away from the other AEs he's competing with) to an exclusive restaurant, wine and dine you, introduce you to a star, and talk about distribution deals, P&A campaigns, putting you on the five-star hotel circuit, and going to Cannes. Glamour will be everywhere.

Your job, after making your great little film, is to not be seduced by a limo or titillated by the first distributor with an offer. If six AEs attend the screening and love your film, then literally hold court in the lobby, with your attorney-agent, and set up six lunches in the next two days. Do not wait too long.

> **IMPORTANT POINT**   Get an attorney or agent before attending a festival, but if you don't, attorneys and agents, always in search of new clients, will find you by getting lists of films, one or two months prior, that are in each festival. That's why Hollywood agents and attorneys attend Sundance—they're hoping that some yokel pops up with a cheap but sellable film and has no idea what to do.

You're hot, and during the six lunches (don't order too much food—you'll feel sluggish and stupid) over the next two days you negotiate, talk money, and deal memo points (chapter 48). And what's negotiable when you have six offers? Everything!

Let's look at how different these six offers can be:

First offer: AE #1 tells you he's from Fox's independent division and loves your film. You appear nonchalant. He asks what your budget was, and you respond, knowing you spent $300,000, with, "Oh, just under $1 million." He'll be taken aback by your understanding of how to talk and play the Hollywood game and may offer you a flat amount—maybe $2 million—to outright buy your film.

AEs will always ask what your budget was, and if you hadn't read this book you would have proudly told them the exact penny. Thus, you would have started a negotiation by telling the buyer, the AE, exactly how much money you owe. Duh! Always remember, AEs are not dumb. They know what it costs to make a film and can probably guess your budget within 15 percent of your actual cost. But the AE will always ask because you're probably naive enough to tell them the exact penny cost. Remember, what your budget was is nobody's business.

Let's assume the AE asked, you replied properly, and now the AE guesstimates you made your film for about $300,000 and he offers $2 million. Get ready to grab it, if it's the only offer. But if there are several other distributors that want to talk with you, then take 48 hours to hear their offers. Let's listen . . .

Second offer: AE #2 is from Paramount's contemporary classics (that's an oxymoron) division, and starts to play the "What's your budget" game. Quickly discovering you know how to play, he offers that standard 50–50 net deal (chapter 48)—by giving you enough money ($300,000) to pay off your investors, plus a large P&A budget ($5,000,000), charging a distribution fee (35 percent), and splitting (50–50) profits with you.

Sounds good!? Careful. You better realize that you'll never see a penny of the profits because Hollywood creative bookkeeping (chapter 48) ensures there won't be any, but you should be happy that your investors got paid back and that the distributor is going to market you into a celebrity.

Third offer: AE #3 tells you he's from Sony, and asks if you've heard of the studio. They love asking if you've heard of them. You acknowledge, "Yes." He'll ask if you've had any other offers that he should beat. You tell him Paramount's offer of $5 million P&A and 50 percent of profits.

The Sony exec says, "Let's take a look at Paramount's offer. They're charging you $5,000 a print. What a ripoff. Prints only cost $1,500 and that's all we'll charge you. Next, we'll only charge a 30 percent distribution fee, give you 70 percent of profits, and still give you $300,000 to pay off your investors."

This deal, on the surface, sounds better than Paramount's, but after studying it you realize that the $300,000 is probably the only dollars you will ever get. You won't see a penny of profits but you should, once again, be happy that the investors got reimbursed and that your name is marketed.

Fourth offer: AE #4 works for a small distributor trying to beat out a big distributor. You probably won't know the name of his company but he'll tell you a couple of films he distributed last year that you recognize. Then he'll caution you about large distributors who make 500–1,000 prints, throw it out there, and if it hits in the first weekend, keep it there. But if it doesn't hit, they pull it, recoup losses with a quick video/DVD or cable sale, and you'll spend the next six years bitching about how they didn't market your film properly.

The small distributor will tell you his company only distributes three films a year, so they must make every film profitable. He'll spend $500,000 instead of $5 million on P&A, but he'll spend it effectively. He'll only strike 20 prints, one for each art house in the top 20 markets, but promises to keep your film in each theater for eight weeks, and every day he'll put a two-column-inch ad in every newpaper where the film is playing.

Then, after two months, even if no one goes to the 20 theaters, he'll make a large "third window" (chapter 46) sale to a video/DVD distributor and split 50–50 with you. Plus, if your film performs well when in theaters, like *Blair Witch, Crouching Tiger,* or *My Big Fat Greek Wedding,* he'll make more prints, take bigger ads, and increase the revenues.

With this offer, you'll get less exposure (small P&A budget), but besides paying off your investors, you'll get a better shot at making profits thanks to an almost guaranteed video/DVD sale.

Fifth offer: This is a hardass AE. He says, "Gimme your film, I'm gonna screw you." You jump back, shocked with this approach. But it was honest. It's difficult to explain to a first-time filmmaker, who doesn't know the difference between a film and a movie, that all they have is a film that has no value without the P&A money. This distributor will spend P&A money on your film.

He goes on: "I'll probably lose money during the theatrical window (he's being honest), so I have to keep the other video/DVD and cable revenues for profit. Try to negotiate away any of these and I'll do creative bookkeeping. Honest!

"Now, here's why it's a good deal for you," he says. You listen and realize that this is the first distributor offering you a "split-rights deal." The distributor only wants North America and leaves you all foreign rights (chapter 45). The other distributors (offers 1–4) assumed they get world rights.

This also is a good deal, for once your film plays in North American theaters, the world thinks of it as an American Movie. Then one or two months later, you take your film, now a Movie, to a foreign market and cash in for $3–$10 million. If your film never becomes an American Movie, and just screens at a festival or two, you'll be lucky to get $10,000–$20,000 from the foreign market.

Sixth offer: This approach is similar to offer 5. AE #6 says he just wants North American rights. He'll make it into a Movie. You keep the foreign rights and cash in. Plus, he'll beat offer 5 by throwing in North American cable rights.

Although it sounds better, this is almost the same as offer 5, because the distributor, who's giving you North American cable revenues as the alleged bonus, will stipulate in the contract that you can't exploit the cable window (chapter 47) until 90–180 days after it is in video/DVD stores. And after it is in video/DVD stores it loses most of its value to the pay-cable networks.

If you can get these six offers in a two-day period, you're hot. You will be front-page news in *Daily Variety,* the *Hollywood Reporter,* the *New York Times,* and the *Los Angeles Times.* The buzz will be loud, it will snowball, and you'll have the leverage to make counter-offers.

You go back to Distributor #1, with his $2 million world buyout offer and counter with, "I'll take $5 million for North American rights only." You go back to Distributor #2, with his 50–50 net deal and $5 million P&A budget, with a counter-offer of $2 million up front, a $5 million P&A budget with prints charged at $1,500 each, and 50 percent of the video/DVD or cable window, whichever comes first. You go back to the other distributors with counter-offers.

Six lunches. Six offers. You're a hit. Be ready to start talking deal as soon as your film has had its festival screening. But don't negotiate for yourself or the AEs will swindle you. Whatever you do, when talking to distributors at festivals, first get an entertainment attorney (aka producer's rep), and only allow the distributor to have North American rights, unless they pay you an ungodly amount of money.

Always keep your foreign rights, allow your film to be made into an American Movie, and then cash in your foreign revenues at a film market. Whoops! We're getting ahead of ourselves and I feel that you're starting to vicariously feel that you can negotiate with distributors. Whoa, Nelly! This chapter was just about film festivals. Now let me give you a couple more chapters, starting with film markets (chapter 45), then going on to comprehending windows (chapter 46), and concluding with understanding the cable and video/DVD sales (chapter 47), before you are ready to negotiate (chapter 48) with a distributor. Now, on to film markets.

TO DO:

1. Secure a list of film festivals.
2. Determine the major festival dates.

BOOKS

The Ultimate Film Festival Survival Guide
C. Gore, 451 pp., $22.95
The only book that tells you how to work a film festival to ensure a distribution deal.

Film Festivals
S. Gaydos, 199 pp., $15.00
A *Variety* reporter details how festivals work and how they can make or break your film. With an annotated festival list.

The Film Festival Guide
A. Langer, 296 pp., $16.95
Over 500 festivals listed, described, and categorized by date, subject matter, and nation.

The International Film Festival Guide
S. Stolberg, 402 pp., $19.95
A festival resource guide. Besides compiling festivals, it also lists contacts of film buyers from around the world.

 GLOBAL FESTIVAL DIRECTORY

Sundance Film Festival
Program director: Geoffrey Gilmore
PO Box 3630
Salt Lake City, UT 84110-3630
Ph: 801-328-3456

California Headquarters:
8857 W Olympic Blvd
Beverly Hills, CA 90211

Ph: 310-360-1981
Fax: 310-360-1969
Web: www.sundance.org

Slamdance International Film Festival
Program director: Peter Baxter
5634 Melrose Ave
Los Angeles, CA 90038
Ph: 323-466-1786
Fax: 323-466-1784
Web: www.slamdance.com

Palm Springs International Film Festival
Program director: Mitch Levine
1700 E Tahquitz Canyon Way
Palm Springs, CA 92262
Ph: 760-322-2930
Fax: 760-322-4087
Web: www.psfilmfest.org

Berlin International Film Festival
Abteilung Programm
Potsdamer Straße 5
D-10785 Berlin, Germany
Contact: Dieter Kosslick
Ph: 49-30-25-920-444
Fax: 49-30-25-920-499
Web: www.berlinale.de/

Rotterdam International Film Festival
Contact: Simon Field
PO Box 21696
Rotterdam 3001 AR The Netherlands
Ph: 31-10-890-9090
Fax: 31-10-890-9091
Web: www.filmfestivalrotterdam.com

Santa Barbara International Film Festival
Program director: Jon Fitzgerald
2064 Alameda Padre Serra, Suite 120
Santa Barbara, CA 93103
Ph: 805-963-0023

Fax: 805-962-2524
Web: www.sbfilmfestival.org

South by Southwest Film Festival
Program director: Nancy Schafer
PO Box 4999
Austin, Texas 78765
Ph: 512-467-7979
Fax: 512-451-0754
Web: www.sxsw.com

LA Independent Film Festival
Program director: Richard Raddon
8570 Wilshire Blvd, 2nd Floor
Beverly Hills, CA 90211
Ph: 323-951-7090
Fax: 323-937-7770
Web: www.lafilmfest.com

Seattle International Film Festival
Program director: Darryl Macdonald
911 Pine St, Suite 607
Seattle, WA 98101
Ph: 206-464-5830
Fax: 206-264-7919
Web: www.seattlefilm.com

Cannes Festival International du Film
Program director: Giles Jacob
3 Rue Amélie
Paris 75007 France
Ph: 33-1-53-59-6100
Fax: 33-1-53-59-6110
Web: www.festival-cannes.fr

Hong Kong International Film Festival
Program director: Angela Tong
181 Queens Rd Central, 22nd Floor
Hong Kong
Ph: 852-2970-3300
Fax: 852-2970-3011
Web: www.hkiff.org.hk

Karlovy Vary International Film Festival
Program director: Eva Zaoralova
Panska 1
11000 Praquew 1
Czech Republic
Ph: 420-221-411-011
Fax: 420-221-411-033
Web: www.iffkv.cz

Edinburgh Film Festival
Program director: Shane Danielsen
c/o Filmhouse
88 Lothian Rd
Edinburgh EH3BZ Scotland
Ph: 44-31-228-4051
Fax: 44-31-229-5501
Web: www.edfilmfest.org.uk

Hollywood Film Festival
Program director: Carlos de Abreau
433 N Camden Dr, Suite 600
Beverly Hills, CA 90210
Ph: 310-288-1882
Fax: 310-475-0193
Web: www.HollywoodFilm
    Festival.com

Montreal World Film Festival
Program director: Serge Losique
1432 de Bleury St
Montreal, QUE H3A 2J1 Canada
Ph: 514-848-3883
Fax: 514-848-3886
Web: www.ffm-montreal.org

Telluride Film Festival
Program director: Stella Pence
379 State St, Suite 3
Portsmouth, NH 03801
Ph: 603-433-9202
Fax: 603-433-9206
Web: www.TellurideFilmFestival.com

Toronto International Film Festival
Program director: Piers Handling
2 Carlton St, Suite 1600
Toronto, ONT M5B 1J3 Canada
Ph: 416-967-7371
Fax: 416-967-9477
Web: www.e.bell.ca/filmfest

Venice International Film Festival
Program director: Alberto Barbera
Ca'Giustinian
San Marco 1364
Venice 30124 Italy
Ph: 39-41-521-8878
Fax: 39-41-522-7539
Web: www.labiennaledivenezia.net

Hamptons International Film
    Festival
Program director: Denise Kassell
3 Newton Mews
East Hampton, NY 11937
Ph: 631-324-4600
Fax: 631-324-5116
Web: www.hamptonsfest.org

New York Film Festival
Program director: Sarah Bensman
c/o Film Society of Lincoln Center
70 Lincoln Center Plz
New York, NY 10023-6595
Ph: 212-875-5610
Fax: 212-875-5636
Web: www.filmlinc.com

Raindance Film Festival
Program director: Elliot Grove
81 Berwick St, Soho
London W1F 8TW England
Ph: 44-207-287-3833
Fax: 44-207-439-2243
Web: www.Raindance.co.uk

Tokyo International Film Festival
Program director: Yasuyoshi Tokuma
4f Landic Gniza Building 11
1-6-5 Ginza, Chuo-ku
Tokyo 104 Japan
Ph: 81-33-563-6305
Fax: 81-33-563-6310
Web: www.Tokyo-FilmFest.or.jp

Pu-San International Film Festival
Program director: Kim Ji-Seok
Yachting Center, Room 208
1393, Woo I-dong
Haeundae-ku, Pusan 612-021 Korea
Ph: 82-51-747-3010
Fax: 82-51-747-3012
Web: www.piff.or.kr

Hawaii International Film Festival
Program director: Chuck Boller
1001 Bishop St
Pacific Tower, Suite 745
Honolulu, HI 96813
Ph: 808-528-3456
Fax: 808-528-1410
Web: www.hiff.org

Mill Valley Film Festival
Program director: Mark Fishkin
38 Miller Ave, Suite 6
Mill Valley, CA 94941
Ph: 415-383-5256
Fax: 415-383-8606
Web: www.finc.org

TriBeCa Film Festival
Program director: Maggie Kim
375 Greenwich St
New York, NY 10013
Ph: 212-941-2400
Web: www.TribecaFilmFestival.org

ONLINE FILM FESTIVALS

Atom Films
www.atomfilms.com

Big Film Shorts
www.BigFilmShorts.com

Bijou Café
www.BijouCafe.com

The Bit Screen
www.theBitScreen.com

Dfilm Moviemaker Festival
www.dfilm.com

Festival Database
www.movies.com

Get Out There
www.GetOutThere.bt.com

Got Film Fest
www.GotFilmFest.com

IFILM
www.ifilm.com

Internet Festival
www.cinema-sites.com

ManiFestival
www.ManiFestival.com

Million Dollar Festival
www.chrysler.com/filmfest

New Venue
www.NewVenue.com

Rad Digital Film Festival
www.radproductions.com

Underground Film.Com
www.UndergroundFilm.com

Web Festival Directory
www.filmfestivals.com

Webdance Film Festival
www.WebDanceFilmFestival.com

Zoie Film Festival
www.ZoieFilms.com

FILM MARKETS

"Foreign Sales"

Film festivals and film markets have nothing in common. They are night and day. Festivals are about fluff and awards. Markets are about foreign sales. You go to a festival to win awards with the subtext of attracting a North American distributor. You go to a market to sell (the proper word is "license") your film around the world, nation by nation.

Festivals have reviewers and moviegoers, and, under the surface, acquisition executives. Markets have buyers and sellers, and, under the surface, foreign bankers. While there are 300–2,000 film festivals a year, there are just 3–9 film markets a year, with each market having over 1,000 buyers and about 100 sellers in attendance.

WHO ARE THE BUYERS?

To Hollywood the world is divided into two territories: (a) North America and (b) foreign. And, while North America is comprised of America and Canada, foreign is subdivided into 30 nations (Japan, Italy, Thailand, Brazil, South Africa, etc.) and 5 territories (Middle East, Scandinavia, East Africa, etc.).

Each of the 30 nations and 5 territories has companies (theatrical distributors, cable networks, video/DVD distributors, etc.) that make feature films in their own language for their nation, but also buy (license) the rights to market American films in their nation. Thus, each foreign company sends buyer(s) to film markets to look for American movies to bring back to their respective nation or territory.

There are 40–50 buyers (employees of film distributors, cable networks, broadcasters, and video distributors) from Japan attending a film market, plus 40–50 buyers from Germany, 30–40 buyers from France, 15–20 buyers from Spain, 7–10 buyers from Portugal, etc. If you add up all the buyers from the 30 nations and 5 territories, you will discover over 1,000 of them. And at a market you can make a total of 35 sales (30 nations plus 5 territories).

WHO ARE THE SELLERS?

The 100 sellers at a film market consist of 6–7 mini-major distributors, 20–25 independent distributors, 25–30 companies that specialize in foreign sales (no North American distribution), 25–30 foreign distributors, and 10–15 filmmakers with a "split rights deal."

And what are you? You are a seller, with a "split-rights deal," and will either join the market to sell your film globally or license a distributor to do it for you.

WHAT ARE SPLIT RIGHTS?

Let's talk a little bit about dealmaking. When you obtain a distributor (usually at a film festival), after the amount of money up front, the second item you negotiate is what territory the distributor is acquiring the rights for. It could either be:

1. World Rights
2. North American Rights
3. Foreign Rights
4. Split Rights

If you get a distributor who purchases the world rights for your film, then there is only one deal. However, if you get a distributor who only wants North American rights, then you'll get a second distributor for foreign rights. This becomes a "split-rights deal," in which you're splitting the world into North American rights and foreign rights.

THE FILM MARKETS

Every year, there are three large film markets, spaced four months apart, lasting 10 days each, which the 1,000 buyers attend. Thus, no matter when you finish your film, there is always a market coming up in the next couple of months.

The big three markets are:

1. American Film Market (winter, Santa Monica, California, 310-446-1000)
2. Cannes (spring, Cannes, France, 33-1-4561-6600)
3. MIFED (fall, Milan, Italy, 39-2-4801-2912)

The secondary markets, with foreign buyers in attendance, are:

4. IFFM (spring, New York, 212-465-8200)
5. London Screenings (fall, London, 44-181-948-5522)
6. Raindance (fall, London, 44-207-287-3833)
7. Munich (summer, Germany, 49-89-38-1904-0)
8. Berlin (winter, Germany, 49-30-254-890)
9. MIP Asia (fall, Hong Kong, 33-1-4190-4400)

The secondary markets are hybrids, part festival and part market. They are festivals in that they screen films and dispense awards. They are markets in that foreign buyers attend in search of product. Cannes is also a hybrid in that it is both a festival and a market.

You've been excited about going to Cannes, getting a $15 cappuccino and participating in the glitz and glamour of this seaside resort. Did you know that the same 1,000 buyers and 100 sellers attend the American Film Market (AFM) in Santa Monica, California, where just as much money changes hands, there's a beach, and a cappuccino only costs $5? Why go to France when you can save money, hang out with stars, and get a tan in sunny California?

The AFM takes place at the Sheraton Loews Hotel in Santa Monica over the last week of February and the first week of March. It is free to anyone. Have a valet park your car (please make a grand entrance), enter the hotel's courtyard, dress in black and gray, stroll to the pool, saunter to a chaise longue, order a cappuccino (big tips impress), and have yourself paged for the remainder of the day. 🔲 *All the sleazeballs in the film industry hang out in film markets' hotel lobbies.*

When you attend a market, you'll notice that the Big Eight (Warner Bros., Paramount, MCA/Universal, Sony, Disney, Fox, DreamWorks SKG, and MGM/UA) are not there. They don't have to be. Warner Bros. is so large that it has an office in Berlin to distribute its films in Germany, as well as offices in Tokyo, Sydney, Johannesburg, Buenos Aires, Rome, Bombay, etc. The major distributors are so large that they distribute their films globally themselves, nation by nation.

However, the mini-majors, which are large North American distributors like Miramax and New Line, don't have offices in foreign nations. They attend a market and sell the rights to their films to a foreign distributor (buyer) in each nation. Thus, the mini-majors and the independent and "exploitation" distributors, who likewise have no foreign offices, band together for 10 days, rent a hotel, and hold a market.

During the market, each of the smaller distributors (now called foreign sales agents) books a hotel room (takes out the beds and replaces them with large HDTV monitors and a small buffet) or suite and uses it as a temporary sales office, plastering the room with posters of their films for sale. The foreign sales agent then stands at his hotel room's door, waiting to collar any foreign buyer walking through the halls. "Come on in. Let me show you what I have." The potential German or Korean buyer walks in, the seller slides a tape of the movie for sale into the VCR, screens a trailer, and peddles.

IMPORTANT POINT   If you want to license your film to a foreign country, join the next market, rent a hotel room and/or exhibit booth, and sell. Anyone can join if you write a check.

To join AFM as a seller costs $15,000. Then you rent a hotel room ($250–$2,000/day) for 10 days; rent monitors and VCRs ($3,000); provide a daily buffet ($2,000–$5,000); design and print posters ($3,000–$5,000); take out ads in the trades ($5,000–$20,000); book screening time ($1,000); and throw a posh party ($10,000–$100,000).

In the hotel room, if the foreign buyer wants to purchase the rights to your film for his nation for a small amount of money, then he is satisfied with viewing only a couple of minutes of the film on tape. However, if you want a large sale from that buyer, he'll want to see the entire 35mm film projected in a movie theater.

When the big three markets take place, the local cinemas in Santa Monica, Cannes, and Milan are closed off to the general public and are made available only to market members for screenings to foreign buyers. You could have a screening, on the second or third day of the market, in a theater that seats 400 people, for five or six people—a German buyer, a

French buyer, a Mexican buyer, a Korean buyer, a South African buyer, and a Brazilian buyer. Remember, they are not in competition with each other.

Then, after the screening, you and your salesman immediately turn to each buyer and try to close the sale. If they offer a large sum, you sign a contract giving them the exclusive right to exploit your film in their nation or territory for a period of four to ten years. Remember, there are 30 nations and 5 territories, for a total of 35 potential sales.

Now, what do you do once you've made a sale? Paperwork. Lots of paperwork! Let's say you are successful and made 20 sales at either AFM, Cannes, or MIFED for a total of $4 million. You are now in the import-export business. Each buyer is afraid that if he just gives you a check, you may never send him a print (second-generation negative) with an M&E track.

Therefore, the buyer only gives you a 20 percent down payment with the signed contract. Then, upon returning to his country, he deposits the remaining 80 percent into a bank escrow account, or establishes a letter of credit (LC), with instructions to release the money into your bank account when your second-generation negative and M&E track clears customs in his nation. This entails a lot of paperwork.

Do you really want to handle your own foreign sales? It's expensive to join a market. Plus, you must be an excellent salesman. And, if you're successful, you'll deal with a ton of contracts and international banks during the collection process.

The second, and simpler, way to sell your film's foreign rights is to stop trying to eliminate the middleman and make just one sale to a distributor who specializes in the foreign market, and walk away. To do this, rent a screening room ($75–$200/hour) in New York or Los Angeles one month before the market and have distributors who specialize in foreign sales look at your film. After the screening, they politely tell you they'll "run the numbers" and get back to you. Here is what "run the numbers" means.

The distributor, now acting as a foreign sales agent, asks his employee who handles European sales, "If I pick up this film, what can you get from England? From France? From Germany? From Spain? From Portugal? From Greece? From Turkey? From Scandinavia?" And so on. He asks his Asian salesman, "What can you get from Japan? From Taiwan? From Korea? From Singapore? From Australia? From the Philippines? From China?"

He asks his South American and African salesmen the same questions. They run the numbers.

Let's say they run the numbers (30 nations and 5 territories) and tally $4 million. The distributor, feeling comfortable that if he buys your film's foreign rights for 50 percent of the $4 million his salesmen will generate a healthy profit, will probably offer you $2 million. If this happens, take the check and walk.

The third way to sell international rights is when a foreign sales distributor runs the numbers and is not comfortable with the projected sales. However, if he knows your film has been accepted at a popular festival (Sundance, Toronto, Telluride), where it'll get critical acclaim and exposure, he'll offer you a commission deal. He'll represent your film at the market and get a commission (30–40 percent) from each sale. Sometimes it is actually more lucrative to take a commission deal, rather than a one-shot cash sale.

So, there are three ways of selling at a film market. First, join the market and sell your film yourself. This is expensive, but if you succeed you will be wealthy and return to the market the following year with a slate of 7–10 films. The second way is to screen your film for foreign sales agents, who run the numbers and give you a cash offer (a single check), and walk away. Third, and most common, is to get a foreign sales agent, who represents your film at film markets on a commission deal.

Reiterating, because it is important: What you have discovered with the last two chapters is that film festivals and film markets have nothing in common. Film festivals are about awards and securing a distributor for a North American distribution deal, while film markets are about licensing your film's foreign rights.

Next, to further put together the film business puzzle for you, let's take a deeper look into the distribution deal and discover what "windows" are.

TO DO:

1. Call AFM and get a list of its member companies.
2. Name the top seven nations, with their buyers, that you'll sell to.

BOOKS

Variety International Guide
P. Cowie, 408 pp., $26.95
Takes you nation by nation and
explains what they're producing and
buying from independent filmmakers,
with contact lists.

Distributors
HCD staff, 224 pp., $59.95
A detailed list, including names and
contact info, of all the foreign buyers.

The International Movie Industry
G. Kindem, 417 pp., $25.95

When selling your film around the
world you should understand each of
your markets. This book details the
film industry in 19 countries and 6
continents.

*Marketing and Selling Your Film Around
the World*
J. Durie and N. Watson, 165 pp., $19.95
This excellent book explains the
foreign sales process from A to Z.

The International Film Festival Guide
S. Stolberg, 402 pp., $19.95
Lists nation by nation the buyers to
contact who might distribute/purchase
your film.

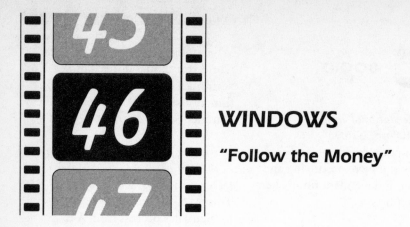

WINDOWS

"Follow the Money"

Everyone wants movies. You've made a film. Question: When is a film a movie? Answer: When it's in a movie theater. Why? Because when it's in a movie theater, there are newspaper ads. When there are newspaper ads the consumer thinks that the film, now a movie, has a value—the $9–$10 ticket price for admission. Now everyone from cable networks to video/DVD distributors to hotel/motel owners will pay for your movie.

> **AUTHOR'S NOTE** This is a very important chapter, especially if you want to make deals and become a Hollywood player. Read it carefully.

Television networks want movies!
Basic-cable networks want movies, but before they're on television!
Pay-cable networks want movies, but before they're on basic cable!
Pay-per-view (PPV) companies want movies, but before they're on pay cable!
Video/DVD stores want movies, but before they're on pay-per-view!
Video-on-demand (VOD) networks want movies, but before they're in video/DVD stores!
And, theater owners want your films—but before everyone!

As you can see, there is a pecking order in Hollywood and each buyer (licensee) wants your film (caveat: if it becomes a movie) for a specific "window."

WHAT THE HELL IS A "WINDOW"?

A "window" is a precise period of time, usually measured in months, when a company is permitted exclusivity to acquire revenues from either the screening, renting, or selling of your movie for their specific (video, cable, broadcasting, etc.) industry.

Thirty years ago a distributor would place your film in theaters, pay for ads, and keep it there as long as box-office revenues were greater than ad expenses. Then, when the glamour of the film wore off and the ad costs were more than the box-office revenues, the distributor pulled the film and sold it to a television network for airing 15–24 months later.

This 15–24 month period, from when a film was in a theater to when it appeared on television, was the "window." And producers, 30 years ago, received revenues from theatrical distributors, television networks, and nominal dollars from the foreign market.

Over the last 30 years, however, this 15–24 month window became divided into sub-windows as new revenue sources appeared. Thus, today, producers generate revenues from PPV/VOD (pay-per-view and video-on-demand) companies, video/DVD distributors, and cable (pay or basic) networks, as well as the theatrical distributors and broadcasting networks. Further, foreign market revenues have exploded from nominal dollars to megabucks during this period.

THE SEVEN SUB-WINDOWS

The flow of revenue, from the seven sub-windows, to a producer for a distributed feature film in North America has an established order. Further, besides sub-window revenues, there are additional dollars from ancillary markets (merchandising and licensing, music rights, publishers, educational markets, airlines, product placement, etc.) and from the foreign market. But for this chapter I'm referring to only revenues from the windows within North America.

THE WINDOW REVENUE PUZZLE

Now let's take a look at how, if you move one piece of this window-puzzle out of place and give it a higher (closer to theatrical release) window, the entire revenue flow disappears.

Movie Profits
Market • Sell

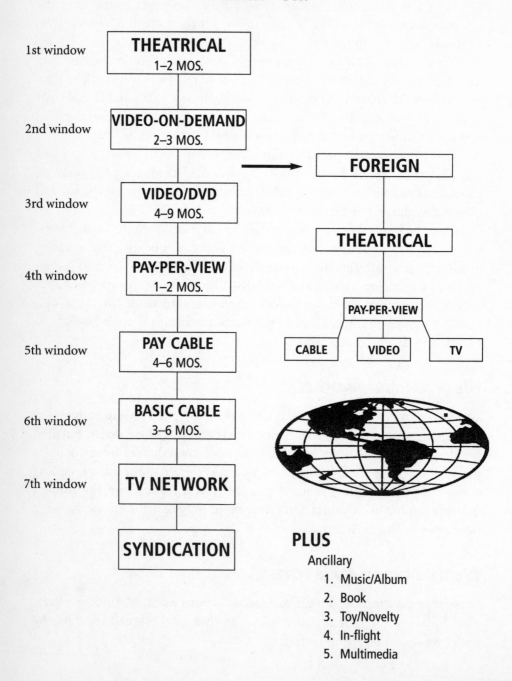

1st window	**THEATRICAL** 1–2 MOS.
2nd window	**VIDEO-ON-DEMAND** 2–3 MOS.
3rd window	**VIDEO/DVD** 4–9 MOS.
4th window	**PAY-PER-VIEW** 1–2 MOS.
5th window	**PAY CABLE** 4–6 MOS.
6th window	**BASIC CABLE** 3–6 MOS.
7th window	**TV NETWORK**
	SYNDICATION

FOREIGN

THEATRICAL

PAY-PER-VIEW

CABLE   VIDEO   TV

PLUS
Ancillary
1. Music/Album
2. Book
3. Toy/Novelty
4. In-flight
5. Multimedia

Let's say a couple of years ago, in search of $10 million, you fly to Atlanta, Georgia. You get off the plane and run into Ted. You know, Ted Turner, the owner of (6th window) basic-cable (TBS, TNT, and CNN) networks.

You pitch him your $10 million idea and he stops you, stating, "Karma, karma." Remember, Ted at one time lived with Jane Fonda. She taught him karma. Ted goes on: "I feel karma. I'm sure your idea is great. Don't even tell it to me. Not even the title. It's a done deal. I'll give you the $10 million. All I ask is that you get a distributor."

You are ecstatic. All you have to do to get $10 million from Ted's TBS network, to finance your film, is get a distributor. In such a case, I'd instantly get on a plane and go to any theatrical distributor and offer them the following: "IT'S FREE! IT'S FREE! PLEASE, PLEASE, PLEASE DISTRIBUTE IT!"

I don't know about you, but if I could get $10 million to make a film, get an opening title credit and a $200,000–$400,000 salary, live in a five-star hotel suite for two months, hang out with famous people, and all I had to do was get a distributor, I'd be on my knees begging them to take it for free if needed.

> **IMPORTANT POINT**   Due to the excessive cost of prints and ads, 80 percent (that's four out of five) of films today lose money during their theatrical window. I repeat, four out of five films lose money. That is correct. Four out of five films lose money. Bummer! However, that is only during the theatrical release window.

Guess what. The distributor, even if offered the free deal, will probably pass. For, as soon as the distributor hears that Ted (TBS network) is financing the film, the deal is killed, and it has nothing to do with personalities or egos. TBS is a basic-cable (6th window) network and Ted wants a movie for TBS. Ted is not a movie distributor. Thus, he will give you the money to make a film if you get a distributor, who pays for the P&A (so it's not really free) to make it into a movie.

The distributor knows what you don't know but do now—that the basic-cable network will only give you the money if it jumps a couple of windows and obtains exclusivity for a 60–90 day period (aka the 2nd window) after it's in theaters. Then the basic-cable network will broadcast it 20 times a month and promote it as a TBS exclusive.

Now, for the problem the distributor faces. Distributors know (I realize

I'm repeating, but it's a very, very important point) that four out of five movies lose money during the theatrical window but eventually profit from the "back end" revenues garnered from the VOD (2nd window), video/DVD (3rd window), PPV (4th window), and pay-cable (5th window) sales that follow. However, when a basic-cable network's (6th window) airings jump to the 2nd window, this instantly kills the 3rd, 4th, and 5th window revenues. Why?

Would you, the consumer, rent a video/DVD after you saw it 20 times on a basic-cable network? No! Would you, the subscriber, be happy with HBO or Showtime, who charge you $15 a month for movies, if you see things that have already aired on a basic-cable network 20 times last month? No! I hope you're getting the point.

Hence, the only chance the distributor has to profit on the above deal you're offering is by hoping that either (a) the movie gets an excellent box-office gross or that, when combined with (b) foreign revenues (assuming the distributor kept them) and (c) a broadcasting sale 15–24 months later, the movie will generate a profit.

IMPORTANT POINT   Each industry (broadcasting, basic cable, pay cable, video/DVD, VOD, PPV) has an established window—break the order and lose all the revenue.

Thus, if you let a TV network (ABC, NBC, CBS, etc.) air the movie before it is on basic cable (6th window), it kills the basic-cable sale.

If you let a basic-cable network (USA, A&E, Sundance, etc.) air it before it's on pay cable (5th window), it kills the pay-cable sale.

If you let a pay-cable network (HBO, Showtime, Starz, etc.) air it before it's in video/DVD stores (3rd window), it kills the video sale.

If it's in video stores (Blockbuster, Hollywood Video, etc.) before it goes on VOD (2nd window), it kills the VOD sale.

Even worse, if you let a TV network (7th window) air it before it's in video/DVD stores (3rd window), besides killing the video sale, it kills the PPV (4th window), pay-cable (5th window), and basic-cable (6th window) sales.

If you can learn how to put the windows together, in a manner that satisfies each of these projected revenue sources, you will be able to become a global producer like Joe Roth, Arnon Milchan, Nik Powell, Brian Grazer, Elie Samaha, or Ed Feldman and will be able to finance big-budget movies. For example, secure 10 percent of your film's budget from a broadcasting network by guaranteeing them exclusivity for the 7th window. Then get 15 percent of your budget from a basic-cable network that wants 6th window exclusivity. Next, get 20 percent of the budget from a pay-cable network that wants exclusivity for the 5th window, and an additional 35 percent of the budget from the video/DVD distributor who wants the 3rd window.

Assuming that you get a theatrical distributor with a solid P&A budget, you have just procured 80 percent of your movie's financing.

Secure the remaining 20 percent from a combination of (a) a theatrical distributor who loves the project; (b) an investor who hopes that the audiences come in droves; (c) a foreign sales agent who lays it off with pre-sales to maybe 5 (Italy, Germany, Japan, England, Argentina) of the 30 nations and keeps the remaining 25 nations as guaranteed profits, even if the film bombs in North America; and (d) a co-producer with government financing, if the film is shot in their nation, or (e) a bank that does "gap financing" (collateralizes unsold windows and markets).

Get the picture? Can you see the pieces of the revenue puzzle? Are you seeing how to put this puzzle together to finance your film? Are the "windows" becoming clear to you? Can you see the pecking order? Can you see how to maximize revenues after your film is in theaters? If so, you are starting to think like a dealmaker—welcome to Hollywood.

If your film gets a distributor, and becomes a movie, there will be excellent revenues from the cable (pay) and/or video/DVD industry, each of which wants extended exclusivity windows. Therefore, it is important to obtain a more in-depth understanding of these two industries who are competing for product (your film, that becomes a movie) for airing or renting.

TO DO:

1. Read movie posters looking for co-producer or co-production names. Then guess which territory or window that name represents.

BOOKS

The Blu-Book
Hollywood Reporter staff, 636 pp.,
$74.95
The most thorough directory of companies who will license your film for
the video, cable, TV, and ancillary
markets. A must-have!

CABLE AND VIDEO/DVD

"Maximize Revenues"

A company from either the cable and video/DVD industries (caveat, "if your film becomes a movie") will want to license it and pay big bucks. Therefore, let's take a couple of moments to understand a little more about these two revenue sources.

THE CABLE WORLD

Cable networks have voracious appetites. They program 24/7/365, which translates to almost 9,000 hours per annum. This means that each cable network sets aside a large amount of funds to purchase and make movies to fill this 9,000-hour-per-annum void. But how do you get some of this money and who do you call?

First, you should understand that the cable industry breaks down into six subcategories that a subscriber receives when purchasing a package, comprised of 40–50 channels, from a cable or satellite operator for $30–$80 a month. The six cable subcategories are:

1. Local Origination and Public Access (LO/PA)
2. Lease Access
3. Basic Cable
4. Pay Cable
5. Pay-Per-View (PPV)
6. Video-on-Demand (VOD)

LO/PA

LO (local origination) or PA (public access) are those blurry, poor-quality channels that program those stupid talking-head interview shows with a woman talking to a plant, or a local yokel demonstrating the best yoga position for guzzling wine. These channels are mandated by law to be free for the public to use. Why?

When a cable operator applies for a community's cable franchise, in return for the quasi-monopoly the FCC (Federal Communications Commission) dictates that the cable operator must provide free access to the facilities (equipment and studio) for the community's constituents. It also must set aside at least two channels, LO and PA, for these community producers to air their shows for free. Thus, the local high school game or the city council meeting is seen.

> **SHOW ME THE MONEY**   Although it is easy for independent filmmakers to air their film on these channels, there is absolutely no money permitted to be made on an LO or PA channel.

Lease Access

Lease access channels have slightly better programming than LO/PA channels, and you actually see telephone numbers superimposed on the screen that create subtle infomercials (advertising is strictly forbidden on LO and PA programs) and ads. Lease access channels are where you see people peddling everything from real estate to furniture to naked massage parlors.

> **SHOW ME THE MONEY**   You can rent (lease) these channels from your local cable operator ($50–$200 an hour) cheaply, show your movie or program, sell ads to the local gas station or psychic at $25–$100 for 30 seconds, and even display a phone number. These channels were becoming a cottage industry until the late '90s, when the Internet popped up and killed it.

Basic Cable

All other cable channels with commercial programming (which means they run ads) fall into the basic-cable category. When you subscribe to cable, you're usually offered a "basic package" of 40–50 channels. Aside from two or three LO/PA and the three or four lease access channels, a majority of the other channels, except for pay cable and PPV, are called basic-cable networks.

SHOW ME THE MONEY   Basic-cable networks license feature films from independent filmmakers, but pay very little ($10,000–$100,000) for multiple non-exclusive airings, unless they get the movie for the 5th window (chapter 46), before it airs on any pay-cable network. These basic-cable channels are:

1. Independent Film Channel (516-803-3000)
2. Sundance Channel (212-654-1500)
3. A&E Network (212-210-1400)
4. USA Cable (212-937-0954)
5. Lifetime (212-424-7000)
6. TBS/The Superstation (404-827-1700)
7. TNT (404-827-1717)
8. ABC Family (212-782-0600)
9. Bravo (212-561-3300)
10. Disney Channel (818-569-7500)
11. Nickelodeon (212-846-4985)
12. History Channel (212-210-1400)
13. Sci-Fi Channel (212-413-5000)
14. MTV (212-258-8040)

Well, $10,000–$100,000 sounds like nice money, but it may not be enough to pay back your investors. The real money ($5–$20 million) is in procuring a pay-cable, not basic-cable, sale for your movie.

Pay Cable

Pay cable is where the big bucks are. However, 📁 *pay-cable networks only buy movies, and the problem is you've made a film.* Once again, there is a big difference between a film and a movie. I'm repeating this solely due to the importance of the concept that "you've made a film" and "a film becomes a movie when it's in a movie theater"—that is, it's shown in front of a paying audience. Movies are not free, and when a film is in a movie theater, there are newspaper ads. When there are newspaper ads, the consumer subliminally believes that the film, now a movie, has a dollar value, which is the ticket price of almost $10.

The problem for pay-cable networks is, the major studios' movies (20–30 movies a year each), when combined with the mini-major and independent distributors' movies and a couple of foreign flicks, amount to only 250–300 movies a year—and this ain't enough product to satisfy 9,000 hours per annum of programming needs.

For feature film producers, pay-cable channel sales are where the big dollars ($5–$20 million) are. This assumes that when you get a distributor (chapter 48) who makes your film into a movie, you are able to keep the fifth window's revenues (chapter 46) for yourself. The pay-cable channels are:

1. HBO (212-512-1000)
2. Cinemax (call HBO)
3. Showtime (212-708-1600)
4. The Movie Channel (call Showtime)
5. Encore (720-852-7700)
6. Starz (call Encore)

HBO owns and buys for Cinemax. Showtime owns and buys for the Movie Channel. And Encore and Starz are really the same company. So actually there are only three companies that dispense the big bucks: HBO, Showtime, and Encore/Starz. Further, each of these networks demands exclusivity for the pay-cable window. So you can only sell to one of the three.

SHOW ME THE MONEY For you, the independent filmmaker, with a darling film that has never had a national newspaper ad campaign, there won't be a pay-cable sale. However, if you get a distributor with a P&A budget, there will be a big sale. But, in all likelihood the distributor, not you, will pocket the money from this sale. ■ *He who controls the P&A keeps the profits.*

PPV (Pay-Per-View) and Video-on-Demand (VOD)

There are approximately 110 million homes or apartments in America with TV sets in them. Of those homes, about 90 million subscribe to cable (80 percent cable penetration) or satellite services for an additional 20–80 channels. And these subscribers have pay-per-view capability, so about 90 million households in America can pay to see a movie in their living rooms before it airs on a pay-cable network.

SHOW ME THE MONEY   In the late '80s and early '90s, the studios thought they were going to make a killing in revenues thanks to 90 million homes with pay-per-view. They planned to make movies in the $3–$5 million range, call them $12–$15 or $15–$20 million films, put them in theaters with a one-week $5 million advertising campaign, then pull them and put them immediately on PPV while still fresh. The studios were sure that they'd get one out of ten cable or satellite subscribers to pay $6 to see a movie that is still in theaters. With 9 million PPV sales (10 percent of 90 million homes) at $6 each, this $3–$5 million one-week distributed movie would gross $54 million from PPV. Wow!

PPV bombed. Here's why. You, the consumer, are lazy after a day's work and feel it is a hassle to order a movie between the hours of 8 P.M. and 11 P.M. You must memorize a phone number, get up from the couch, find the phone, dial, and then wait 10–30 minutes for the movie to be ready. Consumers at home want instant gratification.

However, PPV has found a small niche in the hotel/motel industry, where a more sophisticated remote and cable box allows you to just point at the TV and—poof!—15 seconds later, the movie pops up. Although it lies under the category of pay-per-view, this is actually called video-on-demand (VOD).

It is my opinion that VOD will get large, even humongous, but not until everyone gets a "digital cable box" at home that is as instant as the boxes in hotels. As of today, approximately 50 of the 12,000 cable systems offer them. However, cable operators are now feeling a need to update their boxes, because of competition from companies like DirecTV and Dish Network, which also distribute the same networks to your home but via satellite and—*the Web*.

In the interim, the 2nd window has been given temporarily to the VOD industry, along with in-flight airline sales. This, in turn, has pushed the video/DVD industry to the 3rd window, with the 4th window presently belonging to the PPV industry. The 5th window now goes to the pay-cable networks, with the 6th and 7th windows, respectively, being occupied by the basic-cable and terrestrial broadcasting networks.

The Cable Bottom Line

Although there is no money from the public access channels and little revenue from lease access channels, there is some basic-cable revenue and the big bucks from a pay-cable network. However, this big check usually goes to the distributor who put the P&A money into making your film a movie.

Finally, although pay-per-view initially bombed, thanks to the Web and broadband (chapter 50) and the instant capabilities of VOD, billions in revenue will eventually flow to filmmakers in the forthcoming decade. And, hopefully you will be ready with your film when that day arises.

THE VIDEO/DVD WORLD

If your film has a major release (1,000–2,000 prints), there is probably $50–$80 million in revenue from the video/DVD industry. Make a film with a limited release (20–50 prints) and there is probably $5–$8 million in revenue from the video/DVD industry. Make a film, however, with no release (no newspaper ads) and you're lucky to get $10,000.

The video/DVD industry has been profitable in foreign nations for 30 years. It is only in the last 10–15 years that videos, and now DVDs, have become a massive revenue source for studios and moviemakers in America, with five categories of product:

1. Sell-through videos: These are the videos/DVDs (animation and family) that distributors believe will be more profitable by selling ($14.95–$19.95) directly to consumers rather than selling ($89.95–$109.95) to video stores for rentals.
2. Direct-to-video (DTV): Also called "made-for." These are the low-budget genre titles (horror, T&A, etc.) sold to Blockbuster or Hollywood Video ($19.95–$29.95) as shelf filler, that teenagers rent for $2–$3 for a 4–5 day period.
3. Special-interest videos: These are the how-to tapes on exercise (*Fonda Does Tai Bo*), auto repair (*Max Your Manifold*), cake decorating (*Martha Stewart Does Everything*), etc. that are sold via infomercials and at Kmart stores.
4. Rental videos: These are the videos/DVDs of movies (those newspaper ads), sold to the 25,000–40,000 video stores for $89.95–$109.95 each, that consumers rent at $3–$4 a day.
5. DVD: These are the movies that are now packaged on DVDs (nicknamed "film-schools-in-a-box") and sold for $19.95 directly to the consumer at video rental stores at the same time that you can rent the VHS for $2.95 a night from the store that bought the same movie for VHS rental at $69.95 to $107.95.

Video/DVD Stores

There are at least 25,000 video/DVD stores, mostly owned by chains with full shelves like Blockbuster and Hollywood Video that don't buy just anything. 🗄 *Video stores, just like pay-cable networks, want movies ... not films.*

> **SHOW ME THE MONEY**   If your film becomes a movie (full-page newspaper ads) there will be 20–30 cassettes (selling at $69.95–$107.95 each) sitting on Blockbuster's "New Releases" shelves. Twenty cassettes times 25,000 stores times $107.95 amounts to over $50 million.

Now, let's assume you have made a film (no newspaper ads). It's a good film. It played at Sundance, got honorable mention in Berlin, won the first-time filmmaker's award at Houston, got a screenwriter's award at Philadelphia, but, for whatever reason, it didn't get a distributor. You bombed. But it ain't that bad. There is still money to be made. You'll find a small video/DVD distributor to design and mail a flyer ($2 each) to 25,000 video/DVD stores, offering the tape at a lower price of $29.95, in the hope of getting one out of five stores to order one cassette each.

> **SHOW ME THE MONEY**   With two out of five stores ordering one cassette each, it means you will sell 10,000 units at $29.95, which is a gross of only $300,000.
>
> But these stores don't buy non-distributed, no-name films at retail. They get them at wholesale, 40 percent off. So subtract $120,000 from the $300,000. This leaves $180,000. Wait, it gets worse. The video/DVD distributor spent about $50,000 for marketing, which he subtracts from the $180,000. That leaves only $130,000.
>
> Now, do you think the video/DVD distributor, knowing that he stands to recoup only $130,000 after expenses, will pay $130,000 for the video rights to your film? He will probably offer you $50,000–$75,000 at the most!

So, if your film plays at a couple of acclaimed festivals and wins awards but doesn't get a theatrical release ... then my gut says you'll be lucky to get $50,000–$75,000 from the North American video/DVD industry. But if you know how to maximize revenue (chapter 46), you'll combine this video/DVD revenue with a late-night cable sale ($50,000–$100,000) and 5–10 sales ($5,000–$50,000 each) to foreign nations (Japan, Germany,

France, Korea, England, etc.) that love American independent films, and generate $150,000–$500,000.

What About Those "Made-For"?

Now, I know what some of you are thinking: "Well, how about those cheap made-for-video things?" Yes, there are films produced solely for home video/DVD (video rental), and they're profitable if manufactured cheaply. Technically they are called direct-to-video (DTV).

When someone announces that they are making a film for the home video market, they are telling you right up front, 📷 *"This film sucks. It might even be a piece of shit."* However, skew it to a demographic, make it cost-effectively ($75,000–$150,000), put someone in it (a name, but only a "B" name), have lots of T&A, action, or horror, and sell it as a genre product. Then, when combining the video/DVD revenues with foreign market sales, you'll probably make a small profit.

Have you heard of David Heavener? A video/DVD with his name on the box might sell 15,000 units at $30 each, grossing $450,000. How about Cynthia Rothrock or Shannon Tweed? These names will sell 20,000–25,000 units, grossing $600,000–$750,000. Names like Andrew Stevens, Harry Hamlin, or Jason Priestly can get you one or two cassette sales per store and your movie will garner 25,000–50,000 units in sales, generating over $1 million.

How about Lorenzo Lamas? Rutger Hauer? Eric Roberts? Mickey Rourke? Van Damme? Jet Li? Increasing name recognition produces more and more cassette sales. And in the past two years the black hip-hop video market has been profitable. So get a rapping name like Master P, Snoop Doggy Dogg, Dr. Dre, Jay-Z, or DMX and you should profit.

Finding a Video/DVD Distributor

All video/DVD distributors are members of the Video Software Dealers Association (VSDA), a trade association of video retailers and distributors. The VSDA has an annual convention in Las Vegas where all video distributors rent space, display their forthcoming titles, and try to sell to video store owners. This presents a wonderful opportunity for new filmmakers to meet every video distributor at one time.

The Video/DVD Bottom Line

If you want to make big bucks from the video/DVD industry, then make sure you get a theatrical deal with a film distributor who (big point) permits you to keep the 3rd window video/DVD revenues. If you don't get a theatrical distributor, expect little to no revenue. However, if you manufacture your film cheaply, win some festival awards, or at least have a recognizable name, you could generate a profit when combining the video/DVD revenues with a cable sale and foreign revenues.

More and more I'm sure that you are seeing the importance of obtaining a distributor with a P&A budget to ensure profits. Therefore, let's now learn about the world of distributors—how to get one, how to negotiate, and how to ensure profit.

TO DO:

1. Watch HBO, Showtime, and Encore/Starz.
2. Order two PPV movies from your cable system.
3. Count DTV videos at Blockbuster.
4. Attend the next VSDA convention.

 BOOKS

The Blu-Book
Hollywood Reporter staff, 636 pp.,
$74.95
Lists all the cable networks and video
distributors who might purchase the
rights to your film.

THEATRICAL DISTRIBUTION

"Negotiate the Deal"

You are nothing without a distributor! Every chapter up until now has been involved with taking the idea/dream that is in your head, making it into a 90-minute narrative film, and getting some awards at film festivals. But without a distributor you are still nothing.

> **WARNING** This chapter will be a bummer. All the positive energy I created, by demystifying Hollywood, will be instantly forgotten once you realize how distributors screw first-time filmmakers. However, don't be depressed. For, once I give you the realistic information, then I'll show you how to obtain a distributor with a deal that allows a profit. But first, let me depress you.

I'm sure you've heard that distributors are sharks who prey on naive first-timers. It's true! But I don't like this analogy, for it reeks of the pity-pot and the poor-me syndrome. To me, distributors are more comparable to attorneys. Everyone hates them. Everyone has an attorney joke. But, like it or not, we need attorneys. And, like it or not, you need a distributor.

WHY YOU NEED A DISTRIBUTOR

There are two reasons why you need a distributor: First, they have the P&A money to make your film into a movie. YOU DON'T! Second, they have the ability to collect from theater owners. YOU DON'T! Ask yourself, "How am I going to collect from a theater owner in a shopping center in Akron, Ohio?"

The answer is a distributor. Distributors, middlemen between filmmakers and exhibitors, take your product, create an advertising campaign, place newspaper ads, set up interviews, strike prints, book theaters, freight prints, make your film into a movie, and oversee the collection and distribution of revenues.

A distributor, with 3 to 30 films a year, has the power to collect from theater owners, because the owners want the distributor's next film. You only have one film. Attempt self-distribution and you'll spend your entire life in small claims court trying to collect from each and every theater owner. Therefore, it is imperative to have a distributor who has the power to collect. Your problem then becomes collecting from the distributor.

Remember, marketing a film usually costs more than making the film. Thus, the P&A money is imperative. Without it your film is only a film. And, remember, no one buys films. You ain't got any P&A money—you barely had enough money to make the film and attend a festival. But the distributor does. And 📁 *he who has the P&A money has the power—and distributors have P&A money.*

THE BASIC DISTRIBUTION DEAL

Let's assume you've done everything right. You got a great script. Picked the right actors. Shot on budget. Entered the proper festival. Audiences came. You won an award and are talking with distributors.

The initial deal you're offered 19 out of 20 times is called the "standard distribution deal," which on the surface sounds fair and is what distributors claim everyone gets for his first film. Don't believe them! The deal will appear equitable, but it isn't. The distributor will offer it by saying, "I love your film. Let's partner. I'll distribute, take my standard distribution fee, recoup my expenses, and split profits 50–50 with you."

It is technically called the "50-50 Net Deal" (aka standard distribution deal), and you'll never see a penny. Let's take a deeper look at what the distributor is really saying with, "*Let's partner. I'll distribute,* take my *standard distribution fee, recoup my expenses,* and *split profits 50–50 with you.*"

A. *Let's partner:* "You pay for the film. We collect the revenues."
B. *I'll distribute:* "We make all decisions and stay in control."
C. *Standard fee:* "Our standard fee is as much as we can get."

D. *Recoup expenses:* "That pied-à-terre in New York, condo in Gstaad, hooker in L.A., etc."

E. *Profit split:* "Fifty percent of nothing is nothing."

Assume you "pitch" (orally present) an idea to a distributor and get $1 million to make the film. Once it's done the distributor agrees to put $3 million into a P&A campaign and on the opening weekend the film grosses $10 million. Wow! Don't count your chickens. Thirty days after the $10 million weekend you get an accounting statement showing that your film is losing $3 million. Your jaw drops. You're astonished. You ponder, "How can this be?"

Simple, here's how. I'm assuming you accepted a standard (50-50 Net) distribution deal with the production money. The good news is that on its first weekend of release your film grossed $10 million. It's a hit. This is great, but remember that the word "gross" is not the word "profit," and you split profits not grosses. And the accounting statement you receive will look like this:

	Box-Office Gross	$10,000,000
(Minus)	Exhibitor's Fees (50%)	($5,000,000)
EQUALS		
	Distributor's Gross	$5,000,000
(Minus)	Distributor's Fee (35%)	($1,750,000)
EQUALS		
	Producer's Gross	$3,250,000
(Minus)	Production Expense	($1,000,000)
	Production Interest	($250,000)
	Prints and Advertising	($3,000,000)
	Overhead	($2,000,000)
EQUALS	**Net Loss**	**($3,000,000)**

Gross, specifically box-office gross, refers to the money theater owners collect from audiences. Now, distributor, being the marketing geniuses they are, know that many people didn't see your film this weekend. So how do they get them to attend on Monday, Tuesday, Wednesday, etc.? The answer is, they publicize *what the film grossed, not what the film profited or lost.* The gross dollar amount is always a large number. Ask yourself. What would you rather see, a film that *grossed $10 million* or a film that *lost $3 million?*

Let's follow the money trail and discover how a $10 million grosser becomes a $3 million loser. First, the theater owners (not the distributor) collect the $10 million, take their cut (usually 50 percent) of the Box-Office Gross, and send the remaining money, now called Distributor's Gross, to the distributor, who has paid for all the prints and ads. Your **$10 million Box-Office Gross** has just become a **$5 million Distributor's Gross.**

The distributor now deducts 35 percent ($1.75 million) for his distribution fee from the $5,000,000 leaving a **$3.25 million Producer's Gross.**

Next, remember, if the distributor gave you $1 million to make the film, they want that money back. Actually, distributors don't give you money, they loan it to you and want their loan back—with interest that is usually at 25 percent. Now, deducting the loan ($1 million), typically called a production expense, and interest ($250,000), from the producer's gross leaves $2 million. The number is getting smaller and smaller and . . .

Next, the distributor recoups his $3 million P&A costs. Subtract a $3 million expense from the $2 million Producer's Gross and there is no form of New Math that will show a profit. Your film is now at **$1 million in losses.** Add to the $1 million in losses $2 million in distributor's overhead and your film is now at **$3 million in losses.**

I told you this chapter would be a bummer.

LET'S GET REAL

Directors and/or producers are like architects in the real estate world. Builders option a property (idea/story), hire an architect (writer), get the blueprints (scripts), and construct (direct/produce) the building. When the building is done, the builder (distributor) sells, and if there's a profit do you think an architect expects to split 50–50 with the builder? No way! Not even I. M. Pei or Frank Gehry, world-famous architects, expect to participate in profits. They are happy to be well-paid artists (aka employees or contractors).

If you get funding from a distributor to make a film, be happy. Stop being naive. Don't expect profits. Be happy with the funding, the excellent salary, the celebrity exposure, and the ability to launch your career. But don't expect profits—you never took any financial gambles.

Distributors rationalize, behind closed doors (I lean toward agreeing with them), that since they take all the financial gambles, pay you well, and make you into a celebrity, that that is enough. *Forrest Gump* has grossed almost $250 million, and director Bob Zemeckis hasn't seen profits yet. Is Zemeckis bitching? Probably a little, but he knows that he is extremely well paid, is treated like an artist, and is happy.

There will be no profits. And if there are, the distributor will probably do creative bookkeeping (they just make the overhead number larger) to hide them. Then your only recourse is to hire an attorney, sue, and spend the next nine years in court. Once again, I promised that this chapter will initially be a bummer. Did I deliver?

Now let's get upbeat.

What I've just described is the scenario where a distributor finances you. That, essentially, is called "studio dealmaking." This book is not about studio dealmaking. It is about "independent filmmaking." You get your own money, not a distributor's money, and you with your investors take the financial gamble. You make the film outside the system and then bring it in by attending a festival or two.

Now, if your film hits at a popular film festival, in front of a paying audience, do you deserve a distribution deal that will garner you profits? Absolutely!

BEAT THE DISTRIBUTOR

When you only have one distributor offering you one distribution deal, nothing is negotiable. Don't try to play the "I'm talking to other distributors" game. *To get a good deal you must have more than one distributor making offers—then you can negotiate.* Let's assume your film has premiered at a festival, the theater sold out, the audience loves it, and there are seven to ten acquisition execs wanting to talk deal with you in the theater's lobby. Now you can negotiate.

Deals vary from distributor to distributor. Further, within a distribution company, deals vary from producer to producer. Even further, with each producer, deals vary from film to film. Nothing is standard, except that there are three basic types of distribution deals. They are:

1. The Flat-Fee Deal
2. The Net Deal
3. The Gross Deal

Flat-Fee Deal

By far the simplest deal. Technically it's called a "buyout." The distributor agrees to give you X dollars for either "world," or "foreign," or "North American" rights, plus "non-theatrical" and "Internet" rights. One check and you walk away.

With the flat-fee deal, you simply negotiate the buyout amount, who becomes the copyright owner, and some minor marketing and promotion points.

> **IMPORTANT POINT**   Never expect to see another penny from the distributor after you receive the buyout amount, even if a percentage of profits is put in as an alleged bonus. Therefore, be sure that the buyout amount is enough to pay back your investors and give them a small profit—and two tickets to the opening-night premiere in L.A. and New York.

Gross and Net Deals

When negotiating, if you don't get any money up front with a flat deal, then make absolutely sure you get a small percentage of gross (box-office, distributor, or producer) rather than a large percentage of profits. For, with respect to profits, the distributor's creative bookkeeping system ensures that there probably won't be any, and 50 percent, 70 percent, or 90 percent of nothing is still nothing.

The types of gross and net deals are:

1. First Dollar Gross Deal: Very unusual to get, unless you're Spielberg or Lucas or Cruise, and they only get a percentage of box-office gross with a proven sequel like *Jurassic Park* or *Star Wars* or *Mission Impossible.*
2. First Dollar Split Deal: If you accept no advance payment or guarantee, then it is fair to negotiate a 50–50 split of the distributor's gross (dollars received from theater owners), but not box-office gross.
3. Adjusted Gross Deal: Although called a gross deal, it invariably is a net deal. The producer receives an advance and then allows the distributor to recoup expenses before splitting.

4. 70–30 Major Deal: A combination net/gross deal. The distributor recoups specific expenses first and everything remaining is split 70 percent distributor and 30 percent producer.

5. Sliding Scale Deal: Similar to the 70–30 deal, with the split ratio changing to 65–45 after the first million, then 60–40 after the fifth million, 55–45 after the tenth million, etc. The dollar amounts and split ratios vary from film to film.

6. 50–50 Net Deal: As previously discussed, the distributor gets a fee, recoups expenses, and then splits any remaining dollars (yuk-yuk) 50–50 with the filmmaker.

When negotiating, 🗎 *distributors always want a simple deal. You, the filmmaker, want a complicated deal.* I know this seems weird. But the simpler the contract (two or three pages), the more vague the language. The more vague the language, the easier it is for a distributor to do creative bookkeeping and legally steal from you.

You, on the other hand, want a specific (40–60 pages) contract with all T's crossed and I's dotted. Problem is, you don't know what the T's and I's are. To help you, here's an outline of 29 points to define and negotiate. Each one should take up a page or two in the final contract. These points are known as the "deal memo" points.

The 29 Deal Memo Points

1. Payment: Cash amount the distributor is paying, and when the payment is due.

2. Guarantees: Minimum amount of money the distributor promises to deliver to you over a period of time, usually 1–10 years.

3. Distribution fees: Percentage of distributor's gross the distributor receives as his fee (not his expenses). It could be between 15–40 percent but is usually 35 percent.

4. Credits: Define all opening title credit(s), specifying the size of the print and length of time onscreen (aim for a three-second beat).

5. P&A budget: Dollar amount to be used for promotion (newspaper ads, radio and TV spots, posters, billboards, Web site, etc.). Specify the number of prints and the cost charged per print.

6. Advertising approval: The right to approve "the hook" and the look of the marketing campaign.

7. Trailers: A commitment to exhibit a specified number of trailers in theaters prior to the film's actual play date.

8. Play dates: Secure a guaranteed number of theatrical play dates (a play date is one print in one theater for one week) within a specific number of cities.

9. Release exclusivity: A promissory statement (affidavit) stating they won't release a competitive film during the period they're releasing your film.

10. Definitions: Clearly define all the terms (gross, box-office gross, producer's gross, adjusted gross, film rentals, distribution revenues, net receipts, profits, net profits, producer's net profits, etc.) in the contract.

11. Distribution expenses: Clearly define what is and what isn't allowed as a distributor's expense.

12. Capping expense: Do not allow the distributor carte blanche on expenses. State a specific cap, with the distributor needing written approval before spending additional funds.

13. Cross-collateralizing: Never allow distributors to place expenses related to your film in a "pool" of films they're distributing. Otherwise all their other films' expenses will be charged to you.

14. Overhead: This is a killer word. Make sure you clearly define what is and what isn't overhead.

15. Deferrals: Clearly define at what point deferrals, if there are any, are to be remitted and to what account they are to be charged.

16. Investor recoupment: Specify when investors commence to recoup their investment, when (and if) they receive interest on their investment, and finally, when they receive their share of profits (if any).

17. Ownership: Establish who owns the copyrights and the negative.

18. Licensing period: State the years the distributor has the right to sell and/or distribute your film to each territory or ancillary market.

19. Packaging: Establish that the distributor cannot "package" your film with others without your written consent.

20. Break-even point: Stipulate at what box-office gross dollar the distributor declares that the film has broken even, and state how revenues are to be split with the producer and investors.

21. Gross floor: Specify a fixed amount, after which the filmmaker/investor group must commence to receive revenues also.

22. Interest rates: State the exact interest rate charged if the distributor funds (loans money for) the film, and when it is recouped. Do not permit the distributor to keep the interest growing and growing. This will kill any chance of reaching a break-even point and profits.

23. Sub-distributors: If the distributor subcontracts out distribution in certain territories, define the terms that these sub-distributors can charge the distributor, who in turn will charge you.

24. Windows: Specify the period of time for which companies in each ancillary market (PPV, VOD, video/DVD, cable, broadcasting, etc.) can market the licensing rights to your film.

25. Ancillary markets:

    a. Home video/DVD
    b. Cable: basic, pay, PPV
    c. Broadcasting: network, syndication, and public
    d. Foreign theatrical
    e. Foreign ancillary
    f. Music: albums, songs
    g. Literary: novelization, serialization
    h. Merchandise and toys
    i. Satellite
    j. Internet
    k. Airlines, cruise ships, etc.
    l. Military: Army, Navy, etc.
    m. Educational: schools, libraries, etc.
    n. Future technologies

26. Insurance carriers: Specify whom the distributor's insurers are, and make sure you have a copy of each policy.

27. Laboratory access: Never give the distributor access to your negative at the lab. This allows you to monitor him whenever he needs a print.

28. Auditing and enforcement: Verify bookkeeping statements. You need access to the distributor's books, and should there be a dispute, clearly define how the audit will be handled.

29. Binding arbitration: If the audit is in your favor, you will discover you lack the power to enforce it and can't afford litigation. A

quicker way is to circumvent suing and arbitrate, but be sure that it is "binding."

There is a lot of ground to cover in your negotiations. And you can only negotiate if you have leverage. And you will only get leverage, as stated, by having more than one distributor at a film festival wanting your film. But if this occurs what you basically want is:

1. Money: An up-front payment or guarantee
2. Percentage: Remittance from gross, not net
3. Contract: Detailed rather than simple
4. Audit: Ability to verify everything in #1, 2, 3
5. Arbitration: Ability to enforce the contract

ENFORCEMENT, AUDIT, AND ARBITRATION

You are not educated enough to know all the games a distributor can play. Although I've given you 29 deal memo points to start, it is imperative to conduct all negotiations with an entertainment attorney who, besides (1) knowing how to negotiate, (2) understands how to combat creative accounting, and (3) has practiced law long enough to know how to enforce contracts with audits and "binding arbitration," without spending a decade in court.

Maybe you want to try self-distribution?

––––––––––

TO DO:

1. Find an entertainment attorney to be your "producer's representative."

 BOOKS

deal. Over 800 companies and 5,000 individuals listed.

Distributors
HCD staff, 224 pp., $59.95
The most thorough list of distributors to contact for a theatrical distribution

Film Finance and Distribution
J. Cones, 558 pp., $24.95
You can't negotiate a deal if you don't know the terms. This book is the perfect dealmaker's dictionary.

Feature Film Distribution
J. Cones, 306 pp., $52.00
A must. A step-by-step explanation of each of the major points in a theatrical distribution deal.

The Biz
S. Moore, 364 pp., $27.95
A comprehensive guide to negotiating a distribution deal that is loaded with what to and what not to negotiate.

Movie Money
B. Daniels and S. Sills, 380 pp., $19.95
Movie accounting, although boring, is imperative to understand if you desire to ensure profits. This book explains it all.

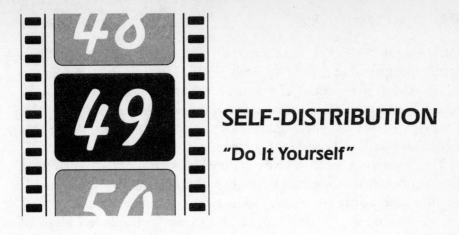

SELF-DISTRIBUTION

"Do It Yourself"

You have a moment of clarity. You see the big picture and realize that only distributors make money. You pause. You ponder. Why not eliminate the middleman, distribute yourself, and keep all the grosses? Book a theater, prepare press kits, design ads, hire a publicist, deliver the prints, and collect ticket revenues. Doesn't sound so difficult. Well, it is. Imagine doing this simultaneously in 200 cities in America.

However, if those logistics don't intimidate you, let's investigate a little further. The four methods of self-distribution are:

1. Four-wall
2. Roadshow
3. Major test
4. University venue

I'll discuss a fifth method, the Web, in chapter 50.

1. FOUR-WALL

This is simply renting the "four walls" of a theater, paying for your own ads, sitting in the ticket booth, and collecting the money—if the audience comes. You do everything. You don't split with anyone. Not the theater owner. Not the distributor. You get 100 percent of the box office.

Here's how it's done. You call the theater and ask the owner what his "nut" or "allowance" (aka house nut or house allowance) is, which represents the theater owner's minimum weekly operating expenses (insurance, payroll, mortgage, etc.). The owner fibs, inflates his nut, and says, for example, "$5,000 per week." Offer him $7,000 and watch how quickly he grabs it. You've booked a theater and your other expenses are only the local newspaper ads and the employees, if not yourself, to sit in each theater's ticket booth and collect the revenue.

Thirty years ago there was a film (*Billy Jack*) that profited massively in this manner, when a filmmaker bought back the rights to distribute his own film from a distributor who thought it was unmarketable.

Four-walling is very uncommon, and in the past decade I know of only three successful ventures. The first is Miller Films (owner, Warren Miller) based in Colorado. He does those skiing and surfing movies with titles like *Catch the Wave* or *Beat the Avalanche.* He makes a film, books a church or auditorium, brings his own 35mm projector and sound system, does a mail-order campaign to local ski and surf bums, supported with fliers in sporting goods stores, creates a concertlike event, charges $10–$20 a ticket, and keeps all the box-office receipts.

Next, Joe Berlinger and Bruce Sinofsky became self-distribution legends with *Brother's Keeper,* which in 1992 played in 250 cities and grossed almost $1.5 million. It is jokingly said that they made more money on the lecture circuit talking about self-distribution than they did by self-distributing. Today, Berlinger and Sinofsky, thanks to their four-walling experience, are traditional art-house distributors, with films like Sundance entrant *Paradise Lost,* and get traditional 90–10 splits (theater gets its "house nut" first, then what's left is divided 90 percent to distributor and 10 percent to theater owner) and share the costs with theater owners.

Finally, *Spike & Mike's Animation Festival* is a successful four-walling operation. However, *Spike & Mike* is not a single film but an animation festival (15–20 cartoon shorts) that cycles America biannually. This roadshow festival has gained a following, and the producers also give theater owners a small guarantee. So it is not a true four-wall situation.

Other than costs, the biggest problem with four-walling is that you stop being a filmmaker and become a distributor. Paperwork. Traveling. Collecting. Do you really want to live out of a suitcase, carrying your three prints as you drive from city to city crashing in cheap motels, sitting in ticket booths hoping that some local yokel gives you $7 (movie tickets are cheaper in the sticks)?

IMPORTANT POINT   Don't be naive and think about partnering with theater owners to cut out the distributor middleman. 🖼️ *If you thought distributors were crooks, try collecting from theater owners.* Always remember that theater owners are swindlers and if you book a theater, pay for the newspaper ads, send a print, then innocently wait to receive your share of box office revenues, you'll end up in every small claims court trying to collect. Remember, you only have one film.

Four-walling sounds exciting. You can even pencil out the numbers and think you'll make a profit. But don't do it. Only Miller Films and Spike & Mike, in the last 20 years, have succeeded at it. However, if you persist in thinking about four-walling, here are some theater owners to start with who play the game:

1.	The Quad	New York, NY	Ron Lesser	(212) 925-4776
2.	Plaza Twin	Brooklyn, NY	Mr. Delphi	
3.	Cinema Village	New York, NY	Ed Arentz	(212) 683-1159
4.	Coolidge Corner	Boston, MA	Sasha Berman	(617) 734-2501
5.	Cine-Magic	Pittsburgh, PA	Arlene Wrener	(412) 281-9893
6.	Ritz Theater	Philadelphia, PA	Ray Bosel	(941) 349-9597
7.	Wilmette Theater	Chicago, IL	Richard Stern	(847) 251-7411
8.	Drexel Theaters	Columbus, OH	Jeff Frank	(614) 231-1050
9.	Key Theater	Washington, DC	David Levy	(202) 965-4401

2. ROADSHOW

Instead of renting the theater for the week, or hoping a distributor prepares a 100–1,000 national print release, you decide to strike three to five prints and make 90–10 deals with theater owners city by city. This is a roadshow.

Roadshow distribution, with over 200 markets or cities in America, goes slowly and takes 12–18 months. It will start in a small college town like Austin, Texas, or Hartford, Connecticut, with only two or three prints. If successful, you'll pay the film lab again, strike 5–10 prints, and expand to a small metropolitan city like Portland, Oregon, or Tampa, Florida. If successful again, you'll pay the film lab again and saturate multiple cities or states within a geographic region with 20–30 prints. Then you'll go from region to region with these 20–30 prints until you have covered all of America. Whew!

To ensure you'll collect from theater owners on your 90–10 deals, you should partner with a small independent distributor (Tara Releasing, Strand Releasing, Frameline, or Greycat Films) with a pipeline of films to guarantee collection from the theater owners. Since you're supplying the film and the P&A money, you will be able to make an excellent deal (15 percent distribution fee, not 35 percent, and keep the window revenues) with the distributor, whom you're really renting for their ability to collect.

Examples of films in the last decade that have succeeded with this approach are:

1. *Together Alone,* Frameline. Grossed $46,000.
2. *Henry: Portrait of a Serial Killer,* Greycat Films. Grossed $732,000.
3. *All the Vermeers in New York,* Strand Releasing. Grossed $157,000.
4. *The Vanishing,* Tara Releasing. Grossed $952,000.

As you can see, the list is short.

3. MAJOR TEST

This is a combination of four-wall and roadshow. You test (four-walling) your film in two or three (roadshow) markets, choosing those where you believe the demographics are perfect for your film. After you have received the grosses, you report the numbers to distributors and hope they purchase distribution rights from you, strike 100–500 prints, and release your film on a national scale.

To attempt this, contact a regional booking service, which, for a small fee, will book three to five theaters in a region that is covered by one or two newspapers and several regional radio talk shows. This allows you to focus all your energy on publicizing your film to those newspapers and radio shows. Examples of regional bookers are:

1. Clarke Theater Service	Port Huron, MI	Bob Hines	(810) 982-9935
2. Lesser Theater Service	New York, NY	Ron Lesser	(212) 925-4776
3. Independent Theatres	Charlotte, NC	Steve Smith	(704) 529-1200

4. George Mansour	Boston, MA	G. Mansour	(617) 266-9129
5. Morris Projects	Sarasota, FL	Dick Morris	(941) 364-8662
6. Pacific Film Resources	Oakland, CA	J. Klingelhofer	(510) 654-7324

4. UNIVERSITY VENUE

Just about every college and university has a student film theater. It is not difficult to contact the student in charge and book the theater. They usually project 16mm, not 35mm. They expect you to send a poster and artwork for their school newspaper. Many times the actual filmmaker goes along with the film and presents a Q&A session or a seminar on how he produced his movie.

This is another route. But I know of no one who has done this, succeeded, and continued to do it. However, if you are a college junkie and depressed that you ever left academia, this is a cool way to get back on campus and another shot at being the BMOC that you weren't 15 years ago.

The bottom line is that although self-distribution is a noble thought, it rarely succeeds. The route to go, which 999 out of 1,000 filmmakers try, is to attend a film festival and attract a distributor who takes over all the expenses and logistics of distribution. However, there is a ray of hope. Hollywood is changing. We are in the information age and something has popped up that no one ever thought of a decade or two ago—the Web. And thanks to the Web, broadband, and digital production (chapter 50), a filmmaker like you can now distribute around the world literally from your home office.

TO DO:

1. Find out which theaters in your city are rentable.
2. Hire a publicist or purchase Bacon's Directory.
3. Find a list of sub-distributors.

BOOKS

Self-Distribution Toolkit
I. Mookas, 185 pp., $39.95
The only book that is totally dedicated
to distributing your own film.

Exhibitor's Guide
K. Bowser, 176 pp., $39.95

This book lists all the major theater
circuits, film booking services, and
university venues that you'll contact if
self-distributing.

*Marketing and Selling Your Film
    Around the World*
J. Durie and N. Watson, 165 pp., $19.95
Details how to sell your film around
the world.

DIGITAL FILMMAKING

"The Future Is Here"

Two innovations have permanently altered the film industry. The first is the presence of inexpensive equipment (digital cameras and computer editing systems) as a means of production, and the second is the Web/Internet (broadband and DSL) as a means of distribution.

DIGITAL FILMMAKING A–Z

A revolution has occurred. ![TOP SECRET] ***Hollywood is no longer the rich boys' game.*** Up until a couple of years ago, if you wanted to make your first feature, you needed at least $70,000–$90,000 for a 16mm one-week shoot. Although minuscule compared to a $5 million low-budget studio feature, $70,000–$90,000 is still a large chunk of cash. And only children of the country club set, who attended four-year $100,000 film schools, could afford this type of toy.

Now, wannabes with a cheap digital camera and little to no film schooling are attempting feature film production. Filmmaking is popping up in every ghetto, church community, and hamlet in America. Everyone who has a story to tell now has the visual opportunity to tell it. So, let's get to the nuts and bolts of digital filmmaking.

However, whether shooting digitally or using a 35mm film camera, it still comes down to the same basics: the script, the actors, the format, the camera, the lights, the sound, the crew, the shoot, the edit, and the distributor. Let's take these basics one by one.

The digital script: It is no different than a film script, and the adage of "If it ain't on the page, it ain't on the stage" still applies. What is different, however, is the number of locations in your script. When shooting your first film with 35mm film your script must adhere to the keep-it-simple stage play formula. But because digital cameras are so light and your crew is so small, you can now handle numerous location moves during production and shoot a more expansive script.

The digital actor: Actors are actors. Be it a digital shoot or a film shoot, if you sign with SAG, the rate you pay them is the same and the way you cast them is the same. The difference is that because digital tape is extremely inexpensive, you'll allow the actor(s) a second take, a third take, and a fourth take. Although there will be more footage to edit, their performances should be better.

The digital format: Of the digital formats (mini-DV, DigitalS, DVCAM, DVPRO), you'll probably use mini-DV, with 60-minute tapes from Sony (DVM60PR or DVM60EX) or Panasonic (AY DVM-60) costing $10 each. Purchasing 9 hours of 35mm film, to shoot a 90-minute movie, costs about $25,000 whereas the equivalent hours of mini-DV tape barely cost $100.

The digital camera: Purchase ($3,000–$4,000) or rent ($500–$750/week) a high-quality prosumer camcorder that accepts mini-DV tape. These cameras have excellent lens quality, capture at least 410,000-pixel resolution, have three CCDs (charged coupled devices, i.e., three chips) of at least one-third inch, audio XLR microphone attachments, time code recording, and IEEE 1394 (aka Firewire or I-Link) interface capability, with a zebra function and an image stabilizer that can be shot with a 16:9 aspect ratio.

The cameras that fit the above parameters are the Canon (XL-1s or GL2), Sony (DVX2000 or PD150A), JVC (550DVU), or Panasonic (VX100). Most professionals buy the Sony PD150A and most first-timers go for the Canon XL-1s. They're both cheap and, for the money, very good. The Panasonic VX100 is the last to be manufactured. Thus, it is labeled state-of-the-art, for it has 24P (read books on digital filmmaking) capacity.

The digital lights: No such thing. There is no specific light that you rent solely because you're shooting digital. Lights are lights. Remember, film captures only 50 percent of what the human eye sees, and video captures even less than film. Thus, you should actually spend more time lighting video than film. However, I know you won't. So make sure you purchase ($2,000) or rent ($400/week) at least a four-light portable kit from either

Arriflex, Mole Richardson, Lowell, or NRG and a large soft fill light from Chimera—and light the same way (chapter 22) as if lighting for film.

> **IMPORTANT POINT** When guerrilla filmmaking at someone's house or office, if you tie in to the building's power, never use more than 2,000 (normal fuse-box capacity) watts when lighting a scene, or you'll blow the fuse. Thus, make sure your lights, plugged in to any one socket at any time, don't overwhelm that fuse when placing your key (600–700 watt), back (two 200–300 watt), and fill (100–200 watt) lights. Also, set all your lights on eight-foot stands. This will throw the shadows out of the picture frame and onto the floor.

The digital filters: When shooting with film cameras, you utilize filters to achieve a certain "look." You do the same, possibly even more, when using video cameras. Digital, which is video, has a visual appearance, "a look," that is too sharp and clear for film projection. The high-contrast look of video many times emphasizes blemishes and wrinkles. Thus, to soften video to make it appear more like film, have filters attached to the camera. The ProMist from Tiffen or the Diffusion from Cokin both create a warmer look.

The digital sound: You have no idea how important this is. Don't get lethargic with sound. It was only last year that I heard an AE say, "I finally saw a digital film that I could hear." Microphones, always important, are even more important to the digital filmmaker who depends less on the visual image and more on the script, story, and sound. If you can't hear it, it stinks. The recording device in your digital camera is good, but the microphone that captures the sound sucks. Think microphone(s) when renting—with the bottom line being that you'll probably spend more for a soundperson with microphones than you will for the cameraman and the digital camera you are so in love with. Think sound! Think microphones!

The digital crew: If shooting 35mm you'll have a 25–30 person crew with two or three trucks and vans. When shooting digital your crew is reduced to seven to nine people with only two vans (one for crew, one for cast). You'll have a camera operator (one for each camera), a light person, a sound/boom man, a hair–makeup person, an art person, someone with a clipboard, and an assistant or two, all of whom you still have to feed.

The digital shoot: Same as film. Rehearse, block, shoot. Know your schedule and stick to it. The benefit of shooting digital over film is that because the cameras are so cheap, you'd be foolish not to use multiple cameras, instead of one, and obtain much better coverage. Therefore, rent three cameras not one, and shoot big-budget style rather than one-camera low-budget style.

IMPORTANT POINT   When shooting, use camera #1 for a master shot and cameras #2 and #3, running simultaneously, for the two over-the-shoulder medium shots or one over-the-shoulder medium and one close-up, action, or reaction shot. The end product is excellent coverage quickly and inexpensively.

The digital edit: With film you physically splice and perform a linear edit; with digital you perform a non-linear edit (NLE) by rearranging shots in a computer. All you need to know is that you'll edit with a computer, using either a hardware turnkey system (Avid Media Composer or Xpress, Fast.silver, Media 100, etc. at $8,000–$15,000) or a "software only" program for Mac (Final Cut Pro 3.5 or EditDV) or PC (Adobe Premiere 6.2), which you'll install into a NLE computer system ($2,000–$8,000) you built. Remember, your end product will be tape.

IMPORTANT POINT   For best quality, if you captured your scenes in a mini-DV format, take the selected takes and bump them up to D-Beta and sync in your DAT audio, if you can afford it. This will give you twice the resolution and color space of an image than transferring it to your NLE system directly from DV and then recording it back after printing.

The transfer to film: How are you going to screen your completed digital film (actually mini-DV tape) in a theater? You have one choice. Transfer the tape to 35mm film, which costs approximately $400 a minute—$36,000 for 90 minutes. There are numerous companies (4MC, Burbank, Calif.; Sony High Definition Center, Culver City, Calif.; DuArt Film lab, Manhattan, N.Y.; Swiss Effects, Zurich, Switzerland; Tape House Digital Film, Manhattan, N.Y.; FilmTeam, Austin, Texas; etc.) that have refined this process.

IMPORTANT POINT   Why pay for the costly transfer? Every major film festival (Sundance, Cannes, Toronto, etc.) has a $125,000 digital projector (Barco, DLP/Texas Instruments, etc.) for screenings. Don't pay to transfer to a 35mm print. Project your digital movie with a digital projector.

Then, if a distributor picks up your film (actually mini-DV tape), his company will pay for the 35mm film transfer, as was done with *The*

Cruise, Celebration, The Blair Witch Project, Chuck & Buck, and *Anniversary Party.*

Digital distribution: Next year there will be almost 1,000 no-budget digital features made. Naturally, each filmmaker expects his to be picked up by a distributor at a festival, transferred to film, and treated like an independent feature.

Let's run the numbers. Of the 1,000 digital features next year, Sundance will accept only 13. Of the 13, four, at the most, will be picked up by a distributor, transferred to 35mm, treated like a film, and put in theaters. What happens to the other 996? First, if your film was one of the 13 that got into Sundance but wasn't picked up by a film distributor, because of the Sundance cachet you will still have some cable (Sundance Channel, IFC, Bravo, etc.), video (Sundance section at Blockbuster, etc.), and foreign TV sales (England, France, Germany, etc.), and because your film was made for such a small amount you more than likely will make a profit.

Now, what if you're not one of the 13 selected and you're one of the other 987 (odds are you will be)? What do you do? Do you quit and go to med school? Possibly, but you have one last shot—to self-distribute, which is finally a viable option thanks to the existence of the Web.

THE WEB

The Web, started in 1969, has allowed the average filmmaker to compete with big business. 📁 ***Movie studios are running scared. They no longer have all the power.*** Their stranglehold is breaking up. Until now, filmmakers have been totally dependent on distributors because of their P&A money and ability to collect from theater owners. This is the twenty-first century. The revolution is here.

Several years ago two low- to no-budget films (*pi* and *The Blair Witch Project*) were released by a small distributor, Artisan Entertainment, with very little P&A money. What Artisan did have was a couple of young executives who knew how to market and reach an audience on the Web. And the result is history.

The Web is communication anarchy. No one owns it. No one controls it. Anyone with a computer, a modem, and "streaming" capabilities can get instant access to everyone in the world who also has a computer and modem. For filmmakers with a film but no distributor this is a dream.

From now on, everyone who makes a film should think strongly about being his own distributor. Be a Web Self-Distributor (WSD). The old game plan of making a film, attending a festival, and attracting a distributor is still good—but now there is a backup. In the twentieth century, self-distribution (chapter 49) just wasn't viable, but today, in the twenty-first century, self-distribution is affordable, and money is easy to collect, thanks to the Web.

SHOW ME THE MONEY

Let's assume you didn't get a distributor at a film festival. Digitize your film, if it isn't already in that format, and place it (stream it) in the sky (the Web) for anyone with a fast modem to pull down and view.

What should you charge? The studios are about to distribute their classic films, cartoons, and shorts like the Three Stooges via the Web for what they call "micro-charges," which will be an extremely small amount. I actually call this a "what-the-fuck" charge—charge 42 cents.

Suppose you enter a chat room with other filmmakers. After chatting about what's wrong with Hollywood, someone in the room announces that he/she has just seen an interesting film on the Web and types in the film's URL (Web address). You instantly surf to it. The opening page is catchy, with a slick Flash animation, and you see that for only 42 cents you can hit a button and check out this recommended film. Would you do it? I bet you'll say, "What the fuck."

Now, let's assume that from the one billion computers in the world you only get 200,000 unique visits (hits) to check you out in week one. That's 42 cents times 200,000, or $84,000 directly into your bank account. Next, what if half of those Web viewers want to see it with better quality, and download it onto their hard drive (archiving) for 76 cents for multiple viewings. That's 100,000 times 76 cents, or $76,000. Next, what if half of these consumers want to order a CD, tape, or DVD (enhanced with interviews and filmmaker stories) of your film so they can collect it and view it whenever they want to, for only $7.95. That's 50,000 times $7.95, or $397,500.

Let's run the numbers on a digital feature you made for $10,000–$60,000, which couldn't get into the local mom-and-pop film festival and was never picked up for release by a theatrical distributor. You kick in your WSD backup plan and gross:

A. Streaming @ $0.42	$84,000
B. Archiving @ $0.76	$76,000
C. CD, Tape, or DVD @ $7.95	$397,500
	$557,500*

A film you made for only $10,000–$60,000 (real actors, real sets, real script), with a cheap digital camera, that couldn't get into the local film festival and was not picked up by a distributor, can still generate millions in revenue. That is if you market it properly and distribute it (with the help of your resident geek) via the Web.

Yep, there are millions in revenue to be obtained for your film, with no middlemen, no distributors to sue, and no theater owners to collect from, thanks to self-distribution on the Web.

HOW TO WORK THE WEB

Call your local ISP or resident geek, and obtain a basic understanding of the eight following areas that have to do with Web self-distribution:

1. URL
2. Digitizing
3. Encoding
4. Search engines
5. Streaming and ISP
6. Encrypting
7. Merchant account
8. E-cash

URL (cyber squatting is fun): Get a Web address! Don't wait. Get a URL (uniform resource locator) or DNS (domain name system). I don't know the difference between the two and I don't care. To me, they're synony-

*Author's note: $557,500 is damn good for a no-budget film that couldn't even get into the local film festival . . . and this is only for the first *week* your film is on the Web.

Further, this assumes 200,000 unique visitors. What if you get 1 million, 3 million, or 10 million from all over the world? What if, as you get successful, you raise your price from $0.42 to $0.83 for streaming? From $0.76 o $1.45 for archiving? From $7.95 to $12.95 to buy the DVD or tape?

mous with cyber address. Think of cyber addresses as real estate. They ain't making any more. The moment you know the title of your film, surf the Web, type in www.networksolutions.com, and grab your Web address (URL or DNS), which is usually your movie's title and then ".com." The fee, at the most, is $35 a year.

Digitizing (proper format, part I): Make sure your film is in the proper format for Web distribution. If you have shot on 16mm, 35mm, or an analog video, you'll utilize a film-to-digital transfer machine to put it on the Web. The machine can cost upwards of $100,000 to buy, so rent time. A film-to-tape transfer is nowhere near as expensive as a tape-to-film transfer.

Encoding (proper format, part II): Make sure your film is easy to stream and download. Select your codec and bit rate. "Codec" is an anagram of "*com*pression" and "*dec*ompression." There are three delivery codecs— Quicktime (for Macintosh computers) and either RealVideo or Windows Media Player (for PC users). Also, home users have several bit rate speeds of 56K to 300K. To encode your video for all possible codecs and bit rate combinations utilize a program called Terran Interactive's Media Cleaner Pro ($400). Other encoding programs include DVDSP (Mac), BitVice (Mac), Cinema-Craft (Windows), Pro Coder (Windows), and Media Cleaner (Windows).

Search engines (marketing and spider food): Make sure that surfers find out about your film. Filmmaking, even on the Web, is a marketing industry. Hit those chat rooms. Post gossip on bulletin boards. Get listed on search engines and maximize your rankings with metatags. Put "spider food" (keywords that search engines latch onto) in your Web site. Get your URL at the top of the search engine's list. Take out some banner ads and sponsored links (search-engine keyword ads) and create a buzz.

Streaming and ISP (delivery system): Get your film to the consumer. Unless you are buying some very expensive routers you will need an Internet service provider (ISP) to get your stream into the Web. The two streaming methods to talk through with your ISP are "HTTP streaming" ($20–$100/month), known as progressive download, or "true streaming" ($100–$300/month), which requires the ISP host to license and install software for each codec.

Encrypting (security system): You don't want freeloaders visiting your site and screening your film for free. At the writing of this book, there is no perfect way to totally safeguard your video stream from visual pirates, called "flick-hackers." If the government can't do it, you won't be able to either. But the good news is, if you're only charging 42 cents, what hacker is going to waste his time?

Merchant account (how to collect): Get viewers' credit card numbers. Establish a credit card merchant account with Visa, MasterCard, and American Express that charges a 3 percent–4 percent fee. SVOD (subscription video on demand), where a viewer subscribes with a set monthly fee, is coming quickly.

E-cash (get the money): Cash still works, even on the Web. Many potential viewers either don't have credit cards or are concerned about posting their credit card information on the Web. To collect from these individuals, use companies that set up small pools of consumers' money that can be transferred from one site to another for a nominal fee.

Today, every filmmaker with a little Web streaming information can distribute globally, and when you include the potential streaming, archiving, and CD/VHS/DVD merchandising revenues, the profits can become massive. Plus, there is no middleman and these revenues go right into your pocket—you, the twenty-first-century filmmaker.

If you don't believe me, take a look. I put my money where my mouth is and created a streaming film school (www.WebFilmSchool.com) and will distribute film education, replete with diplomas, on the Web.

TO DO:

1. Call ISPs and ask their fees to stream (HTTP or true streaming).
2. Establish a Visa/MasterCard merchant account.

 BOOKS

The Digital Filmmaking Handbook
B. Long and S. Schenk, 548 pp., $49.95
The best single book to get on digital filmmaking; takes you from soup to nuts.

Building a Home Movie Studio and Getting Your Films Online
K. Lancaster and C. Conti, 239 pp., $19.95
A must. An indispensable guide to producing your own films and exhibiting them on the Internet.

Producing Great Sound for Digital Video
J. Rose, 428 pp., $44.95
Never use the microphones that come with the three-chip cameras. Discover how to capture great sound.

Audio Post-production for Digital Video
J. Rose, 256 pp., $44.95
Very important! Post-sound is the Achilles' heel of digital filmmakers. This book teaches the dos and don'ts.

Lighting for Digital Video and TV
J. Jackman, 416 pp., $44.95
Extremely important. Reveals the lighting secrets to get a great visual image like the Hollywood pros do.

Digital Video Handbook
M. Collier, 266 pp., $24.95
Covers the creative and technical aspects of digital filmmaking.

Digital Moviemaking
S. Billups, 246 pp., $26.95
This book describes how to use a credit card and make a digital feature.

Little Digital Video Book
M. Rubin, 177 pp., $19.95
A friendly non-intimidating intro to digital filmmaking for the short-film moviemaker.

Digital Filmmaking 101
D. Newton and J. Gaspard, 281 pp., $24.95
If your creativity is high and your cash is low, this book will show you how to produce digitally.

The Complete Idiot's Guide to iMovie 2
B. Miser, 357 pp., $19.99
The simplest way to make movies with a cheap camera and your Macintosh.

Making iMovies
S. Smith, 138 pp., $39.99
This book and a digital video camera, an iMac DV computer, and iMovie software can have you making a movie in 30 minutes.

Windows Movie Maker Handbook
B. Birney and S. McEvoy, 366 pp., $32.99
If you are working with Windows software to edit your film, then this is the book. Includes CD-ROM.

Digital Cinematography
P. Wheeler, 189 pp., $34.95
Clear description of all the expensive high-end cameras that use the 24P format.

FAME AND FORTUNE

"The Game Plan"

LET'S TALK DOLLARS

It's a golden era for independent filmmakers. Revenues, during the past three decades, have increased massively. The end result is that fame and fortune are happening for first-timers more and more than at any time in history.

Thirty years ago a successful independent film ($1 million budget and $2 million P&A) would gross $9 million to $13 million. Today (thanks to all the "windows," "revenue sources," and "technologies"), that same modestly successful film should gross $72 million to $130 million. That's a whopping 700–900 percent revenue increase.

In 1972, when there were only two windows (theatrical and broadcasting) in North America, if you made an independent film, attended a festival, got a distributor, and it was a modest box-office success, it would probably gross $10–14 million (1st window) at the box office. From this the distributor received $5–$7 million (50 percent), sold foreign rights for $2–$3 million, and waited 18 months (2nd window) for a $2–$3 million broadcasting sale—generating distributor revenues of $9 million to $13 million.

1st Window	Theatrical (USA)	$5–$7 million
	Theatrical (Foreign)	$2–$3 million
2nd Window	Broadcasting (USA)	$2–$3 million
	Total Gross:	**$9 million–$13 million**

Today, once again assuming that the film is a modest box-office hit, let's pencil out the revenues.

First, it will gross (1st window) $30–$50 million (remember, *The Blair Witch Project* grossed over $150 million and *My Big Fat Greek Wedding* grossed over $220 million). Theater owners will take their 50 percent cut and send the remaining $15–$25 million to the distributor. Next, with a $30–$50 million North American gross the foreign market will generate $35–$60 million. Then, back in North America, the movie will get a $1–$3 million (2nd and 4th windows) VOD and PPV sale. Next, the video/DVD (3rd window) rentals and sales will garner $12–$20 million, with a pay-cable sale (5th window) getting an additional $5–$10 million. Finally, the basic-cable and broadcasting (6th and 7th windows) industries will generate $1–$2 million and $3–$10 million sales—yielding a total revenue of $72 million to $130 million.

1st Window	Theatrical (USA)	$15–$25 million
	Theatrical (Foreign)	$35–$60 million
2nd Window	VOD (USA)	$0.5–$1.5 million
3rd Window	Video/DVD (USA)	$12–$20 million
4th Window	PPV (USA)	$0.5–$1.5 million
5th Window	Pay Cable (USA)	$5–$10 million
6th Window	Basic Cable (USA)	$1–$2 million
7th Window	Broadcasting (USA)	$3–$10 million
	Total Gross:	**$72–$130 million**

Thus, $9–$13 million in revenues in 1972 has grown to $72–$130 million today. Fame and fortune in the film industry is more possible today than at any time in the past. It is never guaranteed, but it won't happen if you don't give it a shot. Thus, start with a dream—everything does—and follow the game plan.

THE GAME PLAN

1. Get the script! This is not difficult. Then make it great. This is difficult. Getting 90–120 pages of typing is easy, but getting the great script is amazingly difficult. And what's harder than getting the great script is getting the great script that takes place in one location. Get this and you have liquid gold.

2. Get the money! Be a salesman. Select your cinematographer. Get use of his demo reel. Set up a wine-and-cheese screening. Offer investors 50 percent of profits, first position, and 25 percent interest on their money. Ask the closing statement ("How much may I put you down for?" or "How many units do you want?"), create silence, and close the deal.

3. *Hire the right people:* Start pre-production. Get your production directory. Hire your key people (cinematographer, production manager, production designer, assistant director, and production coordinator) and have them hire the crew.

3a. *Publicity (trades):* Simultaneously start marketing to distributors' acquisition executives by getting listed in the trades' (*Daily Variety* and the *Hollywood Reporter*) Film Production Charts and with Film Finders.

4. *Get ready to shoot:* Get organized. Rehearse actors, make vendor deals, secure locations, do paperwork. Make the storyboard. Get your shot list. Get your checklists. Build sets. Rehearse actors again. Have your final meeting, dispense the cast and crew list, and give an inspiring speech.

4a. *Publicity (1st contact):* Acquisition executives will start calling. Don't get excited; create a mystique by maintaining coolness and you'll contact them when your film is ready to be seen. Say, "Thank you" and hang up.

5. *Start the shoot:* Start production. Don't be frightened. First get a master shot and then go in for coverage as you get 25–35 shots per day with lighting and camera movement, as you stay on budget (say no) and on schedule (get the master) until the final Martini Shot is accomplished.

5a. *Publicity (photo stills):* While shooting, get your "staged" pointing photos, which are needed for enhancing the press kits.

6. *Finish the shoot:* Power through. Get up at 5 A.M., shoot until 6 P.M., plan for tomorrow until 8 P.M., view dailies at 10 P.M., crash at 12 P.M., wake up at 5 A.M., and start again. Filmmaking is exhausting. Be ready for three weeks of 18-hour, anxiety-ridden, tension-packed days. Don't stop. Keep shooting until every page is shot.

6a. *Publicity (invitations):* During the shoot, invite the acquisition executives who phoned during pre-production, and have them visit the set. Play them against each other.

7. *Finish the film:* Start post-production. Don't get lazy. Finish your film with the same dedication that you started with. Do the film edit, the sound edit, the ADR, the Foley, the score, and the re-recording session. Then finish with optical transfers, negative cutting, and color correcting at the lab until you have an answer print.

7a. Publicity (press kits): Prepare 100 press kits and mail 40–50 of them to the acquisition executives, titillating them again, keeping the remaining press kits for film festivals and for the ensuing publicity.

7b. Publicity (film festivals): The AEs, who came to your set and saw the other interested distributors, will phone and want to see your film. Notify them of the festival you entered, have them attend to see that the theater sells out and the audience leaves raving. This buzz (the raving), which can't be bought, is worth millions.

If this happens, you are about to make a killing.

8. Negotiate the deal: Attend your festival screening with your agent who negotiates with the AEs, who are lined up to talk to you in the lobby of the theater where your film has just played.

Your agent negotiates, one by one, each deal memo point: first, how much money; then what territory; next the P&A; then the distribution fee; then the windows; then expenses, overhead profits, etc., etc., etc.

If you have several distributors submitting offers you'll weigh them against each other and counter-bid. Voilà! You are a winner and have just made the next *Easy Rider; sex, lies and videotape; Blair Witch;* or *My Big Fat Greek Wedding.*

Keep the game plan simple. It becomes: *Get the great script. Cast excellent actors. Make equipment deals. Hustle AEs. Shoot your film. Attend festivals and negotiate.* This is your road map, but I must put in one more step, trait, quality, whatever, which is needed to ensure fame and fortune.

Many people in Hollywood say there is a lot of luck within the film industry. I don't buy that. *I am not a person who believes in luck or coincidence or kismet . . .* All that I know is that THERE IS A GOD and IT IS NOT ME.

I am a very self-centered, egotistical individual (I'm not proud of that) who for a long time believed that God created me first and then created the universe for me to play with. Then one day I had a moment of clarity and realized that the universe was created before me, and that God, in whatever form he/she/it is, put me here to make it a better place. What an amazing revelation that was.

All of my life I've been making deals with the devil. You know, looking for the faster, easier way to do everything. Then one day, about 20 years ago, I made a deal with God, and all he/she/it asked me to do was to simply *show up every day (that means get out of bed), go to work, and do a good deed for someone without telling anyone about it.* The key point is to not tell anyone about the deed. If I tell anyone it becomes ego.

Thus, each day that I do a good deed and don't tell anyone about it, I make the universe a better place and God rewards me with a "good deed chip." Then, if I accrue enough good deed chips, God will someday permit me to cash in so that I may be able to attain a higher-visibility (aka fame and fortune) status and utilize this elevated stature to help more people with a good deed. And become a George Clooney, who, immediately after the 9/11 tragedy, used his fame to raise $400 million.

Here's what I mean by the subject of God and that there is no luck or co-incidence in the film industry. For instance, what if you did everything that I taught perfectly? You got the great script, actors, crew, deals, publicity, made the great film and marketed it properly . . . But at the festival you screened there are seven other darling films. Damn! You got lost in the shuffle. But if you attended a festival two weeks prior or three weeks later you would have been the only darling film at that festival—and gotten the great deal.

Who controls that? I don't! You don't! And there is no amount of information or money that permits you to control what happens in the rest of the world. However, there is an entity that controls everything—and that entity is God, in whatever form you believe God to be.

Thus, God, not luck or coincidence, has a lot to do with success in the film industry. I have two friends who are outrageously successful. I truly don't want either of their lives, for they are literal prisoners of their fame. But the point is, they are both extremely sweet and nice.

I know that there is an image that Hollywood is populated by a pack of sharks and whores. I'm sorry to burst your bubble. I've been in Hollywood for 20 years and the people that I know who are very successful are all workaholics, write all the time, and are extremely nice.

Thus, if you want fame and fortune in the film industry, it comes down to three simple things.

1. Script
2. Talent
3. God

Therefore, the game plan is simple. Get the script, make it great, hire good people, apply your talent, and, if you are truly a good human being, I have no doubt that you'll achieve everything you desire. Now shut up.

Put down this book, go help someone (think of this as your final "To Do"), and start writing . . . Good things will happen.

God Bless and Happy Filmmaking.

———————

 AWARD GIVERS

Academy of Motion Picture Arts and
    Sciences (AMPAS)
8949 Wilshire Blvd
Beverly Hills, CA 90211
Award: Oscar
Contact: John Pavlik
Ph: 310-247-3000
Fax: 310-859-9351
E-mail: Publicity@Oscars.org

American Cinema Editors (ACE)
100 Universal City Plz, Bldg 2282,
    Room 234
Universal City, CA 91608
Award: Ace
Contact: Jenni McCormick
Ph: 818-777-2900
Fax: 818-733-5023
Web: www.AmericanCinema
    Editors.com

American Film Institute (AFI)
2021 N Western Ave
Los Angeles, CA 90027
Award: AFI Award
Contact: Leah Krantzlar
Ph: 323-965-1990
Fax: 323-467-4578
Web: www.AFI.com

American Society of
    Cinematographers (ASC)
1782 N Orange Dr
Hollywood, CA 90028

Award: ASC Award
Contact: Patricia Armacost
Ph: 323-969-4333
Fax: 323-882-6391

Art Directors Guild
    (IATSE Local 876)
11969 Ventura Blvd, Suite 200
Studio City, CA 91604
Award: ADG Awards
Contact: Scott Roth
Ph: 818-762-9995
Fax: 818-762-9997
E-mail: adoffice@ni.net

Broadcast Film Critics Association
    (BFCA)
9220 Sunset Blvd, Suite 220
Los Angeles, CA 90069
Award: Critics' Choice Awards
Contact: Joey Berlin
Ph: 310-659-7284
Fax: 310-860-2651
Web: www.bfca.org

Hollywood Foreign Press Association
646 N Robertson Blvd
West Hollywood, CA 90069
Ph: 310-657-1731
Fax: 310-657-5576
Award: Golden Globe
Contact: Michael Russell
Ph: 310-939-9024
Fax: 310-657-5576
E-mail: info@hfpa.org

Independent Spirit Awards (IFP/West)
8750 Wilshire Blvd, 2nd Floor

Beverly Hills, CA 90211
Award: Spirit
Contact: Diana Zahn
Ph: 310-432-1240
Fax: 310-432-1241

International Documentary
   Association (IDA)
1201 W 5th St, Suite M320
Los Angeles, CA 90017
Award: IDA Awards
Contact: Sarah Peterson
Ph: 213-534-3600
Fax: 213-534-3610
Web: www.documentary.org

National Society Film Critics (NSFC)
Brooklyn College Film Department
2900 Bedford Ave
Brooklyn, NY 11210
Award: NSFC Award
Contact: Elizabeth Weiss
Ph: 212-989-1767
E-mail: LizFilm@NYC.rr.com

Producers Guild of America (PGA)
8530 Wilshire Blvd, Suite 450
Beverly Hills, CA 90211
Award: Golden Laurel
Contact: Cherish Peterson
Ph: 310-358-9020
Fax: 310-358-9520
Web: www.ProducersGuild.org

Screen Actors Guild (SAG)
5757 Wilshire Blvd
Los Angeles, CA 90036
Award: SAG Awards
Contact: Kathy Connell
Ph: 323-549-6707
Web: www.sag.org

Writers Guild of America (WGA)
7000 W 3rd St
Los Angeles, CA 90048

Award: WGA Honorary Awards
Contact: Ryan DeKorte
Ph: 323-782-4574
Fax: 818-761-3814

Academy of Television Arts & Sciences
   (ATAS)
5220 Lankershim Blvd
North Hollywood, CA 91601
Award: Emmy
Contact: Julie Shore
Ph: 818-754-2800
Fax: 818-761-3814

Sundance Film Festival
8857 W Olympic Blvd
Beverly Hills, CA 90211
Award: Grand Jury Prize
Contact: RJ Millard
Ph: 310-360-1981
Fax: 310-360-1969
Web: www.Sundance.org

Cannes Film Festival
Association Francaise du Festival
   du Film
99 Blvd Malesherbes
Paris 75008 France
Award: Palme d'Or
Contact: Gilles Jacob
Ph: 33-1-4561-6600
Fax: 33-1-4561-9760
Web: www.filmfestivals.com/cannes

Toronto Film Festival
2 Carlton St, Suite 1600
Toronto, ONT M5B 1J3 Canada
Award: Metro Media Award
Contact: Sarah Brooks
Ph: 416-967-7371
Fax: 416-967-9477
Web: www.e.bell.ca/filmfest

Berlin Film Festival
International Filmfestpiele Berlin
Abteilung Programm
Potsdamer Straße 5
D-10785 Berlin, Germany
Award: Golden Bear
Contact: Dieter Kosslick
Ph: 49-30-259-20-444
Fax: 49-30-259-20-499
Web: www.Berlinale.de/

Academy of Canadian Cinema &
   Television
172 King St East
Toronto, ONT M5A 1J3 Canada
Award: Genie (The Canadian
   Oscar)
Contact: Erin McLeod
Ph: 416-366-2227
Fax: 416-366-8454
Web: www.Academy.ca/index.htm

British Academy of Film and
   Television Arts
Freud Communications
19-21 Mortimer St
London W1N 8DX England
Award: The Orange (The British
   Oscar)
Contact: Julian Henry

Ph: 44-207-291-3000
Fax: 44-207-637-2626

Australian Film Institute
49 Eastern Rd
South Melbourne, VIC 3205 Australia
Award: AFI Awards (The Australian
   Oscar)
Ph: 61-3-9696-1844
Fax: 61-3-9696-7972
Web: www.AFI.org.au

European Film Academy
Kurfurstendamm 225
10719 Berlin, Germany
Award: European Film Award (The
   European Oscar)
Contact: Nik Powell
Ph: 49-30-887-1670
Fax: 49-30-887-1677
Web: www.EuropeanFilmAcademy.org

British Independent Film Award
81 Berwick St
London W1V 3PF England
Award: BIFA
Contact: Suzanne Ballantyne
Ph: 44-207-287-3833
Fax: 44-207-439-2243
Web: www.BIFA.org.uk

Index

Page numbers of illustrations appear in italics.

ORDER FORM

24-hour shipping for all filmmaker's resources

FOUR WAYS TO ORDER

1 Call	**2** Fax	**3** Mail	**4** Web
1-800-366-3456 1-310-399-6699	1-310-581-0919 (Fill out and fax form)	PO Box 481252 Los Angeles, CA 90048	www.WebFilmSchool.com

Title (Books/Video/Audio/CD)	Price	#	Total $
1.			
2.			
3.			
4.			
5.			
6.			
7.			
Subtotal			
Shipping (See chart)			
8.25% CA sales tax			
Total enclosed			

Make checks or money order payable to "Hollywood Film Institute"

USA shipping:
(All orders must be prepaid)
UPS Ground
1st item: $3.95
Add $2.00 per each additional item
UPS 2–3 Day Express
Add $12.00 to
UPS Ground price

Overseas shipping
(All orders must be prepaid)
Surface: $12.00 per item
Airmail: $25.00 per item

(Check one) ___ MasterCard ___ Visa ___ Amex ___ Check/MO

Credit card number _____

Expiration date _____

Cardholder's name _____

Cardholder's signature _____

SHIP TO:

Name _____

Address _____ Apt. # _____

City _____ State _____ Zip _____

AIN'T IT COOL?

Hollywood's Redheaded Stepchild Speaks Out
by Harry Knowles with Paul Cullum and Mark Ebner
Foreword by Quentin Tarantino

If you love the magic but hate the hype . . . if your heroes have always been twenty feet high . . . if the eyes of the ten-year-old celluloid junkie inside grow wide when the white light fires up the silver screen . . . you dwell in the land of Harry Knowles, the college dropout who reigns as the Roger Ebert of his generation. Now Harry tells how he started a movie-based Web site purely for his own enjoyment—and became the most feared, sought-after outsider in the entertainment industry.

"Reads like the dream diary of the ultimate lay movie fanatic and would-be filmmaker. The author wrestles carte blanche access to the pearly studio gates. . . . Ain't *that* cool?"

—Kevin Smith, actor/writer/director